Critical Dialogues in Southeast Asian Studies

Charles Keyes, Vicente Rafael, and Laurie Sears, *Series Editors*

Critical Dialogues in Southeast Asian Studies

This series offers perspectives in Southeast Asian Studies that stem from reconsideration of the relationships among scholars, texts, archives, field sites, and subject matter. Volumes in the series feature inquiries into historiography, critical ethnography, colonialism and postcolonialism, nationalism and ethnicity, gender and sexuality, science and technology, politics and society, and literature, drama, and film. A common vision of the series is a belief that area studies scholarship sheds light on shifting contexts and contests over forms of knowing and modes of action that inform cultural politics and shape histories of modernity.

Imagined Ancestries of Vietnamese Communism:
Ton Duc Thang and the Politics of History and Memory
by Christoph Giebel

Beginning to Remember: The Past in the Indonesian Present
edited by Mary S. Zurbuchen

Seditious Histories: Contesting Thai and Southeast Asian Pasts
by Craig J. Reynolds

Knowing Southeast Asian Subjects
edited by Laurie J. Sears

Making Fields of Merit: Buddhist Female Ascetics and Gendered Orders in Thailand
by Monica Lindberg Falk

Love, Passion and Patriotism: Sexuality and the Philippine Propaganda Movement, 1882–1892
by Raquel A. G. Reyes

Gathering Leaves and Lifting Words: Intertexuality and Buddhist Monastic Education in Laos and Thailand
by Justin McDaniel

The Ironies of Freedom: Sex, Culture, and Neoliberal Governance in Vietnam
by Nguyễn-võ Thu-hương

THE IRONIES OF FREEDOM

SEX, CULTURE, AND

NEOLIBERAL GOVERNANCE IN VIETNAM

NGUYỄN-VÕ THU-HƯƠNG

UNIVERSITY OF WASHINGTON PRESS *Seattle and London*

This book is published with the assistance of a grant from the Charles and Jane Keyes Endowment for Books on Southeast Asia, established through the generosity of Charles and Jane Keyes.

University of Washington Press
P.O. Box 50096, Seattle, WA 98145 U.S.A.
www.washington.edu/uwpress

Library of Congress Cataloging-in-Publication Data
Nguyen-Vo, Thu-Huong, 1962–
   The ironies of freedom : sex, culture, and neoliberal governance in Vietnam / Thu-huong Nguyen-võ.
      p.   cm.—(Critical dialogues in Southeast Asian studies)
   Includes bibliographical references and index.
   ISBN 978-0-295-98865-8 (hardback : alk. paper)
   ISBN 978-0-295-98850-4 (pbk. : alk paper)
      1. Prostitution—Vietnam.   2. Prostitution—Government policy—Vietnam.
   I. Title.
   HQ242.5.A5N48   2008
   306.7409597—dc22   2008020390

Chapter 4 originally appeared in slightly different form as "Governing Sex: Medicine and Governmental Intervention in Prostitution," in *Gender, Household, State: Đổi Mới in Vietnam,* ed. Jayne Werner and Daniele Belanger (Ithaca, NY: Cornell Southeast Asia Program Publications, 2002).

The paper used in this publication is acid-free and 90 percent recycled from at least 50 percent post-consumer waste. It meets the minimum requirements of American National Standard for Information Sciences—Permanence of Paper for Printed Library Materials, ANSI Z39.48–1984.

CỦA BA MẸ

Contents

Acknowledgments

OUT OF CONVENTION, this book bears one name, but it owes its life to many. Although I bear responsibility for whatever faults you may find with it, I owe my work to so many who rendered their generous assistance along the way. I take this opportunity to acknowledge those debts. If I do not name all individuals in all cases, it is to avoid bringing unnecessary complications to their lives.

My biggest debt is to the working women who shared with me their stories under very difficult circumstances.

Hòang Chính Nghĩa, Hòang Lê Ngân, Hòang Lê Ngự, Hòang Chính Nghi and Thúy, and their family welcomed and helped me in more kind ways than I can name.

In Saigon, the Women's Union, the Health Bureau, the Institute of Social Sciences, a shelter for young women, and CARE International, particularly Michaela Raab, all helped me with information and access. I received an overview of government policies relating to women and social issues from the Ministry of Labor, Invalids, and Social Affairs and from other women activists and researchers in Hanoi.

The Andrew W. Mellon–Woodrow Wilson Career Enhancement Fellowship, the University of California President Fellowship for Research in the Humanities, and the UCLA Asian American Studies Center gave me precious time without which this book could not have been written.

My sponsoring editors at the University of Washington Press— Vicente Rafael, Michael Duckworth, Charles Keyes, Beth Fuget, and others—and my anonymous reviewers gave their time, support, assistance, invaluable critiques, and generous suggestions.

Thiên Hương Ninh pored over the text for many hours. Dorothy Solinger, Nancy Naples, David Easton, Đòan Nam Hậu, Esha De,

Namhee Lee, Min Zhou, Shu-mei Shih, King-kok Cheung, Cindy Fan, Don Nakanishi, Valerie Matsumoto, Alejandra Marchevsky, and Chorswang Ngin, at the University of California, Irvine; the University of California, Los Angeles; and California State University, Los Angeles, gave me intellectual companionship and mentorship. Many of my friends or colleagues in other places—Jayne Werner, Nguyễn Hưng Quốc, Trân Bích Ngọc, Helle Rydstrom, Lisa Drummond, Kim Ninh, and many others—rendered mentorship, assistance, and ideas.

This book was conceived and written in part by Kristen Hill-Maher and Allaine Cerwonka, who gave me their analytical insight and deep friendship.

Finally, my family—particularly Huy, Thế-an, Hồng Châu, Hương Anh, and Minh—who supported me and put up with my preoccupation.

I thank you.

Introduction

BEFORE THE HEAT would define the day one early morning in June 2002 at the center of Ho Chi Minh City, an area still called Saigon by its residents, crowds gathered in front of the old French-built Opera House, which now has reverted to its theatrical functions after various incarnations through Vietnam's postcolonial history. Young faces of uniformed students in lethargic poses filled the ranks. Surrounding them were banners and posters in primary colors. One large poster depicted a human form shackled to the words DRUGS and AIDS. Adjacent to it was a banner exhorting the "construction of a healthy cultural environment to help push back drug addiction and other social evils." A red banner hung across an intersection promising to "sternly punish drug-related criminals to protect social order." Representatives from local Communist Party and government organs stood up to give speeches behind a podium perched on top of the steps of the Opera House and framed by its vaulting entrance. As the sun climbed, the event became a procession, announced by slogans and songs from loudspeakers and flanked by rows of motorcycle police down tree-lined boulevards. It turned out to be an "anti-social evil" rally, set to coincide with the International Day of Drug Awareness on 26 June.

The physical surroundings of this latest anti-social evil rally consisted of refurbished posh hotels, multiplex theaters, and high-end retailers carrying global brands, catering to both a tourist and a domestic clientele of newly affluent Vietnamese who make their money in the new market economy. Many now populate the various night scenes of narcotics and commercial sex, as Vietnam embarks on the marketization and globalization of its economy after its victory against French colonialism, American imperialism, and decades of socialism.

The mode of intervention in society in this new context had been set by the government's approach to "prostitution" as a "social evil" as of the mid-1990s. The themes of the day's anti-social evil campaign— disease in medical knowledge, Vietnamese culture, and social order— were taken directly from strategies that the government has been using to fight prostitution. As with prostitution, tension exists between "knowledge of the real" and what is true in Vietnamese tradition and culture. On the one hand, the government refers to knowledge both of real social practices and of the (medical) expertise designed to address them. The Ho Chi Minh City Health Bureau since the mid-1990s has run a semipermanent exhibit with photographs that link prostitution to sexually transmitted diseases including AIDS. On the other hand, the government exhorts adherence to tradition and order. Governmental Decree 87, for example, in the late 1990s inspired similar rallies, street banners, and exhibits in which the government linked prostitution as a social evil to "poisonous cultural products." Making this linkage, the government resolved to build a healthy Vietnamese culture to fight prostitution.

The government was not the only entity interested in commercial sex. In 2003, the movie *Gái nhảy* (Bar Girls) opened in Vietnam with unprecedented box office receipts and blazed the trail for a commercially viable domestic film industry. The plot revolves around the lives of two women in the sex trade, replete with nudity, booze, heroin, violence, and death. The success of this film has been based in part on its claim to a new brand of social realism in the time of a market economy in Vietnam, a representation of "real" life that both reflects and reworks prevalent governmental representations of society and its ills.

What is it about commercial sex that makes it such a busy site of commerce, of governmental intervention, and of representation in popular culture in Vietnam at the present moment? What do the specific forms of these economic, governmental, and representational practices reveal about neoliberalism as the market takes root and Vietnam becomes integrated into the neoliberal global economy?

To answer these questions, this book combines methods and theories from the social sciences and humanities to examine (1) commercial sex as a function of government-initiated neoliberal market freedoms; (2)

the government's shaping of citizens and their desires through intense intervention in what the government represents as the empirical "social evil of prostitution" set against authentic Vietnamese tradition; and (3) the depictions of this social evil in a popular culture that currently responds to both the market and the government, as the latter sets the terms of discourse between the empirically real and the authentically true. I consider how various constructions of femininity reflect struggles over how reality should be represented as well as how the liberalizing society in Vietnam should be governed. Vietnam in the late 1980s "opened up" and joined the global economy after decades of war and socialism in the new policy of Đổi Mới, making it a good case study of how a former socialist government adapts to the market and to its neoliberal insistence on the freedom to choose for entrepreneurs and consumers, who may operate not just in the national context but in a transnational one as well.

Mass-mobilization rallies may still give off a familiar whiff of the all-encompassing state under the Vietnamese Communist Party, but the manner, object, and context have drastically changed. The foremost difference lies in the presence of, and reference to, a market, one that fully participates in the current global economy in both consumption and transnational production in the flexible mode of capital accumulation with all of its effects of inequality.[1]

Such an economy currently relies on a kind of freedom of choice much celebrated by neoliberal champions: the freedom to make entrepreneurial and consumerist choices. What underlies both the government's approach to a social problem and the rise of a popular culture fascinated with a social phenomenon such as commercial sex is the presence of these neoliberal freedoms in the market economy.

I argue that the techniques of governance in Vietnam have been shifting from the former Leninist mode, in which the state monopolized power and recognized no society or realm outside itself. Certain features familiar in their use of repression now have a different object and serve a different purpose. As society in Vietnam liberalizes and integrates into the global economy, the government must now govern the newly privatized intimate desires of citizens and the kinds of "social problems" such desires create. Governing for the neoliberal global market requires both a "realist" recognition and promotion of market freedom, on the one hand, and, on the other hand, measures of repression based on notions of "the true"—true Vietnamese traditional femininity, in this case. Such differentiated governance is class and gender specific in order to produce different kinds of producers and consumers for the market. While middle-class urban women are taught how to provide good but clean conjugal sex with new empirically based expert knowledge to guide their consumerist choices, lower-class sex workers are taught Vietnamese traditional femininity and subcontracted piecework in rehabilitation camps.

Governmental practices produce ideological effects by providing the terms that citizens use to understand themselves and their place in society. However, the production of ideology is no longer just the purview of the state. For the first time in decades, the generation of symbolic meanings for society has now also become part of the domain of a commercially viable popular culture, most notably in the new films that stake a claim on a new genre of social realism. This new social realism serves up the sensationalized dangerous undertow of excess enjoyment that drives market choices. The focus on commercial sex as the racy side of the market allows such films to pose the dangers of market freedom and simultaneously integrate it into some normative order at a symbolic level. Looking at the rise of popular culture in Vietnam allows one to say something about ideology and governance in relation to the neoliberal market: the language of commodities itself can become *the* symbolic order integrating both the enjoyment underlying market freedom and the terms of its differentiated governance.

NEOLIBERAL GLOBALIZATION, GOVERNANCE, AND REPRESENTATIONS OF SOCIETY

While the empirical materials in this book center on Vietnam, many of the theoretical themes in the book apply more broadly. Pierre Bourdieu calls attention to the "imposition on the entire world of the neo-liberal tyranny of the market."[2] Similarly, Jean Comaroff and John Comaroff name today's global moment neoliberal globalization and emphasize its "fetishism of the free market," in which the "rights" of businesses and consumers are guaranteed by law to "possess, to signify, to consume, to choose."[3] This diagnosis of the global spread of neoliberal freedoms raises questions in relation to government. The first asks what role a national government would play in neoliberalist globalization. The second, perhaps the more fundamental question, asks how a government would govern with these neoliberalist freedoms that Jean and John Comaroff have enumerated.

Forces of globalization have often been theorized as undermining the sovereignty of the nation-state or national government. Jürgen Habermas, for example, reiterates the specter of the "globalization of commerce and communication, of economic production and finance, of the spread of technology and weapons, and above all of ecological and military risks" as progressively undermining national sovereignty.[4]

Many scholars have theorized about, and documented the current phase of, global capitalism, which since the early 1970s has involved greater flexibility in production and distribution. Significantly, these new strategies include offshore production, outsourcing, and subcontracting to take advantage of the cheap labor that results from diverse labor disciplinary practices based on different patterns of living arrangements, authority relations, and gender constructions.[5]

What this economy entails in the area of labor use is the demand for flexibility, which translates best to the system of piecework subcontracting such as that of the electronics and garment industries in which feminine labor and space-time differentiation play a pivotal role.[6] The result has been an international division of labor taking advantage of "traditional" femininity translated into worker attributes of docility, dexterity, and the tolerance for tedious work on the global assembly line. Chandra Talpade Mohanty has noted that tolerance for tedious work has "racial and gendered dimensions" since it draws on "stereotypes which infantilize Third-World women and initiates a nativist discourse of 'tedium' and 'tolerance' as characteristics of non-Western, primarily agricultural, premodern (Asian) cultures."[7]

Is this model of the Asian female worker solely the product of global economic forces that transcend national boundaries and render national governments irrelevant? Despite warnings about the increasing irrelevance of the nation-state in globalization, Anthony Giddens continues to insist on certain capabilities of the nation-state like its monopolistic control over the means of violence at home and abroad and its deployment of Foucauldian disciplinary technology.[8] Debating the literature on empire, David Harvey posits the nation-state must obey the "territorial logic" in its attempts to pull economic advantages toward its spatial domain.[9]

How would national governments do this? Coining the term "flexible citizenship," Aihwa Ong argues that the Southeast Asian "tiger" states increasingly focus on "producing and managing populations that are attractive to global capital" through "differential deployment of state power," subjecting populations to different zones of "political control and social regulation by state and non-state agencies."[10]

Ong's flexible citizenship argument builds on Michel Foucault's later work on governmentality, which focuses on certain modes of Western modern governance that must seriously take into account the freedom to choose on the part of individuals who are also sovereign citizens.[11] Such political and social organization privileging freedom may be "overdetermined," as Charles Taylor would say, because of a "modern understanding of moral order" centering on individuals and their agency.[12] Or perhaps the explanation lies in the Marxist analysis that capital must depend on "legally free laborers who can move and sell their labor as they see fit."[13] However, the larger context of colonialism through much of modern times renders both claims, Taylor's that freedom is central to the modern West's moral imagining and Marx's that free labor is central to capital, paradoxical at best. Rosa Luxemburg saw that capital must also depend on unfreedom in class rule either domestically or internationally, where capital's "predominant methods are colonial policy, an international loan system . . . and war."[14]

This is reminiscent, not only of contemporary capital's outsourcing to take advantage of laborers who do not have the freedom to move to where their labor would fetch more, but also of the less-than-free labor produced when metropolitan nation-states racialize populations and police "illegal" immigrants within their borders. If these claims of freedom in the moral and economic realms are questionable when seen in the larger context that the West has created for itself, I now examine the Foucauldian claim that freedom is at the center of the West's modern mode of governance.

Foucauldian formulations of governmentality have dealt most systematically with the question of freedom and governance. Partly in response to criticism directed at his preoccupation with discipline in his earlier work, and partly in response to the rise of neoliberalism in the 1970s and early 1980s in the United States and the United Kingdom, Foucault started to work on the puzzle of the art of liberal government within an approach that draws attention away from theories of the state to point it toward the mentality and techniques of governance, coined "governmentality."[15]

Linking the microphysics of disciplinary power to the level of governance, Foucault finally confronted the problematic of freedom. Theorists, whom Alan Hunt has labeled "neo-Foucauldian," many writing from the United Kingdom at the end of the 1980s and through the 1990s, take this approach further in their exploration of the modes of governance and possibilities for the exercise of freedom at the height of neoliberalism in the United Kingdom.[16]

According to them, liberal governance persuades by positing its own limits, its non-totalizing power, in two related ways. Liberal governance asserts the inviolability of free subjects, and it acknowledges a socioeconomic realm with autonomous dynamics knowable through empiricist knowledge generation rather than through either normative or state reason. The second could be thought of as a correlate of the first. The free agency may result in sociological patterns, but it also contributes to the epistemological limits of government and forces it to rely on a mode of realist representation regarding the social realm.

Liberal government involves, as Paul Gordon writes, "the idea of a kind of power which takes freedom itself" and the conduct of the free subject as "the correlative object of its own suasive capacity."[17]

In simpler terms, liberal governance persuades and controls by positing the individual subject's freedom to choose. Nikolas Rose has argued that the freedom to choose has been the problematic of Western modern governance albeit in different configurations: from early liberalist institutions organized around the notions of autonomous individuals and the free market of the late eighteenth to mid-nineteenth century; to the emergence of the "social" from the turn of the twentieth century to mid-century, culminating in the welfare state providing people with the social conditions necessary to exercise their freedom; to the neoliberalist recuperation since Ronald Reagan and Margaret Thatcher of the free market to liberate economic agents from dependence on and constraints by the welfare state, bringing market logic into realms hitherto imagined as outside of the market (i.e., the corporatization of government, the school, and philanthropy).[18]

But current neoliberal leaders who insist on free market forces and free economic agents are also the ones implementing the use of imprisonment on a massive scale. In the United States and the United Kingdom, as the heartlands of neoliberalism since Reagan and Thatcher, more and more find themselves in prisons whose carceral logic precludes any kind of freedom of choice. In the United States, 7 percent of the male adult population remains under the control of the criminal justice system, a rate that Jonathan Simon has lamented as unprecedented in the history of societies.[19]

This contradiction in how freedom may be deployed in the economic sphere but suppressed in the cultural and social spheres suggests that modern governance should be understood as it is practiced in particular contexts, as contingent on political and economic appropriation and contestation, and that it not be taken for granted that there is one central concept around which Western or liberal governance may be organized. In the global economic context, perhaps it would be fruitful to see certain freedoms, namely, the currently dominant neoliberal entrepreneurial and consumerist choices, as the features with which particular governments operate, depending on their positions in the global capitalist system and other historically specific factors. Such an examination of how governments respond to these freedoms as they spread via globalization can reveal the fissures and political nature of governance in the particular contexts of the "modern West" itself, dissolving the Orientalist/Occidentalist character of the theoretical discourse on modern governance.

VIETNAM AND PARADOXICAL MODES OF GOVERNING IN NEOLIBERAL GLOBALIZATION

In response to Vietnam's political reforms allowing for marketization to take place since 1986, scholars have studied Vietnamese politics and governance in terms of liberal factions that are reform-minded, forward-looking, and open to the global economy with its political or cultural values, versus conservative factions that are backward-looking and authoritarian, to explain "contradictions" in pronouncements and policies.[20] At the same time, other researchers have noted the commercialization of agencies at all levels of government during Vietnam's marketization and the rapid establishment of global modes of production with a multileveled subcontracting system to take advantage of cheap and docile labor in Vietnam.[21]

It seems the "conservative forces" are not stopping the marketization and globalization of Vietnam. An alternative explanation is needed for the contradictory practices and pronouncements that sometimes promote global exchanges and at other times toe a conservative, inward-looking "traditional" cultural and political line, one that does not particularly correspond to the proletarian revolutionary discourse of socialist days. *I propose to look at this contradiction in governance not as a result of just historical residuals but as a paradoxical product of how this government deals with the neoliberal freedoms of a new transnational market economy.* Where history is most evident is not in the presence of conservative elements but in the continued prominence of the Vietnamese state, whose Communist Party and governmental units own the majority of big enterprises, including those involved in transnational and cultural production. Ironically, the Vietnamese socialist state is the biggest stakeholder in the market that is a part of the neoliberal global economy.

Since this economic liberalization, commercial sex has become a fix-ture in Vietnamese society not just through tourism but also through transnational business practices. The government has responded in high-profile and far-reaching intervention measures while it must take into account the free market with its entrepreneurial and consumerist choice. A redefined "social evil of prostitution" allows the government to work out state-society relations as well as to shape citizens in relation to their most intimate desires in the free market.

Some recent studies draw the connection between local economic structures and acts of sex consumption, or between the global economy and commercial sex.[22] Others call attention to "how public institutions use issues of intimate life to normalize particular forms of knowledge and practice and to create compliant subjects."[23]

My analysis brings together these three approaches by strengthening the link between sex and governance for the local market economy with its transnational connections. It makes clear that a government's simul-taneous use of freedom and tradition, the empirically real and the true in discourses about citizens as subjects of intimate desires, works to feed the differentiated needs of the market, whether in terms of racialized, classed, and gendered labor or in terms of an ideology of identity-based consumption. An examination of the sex trade and the Vietnamese government's intervention measures should allow a glimpse into how freedom in the neoliberalist market context of globalization is appropriated, contained, and used by the government and the men and women it governs. I suggest that the governing of sex and desires in the Vietnamese neoliberal market does two things. First, the gov-ernment's promotion of entrepreneurial and consumerist freedoms in the market has unleashed a new nativist and masculinist sexuality fu-eling the sex trade. Concurrently, a new middle- and upper-class fem-inine sexuality is also being shaped in relation to consumption. In many ways, the government has privatized desires from their public man-agement through surveillance by the old Leninist party–state organs. Second, through its responses to the introduction of choice in the eco-nomic realm, the government seeks to produce gender, sexuality, and class-differentiated producers and consumers, employing simultane-ously *different modes* of directing the behavior of a differentiated citi-zenry. On the one hand, public health intervention may rely on a "re-alism" based on social empiricist and medical knowledge to shape choices on the part of consumers like women of the middle and upper classes. On the other hand, policing and carceral rehabilitation will call on coercion and a "true" traditionalist culture in governing its target population of lower-class sex workers because Vietnamese "traditional" femininity has become a labor commodity in global production. Gov-erning with the neoliberal market entails producing different kinds of producers and consumers with different levels of access to market free-doms as a site of value and meaning generation. What kinds of pro-ducers and consumers a government produces depends on historical institutions and the economic-political positions of that government at home and abroad.

The mode of governance that makes use of both choice and repres-sion in Vietnam echoes what other scholars have noted in Asia and many other places where the neoliberal market economy has made inroads. For example, Richard Robison finds in places like Russia, Thailand, China, and Indonesia "hybrids of markets, crony relationships, and arbitrary state power" in the form of authoritarian or illiberal political systems, and he questions the "assumed functional relationships between market reforms, liberal democratic transitions, civil society, and pre-dictable and rational systems of governance."[24]

Robison explains these hybrids in terms of the preference of neolib-erals and their champion, the American empire, for state power in these places that could deal with the "by-products of rapid social and eco-nomic change," thus providing security for American and neoliberal economic interests.[25] Empires, needless to say, always make their de-mands felt in the world. The current empire is reverting to cold war tac-tics of disciplining other states according to American security needs in the "war on terror" and American neoliberal economic interests, as other scholars point out.[26] However, I must insist that there is some-thing more than just imperial security. Ong suggests that "different vectors of capital construct spaces of exception—'latitudes'—that coordinate different axes of labor regulation and of labor disciplining."[27]

I will be so blunt as to say that the global neoliberal economy's requirements for various labor and consumption needs rely on governments that will deliver by promoting choice and applying repression to different segments of their populations with the corresponding modes of seeing and representing society. In turn, these governments rely on the same economy to bolster their own agendas through the use of new technologies of choice in governance as well as through the more familiar repressive ones. This is where historically specific factors must be considered beyond a generalization of the workings of global neoliberalism and the American empire. In Vietnam, familiar repressive measures like arrests and incarceration contribute to the new mix of governing technologies that serve both the differentiated needs of the neoliberal global economy and the Vietnamese government's desire to maintain its monopoly on political power while promoting a base of support in the new ruling classes of Vietnamese society that benefit from that government and this new economy. Thus in this case there is little contradiction between the neoliberal global economy and a government that at times still appears familiar in its repression and Leninist monopoly of political power.

METHODOLOGICAL CONSIDERATIONS

A purely Foucauldian take on the notion of freedom as the organizing intelligibility of liberal governance cannot explain which populations are imprisoned or governed in certain ways. Neither could it explain certain kinds of social fantasies in popular culture that depoliticize such differentiated governance. I advocate a modified Foucauldian approach to both governance and cultural representation that would bring back a materialist dimension in a situated analysis of the politics and culture of neoliberalism. Bringing together an analysis of governmental and social imaginings in modes of representation, this book bridges the divide between social scientific and humanistic methods. Much of my analysis of the sex trade and recent governmental practices relies on my fieldwork in 1996, 2000, 2002, 2005, and 2006. The bulk of my field-work took place in Ho Chi Minh City and its vicinity and included in-depth interviews with twenty-five informants, shorter interviews with another twenty-six informants, and participant observation at selected sites of sexual commerce and governmental intervention. Eleven of the interviews were with sex workers. The rest of the interviews were with state officials involved in the antiprostitution campaign and included public health and rehabilitation officials, nonstate social and rehabilitation workers, peer-group educators, and informants on the clientele. My primary sites for participant observation and/or interviews were a sex-service café; two rehabilitation camps run for sex workers by the Ministry of Labor, Invalids, and Social Affairs in the vicinity of Ho Chi Minh City and Vũng Tàu; a rehabilitation home in a suburb of Ho Chi Minh City operated by private charity, for comparison; the Ho Chi Minh City Health Bureau, part of the Ministry of Health; two peer education groups consisting of "reformed prostitutes" and run by the Women's Union with funding from and under the direction of the Ho Chi Minh City Health Bureau; various program sites related to prostitution and coordinated by the Committee for the Control and Prevention of AIDS, such as an AIDS counseling café and public exhibits; and the abortion clinic at a major hospital for obstetrics and gynecology where many sex workers went for services. I also visited the Ministry of Labor, Invalids, and Social Affairs in Hanoi; Ho Chi Minh City's hospital for sexually transmitted diseases; related activity centers run by the Women's Union and the Communist Youth Union; women's study centers with projects on prostitution; and many commercial places providing sex service.

In addition, I rely on close narrative analysis of visual and textual materials collected in Vietnam between 1996 and 2006. For genealogical investigations into shifting governmental modes of managing empirical and expert knowledge, I rely on journalistic accounts and published denunciations in the press of the 1950s and 1960s, some of which were later compiled into published collections. For genealogical investigations into different modes of realism since the 1950s, I read literary and journalistic writings from the 1950s, at the moment of the consolidation of the socialist state and from the 1980s at the start of marketization. For an investigation into the current mode of social realism, I use journalistic writings from the mid-1990s, when the market began to be more established, and the popular films of 2003 and 2004 that have blazed a new commercial path. Finally, my analysis is supplemented by sex education pamphlets and self-help books, government exhibits pertaining to "social evils," published policy documents and political statements by leaders and officials, and other secondary sources. Unless otherwise noted, all translations herein are mine.

The methods of interviews, participant observation, and textual analysis have become popular in the past two decades because they constitute the meeting point between ethnographic methods in anthropology, cultural and literary analysis, and a post-structuralist attention to "practices." In my analysis of interviews, observations, and texts, I do not look merely to reconstruct events, to uncover the "truth" by sifting through the "distortions of talk."[28] Rather, I take what people say, write, or do on the whole as historically situated practices involving certain understandings, normative rules, and a consciousness of self and others.[29] My interpretations make use of, but are not reducible to, the participants' meanings, since this leaves out the question of the effects of what these actors do. Nor are my interpretations revelations of motivations or meanings hidden from the participants.[30] Rather, I try to decipher the patterns that arise from the practices of persons, groups, professions, and institutions.[31]

In other words, what are the effects of what people understand, do, and communicate? Likewise, I read textual representations in relation to both intratextual/intertextual features and in the contexts of social and political practices.

The researcher in this approach analyzes the contingent formation of meanings and their effects in sets of practices, textual or otherwise. This kind of work should help "wear away certain self-evidences and commonplaces."[32] Encouraged by this possibility, yet disturbed by the dangers of complicity by implication, I want to raise certain ethical issues involved in a study of this kind. I hope, for example, that by unpacking the aestheticization of sex buying, I am not just reproducing the aesthetic experience but am also helping to "wear away the self-evidences." If I analyze the commodification of women as special foods to evoke a sense of place for male entrepreneurial consumers, as I do in chapter 2, I hope that eventually a reader somewhere will next utter the words "specialty dishes" in such a context, not with nostalgia or relish for the exotic, but with questions.

Likewise, the use of words such as *sex worker* and *prostitute* carries implicit moral judgment and thus political implications. One easy way out is to consistently choose *sex worker* over *prostitute* to avoid the negative connotation of the latter. But this strategy avoids what goes into the construction of these meanings in the first place. Shannon Bell has proposed destabilizing the meaning of prostitution and its connection to moral assumptions that cast the prostitute as "other."[33] By showing what goes into the commodification and problematization of prostitutes and prostitution, I hope that readers will question meanings rather than take them for granted.

During my field research, I was amazed time and again by the sex workers' openness to my intrusion in their lives. The women seemed glad to have a chance to tell their stories as opposed to the government's stories or the clients' stories. The women saw me as somehow on their side. But the contrasts in our relative positions of power were all too clear. I would be the one who benefited more from our encounters. In my talks and in my texts to advance my scholarly/career pursuits, their lives would at times appear to audiences on some level as spectacles that are horrendous, exotic, or pitiable. This issue of the exploitation of those less powerful can never be fully resolved with my claims to the Foucauldian hope for the enterprise of critique. I do not have the full answer and do not think I can come up with one—surely nonengagement helps no one. But the tension arising out of my complicity and my consciousness of it at least makes my position uncomfortable enough to force me to continue facing these issues, sometimes productively, sometimes not. It forces me to approach ethics as a category comprising complicated and contradictory, if not complicit, choices. The acknowledgment of complicity should not however be viewed as a ritualistic confession done in the hope of gaining absolution without costs. Rather, it forces me to choose one kind of engagement over another, one mode of representation over another in specific contexts—the details in the ways we interact with those who have more, equal, or less power than ourselves.

The book is arranged in three corresponding parts: (1) market choices as they are manifested in commercial sex, (2) the governance of such choices, and (3) their representation in writings and films. Part 1 examines the rise of commercial sex as part of the socialist government's introduction of neoliberal freedom, namely, entrepreneurial and consumerist choice as it marketizes the economy. In chapter 1, I begin with how commercial sex became integral to entrepreneurs' way of doing business in Vietnam as the government marketized the economy in the late 1980s. My analysis follows the transformation from command economy to market to implicate in the exponential growth of commercial sex an emerging class of men and their practices of using sex buying to conduct business. Chapter 2 continues to explore how commercial sex thrives on the other kind of neoliberal freedom: choice in consumption now becoming a realm of signification and expression of identity. This chapter looks into entrepreneurial men's consumption practices to analyze the processes of commodification of women and sexual access to their bodies. I examine the men's use of female subservient sexual service and the equation of women to special food offerings of particular geographical places in Vietnam to argue that buying sex is an expression of class and national identity for male clients.

Part 2 deals with the genealogy of governance in Vietnam from the 1950s, showing the shift toward the government's intervention into the newly redefined social problem of prostitution. Chapter 3 looks at governance by the Vietnamese Communist Party and its state apparatuses, which sought to curb the autonomy of knowledge and other intellectual activities while enfolding them into an encompassing party-state. This process was most evident when the state purged dissenting writers, artists, experts, academics, and intellectuals during the Nhân Văn– Giai Phẩm affair of the 1950s and the anti-revisionist campaigns of the

1960s. During marketization, the state's effort to contain knowledge shifts toward the new mode of governance organized around medical knowledge and choice. Chapter 4 examines the government's public health intervention in prostitution and the popularity of sex education self-help manuals. This governance is differentiated by both class and gender in that the clinical measures targeting sex workers are more coercive than the discourse of sex, health, and vitality aimed at men and women of the new middle or higher classes. Chapter 5 details the arrest of sex workers and their incarceration in rehabilitation camps and discusses the government's deployment of cultural authenticity in anchoring identities of citizens and directing their choices. The rehabilitation camps for sex workers teach them to be traditional Vietnamese women through subcontracted piecework, with the message that they should embody values that will make them employable in the new economy. Chapter 6 considers the implications that multiple modes of power, using both choice and repression, have for the notion of liberal governance. Together with choice and repression, differentiated governance deploys the empiricism of a social "reality" and the assertion of a true Vietnamese tradition. Governmental practices thus produce ideological visions of self and society.

With the rise of a market for cultural productions, the government is no longer the sole producer of ideological vision. Part 3 looks at cultural productions to address the problem of ideology in governing with a neoliberal market. Chapter 7 traces both state actions and dissent in literary and journalistic writings from the beginning of the socialist state in the mid-1950s to the introduction of marketization in the late 1980s. At both moments in time, the use of the feminine as the marker of the socially real had been reinforced, paving the way for the popular film *Bar Girls* (*Gái nhảy*) and its sequel, *Street Cinderella* (*Lọ lem hè phố*), examined in chapter 8. Both films, in the new genre of social realism, feature the sex trade and the lives of sex workers, setting the way for a commercially viable film industry in Vietnam after decades of socialist government subsidy.

The Foucauldian approach to liberal governmentality forecloses the question of ideology prematurely. It claims that liberal governance really takes as its correlates the freedom of subjects to choose; therefore, freedom does not function as a Marxian false consciousness. As a result, there is not enough attention paid to fragmentation at the level of symbolic representation caused by the neoliberal economy's needs for differentiated labor and segmented access to consumption. Nor is there enough attention paid to ideological constructs in excess of freedom as a governmental notion. Looking at writing and films within the context of economy and governance can supplement an understanding of neoliberalism and the ability of the market to generate a symbolic language based on the commodity fetish to make sense of both freedom and its differentiated governance.

The book concludes with speculations on the case study's theoretical implications for neoliberalism. If governance of neoliberal freedoms is about particular political arrangements of freedom and coercion, about the search for the empirically real and the faith in the true of one kind of tradition or another, then this analysis might be useful in an attempt to understand neoliberal governance elsewhere. It probably has the greatest potential to speak to the differentiated governance in nation-states on the periphery pressured by the global economy to adopt neoliberal policies. Such states are likely to try to produce an expediently differentiated labor force through the use of simultaneous modes of governance based on both choice and repression. The need for differentiated governance does not stop at nations newly integrated into the neoliberal global economy, however. The United States as the heartland of neoliberalism must also combine neoliberalism and neoconservatism with multiple modes of power operating simultaneously to produce an unequal population differentiated by gradations in status that would best serve the needs of market production and consumption in order to maintain the position of this nation within the global economy. It is no surprise that it rallies a cry for freedom while maintaining prisons at home, Guantanamos offshore, and Abu Graibs abroad.

PART I

SEX FOR SALE

Entrepreneurial and Consumerist Freedom

CHAPTER 1

The Hooking Economy

Entrepreneurial Choice and Commercial Sex
in the Liberalizing Economy

COMMERCIAL SEX BECAME INTEGRAL to the Vietnamese economy in
the first decade of marketization despite governmental rhetoric about
how prostitution was a "social evil." With the arrival at the new market
and its neoliberal freedom to make entrepreneurial choices, Vietnam
opened to the global economy. This marketization of course brought
with it the global economy of sex tourism. However, the rise and spread
of the sex trade in Vietnam primarily depended on male entrepreneurs
who turned the use of women for sexual services into routine practices
that remain so today. During marketization, the state, which includes
the Communist Party and government, endowed a class of men with
certain state-owned capital and freed them to make entrepreneurial
choices in an economy that now included private entrepreneurs and foreign capital. Entrepreneurial men used sex buying to establish personal
ties facilitating their access to the means of production and exchange
in an economy that was moving from central command to one that
depended on decisions by entrepreneurs. My analysis follows this transformation to implicate in the exponential growth of commercial sex an
emerging class of Vietnamese men and their economic practices.

PROSTITUTION SINCE THE WAR

After the end of the war in 1975 and the unification of the country in
1976 resulted in the application of socialism over all of Vietnam, the state
defined prostitution as a problem with its causes in the past. As with the
expulsion of the French colonial presence earlier, prostitution at the end

of the Vietnam War was said to be no more than a vestige of the imperialist American presence and the southern puppet regime. The Leninist
party and government had often said during and after the war that South
Vietnam had been one sprawling whorehouse for American soldiers. As
the puppet regime was a whore to American imperialism, Vietnamese
women were turned into whores for the occupying army.[1] The revolutionary society after the Vietnam War therefore had to conquer the social
evils left by American neocolonialism: To lead those fallen sisters back
to a happy future life, the state and the Women's Union organized schools
for the "Recovery of Human Dignity," to cure diseases, provide vocational
training, teach culture, and educate these sisters so that they could
clearly see they needed to get on the path of honest work, of building a
happy life, and of becoming true and legitimate workers.[2]

According to the official line, what needed to be done was the implementation of a new and healthy socialist way of life. The state found
prostitutes to be stripped of human dignity. The forced performance
of labor was to make proletarian subjects of these sex workers, thus
enabling them to recover their humanity.[3] As a vestige of the inglorious
past, it was unimaginable that prostitution continue in the new society.
The state's rehabilitation of existing prostitutes at the end of the war
should have been the end of it. Instances of sex buying and selling were
decidedly fewer and went underground.[4] The official literature narrated
the absence of signs of these practices in the decade following the war
as evidence of the overall success of the new regime. It took a few years
of economic liberalization before conspicuous practices of sex buying
and selling reappeared.

The current volume of sexual commerce in Vietnam is difficult to estimate. One reason is that this activity is illegal, and therefore there are
few ways to quantify it. One estimate puts it at VND144 billion (Vietnam Dong; roughly US$10 million) annually.[5] Another method of quan-
tification reveals a target population bias in its focus on the number of
women involved in commercial sex. These estimates vary, and most
reporters and scholars in Vietnam avoid giving numbers that they have
no way of confirming. Most observers, however, seem to agree that these
numbers have been growing. One researcher from the Center for the

Scientific Study of Family and Women in Hanoi cites a tenfold increase, from ten thousand "prostitutes" in 1988 at the start of Đổi Mới, to one hundred thousand four years later in 1992, to two hundred thousand in 1996.[6] At this rate projections for 2006 would put the figure at roughly half a million women involved in the sex trade.

Beyond their unreliability and the preoccupation with quantities problematically conceptualized, these numbers indicate the prominent presence of a sex market after Vietnam opened its doors to both the market economy and the world. From high-class hotels, dance halls, and bars, to "hugging" karaoke places, "hugging" beer halls, and myriad forms of "hugging" cafes in the city centers and small towns as well as along the roads connecting them, commercial sex in different degrees and forms is readily available in Vietnam today. Where the government looked at prostitution at the end of the war in 1975 as a vestige of the ancien régime, it no longer could do so in the post–Đổi Mới era. It seems more promising to seek an understanding of this phenomenon in the market economy.

I begin this chapter by exploring the ways in which the practices of buying and selling sex undermined the simple story about prostitution as the social product of prerevolutionary regimes, a vestige destined to disappear. So visible to commoners and officials alike, these new practices with regard to commercial sex simply broke the confines of the old narrative and rendered it incredulous. I argue that the growth of the sex industry was intricately tied to the particular ways in which the Vietnamese economy had been liberalized. This state-led liberalization of the economy had preserved the privileged positions of past and present state officials and managers, who are given the freedom to make entrepreneurial choices. I consider the literature on economic liberalization in Vietnam (which mirrors the larger literature on economic liberalization from a command economy), rejecting theories based on neoclassical assumptions of an ideal-type market in which political power guarantees the necessary functioning of the market such as the private ownership of the means of production, among other things. Instead, I opt for approaches that are based on the observation of actual economic practices, especially at the firm level. Such an approach reveals that a market need not conform to an ideal type; rather, it needs certain market choices, in other words, neoliberalist freedoms. Adam Fforde and Stefan de Vylder offer a revealing analysis of "micro-adaptation" by state-agents-turned-entrepreneurs at the firm level as state enterprises became commercialized.[7] This micro-adaptation at the enterprise level exhibited clientelistic features as observed by David Wank in the Chinese liberalizing economy, not as a vestige of a centralized Communist system, but as the process of marketization itself. Wank and other writers on clientelism focus on the patron-client relationships between private operators and state bureaucrats. Here, I rely on Wank's notion that patron-client ties drive marketization by "reducing uncertainty and facilitating market links."[8] In my usage, these ties point primarily to links between and among private and state entrepreneurs. It was a market just as dynamic as any ideal neoclassical market, evident in the phenomenal growth rates boasted by both Vietnam and China in the past decade. However, this was a market in which the flow of materials, capital, and information about the market had to be actively accessed through more personal channels, the personal "hooking up" (*móc nối*) of economic operators. I build on these analyses to argue that these personal connections in Vietnam provided access links among state and private entrepreneurs (foreign and domestic) with the state sector in the pivotal position. It was all about entrepreneurial *access* to the procurement of information, capital, contracts, and materials. Finally, I note that this practice of business hooking primarily took the form of buying sexual pleasure for the facilitators of business by entrepreneurs who sought such access. Illustrations of liberalizing economic practices in personal connections and the place of the consumption of pleasure come from the mid-1990s, when the market had begun to be established after a decade of reforms.

Two points need clarification. One, I am not trying to explain the "cause" of prostitution, be it the "culture," "male biological needs," or something else. In looking for the causes, Vietnamese studies of prostitution center on the women in the trade.[9] Instead, I am trying to see how prostitution as a set of practices had become integral to economic practices in Vietnam during economic liberalization. Two, *economic lib-*

eralization is a common term used in the literature. I use it to denote the adoption of market mechanisms, which started out as the commercialization of state enterprises.

THE SOCIALIST ECONOMY

The economic model that was implemented in the North (the Democratic Republic of Vietnam) from the mid-1950s and nationwide for a decade after the end of the war in 1975 sought to "construct socialism." This meant replacing private property with public ownership of the means of production in the Soviet-style central planning of industrialization; controlling "prices, money, interest, and exchange rates"; and detaching the "domestic market from the world market."[10] This economy recognized solely the state sector, ignored an informal sector, and stayed inaccessible to nations not participating in the Council for Mutual Economic Assistance (among socialist countries). The state determined quantities, prices, purchasing, and marketing. It supplied funds to the state enterprises, collected profits, and absorbed losses. A two-tier price system emerged as the state fixed prices and rationed goods for state wage earners in what was called the "coupon regime" (*chế độ tem phiếu*).

The years preceding reforms in Vietnam saw factories working at half their capacity as well as persistent food shortages.[11] Inflation was running at 774.7 percent in 1986.[12] Forty percent of the population was under the age of fourteen and retained no memory of the glory of the Communist Party–led victories against the French and the Americans. After the disastrous results of one last-ditch attempt at command economics with the currency conversion of 1985, and encouraged by successes with the limited system of contracting out land use (*khoán*) since the early 1980s to farming families, the party decided to embrace reforms. The slogan "Reform or Die" at the Sixth Party Congress in December 1986 heralded the beginning of a new era marked by *tư duy mới* (new thinking) and *đổi mới cơ chế quản lý kinh tế* (reforms in economic management).

Reforms in economic management became the code phrase for the recognition of market mechanisms in the economy. It meant first and foremost incentives to improve performance and productivity tied to the decentralization of economic decision making. Next, it meant the diversification of forms of ownership, giving rise to an officially recognized private sector. This move had the effect of a double opening. Not only did Vietnam open up to the capitalist world economy through foreign direct investment and foreign trade, but it also opened up its state-owned enterprises to competition in the market, which now included private companies.

Most analysts agree that by 1989 Vietnam had some sort of a market economy, although they disagree on the exact nature of this process and its future direction. Fforde and Vylder note that the "two-price" system had been dismantled, as was the "system of central planning based on state allocations of inputs and obligatory production targets for the individual enterprises."[13]

VIETNAM'S LIBERALIZING ECONOMY: THE COMMERCIALIZATION OF THE STATE

The literature on Vietnam's "economic transition" offers two basic assessments, both based on neoclassical premises. The first is an economistic approach, which generally views the Vietnamese liberalizing economic experience as a success. It attributes this success to the fact that Vietnam had made a break with the bureaucratized and centralized Soviet system of the past. Along this line is the assessment that Vietnam's economic success was the result of shock therapy in the form of big-bang microeconomic liberalization and macroeconomic stabilization, which was International Monetary Fund orthodoxy.[14] The second assessment starts from analyses of the Vietnamese political structure and arrives at a more pessimistic conclusion of inertia that resulted from "bureaucratic centralism," which allowed economic liberalization to take place only with the generational transfer of power in the mid-1980s.[15]

Both lines of assessment are based on the assumption that the Vietnamese political organization prior to liberalization was incompatible with a market economy. This kind of an assumption is referred to as liberalist or neoclassical. It insists that a real market must have an accompanying political organization that safeguards private ownership of the means of production (necessary for a free market of the factors of production—land, labor, and capital) and free competition (which requires transparency, good information flows, etc.). Since the Vietnamese socialist system seemed incapable of providing any of these conditions at the beginning of liberalization, a momentous break in policy, either of a big-bang nature or a generational transfer of power, has to be posited.[16] Although there were political pronouncements opening the way for policy changes to accommodate liberalization, the features of the Vietnamese liberalizing economy did not correspond to assumptions of successes based on neoclassical compatibility between economic requirements and political safeguards. Among the Vietnamese "aberrations" from the neoclassical model were the following: land was still held by the state, there were major constraints in the labor and capital markets, there were state-enterprise monopolies geographically and in key commodities, and information about the market as well as about selective bureaucratic intervention was not readily available without good connections. In short, there was no big bang in policies that created market conditions even in the first decade of marketization.

Rejecting an exclusive focus on policy in a top-down approach to marketization, Fforde and Vylder propose viewing it as a process. Although not quite free from liberalist assumptions of the pressures of a growing market whose seeds sprouted from the cracks of political suppression during the socialist years, Fforde and Vylder's process-oriented approach affords two advantages in explaining liberalizing economics in Vietnam. First, it treats liberalization or marketization as an open-ended process rather than as a prescribable transition from command economics to an ideal-type market.[17] Second, it focuses attention on the actual economic practices at different levels, only one of which was the policy arena. This move is oriented toward an area crucial to an understanding of Vietnamese liberalizing economics as well as the place of pleasure in these economic practices. This was what Fforde and Vylder call microadaptation, or the economic behavior at the enterprise level.[18] This microadaptation, in turn, depended on the freeing of entrepreneurs to make choices in the operation of an enterprise according to fluctuations in the market.

Fforde and Vylder argue that experimentation in creative procurement and marketing of products by state enterprises (i.e., informal connections and bartering of matériel, products, access to machinery, etc.), together with the family plots as a precursor of the agricultural contract system, had been going on at least since the late 1970s under command economics, because the goals set by the system were usually not possible to meet. Following some Vietnamese analysts, Fforde and Vylder see liberalizing policies as a recognition of and reaction to this experimentation with "breaking the fence" (*phá rào*).[19] Many Vietnamese economists I spoke to confirmed the presence of this kind of experimentation in practices of breaking the fence in the decade before the official opening up of the command economy in the late 1980s. Political acceptance of decision-making autonomy by state enterprises allowed a kind of market to happen.[20] This official recognition took the form of a certain recognition of the rights of entrepreneurs to make decisions regarding the use of the means of production and exchange as individuals or the government units that began to operate as profit-oriented entities. By the mid-2000s, this recognition has begun to push toward private ownership of property including the means of production and exchange.

As a result of the combination of breaking the fence behavior and official policy recognizing the need for decision making at the enterprise level in the burgeoning market, there was a "commercialization" not just of state-owned production enterprises but also of most government units as these entered into the game of profit chasing in the marketplace.[21] The expression was to "break out and do some business" (*bung ra làm ăn*).

Commercialized, the state-owned work units (*cơ quan*) could make more decisions and diversify their income sources. Profit became the real bottom line. The production enterprise could now make decisions regarding the procurement and marketing of its products. As state subsidies were reduced to further the commercialization of state-owned enterprises, the latter found ways to finance their ventures, some of which came from (1) creative ways to convert their state-assigned assets into income, (2) foreign investment, and (3) the rising private sector. Most work units found themselves free to convert inert assets into profitable ventures, regardless of whether they were production units. For instance, villas and buildings long allocated to the ministries and their local bureaus were turned into profit-making hotels. The General Office of Energy, under the Ministry of Heavy Industry, and Public Security, under the Interior Ministry, were known to offer desirable guesthouses as a result of their choice real estate assets throughout the country. Work units also set up companies in pursuit of profit in the marketplace using their expertise and their government/party connections, in addition to the tangible assets allocated to them as a government or party organ. For instance, the Ministry of Light Industry would be in a good position to set up a Phú Lâm Shoes Import and Export Company or a Tân Tiến Plastic Packaging Company. The Ministry of Construction would be in a good position to set up the Alliance of Construction Material Companies, to which a Ho Chi Minh City Construction Material Company would belong. Fforde and Vylder note that the emphasis on the economy of scale under socialism meant creating one major supplier of many commodities in each district or province. When these units became commercialized, they enjoyed a virtual monopoly.[22] Thus, the results of this commercialization of state units included (1) de facto state monopolies locally and even in sectors not officially protected as state domains (such as mining, communications, and banking) and (2) a blurring of distinction between state entrepreneurs and state bureaucrats. The commercialization of state units, in effect, had turned most bureaucrats into state entrepreneurs.

The Vietnamese economy during liberalization could be characterized by this commercialization of state entities and not their privatization. The state-owned enterprise behaved like a commercial firm in the market, but its ownership did not go to private hands. Fforde and Vylder point out that, even by 1990–91, the "state" (meaning the commercialized state entities) was still the dominant owner of the means of production in industry, with the nonstate share accounting for an estimated 23 percent. The state held monopolies in banking, mining, and communications, among other sectors.[23] Conveniently, this dominance of the state sector testified to the Communist Party's resolve to maintain a "socialist orientation."[24]

commercialization
vs.
privitization

Far from the stagnation attributed to state-owned industries before liberalization, the state-dominated industry and construction sector was the fastest growing, at 14–15 percent annually.[25] The dynamism of the Vietnamese market economy as a whole, with average annual growth rates of 7–8 percent, and the relative dynamism of certain parts of the state-dominated industrial sector required an explanation beyond the bureaucratic inertia hypothesis and the liberalist premise of big-bang privatization.

Two interrelated features of practices at the level of the commercialized state enterprise could shed light on the dynamics of the Vietnamese liberalizing economy. First, the profit incentive as part of the commercialization of the state-owned enterprise went to benefit most if not all in the work unit involved. The profit made was used to "enhance the quality of life" (*cải thiện đời sống*) for members of the work unit. This innovative micro-adaptation to improve the bottom line had become the driving force, with few questions asked, as most state employees benefited. Most stood to gain as bureaucrats became entrepreneurs, nullifying the bureaucratic inertia hypothesis.[26]

Second, the central place of the state-owned sector put state entrepreneurs in a pivotal position in the web of connections that linked economic operators in the Vietnamese market economy. The state entrepreneurs could provide the private entrepreneurs with access to the state-held means of production (land, factories, etc.), access to contracts that the state-owned enterprises were in a better position to win as a result of their state-endowed assets, and bureaucratic advantages in navigating the selective bureaucratic intervention of a state groping to devise control mechanisms in the uncharted territory of a market economy. The need for access found its solution in the clientelist feature similar to what Wank observes to be integral to marketization in China. There was thus no overwhelming need for some kind of big-bang privatization.

The resulting feverish seeking out of profit-generating business tended not to discriminate between legal and illegal economic activities, especially where regulations were less than clear.[27] Sensitive business dealings that might include outright corrupt practices called for familiarity among the economic operators involved. The offer of pleasure had become an important means of acquiring and maintaining these contacts, especially sensitive ones, which allowed economic operators access to the means of production and exchange.

ENTREPRENEURIAL DECISIONS AND THE PLACE OF COMMERCIAL SEX

I have proposed that micro-level practices or behavior in the Vietnamese liberalizing economy be attributed to (1) the profit incentive tied to decentralization of economic decision making translated to bonuses for members of the work unit and (2) the pivotal position of the state-owned enterprises, and thus state entrepreneurs, in their interaction with private entrepreneurs. Both features figured into the "hooking up" among state and private entrepreneurs. Below I illustrate with examples these two features in the Vietnamese "hooking economy" and the use of pleasure to facilitate these "hookings."

The Hooking Economy

Describing how business was done, a private entrepreneur in Ho Chi Minh City said, "It's all inside hooking. Me, too. I have to cultivate my contacts."[28] Here, I look at how hooking provided access for entrepreneurs to the means of production and exchange. I deal briefly with the collective incentive mechanism and then move on to the pivotal position of the state entrepreneurs in these entrepreneurial connections.

Profits within the state enterprises would be used for enhancing the lives of workers in various ways, such as work unit vacations and periodic bonuses.[29] The line between legal and illegal procurement of these enhancements was extremely blurry. The principle of the work unit profit to be divided up among workers had become the driving force with few questions asked. Hiếu, the co-owner of a private interior construction and supply company, reported occasions when the accounting office of a state-owned construction company had engaged in "fixes," where higher prices for American products in the terms of the signed contract were paid for lower-priced Thai merchandise because the supplier had run out of the former. One such occasion resulted in a windfall of more than VND30 million (more than US$3,000), to be divided up among the fewer than ten members of the accounting office. The official monthly salary of each of these accountants averages around VND400,000 (roughly US$40).[30] This kind of profit made for enhancements several times their salaries. What is more, the "victims," who would ultimately pay for this switch, could not be clearly identified. In the meantime, this kind of fix also called for additional "gratitude" on the part of the supplier.

When state-owned units and their workers became driven to improve their bottom line with all their tangible and intangible assets, certain patterns of interaction with the emerging privately owned enterprises became routinized. As state entrepreneurs were eager to strike up deals with one another and with private entrepreneurs, the latter sought out the former as the insiders to aid them in a market with impediments such as numerous local and commodity "monopolies, information asymmetries, and barriers to entry."[31]

More concretely, entrepreneurs in all three ownership sectors—foreign, state, and private—needed access to things held by those in the other two. The foreign investors needed land, production sites, and knowledge about the market and about how business was conducted in Vietnam. The state enterprises were in the best position to meet these needs. The state enterprises, in turn, needed the business contracts— capital from the foreign sector—while they might rely on the small private subcontractors to front the cash.[32] Finally, from their connections with state entrepreneurs, the private entrepreneurs needed the subcontracts and aid in navigating the selective bureaucratic regulations.

The state sector continued to occupy the pivotal position in these cross-sector linkages. Foreign investment totaled US$18.44 billion by 1995.[33] Foreign investment joint ventures and contracts were mainly with state-owned enterprises, especially in the first decade of marketization.[34] This was understandable since the state-owned enterprises were much larger in size and could provide the sites allocated to them and since state production units were better equipped as far as heavy equipment was concerned. By comparison, the typical private enterprise in Vietnam was quite small at this time, with less capital to invest in heavy equipment.[35] In addition, bureaucratic regulations such as "delegated importation and exportation" (*xuất nhập ý thác*) required the private enterprises to import materials and export products through a state-owned company for clearance through the various ministerial controls.[36] Thus, while the state-owned enterprise might need the operating cash from private subcontractors, it acted as an intermediary through which the private entrepreneurs gained access to foreign contracts, materials, distribution, information, and passage through bureaucratic controls.

The advantages enjoyed by the state-owned sector were such that they accounted for part of the difficulty in attempts at privatization. In keeping with the policy of diversification of forms of ownership, the government cautiously experimented with the beginning steps of privatization of state-owned enterprises. In 1993, the government selected nineteen companies to undergo experimentation with conversion into share companies. After two years of this process, only two out of those nineteen companies had converted. Đinh Thơm attributes this failure to the comparative advantages of being a state-owned company and the disadvantages of the private sector, such as lack of a strong competitive environment and a lack of modern technology in industrial production.[37]

These comparative advantages of the state-owned companies over private ones shaped the relationship between these sectors in the fledgling marketplace. Subcontracting was one of the main features of this relationship. Hiếu explained that the state-owned companies were given the big construction contracts, with few exceptions. The reasons included their size, their equipment, and their reputation for backing and support within the government, which would help them navigate the nightmarish bureaucratic waters in Vietnam and ensure completion of the project for foreign investors. A private firm would need unusual connections to the state sector to secure contracts directly rather than through the usual channel of subcontracting. As Hiếu put it: "For example, the director of Construction Company No. 'X' [among the largest state-owned companies] has a twenty-three-year-old son who runs a private construction company. The relatively smaller contracts that come the father's way would be passed on to the son, you know, the villas or six-, seven-story buildings."³⁸

But as Hiếu stated, save a few big companies like "Construction Company No. X," many of these state-owned companies lacked the cash to carry out a contracted project. Subcontracting thus became necessary not just for the usual reasons of specialization and lower costs:

> [Among the state-owned companies], there are some that sound big, this or that General Corporation, but they would exist just as a front to get the big contracts, which they pass on down to their "subsidiaries." Of these, not all are well equipped or well funded. My company has worked with the ones that don't have much. They would call the smaller ones like mine to forward the money. I would have to come up with twenty percent of the value of the contract up front. And then I'd have to cover all expenses after that until I get it back three or four months later.

From this privileged position that resulted from their government-endowed tangible and intangible assets, the big state-owned companies had the power to subcontract out to privately owned companies. Private entrepreneurs during liberalization had often been relegated to the position of the ones doing the asking, while the state-owned companies' officials had been in a position to parcel out morsels of the growing economic pie. Additional government controls only enhanced this relationship. For instance, to import or export materials and products, private companies had to go through the state-owned ones in a system called "delegated exportation and importation" (*xuất nhập ỷ thác*). All the state-owned company would have to do for clearance through the various ministerial controls was to put its company name on paper as the importer or exporter. For this service, the state-owned companies charged the private parties 1 percent of the total value of goods imported if it was of a certain bulk. For smaller loads, the charge was 5 percent, "unless they collude with you to dodge taxes, in which case the percentage is much higher."

If collective incentive on the part of the workers at the small sub-work unit blurred the line between legal and illegal activities, as the accounting office example illustrated, the uneven relationship between the state and private sectors provided the crevices of opportunity for these routine, yet very often illegal, dealings. The governmental controls that loaded the dice in favor of the state-owned companies could be used by private entrepreneurs to their advantage. For example, Hiếu explained,

> Delegated importation is very important. Sometimes, it [the government] gives priority by way of lowered taxes to certain provinces because of floods or because these are fledgling development areas. What we can do then is to delegate our importation to that area through an appropriate state-owned company. Instead of our goods going to Đồng Tháp, for instance, we'd cheat and our goods stay here in Saigon. Then we'd invite customs officials from Đồng Tháp here to inspect the goods, and they'd just tax us here. They [the customs officials] would cost us a percentage. But it's worth it because import taxes here amount to twenty, thirty percent, while it's one percent for these priority areas.

In this situation, the delegated state-owned company would benefit from the official rate of 1 or 5 percent. The workers in the subunit directly involved in this fix would receive the remainder of the higher percentage for participating in this tax-evasion scheme. And the illegal dimension of the transaction drew even more state agents into the game, as the customs unit in Đồng Tháp would have to be paid as well.

This scenario was far from isolated.[39] Another private entrepreneur complained in a letter to an economic publication that the complex, overlapping, and sometimes contradictory regulations and jurisdiction in state management of the construction industry provided plenty of opportunities for official corruption as private entrepreneurs tried to manipulate these constraints.[40] The investigative unit of the Interior Ministry reported in 1996 that the number of discovered cases of corruption involving illegal economic transactions increased 119.5 percent in 1995.[41] The inspector general boasted in an interview that within the first six months of 1996, his bureau of inspection had uncovered "economic management violations," shorthand for economic corruption, costing the "public" a grand total of VND701,137,000,000; US$31,138,000; 1,725 *chỉ* (about a tenth of an ounce) of gold; and 12,664.7 hectares of land.[42] There were political reasons behind these arrests and boasts, but they also suggested that the phenomenon of corruption was rather widespread.

Sexual Pleasure as Market Enjoyment in Entrepreneurial Practices

Vietnam's liberalizing economy was a hooking economy in which personal connections were vital for business, especially sensitive business. Foreign, state, and private entrepreneurs offered the enjoyment of commodified pleasure, especially sexual pleasure, to facilitate and maintain contacts among business partners or potential partners. As a result, these men made up the clientele that fueled the volume and growth of the pleasure industry in the 1990s.

In an economic arrangement where the state sector and state bureaucrats cum entrepreneurs occupied the pivotal position, the private entrepreneurs often found themselves paying for the former's "entertainment" to facilitate business deals. This customarily meant taking the contacts, and others involved, out to *bia ôm*, literally "hugging beer," a catchall term for places that serve various foods, alcoholic drinks, and invariably pleasure through access to women's bodies in a range of semi-sexual to sexual services. Minh, who had dropped out of ninth grade to go work at a *bia ôm* restaurant six years ago and had since worked in a number of different of settings, described what she and her coworkers did: "We have to dance with them [male customers], hug them, all that. Call it making money. . . . This life, it's selling sex, really. You just don't see it there outright."[43] The hostesses served these men in a variety of ways, including wiping their faces with warm towels and pouring their drinks, followed by touching, hugging, and kissing the men. The men were free to touch these women in any way they chose. Should a hostess object, she would be replaced by someone else at the guest's request. Hostesses could be asked to take off their clothes and perform tricks in touching the men. Guests and hostesses could agree on rendezvous places where intercourse could take place. Minh and a coworker, Hằng, explained:

> Minh: If they touch you too much, you feel too violated, and you say something. They would say to you, "I have the money, I have the power.

Remove yourself and call somebody else out for me, someone who is easy, to come and sit with me." If we let them have their way, they would give us good tips. And if things are to both sides' liking, he would ask you to sleep with him. You'd sleep to get the money.

Hằng: What else could you do? It's called selling sex.

Minh: *Bia ôm* restaurants where you sit hugging them at their table to get the tips, that's what's on top. What goes on under that is they ask you to sleep with them if they like you.[44]

In many of these places, especially where there were partitioned rooms such as at karaoke restaurants, sexual intercourse in exchange for money in the form of tips often was part of the "playing."

As this pleasure industry grew in ingenuity both to keep offering ever more exotic fares to the guests and to elude crackdowns unleashed by anti-social evil campaigns, which were most intense in the city, pleasure places flourished in the suburbs and nearby resort towns throughout the latter half of the 1990s. Massage parlors offered a range of services and prices. Karaoke bars abounded where guests could ask service women for sex at prices in the range of US$40–$70 a session. High-class establishments, including five-star hotels, offered service women, with whom a night would cost between $70 and $100. In addition to the core of the *bia ôm* places already described, there appeared "hammock cafes," "thatched-hut cafes," "hugging lounge chairs on the beach," "thousand-star hotels" (at beachside, lakeside, and riverbank outdoor places that are not registered restaurants), "hugging sea bathing," and so on, all of which served primarily as venues for prostitution.[45]

The practice of taking one another out to have a pleasurable time in the manners described became a currency that, according to those involved, afforded deniability, secured contacts in sensitive situations, and served as an expression of gratitude. Hiếu, the private entrepreneur, recalled one go-between who denied responsibility after a business-deal-gone-wrong by saying, "'I didn't take one dong from you.' And what can you say in response? You can't say to him, 'But you ate, drank, and played.'"[46] Outright illegal activities (or more generally "dodging") required discretion. Thus more were drawn into this economic game playing as go-betweens, as potential partners needed to become acquainted and familiarized. Familiarity was an order of business in all sensitive sit-uations that often blurred the line between bending the rules and break-ing the law. Hiếu explained, "It's not like five private companies put in five sealed bids. No, it's all inside hooking. Me, too. I had to cultivate my contact and take him aside and ask him how much is that other com-pany's bid? Tell me and I will give you a lower quote."[47] Some of the con-tracts that Hiếu won through this subcontracting process involved "almost twenty times of taking different people out to *bia ôm*, each time costing me from two to three million dong for one contract worth a few hundred million dong."[48]

There were costs to neglecting this practice, as Hiếu found out: "One time, I could not collect the money due me even when I was willing to give the president of that company a cut.... It was difficult because we didn't wine and dine them."[49] Taking the favor grantors out for an evening of food, drink, and women was an expression of gratitude for a deal-gone-well, especially if there was illegality involved. As some read-ers put it in *Phụ Nữ*, the news organ of the Women's Union: "*Bia ôm* is a super form of bribery. Underlings take superiors out to express 'grat-itude.' Students 'invite' teachers to *bia ôm* to set the 'conditions' for the results of their exams."[50] It seemed this practice, integral to economic practices during liberalization, had become generalized to relationships outside the business realm, although on a much smaller scale.

As an economic practice, this provision of a good time with drinks and women became so obligatory that Hiếu found it difficult to ignore. Lacking readily available males to take the contacts and officials from the state companies out on the town, Hiếu's company had to give these part-ners a percentage to be spent on *bia ôm* on their own. To the extent that this practice was expected in these transactions, a go-between once found it appropriate to take the director of the potential contract-granting state company out to *bia ôm* and called Hiếu's partner, Tuấn, to the restaurant once they were done, to pay for the expenses. The go-between informed Tuấn that his company was responsible for the expenses of that session of *bia ôm* since "the connection fostered was to our benefit and not his. Neither was it for the director of the state company.... That director, I had to give him more than eighty million dong already."[51]

Again, Hiếu's experiences did not appear exceptional in any sense. Newspaper accounts abounded that chronicled the miring of state company officials in the women and corruption scene.[52] More commonplace than these high-profile cases were men like Hoàng, a highly placed official in a big state-owned construction company. Lan, his wife, told me he spent six nights a week in these *bia ôm* restaurants negotiating deals, making or reinforcing his contacts:

> The men now "eat and play" terribly. All cadres. Hoàng knows because he has to wine and dine them. I was very uncomfortable at first. When he started to break out to do business, he would stay out till eight in the evening. I nagged. He stayed out till nine. I nagged. He stayed out till ten, eleven, twelve. He'd come home and go straight to bed. I'd end up talking to myself like a madwoman. Now, he's got a hand phone. He calls home around eleven to tell me he's at some restaurant. So I'd know my husband is at such and such a place. And I'd just go to bed. He has to make money.[53]

Or there was the case of Tình, who was a private hardware supplier. While showing me the nightlife at Restaurant XYZ, Tình attributed his expertise in these matters to the fact that every single one of his contracts had been signed in one of these "eat and play" places.[54] XYZ was a popular pickup point for businessmen and high-class taxi dancers out from the dance halls after twelve at night. Minh and Hằng, who had worked as *bia ôm* hostesses, said most of their customers were there for business, such as to sign contracts or pick up *áp phe*—money-making deals of all kinds, usually involving a commission.[55] By the early 2000s, such practices had become routinized. Công, a light construction supplier described the business scene in a resort town on the coast: "It has become a habit. In the establishments that offer *ôm* (hugging), the people who take others out and those who get taken out are all happy." When asked how things compared to the mid-1990s, Công replied, "It's several times more. But it's less visible."[56]

These practices of entertainment and prostitution had followed business into what were traditionally considered to be nonbusiness realms that had more rigid rules of propriety, but which now fell neatly under the logic of economic liberalization in Vietnam. Diệu, an instructor explained that his school in Ho Chi Minh City was a profit venture initiated by a group of instructors who managed to establish an affiliation with a public university in Hanoi. Profits from the venture went in part to the Hanoi school, of course. But on top of that, there were other expenses: "For example, we can grade the regular exams. But for level-advancement exams, we must bring professors here from Hanoi because only they are authorized to grade them. While they are here, we have to take care of them from A through Z. Of course, there are the airfare and accommodations. But we have to pay for their entertainment and girls every night that they are here as well. It's expected."[57]

One could make a quick calculation and see that the percentage of the value of the economic transactions going into this kind of "familiarization" was quite high. Hiểu complained,

> Almost ten projects out of ten, ten people out of ten have to go in there [*bia ôm*], spending money. What a wasteful amount of money. They [state company employees] make a few hundred thousand a month to take home to their wives and kids. A drinking session at these places costs a few million. For each project of the best ones, the fattest contracts, my company gets a profit of a few dozen million. For the rest, we make a few million in profit each. . . . One contract I just completed, I paid fourteen million on the side to the director of the other company. There was this big one where I paid more than eighty million in entertainment and side payment. Afterwards, we kept thinking how much we could do for the company if we could have reinvested that money.[58]

In the middle-to-low range, a few hours of *bia ôm* for three to four men cost about VND1 million, twice the average monthly salary of a state employee. At the high end, the hourly rate for just renting a chic karaoke room ran up to VND350,000, without the costs of drinks and food and tips for the hostesses. A reader commented in *Phụ Nữ*, complaining about the money these men "throw around": "Whose money is it when the state needs it to pay debts of gratitude to families of martyrs, to help orphans and the poor?"[59] One Nguyễn Trung Thành sent a letter to the same newspaper and expressed concern about the source of money spent on *bia ôm*: "If this money comes from honest sweat and tears, no one would throw it away in such amounts. If it doesn't come from honest sweat and tears, then it must belong to the state, the people, or come from illegitimate business dealings."[60] The pleasure industry in the mid-1990s was fueled by new money, by this process of facilitating economic transactions, many of which were between privately owned enterprises and the pivotal state-owned ones.

My observations and interviews led me to the claim that entrepreneurs made up the bulk of the clientele, and the amount of money made from these entrepreneurial sex activities probably far outstripped money made in other instances of sex buying. While the highly political character of "the problem of prostitution" makes it too sensitive a topic for definitive surveys of the women sex workers about their clientele, other investigators reached similar findings. Relying on informants for his study, Ngô Vĩnh Long also highlights the prominence of the business clientele, domestic and foreign.[61] The Coalition Against Trafficking in Women states in its report based on international journalistic accounts of the late 1990s that "two-thirds of government officials are known buyers of women in prostitution" and that "after Vietnam shifted to a market economy, prostitution became so integrated into trade relations that business deals are often closed with the use of women as incentive or reward to foreign investors, bureaucrats and corporate representatives."[62] According to a 2002 news report, the government itself found "state cadres," including "state-enterprise directors," comprising 38.3 percent of all sex clients.[63] If you add to this figure of state cadres their interlocutors in the private sector, then indeed this client group seems to make up the main clientele of the sex trade from the late 1990s into at least the early 2000s. The use of pleasure to facilitate access to the means of production and exchange among both state and private entrepreneurs, of course, did not account for all instances of prostitution in Vietnam. Foreign tourists and Vietnamese non-businessmen engaged in sex buying.[64] However, it is my contention that the use of pleasure to facilitate business connections was the main engine fueling the widespread commodification of pleasure involving women's bodies for men.

CONCLUSION

Despite vehement government denouncement of prostitution as a social evil, commercial sex was integral to the marketization of the Vietnamese economy. The opening up of the Vietnamese economy to the global traffic of people and money allowed sex tourism to flourish. But much more important, commercial sex became widespread primarily as a result of the governmental freeing of entrepreneurs to make business choices in a marketizing economy. My observation and interviews with the women in the pleasure industry in the mid-1990s, when the market had begun to become entrenched after nearly a decade of liberalization, yielded a picture in which the main clientele consisted of "those doing business," namely, state and private entrepreneurs. Whereas before, decisions about matériel, production levels, pricing, personnel, and so forth were made centrally in a command economy, now they had to be made by entrepreneurs who had been freed to make business choices in the new market. In order for entrepreneurs to make their entrepreneurial decisions, they needed information and access to the resources of other entrepreneurs who had now been freed to do business as well. The use of bought sexual pleasure answered this need for information and access to the means of production and exchange, via personal connections, in a dynamic marketizing economy. In the mid-2000s, the use of commercial sex has become routinized from such beginnings in the 1990s.

CHAPTER 2

Hierarchy and Geography

Class and National Identity in Sex Consumption

JEAN AND JOHN COMAROFF have pointed out the "neoliberal stress on consumption as the prime source of value" that envisions persons as "consumers in a planetary marketplace: persons as ensembles of identity."[1] Buying sex not only facilitated business connections for entrepreneurial men, but it was also a way for them to mark their class and national identity. I examine here the forms of the consumption of sexual pleasure and its commodification. Building on the identity theories of class distinction, and performative subjectivity, I argue that these forms of consumption constituted performances of class and national identity, predicated on a gender difference.[2] Consuming sexual pleasure through women and their bodies allowed men to construct themselves, not just as men, but as Vietnamese men of a certain class.

HIERARCHY: CLASS DISTINCTION IN THE
CONSUMPTION OF SEX

In the previous chapter, I noted that entrepreneurial consumption drove commercial sex. Here, I argue that through the entrepreneurs' consumption of this pleasure, two things happened simultaneously: the consumer exhibited his status by participating in a classifying activity, and this classification and differentiation in turn evoked the perception in society of the social and cultural presence of this class. I discuss the entrepreneurial class, an analytically identifiable group, using Nicos Poulantzas's reworking of the Marxist "class" in relations of production. But the transformation from such an analytically identifiable group to a social and cultural class presence demanded a more Weberian perspective on group status, as well as more recent theories on identity-producing processes. I make clear my usage of *class* in relation to the Marxist and Weberian traditions and discuss the adaptation of Pierre Bourdieu's notion of class distinction through consumption.

The sale and consumption of women were used as tools of status by both the men who were consumers and the women sex service workers in a society undergoing a rapid process of socioeconomic stratification. In the murky beginnings of the formation of classes brought on by economic liberalization, men and women incessantly marked their class with the signs of spending power, asserting the presence of these nascent classes. As such, the status of class, to be read in its enactment, went to differentiate and construct the presence of certain classes even in the face (or more earnestly so because) of their recently acquired wealth. But whether this pleasure trade evenly distributed the signs of class and status among the consumers and the sex service workers is a matter that must be explored. I argue that one class in particular stood to benefit the most in this process of class differentiation via status: Vietnamese men who are the state and private entrepreneurs in the new economy.

Class

The use of *class* in social and political analysis relies on two main traditions: the Marxist and the Weberian. Simply put, the former sees society (in the last instance according to Engels) organized around the prevailing mode of production. Classes are the results of the organization or relations of production. Classes are thus identifiable in relation to the ownership of the means of production and exchange.[3] Capitalist society boasts two main classes: the bourgeois, who own the means of production, and the proletarians, from whose labor a surplus value is extracted.

The growth of the middle class in advanced industrialized countries complicates this picture since significant numbers of this class do not own the means of production, yet neither do they seem to fall increasingly into the ranks of the proletarians. Neo-Marxist attempts to deal with this problem include the work of Poulantzas, who pointed out that the legal ownership of the means of production should not be the sole criterion in the determination of class. There is also the access to or the control of these means of production.[4] The managerial middle class (managers, bureaucrats, supervisors, or those with access to and control of the means of production) then could be classified among the bourgeois in the social division of labor. It is this access to the means of production that is of concern here, since much of the means of production in Vietnam in the 1990s was still legally owned by the "people" and "managed by the state," as was land. It was not until the mid-2000s that property began to pass legally into private hands. This reworked notion of a dominant class based on access to the means of production works well in my analysis of an economy where such direct and indirect access was necessary for the functioning of this economy, as has been shown. It was the economic operators' access to the mostly state-held means of production and exchange that required the personal "hooking" underlying much of the buying of sex. Using Poulantzas's notion of access and control rather than legal ownership, I can identify the state and private entrepreneurs as joined in an emerging class.

If the Marxist literature has dealt at length with "production" in relation to class, the notion of "exchange" in relation to class is elaborated by Max Weber. For Weber, classes have to do with "differential market situations."[5] Thus, it is the position in the relations of exchange that classifies classes for Weberians. Barry Hindess has pointed out that the emphases on production for Karl Marx and on exchange for Weber would lead to a marked difference for an analysis of precapitalist society, but not for capitalist society where both would agree capitalists and workers occupy different class situations, although Weber would see many different class situations within the "working class."[6] For my purposes, the class of entrepreneurs could be identified in relation to both production (land, industrial machinery, etc.) and exchange (procurement of contracts, clearances for imports/exports, etc.).

This analytical classification so far relies on the position of a group in the economy. But occupation of an economic position does not automatically mean this group comes with a socially recognizable class identity. Thus, Poulantzas found it necessary to add "ideological" and "political domination and subordination" to his structuralist class analysis.[7] This is where my use of Weber's notion of "social class" comes in. Weber focused on the ease of mobility as an indicator of the boundary and exclusivity of a social class. This exclusivity has to do with the notion of "status," which "implies a recognition of social differences" and which goes to restrict "social intercourse."[8] There is thus a conjunction between class and status groups, where "class and status differences are interconnected."[9] The wealth at the disposal of a class buys more than a good education for the next generation of class members, as marketing firms are well aware. "A class," according to Bourdieu, "is defined as much by its *being perceived* as by its *being*, by its consumption . . . as much as by its position in the relations of production (even if it is true that the latter governs the former)."[10] This is because "goods are converted into distinctive signs" of distinction or vulgarity, as "representation which individuals and groups inevitably project through their practices" (483).

The key here is the "practices" by "individuals and groups." But how do individuals' practices project a representation apart from those of other classes? The answer may be that these practices are performances of difference. In the case of class status, they are performances of hierarchy and domination. In short, as individuals perform their differentiating status, a differentiated class presence is evoked in hierarchical relation to others.

The pleasure place was a good site for acts of classification because it was, as Bourdieu would say, a site where the "symbolism of social domination and submission and the symbolism of sexual domination and submission" are integrated into "the same body language" (475). The body is shaped by habits (from eating habits to postures and mannerisms) that allow it to occupy a distinct hierarchical social space. Sex, as an activity that directly involves the body, taps into the "socially constituted principles of the sexual division of labor and the division of sexual labor" (475). Moreover, the pleasure place in Vietnam was the site of business hooking, the work activity that identified this economic class. Yet the pleasure associated with food, drink, and sex turned it into a leisure activity. Consuming pleasure was both economically necessary and pleasurable. This was why one would see money made and money spent in large amounts at the pleasure place. It was a way in which these male entrepreneurs claimed the status of a leisure class from their economic position.

Work, Leisure, and Domination

I turn to concrete illustrations in a discussion of the uneven distribution of the signs of status for the buyers and sex service workers. The dual construction of this activity as both work and leisure for the male customers shows how these entrepreneurial buyers of pleasure asserted the status of their class through practices of hierarchy and domination. Participation in this pleasure industry was perceived by those involved as an economic necessity, but one transformed by the leisure aspect of consuming pleasure for male customers. The sex workers' work, however, continued to be cast in terms of necessity. I explore the consumption of signs of status, by the women who earned their money selling sexual pleasure and by their entrepreneurial customers. The sex workers faced much difficulty in gaining status with the money they made. The male customers were thus well disposed to perform class social domination through acts of sexual domination over these women.

As shown, the offer of pleasure and its consumption had become important in the generation of wealth for its participants. Economic activities not only provided the conditions for the thriving of the pleasure trade; they became the justification of the men's consumption of pleasure as well. As Lan grudgingly admitted to the financial necessity of her husband's roaming the pleasure inns six nights out of the week (see chapter 1), one *bia ôm* confessor, who was an anonymous president of some company, wrote to the Women's Union's newspaper to justify his pleasure habits in terms of "saving the company from losses through *bia ôm* as a means to buy off customers, superiors, and underlings."[11] Hằng, the *bia ôm* hostess, saw this practice as a necessity on the part of the man who must go out there and make money. She would look the other way, she said, if her man visited these pleasure establishments.[12] In another article in the same Women's Union's newspaper, on the "social psychology" of the practice of buying sexual pleasure, the author writes, "They [the men who engage in this habit] change their life for the bet-

ter through money. . . . Some do it through tricks, cunning and oppor-
tunism to gain riches."[13] The pleasure habit had become an integral feature of turning tricks, the almost indispensable advancement tool in these
times of liberalization.

Yet this "necessity" was one that involved pleasure in eating, drinking, and sex. Slang like *tới bến* (reaching a "high"), *tươi mát* (fresh and
cool), and *ngon* (tasty—the women and the food) placed these activities in the realm of pleasure for the consumers. And pleasure rendered
this a leisurely activity. One mother writing to a newspaper forum on
bia ôm urged her son to join his friends at these "eat and play" places:
"If you have money, you have to play. *Bia ôm* is a joy, a touch of class for
men nowadays."[14] This "joy," and the connoisseurship in this practice,
bestowed a sense of leisure on a moneymaking activity on the part of
the entrepreneurial customers. This leisure aspect is a mark of class distinction.

For the women sex workers who sold a good time, however, work
remained "necessary." Moral shame and the degrading experience in servitude at work prevented the women from exhibiting enjoyment of their
work, thus depriving them of the possibility of laying claim to status in
the same pleasure activity that for men could be read as the mark of
leisure. I next explore further the women's stories and the mechanisms
that nullified the status signs acquired by the women by way of their
purchasing power.

Most women saw their work as necessary. Hằng and her coworker
Minh reflected on their trade:

> Minh: Most Vietnamese now work this trade for this reason. Too poor,
> no money to stay in school. For example, if there are five or six chil-
> dren in the family. If everyone wants to eat and go to school, how is
> there enough money? One or two sisters must work [selling pleasure]
> to pool the money so the younger ones could stay in school. Now once
> the younger ones are educated, there might be a chance. We'll see then.
> But now, to tell us to just suddenly be rich enough to get an educa-
> tion, how are we to do it?
>
> Hằng: . . . With *bia ôm*, you can work even if you're illiterate. All you
> need is to look a bit pretty. It's really illiterate work. . . . You take the
> money, solve your impoverished parents' problems, fix their place up

a bit, help your brothers and sisters with some money to start up something so they could make a living. What's more, afterward, there's even a bit of security for yourself. You move up in the world.[15]

The women called themselves working women. But the money they made a month on average would put them in the richest category of Vietnamese. Did these women then belong to the moneyed class on a par with the entrepreneurial class in status, or did they belong to the working class by virtue of the social division of labor? Hằng pointed out that, although this work earned good money, "you just have to endure the bitter part."[16] What made this money earning work bitter?

The women felt enough affinity with a high-status group to find the men beneath them unendurable:

> Minh: Sometimes, there are those without money who come in. Sometimes it's the cyclo driver accompanying some businessman who had hired him to ferry some goods, who'd made some profit and tipped him well. The cyclo driver would decide to show some class and come in, drink just a couple beers, and tip me twenty thousand dong [she normally received up to one hundred thousand dong serving a table]. . . . They are smelly and dirty. You must say. . . . They wear these dirty shorts, their faces hairy and black. Their mouths stink. God.
>
> Hằng: With money, they are gods. The customers are gods.
>
> Minh: They'd hug you tight, pull you in. Their breath stinks. God. I'd go out of my mind.
>
> Hằng: We must accept it all.
>
> Minh: I'd get so pissed off I'd want to take a stick and chase them out of there. God, how can a man like that touch me. Outside of that place [of work], on the streets, such a man would be fit to carry my shoes. But he comes in here, and he can hug you.[17]

As their comments suggest, money did bestow a certain status and place the women above some of their customers. The class distance Minh and Hằng felt was expressed in their descriptions of these customers' clothes, odor, and skin color (dark skin denoting a lower status). These men's low-class status went against their performance of sexual domination, which was often read as social domination. This perceived contradiction was expressed in the women's words of revulsion and mental dislocation ("go out of my mind"). As Bourdieu puts it, this kind of contradiction challenges "the socially constituted principles of the sexual division of labor and the division of sexual labor, [and] violates the mental order, scandalously flouting common sense."[18]

There are two issues to explore here. The first is that the relative status of the women was undermined when they were forced to put themselves in a sexually subservient position to these men who were so obviously of the lowest class in society. The second is the ongoing constitution of what was considered "natural" in society regarding social hierarchy and sexual domination. While the women felt revulsion at having to serve the lower-class men, they voiced a resigned sadness when it came to serving the new state and private entrepreneurs. I come back to the second point to explore the enactment of hierarchy and domination on the part of the entrepreneurial consumers of pleasure.

In a number of ways, the status signs bestowed by money were nullified for these women. Money allowed the lower-class man to obliterate the class distance Minh had diligently worked to create. The act of spending money in such a place installed the lower-class/working-class man as a "god" (*thượng đế*), a half-flattering, half-sarcastic term referring to *bia ôm* customers. The women continually described their work as "sour." These *bia ôm* hostesses at first went through a process of selection based on their appearance in order to be taken in by a restaurant. They had to work from ten in the morning until midnight without pay. They lived on the tips given them by the men. They would have to compete with a couple dozen other women at the same restaurant for their time serving customers. They would maneuver to be sent out to a table by giving the supervisor of the hostesses (*tai-pan*) a cut of their tips. Should the customer become displeased with their service or their appearance, they would be replaced by their coworkers. They were at the bottom of the hierarchy at work. Even the men who provided protection to the establishment, the *ma-cô* and *giang hồ* (pimps and gangs), could demand their service for free. Minh and Hằng described this situation:

> Minh: There are those *ma-cô*s protecting the place. They'd come in and decide they like you. They'd say . . .

Hằng: They'd say I want to sleep with that one tonight. And you'd
have to. You wouldn't get a dime. And you'd have to sleep with two
or three of them that night.[19]

What about a class status bestowed by the type of services they provided
and the clientele they served? The range of services and prices varied
widely. The expensive "call girls" (*gái gọi*) who operated via phone links
and the taxi dancers (*vũ nữ* or *gái nhảy*) from the expensive dance halls
would rent out a flat for the purpose of receiving clients who were willing to pay for discretion. The hostesses at the state-owned hotel restaurants were well protected from harassment from customers and police.
The *bia ôm* hostesses worked at privately owned establishments. These,
in order of status, include hotels, karaoke places, hair salons, massage
parlors, and various styles of small cafés either in the alleys of the city,
along the highways, or tucked away in the suburbs and small towns. The
streetwalkers usually were the most vulnerable in terms of the prices they
could charge and the harassment they endured from the police and from
their customers. Of course, a woman from any of the above categories
(but more frequently from the level of *bia ôm* hostesses and on upward)
could become a kept woman (*gái bao*) for a few months at a time for a
foreign businessman or for a Vietnamese official/businessman from the
city or one of the provinces who would come to the city for business on
a regular basis.

There could be a big gap in the prices these women could charge. An
expensive call girl could charge a customer more than a hundred U.S.
dollars a night. Local newspapers report that famous models were available for $700–$1,000 a night.[20] A streetwalker down on her looks and
luck might charge only VND5,000 (50¢) each time. However, despite
the range in services and prices, the women did not see themselves as
belonging to any category exclusively. There were two reasons for this
lack of rigidity in the hierarchy of pleasure providers. First, the women
moved from one kind of service, one mode of operation, to another without too much difficulty provided they did not appear undesirable.
Second, the classes of clientele were not clearly segregated. The class of
men with new money frequented a wide variety of services, from the

expensive dance halls to the humble cafés, for reasons that I explore in conjunction with practices that I argue to be nativist.

Minh and Hằng had worked variously at *bia ôm* restaurants, from rented flats, by rendezvous at hotels, and as kept women. Bé Hai, a beautiful twenty-year-old woman, in the space of three years, had started out working a hotel in Vũng Tàu where she received city men with money to spare, had set up a *bia ôm* place of her own, and was temporarily working the parks and streets in Ho Chi Minh City when I met her. Her abusive partner, an unwanted pregnancy, and debts in this case had led her to this downtrodden state. Stories of downward mobility were abundant. But upward mobility was far from unlikely. This ease in upward mobility was due to the fact that the requirements for entering into a higher category were not forbidding, as Minh and Hằng explained when I asked what kind of women could work the expensive scenes:

> Hằng: All you need is a need for money and have good looks, and you can work.
>
> Minh: All you need is "waiter's" language. People, Vietnamese or foreigners, they are not that interested in talking to you. They just want to see if your face and your body look good. Just a few sentences. The generous ones take you to a restaurant for a good meal. And the others just take you straight to a room to sleep with you. When you're done sleeping, you go separate ways.[21]

While some big state-owned restaurants did require some education and character references, other modes of operation to advance one's price range were available, as women like Minh and Hằng rented their own flat, became connected in a "phone link operation," and improved their presentation of their services. At other points in their careers, though, they might find themselves working the streets, as Bé Hai found herself doing after breaking up with her boyfriend who had helped her run her small *bia ôm* place. Although there were barriers, such as youth, good looks, and other resources (money to rent a flat or to pay off the neighborhood cop, know-how, connections to a phone-link network, etc.), there was a good deal of overlapping and mobility among the categories of prices, services, and clientele. Because of this relative fluidity among the types of services, the women in general did not have a clear and enduring sense of class identity via their work.

Outside of work, the impersonal signs of money and status did not go far enough to earn them respect from people who knew about their work. Minh related how her profession tainted her personal relationship with men other than her clients: "Like while I worked, I had a boyfriend. We lived together. But when I told him I was pregnant, he wouldn't acknowledge it [the child] was his, saying, 'I didn't stay with you to have a kid.' As if we're their toys."[22] "The men, they don't trust you when you work this trade. If you love a man, he wouldn't really love you back. He'd say, 'How can I love that girl. She's with dozens of men a day.' You'd never know if the men really love you or if they just want to spend your money."[23] As the woman's love was rendered non-genuine by her work, she found it hard to believe in the sincerity of the man's love as well.

Indeed, these women were often portrayed as whores out turning their "1,001 tricks." One woman, who described herself as a wife speaking for wives of a class of well-off men who frequent *bia ôm*, lamented the victimization of wives and their husbands by these modern Kiều (Kiều is a literary character who sells herself into prostitution to save her father from imprisonment, from *The Tale of Kiều*). The woman wrote in *Phụ Nữ* that when she asked the men why they choose those *bia ôm* girls over their wives, the answer was that the former seemed to the men so weak and fragile compared to their educated and intelligent wives.[24] It was such that signs of a lack of class (in this case education) on the part of the prostitute were also denounced as ploys, tricks to trap the men. Deception was a pervasive theme. This characterization of the prostitute went to render unbelievable the signs of status and class that she put on with the money she earned. The nonwork that she perceived herself performing ("You just put on the clothes and the makeup and sit there waiting," as Minh said) went to substantiate the wife's negation of her lower-class/working-class status, which would legitimately earn the pity the men bestow on her.[25] She thus remained not fully incorporated into a proper class, be it the moneyed class or the honest working class.

Unlike the *bia ôm* women, with their class identity rendered precarious by readings of moral deceptions, servitude, and the mobility of their trade, the men who partook in this kind of commercial sexual pleasure did find class differentiation. Social stratification had become a hot topic in Vietnam. It was the subject of academic conferences, party discussions, and policy considerations. But the mere category of official income, or of education alone, would not be enough to address the issue of class status.

Income disparity gained ground within a few years of the start of marketization. According to the national statistical office, by 1990, "rich" households accounted for 10–15 percent of the total number of households, while "poor" households accounted for 25–30 percent. The income differential between the two categories was put at fifteen times in the city and ten times in the rural areas.[26] According to this office's 1993 estimate, the differential between the richest and the poorest was put at 27.03 times.[27] Nevertheless, the per capita monthly income of the richest category was put at VND350,000 (about US$35) for the countryside and VND400,000 for the city. Thus, for a "very rich" family of five in Ho Chi Minh City, the monthly income would be VND2 million, or US$200.

The spending power of such a monthly income would definitively not fetch a luxurious lifestyle. The building costs alone of a decent house befitting this class would be roughly US$40,000–$50,000. Consumer goods were higher priced than in the United States. A good motorcycle would cost a couple of thousand U.S. dollars, while a new Toyota sedan would cost well above US$20,000 at the time. As noted, an average session of *bia ôm* would cost at least US$100–$200. Yet a wealthy group of men made their class presence felt in the pink marble facades of multistoried houses, in riding the Dreams and Cubs, in driving the new Hondas and Toyotas, and in partaking of the bustling pleasure scene.

If the official income bracket of the "rich" could not afford and did not signify a wealthy lifestyle, then how was this performance of class distinction possible? Who made up this class, and where did the money come from?

In an article appearing in the official publicist organ of the Communist Party, Bạch Hồng Việt, an Economic Institute researcher, attributes the rapid acquisition of wealth to the transition from a subsidy-based management to a balance-sheet (profit-based) management, where the state work units entered the marketplace, "renting out their buildings and such" to raise their receipts, "to the point where the state employees' official salary becomes a minuscule percentage of their true (undocumented) income."[28] According to Bạch, the "majority of the urban rich" consisted of those in trade and services: "Of these, most had manipulated the loopholes in laws and regulations to evade taxes and fees. Here we must mention the large group of state officials, engaging in the so-called 'general services' at the [state-work-unit-turned companies]. All that is needed is a simple act of 'breaking the wall' in basic construction, or a big contract and they would have sucked from the state five to twenty percent of the value of the contract signed."[29] It seems this class consisted mostly of state officials/entrepreneurs and private entrepreneurs, in ways explored in the previous chapter.

In the anticorruption debates raging in Vietnam, there had been for some time clamoring for an accounting of the state officials' assets. Such clamoring amounted to little. By 2005, National Assembly candidates were required to declare their assets. But as one party member put it, no one took the measure seriously.[30] If the largest part of this class's income was unaccounted for, and if beautiful villas and brand new automobiles would have to be included in an inventory of its wealth, the sources of which would have to be disclosed, then how were the new rich to wear the trappings of class? Deniability certainly played a part. The practice of taking one another out to have a good time with women was an asset in that it facilitated the generation of wealth for the men involved. Furthermore, since their official salary was not an indication of the spending power they commanded, seeking pleasure was a way to sort out the hierarchy of status among men. As one mother thought, *bia ôm* was "a touch of class for men nowadays." A rich respondent to a CARE study stated, "Going for girls is a fashionable trend. . . . It's a rich man's fashion."[31]

These men rarely sought out pleasure alone. The CARE study cited finds that "those who seek prostitutes say they prefer to go looking for them in the company of their men friends. Their comments suggest that going out for sex is a male pastime . . . , for closeness with other men." One high-income respondent is quoted as saying, "We have rarely gone out for sex alone. We always go in a group, it's merry to go in a big group. Usually 2 or 3 people." Another high-income man said, "Usually a group of us have sex with a girl if she's a prostitute."[32] Hiếu related how when a middleman took the director of the state-owned contract-granting company out to *bia ôm*, the director took a few other men with him. Then the middleman started to use the "hand phone to call this and that person." "Worse, he brought his eighteen-year-old son. And just like that, the father [and] a girl, the son [and] a girl, they hug away in there."[33] The group aspect of this activity could be explained frequently by business fraternization. But also, going to prostitution places was a social activity done not for private gratification but in the company of others. The men served as spectators for one another's performance of sexual domination to be translated to social domination.

When asked what kind of men in society frequented their workplace, Hằng and Minh gave the following description:

> Hằng: They could have business deals with each other, pitching in for a good time. Let's say there's a table of five men, each pitching in five hundred thousand dong to have a good time and tip us. Or someone who had signed a contract, making ten million, he would take out his friends who helped him in that deal. Or someone who must take out the very person who would put down his signature on the contract he's after.
>
> Minh: Most of the classy ones are big business people. For the sake of their business, they have to bring each other in here.
>
> Hằng: The person who has the power to sign the contract might want the contract seeker to take him to a specific restaurant, and then say, "I want to sleep with that girl." So the other one would have to get him the girl, and then he'd sign the contract.
>
> Minh: The "big hands" are the ones with money, conducting their business. Next down there are those who are after *áp phe* [usually middlemen receiving a commission].
>
> Hằng: Contract signers are the "big hands." They are the high-level cadres and officials. . . .
>
> Minh: Farther down, there are those with some money who want to have a good time, each pitching in two hundred thousand dong. For a table of five, that's a million there. And then there are those without money [the lower-class/working-class men described above].[34]

If there was uncertainty about the men's class identity in society, the pleasure place was where these men asserted their places in a hierarchy of power, the power to grant economic favors and the spending power of money. Subservience in one's interlocutor denoted a higher status. Subservience in the offer of women was demanded by the favor/contract grantor from the grantee. Even more disturbing was the women's sense that their work sorted out the proper classes of Vietnamese men from an emerging underclass of men:

> Hằng: There are many women who are married but still have to work this trade. Their husbands take them there in the morning and pick them up at night. It's bitter.
>
> Minh: Not enough money to live on.
>
> Hằng: The husbands do not have words (not well educated), unemployed. Stay home to care for the kids while the wife works this trade.
>
> Minh: No one wants it. . . . Even, there are men who have to take their wives to rendezvous places so the wives can sleep with other men. (Minh and Hằng, interview, 19 May 1996)

To the question of whether the men would get jealous, Minh and Hang responded as follows:

> Minh: Yes, they (husbands and wives) often bruise each other's faces up. But the money for the family to go on. . . . And the women who have to do this to make money would not respect their husbands. Because the husbands not only cannot feed them, but beat them up for trying to feed them. Me, too, I resent that. . . . On and on like this. Now the men are unemployed and the women have to ply this trade to feed the men.
>
> Hằng: The young men here do nothing, drifting. They gamble. Down there, you saw them on the staircase on your way up here [referring to groups of young men drunk, playing cards on the landings]. The women that have a bit of looks take it and sell it. The men hang on to the hems of the women's britches to eat. They would latch on to a girl, spend all her money, and then leave. (Ibid.)

This sorting out of classes of men was predicated on the women's subservience in this trade. This class distinction thus constructed itself around a gender difference in both the division of sexual labor (female submission in the pleasure act) and the sexual division of labor (husbands are to support their wives and kids). In this world of pleasure, the customers were gods. Should they be displeased with the sex worker's appearance, manners, or shortcomings in responding to their demands, they could wave her away. This was a deep source of feelings of shame and degradation for the women. At the Vũng Tàu cafe where I spent two weekends, my conversations with the women were frequently interrupted as the women went into the back room for lineups where they were picked by their prospective buyers. When a customer asked for two women to serve him at the table or in bed or to dance with him on the dance floor, he was "playing 'king' [*làm vua*]. Some like it that way. They make so much money they have to find ways to spend it to their heart's content."[35] In the following conversation, Minh recalled how a man presided over her initiation into this service/servitude:

> Minh: I wasn't yet eighteen. Small. Just a kid. I was called to serve this man. He knew it was my first time with a customer. He told me to open his beer bottle. I didn't know how. The beer squirted everywhere. He yelled at me. He knew it was my first time opening a beer bottle, but he still yelled at me. I cried. He told me to set it on the table. I set in on the table. Then he yelled, "No, put it under the table." I put it under the table. I didn't know anything, but thought his tip of six thousand dong was a lot of money. I was happy to get six thousand.
>
> Hằng: Many of these young girls know nothing. The sound of the beer can popping startles them the first time. Then they paint their nails, put on makeup, hold the cigarette to smoke. Then they're ready to sleep with the customers. If they don't, they just won't be able to cover their expenses. (Ibid.)

This repetitive act of class stratification for the male customers was predicated on acts of sexual domination over the women who served them. The lower-class cyclo drivers provoked disgust in their performance of sexual domination because it was not accompanied by any position of social domination. These male entrepreneurs, however, pointed to no such contradiction in their performance of domination. As Minh's initiation scene suggests, there was resignation and sadness as opposed to protestation of something out of the ordinary in the order of things, as in her expressed revulsion at serving the cyclo drivers. Indeed, repetitive acts of sexual domination confirmed the entrepreneurs' position of social domination. However, the women's use of the pleasure trade for class advancement failed to bestow on them a clear class identity, be it the moneyed class or the working class. The distribution of the cultural signs of class thus worked differently for the men who bought and for the women who served. The status possibly acquired by the women with money earned in this trade was nullified by social readings of whores' deception, by the women's own stories of moral shame justified by necessity, and by the degradation of servitude.

A powerful class of Vietnamese was emerging. For many, their wealth came from their position in the state, which afforded them dealings with both foreign capital and domestic private entrepreneurs. Not only that, a large part of this wealth came hidden, as it was illegally siphoned from the state coffers. The murky and precarious possession of their wealth heightened the importance of their wearing the trappings of class. This class's position in the economy had yet to prove its endurance as it sprang forth from the power of the state. Consuming this pleasure not only facilitated the generation of their wealth, but it also marked their class with the signs of leisure. Finally, for this class of Vietnamese men, consuming pleasure in women conveniently served as a way in which performances of sexual domination could be read as social domination, a status befitting their economic power.

GEOGRAPHY: THE NATIVIST AESTHETICS OF VULGARITY

If the sorting out of classes of men (this assertion of social domination) via performances of leisure and sexual domination sounded unproblematic, it was not. There was the aesthetic problem with this class performance in the consumption of sex. Bourdieu points out that aesthetic taste is a major component of the signs of class distinction, particularly in leisure activities. In the case of Bourdieu's French bourgeois, this class distinction in aesthetic taste was showcased in the enjoyment of artistic productions (music, painting, literature, theater, etc.).[36] In the case of the Vietnamese entrepreneurs, representations of this leisure/pleasure activity harked back to the aesthetic experience of the old leisure class's visits with courtesans who were well versed in music and literature, poeticized by that quintessential Vietnamese poet

Nguyễn Du in his nineteenth-century portrayals of Kiều and cô Cẩm.
But these representations were not credible to most people. The
mother's remarks regarding *bia ôm* as a leisurely touch of class (*thú vui
sang cả*) or a magazine letter writer's comparing this activity to the frequenting of courtesans (*kỹ nữ*) in wine/teahouses of "feudal times" were
contested on the same pages on which they appeared with descriptions
of the vulgarity and ugliness of the whole sex and pleasure scene. Theft
of public wealth was a frequent reference as to the speculated source of
the money spent in the pleasure houses. Men's behavior in the pleasure
places was characterized as vulgar and obscene. The *bia ôm* women were
described as dishonest, cheap, gaudy, withered, ugly, and even frightening.[37] There were frequent characterizations of sex as pleasure of the
flesh, on a par with other bodily functions.[38] The high culture of music
and poetry recitals provided by the courtesans of the past, immortal-
ized in Nguyễn Du's Kiều and Cẩm, failed to provide the aesthetic
anchor for this contemporary pleasure scene.

I argue here that something else took the place of the music and
poetry of the past as the source of this contemporary bought-sex-as-
aesthetic-experience. That element was the native motif that tapped the
wellspring of nationalist romanticism. Sexual pleasure, commodified as
native things, did two things for its consumers. One, it aestheticized a
vulgar pleasure-seeking activity unbecoming of the newly acquired
social status of its clients. Two, it excluded foreigners (that other important clientele of the pleasure trade) from a status yardstick, the height
of which would be reached by Vietnamese entrepreneurs only if the foreign harbingers and bringers of prosperity could be discounted.

If class identity had become an urgent, earnest task for those who were
rising with the transformation of the socialist economy, what would be
the reason for the problematization of a Vietnamese national identity?[39]
Perhaps integration into a world capitalist economy went to negate the
glory of war against the foreign capitalist world—a capitulation of cause
and identity. A Vietnamese identification with past moral and ideological
superiority through wars of national liberation / socialist revolution no
longer worked in the face of the new foreign presence on Vietnamese
soil when this presence of tourists and investors provided the key to newly

exalted prosperity. If "Vietnam is a country, not a war," as the saying goes, then what defined this "country" was suddenly up for grabs. Artists, writers, bureaucrats, political power contenders, entrepreneurs of broad and narrow stripes, restaurateurs, madams, pimps, call girls, and street walkers all groped about in the mixed bag of "Vietnamese culture" for the shape of this country, to sell for cash or to wield as a weapon. Below, I provide a brief survey of representations of Vietnamese-ness in the pleasure scene catered to the foreign clientele, looking at official reactions and offering an argument of a domestic essentialization of Vietnameseness in commodified sex that would bestow native-ness on Vietnamese men of status, distinct from, and in opposition to, the sexual-social presence as domination by foreign men. This male nativist resistance to the reminiscent colonial presence of outsiders was this time eagerly fought on the battlefield of women's bodies as purchasable and consumable national boundary markers.

Presenting Vietnam

In front of the state-owned Rex Hotel and Nightclub, valets in "traditional" Vietnamese male garb politely opened doors for guests, most of whom were foreigners. Inside the nightclub, hostesses and taxi dancers moved gracefully across the floor in their female Vietnamese traditional/national dresses called *áo dài*. State-owned restaurants and hotels featured hostesses in *áo dàis*.[40] For most tourists, this scene offered a taste of Vietnam. Not unlike tourist industries elsewhere, the state-owned Hanoi Tourism Company proclaimed its mission to be the "creation of special tourist products [*sản phẩm du lịch đặc thù*], particular to and typical of our nation to gain a healthy competitive advantage."[41]

A barrage of reports by the various news publications of the Public Security organs detailed the tourist scenes in which "foreign guests" sought out a "taste of nice and cool (*mát mẻ*) specialty dishes of Vietnam." These specialty dishes were also referred to as "high-quality goods" (*hàng cao cấp, hàng xịn*, and *đặc sản cao cấp*), "whores deluxe and the tropical night," and so on.[42] These were the call girls who wore their hand phones or beepers, the taxi dancers who doubled up as escorts, and

the official and unofficial hostesses at American-style bars. Minh and
Hằng, who had worked those scenes, said having long hair to go with
the flowing *áo dài* is an "asset." "The foreign guests," those "Hong Kong,
Taiwanese, Korean businessmen really go for the long hair."[43]

It was of no surprise that pleasure geared for foreign consumption would
take on the exotic flavors that typify what is Vietnamese for tourists. Nor
is it any surprise that women come to embody much of this typification
of Vietnamese-ness for foreigners. Anne McClintock has pointed out that
today "women are typically constructed as the symbolic bearers of the
nation," as in the advertisement "Singapore girl, you're a great way to fly."[44]
What then happened in the pleasure market geared to foreign consumption is merely the commodification of that Vietnamese-ness embodied in women, to be bought in the sexual act.

In addition to this foreign-catered scene, there were also sex tours.[45]
Sex-tour and sex-ring organizers supplied young women to foreign
businessmen in Vietnam and also exported them to Phnom Penh,
Singapore, Macao, Hong Kong, and Taiwan as prostitutes and as mail-
order brides.[46] While staying at a hotel in District 10 of Ho Chi Minh
City, I witnessed one such wedding between a Taiwanese man and a local
woman. Among the ceremonial items was a live rooster to test the virginity of the bride. Indeed, "virginity selling" had become notorious as
Chinese businessmen were reported (in the media as well as by many
with whom I spoke) to pay hundreds of U.S. dollars for a virgin girl,
whose defloration would bring luck to his business ventures. Virginity
was one more exotic commodity a hitherto veiled Vietnam had to offer
the world.

To certain quarters in the government, this foreign connection seemed
a culprit on which to place the blame for the social evil of prostitution.
This social evil, in the form of "whorehouses in disguise" and "sex tours,"
poses "extreme dangers to the health of our race, and destroy[s] the moral
foundation of our nation," through the "scourge of AIDS" and through
the bad "influence on the lifestyle of our youth, especially those of the
feminine sex," as one writer of a public security news article commented.[47] In an opinion piece in January 1996, the "official theoretical
and political publicist organ of the Vietnamese Communist Party," *Tạp*

Chí Cộng Sản (Communist Review), reminded its readers of the stakes involved: "What's worthy of saying is not only do these social evils erode the pure and beautiful customs of our nation, creating the decadent lifestyle deprived of human value and dignity, they also serve as the conditions giving rise to other social evils such as thievery, hired killings, spreading the plague of the century [AIDS] destroying the health of our race with consequences on not just one generation but many in the future."[48] Indeed, some quarters of the state saw a clear connection between prostitution and the foreign pollution and erosion of the virtuous foundation of Vietnamese culture. On 12 December 1995, Prime Ministerial Decree 814 (814/TTG) announced the implementation of Government Resolution 87 (87/CP), calling for the insertion of "order and moral principles into cultural activities according to our cultural content" to "eliminate social evils." In short, its twin goals were to build (*xây*) and to combat (*chống*). Vietnam was to build a "progressive culture deeply colored with national characteristics" by cracking down on the dissemination of "decadent, poisonous cultural products" and the three social evils. The three social evils to be combated were prostitution, drug addition, and crime, with prostitution receiving the highest profile. Government Resolution 87 was followed by Government Resolution 88 (88/CP), which called for sanctions of "administrative violations involving these social evils."[49] These official measures were preceded by those issued in the early 1990s. However, the current ones exhibited a new degree of intensity and a clear connection to the protection of Vietnamese culture from foreign pollution.[50]

Governmental reactions in the form of decrees and harassment campaigns responded to power struggles within the party and government. But this official crusade to fill the category of culture as national identity and the pleasure industry's commodification of Vietnamese-ness were locked in mutual mimicry and negation. Despite the government's crackdown on the pleasure industry for eroding "beautiful traditions and customs" (*thuần phong mỹ tục*), the government's and the pleasure industry's representations fed each other in their reinforcement of the category of Vietnamese-ness with essentializing "tradition," a "moral order" signified by the fetishism of dress, hair, and national dishes.[51]

Consuming the Native Land

This mutually reinforcing contest of representing Vietnamese-ness prepared the ground for a new form of pleasure commodity catered to the domestic clientele. In opposition to the commodification of Vietnamese-ness in Vietnamese women for consumption by foreign men, Vietnamese men took to marking themselves as natives in the same act of sexual consumption, disrupting both the government's accusation of prostitution as foreign pollution and the sexual/social presence of foreign men. I turn here to a proliferating form of commodification of women's bodies for a Vietnamese clientele where the consumption of sexual pleasure marked the Vietnamese men as natives with exclusive rights to their domain.[52]

But before going further into an analysis of this native-making process, a brief explanation of the theoretical basis of my analysis is in order. I rely on the notion of repetitively signified subjectivity worked out by Judith Butler with regard to gender. In *Gender Trouble*, Butler discusses her notion of performative gender engaging Foucault's modification of Nietzsche's claim in *On the Genealogy of Morals* that there is no "being behind doing, effecting, becoming," no "doer" behind the deed. Butler reads Foucault in *Discipline and Punish* as rewriting the Nietzschean internalization model, obliterating the distinction of exteriority and interiority. Identities are not internalized because the interior is repeatedly inscribed on the surface. Subjectivities or identities including gender, then, are not essential or prior to the doing; instead, they are performed and thereby constituted in repetitive performances.[53] Modifying and supplementing this notion of subjectivity from *Gender Trouble*, Butler focuses on the materiality of the signification process in her subsequent *Bodies That Matter*: "The process of signification is always material; signs work by appearing (visibly, aurally), and appearing through material means, although what appears only signifies by virtue of those non-phenomenon relations, i.e., relations of differentiation, that tacitly structure and propel signification itself."[54] What I adopt from Butler's discussion is this material signification of the native subject. This notion allows me to argue that the domestic consumption of the female body, mimicking the ingestion of food (both material acts), signified a native status differentiated from that of outsiders.

Based on my observation of the pleasure scene in Ho Chi Minh City (the most economically vibrant city with the biggest foreign presence) and in the surrounding suburban and rural towns along its highway to the resort town of Vũng Tàu and on my interviews with women in the trade, government officials, and individuals from organizations dealing with prostitution, I found that the domestic clientele was by far larger than the foreign clientele. I also found that Vietnamese men of means from the entrepreneurial class did not confine themselves to the high end of the scale, where one found most foreigners. Instead, they tended to sample a much broader spectrum of the food and sex available. Places offering both food and women for sexual services with a native/rural flavor tended to look like they were from the middle to the lower end of the scale. Yet pleasure seekers would find that the money they spent there was not that much less than that spent at the glitzier places. A woman from the high end charged on average about ten times more for her services (about VND1 million, or $100) than did a woman at a small "rural" eating place. But at places where the customers enjoyed the specialty dishes and drinks on top of sex, they might not find themselves saving much money. The "specialty" food was surprisingly expensive, and the shabbiness of the place, rather than subtract from the price customers had to pay, added to the ambience of the humble origin of the food. Customers had to find their satisfaction in some aspect of the experience other than cheaper prices. The clients were mostly state and private entrepreneurs fanning from the city in search of pleasure, often conveniently on business trips. Or they were of the same class from the provinces and on trips to the city, resort towns, or other small provincial towns. As for geography and variety, this clientele was mobile in terms of its grazing habits. A purely economic explanation ("They cannot afford the high end") was far from exhaustive and ran counter to the particular cases I witnessed. Why would these men jeopardize their class status by frequenting these extremely modest-looking places (if not downright poor and dirty with prices that did not match their appearance)?

In her discussion of nationalist resistance against the colonial cultural economy of domination, McClintock repeats Frantz Fanon's critical ventriloquy of "the long Western dream of colonial conquest as an erotics of ravishment."[55] As conquest had long been rendered in metaphors of male sexual domination, guarding the land against such conquest had long been confused with guarding the women. Many Vietnamese men expressed to me the pain of seeing busloads of Asian businessmen on sex tours in their city. Even a common newspaper account of different cafés in Ho Chi Minh City would note Vietnamese men's sensitivity to the sight of Vietnamese women going for foreign clients; as one Ho Chi Minh City reporter wrote: "Usually around 5:00 p.m. or a little later, many taxis would stop at the curb, and many pretty 'little sisters' would step out, nonchalantly head for the Western men's tables and . . . sit down. My friend once got a case of 'national pride' and angrily asked: 'Why won't they come to us?'"[56] Another newspaper article raised the humiliating spectacles of the "foreign males who act inappropriately towards Vietnamese women" and "young women who accompany foreigners in public in suggestive dress and heavy make-up."[57] The article was titled "We Are Masters of the House," for good measure. Another newspaper piece censured the tourist bureau of Hue (a former imperial capital) for "offering banquets in which a foreign male sits in regal outfit on a throne, with a Vietnamese queen and two Vietnamese servants positioned on either side."[58] The rhetoric of nationalist anticolonialism had thus been relocated from the battlefields of wars won to the site of the female body, to its mannerisms, its location in public spaces, and its markings. Before, denunciations of the whoring Southern regime, which boasted of streets lined with bars and of prostitutes on the arms of American troops, were used as fodder for the war efforts by the North. Now, there was no war (that masculine activity) other than the one waged over women. If before, the proper nouns of Vietnamese geography—Điện Biên Phủ, the Ho Chi Minh Trail, and the Củ Chi tunnels—were written in the glory of blood, place-names were now projected onto the female body, to be staked, guarded, claimed, mastered, and internalized in other ways.[59] One way was the commodification of the sexual act mimicking the act of the ingestion of local edible offerings.

Hằng described her relationship to her male customers at the *bia ôm* restaurant in this way: "In that place, I am their cake. They buy it, they eat it any way they want."[60] Minh said she felt "worse than selling fish" when the guests refused to tip her for her services, as if people keep poking the fish flesh at the market without wanting to buy it.[61]

As women expressed their feelings of being devoured or their vulnerability at being rejected as a not-good-enough piece of edible flesh, metaphors of food repeatedly showed up in references to these pleasure practices. Some ethereal qualities in women were being commodified in things solid enough to be bought and eaten. One Nguyễn Đình Đạm, in justifying his *bia ôm* habit, likened his wife to dry squash fibers (*xơ mướp*) and the *bia ôm* hostesses to young gourds (*bầu non*), both vegetables used in rural dishes.[62]

As food, this pleasure was given a sensory locus, taste. In interviews with hundreds of male clients of prostitutes in Vietnam for an attitude study, CARE project workers note how "food [is] a common image used by men to justify their desire for variety in sexual partners." One man is quoted as saying, "Just like food, if you eat one kind of food for a long time, you will lose your appetite, and you want to eat other kinds of food."[63] Công, a male entrepreneur, told me in 2002 that as the practice of entrepreneurs' and government officials' (who often doubled as state entrepreneurs) taking one another out for food and sex became routinized, people no longer liked to eat "dishes like beef, chicken, fish, pork. . . . Now when people play, they like to eat only the most exotic things like game meat, and now even snakes, centipedes, boa constrictors, cicadas and other insects."[64] This search for new flavors left a trail of the exotic, as gustatory delights and erotic pleasures mingled. Up and down Vietnam, snake blood was the new craze. I saw in the streets how cooks demonstrated ripping out a snake's heart and dropping it in a cup of sake, to be drunk by men as an aphrodisiac as they enjoyed the snake blood beaten into a custard-like cake.

But why snakes? What form of the exotic was being served up? It was not an exoticism that called forth the foreign, as from another land. Rather, it was the indigenous quality that it acquired that was eagerly bought and sold. Perhaps the production of this cultural meaning could be better understood by considering the passage below written by Sơn Nam, the inventor of the notion of *văn minh miệt vườn* (orchard civilization of the rural south) and icon of nativist claims to local wisdom against the onslaught of Western knowledge since colonial days.[65] In a collection of economic writings about the burgeoning Vietnamese market economy, Sơn Nam offers his understanding of the current "money-spending culture":

> Some Frenchmen of modest backgrounds in the mother country came here to the "Pearl of the Orient" [Saigon] and could live like princes, leisurely eating and playing at the Continental or Majestic, liberally opening champagne bottles. The Vietnamese in Saigon became prideful. In however ways the French could play, the Vietnamese, although people of the colonies with "yellow skin and flat noses," could outplay them. They too could buy villas for their kept lovers, acquire attractive actresses, smoke opium, and outspend the French in French restaurants . . .
>
> The [Chinese] husbands could freely pursue their business at some cafés where they collected news and information relating to buying and selling, met their friends, took these friends and acquaintances to eat. When they ate and drank, they could more easily come to some understanding, or request loans, the refusal of which would not be too embarrassing in such a cordial setting . . .
>
> But with the Vietnamese, spending money originated from special circumstances. These were the people who opened up the [southern] land for the past three hundred years. . . . The French and the Chinese view Saigon as their temporary home. When necessary, they could just pick up and leave for France, Singapore, Phnom Penh, Bangkok. But us, we hold on to our fatherland. The first steps of opening up the land involved clearing swamps and jungle, struggling with disease, tigers, and crocodiles. [The Vietnamese settlers] cleared trees, dug water drains, dredged up mud to cover their walls, to build their houses, to feed the betel and coconut palms. They ate everything the land had to offer. . . . They ate eels, turtles, frogs, snakes, young *bần*, guava, mango leaves, shoots, water lilies, roots, etc. Southerners are now willing to spend a lot for these culinary delights.[66]

How the settlers lived, worked, and ate in the most fertile part of the Mekong Delta was what Sơn Nam refers to as "orchard civilization." The term has since acquired a more general meaning of southern rurality. This rurality conjured up ties and thus allowed its practitioners to lay claims to the land. According to Sơn Nam's account, what distinguished the Vietnamese way of pleasure seeking from the wanderlust of the fortune-seeking Westerners, or from the *guanxi* (relations) among local Chinese businessmen, was this indigenousness that could be demonstrated in what the Vietnamese ate. The eels, turtles, frogs, snakes, leaves, shoots, water lilies, roots, and so forth were exotic in their fantastic varieties. Yet they all came from one source, the land, to be tasted and appreciated as distinctly local offerings. What was rural was at once welded into what was native.

Much of the commodification of pleasure geared to domestic consumption framed sex in native gustatory desire. There were now stretches of "fifteen kilometers of eating and playing." This phrase referred to stretches of highway lined with shops specializing in local culinary flavors mixed with exotic ways in which men could enjoy women. One such stretch was in the Sông Cầu area. Another ran from the Saigon Bridge to Thủ Đức on the Hanoi Highway. According to one reporter for a Public Security newspaper, the Sông Cầu stretch in central Vietnam acquired its reputation "because here there are many specialty dishes (*món ăn đặc sản*), from the marshes and the sea, that are fresh and delicious. . . . And the red lights come on as night falls. The girls who attract customers to the food are young and agile, with powdered cheeks and colored lips, alluring enough to serve 'the gods' as they reach the desired degree of *bia ôm*."[67] According to another magazine report, the Saigon–Thủ Đức stretch offered the latest form of *bia ôm*, "hammock cafés," where guests in hammocks hung between trees could be "hugged" by "'rice tantalizing' [*ngon cơm*, meaning either that the women are dishes that make the accompanying rice taste good or that the quality they bring makes the meal taste good] girls of sixteen and seventeen." Afterward, the guests could "land" with their young hostesses in the tiny thatched huts safely tucked away among the trees. "Knowing we were looking for 'fresh and cool' services [*dịch vụ tươi mát*] on the highway, the motorcycle taxi driver slapped his thigh: 'If you haven't tried the thatched huts, you don't know anything about eating and playing on the highway.'"[68] Edible greenness/youth, freshness, the coolness of the shade in the orchard, and hammocks and thatched huts among the trees all evoked rurality. Although men of money frequented a wide range of pleasure services, from the expensive dance halls and call girls to the rustic roadside cafés, women and their provision of sexual services had come to be designated by the code word *tươi mát* (fresh and cool). As with Son Nam's celebration of *văn minh miệt vườn* in the knowledge and ability to enjoy native offerings, the assertion about "knowing" in the last quotation also highlights the casting of these as secret pleasures accessible to only those initiated into a native way of being and knowing.

In the resort town of Vũng Tàu, a popular playground of the Saigon nouveau riche, the cyclo driver who gave me a tour of "Vũng Tàu by night" casually told me that the restaurants with advertisements of specialty dishes are the ones that offer the "chicks/hens with red nails/claws" (*gà móng đỏ*). This mocking phrase was slang for "prostitutes," referring to their red nail polish, and I heard it used in conjunction with the women who work on the outskirts of the city and in this resort town. Again, there was the same rural ambience as young women gathered to wait for their customers late at night under dimly lit fruit trees in places not formally named but simply called one mango orchard or another. Most of these young women wore *đồ bộ*, the same top and bottom set that had come to designate the un-Westernized rural. The innovation was that they were now sleeveless, cut to reveal, and made of brightly colored, clingy silklike materials. Even in Ho Chi Minh City, with its modern, Western outlook, many of these young women wore *đồ bộ* while working the small eating places or the streets. One police newspaper in 2005 refers to the "salty ruralness" (*chất quê mặn mòi*) of sex workers that attracted clients.[69]

According to my observations, informal estimates by Vietnamese who worked with prostitutes, and some researchers' surveys, many of the young women in the urban and suburban areas and a good majority in the pleasure trade along the highways, or in the resort towns, came from rural areas. In one study, 47.2 percent of respondents said they came from farming backgrounds, by far the largest of any background/occupational group.[70] This was another way that these young women embodied rurality for their customers. The availability of these young rural women was facilitated by conditions in the countryside, where economic growth had shown signs of reversal after the initial gains in agricultural production at the beginning of liberalization in the 1980s. In 1990, the per capita gross domestic product in rural areas amounted to 31 percent of that in urban areas. By 1994, it had dropped to 19 percent.[71] According to statistics generated by the Farmers' Union, 10 percent of peasants in the Mekong Delta in the south did not have access to land. In each province, there were approximately ten thousand to fifteen thousand families who had to find employment as hired farmhands. In Trà Vinh Province, the number of households with no land holding climbed to 14.4 percent in 1997.[72]

One man, experienced in "playing," declared, "Plain *bia ôm* is old stuff! Now, it's the hammock cafes! Cool breeze, clear sky in the suburbs, you've reached the other side, you're 'there.'"[73] One newspaper notes how *bia ôm* had originated in the city and spread to the countryside.[74] As the search for the locally exotic deepened and widened, pleasure as a commodity increasingly took on rural colors as it spread through the countryside.

The rural place-names of the nation's geography, its rural soul, were compressed into the materiality of native "specialties" that could be brought to the city. These pleasures from food and women's bodies could be "discovered" in the city if one looked deep enough. The following passage appeared in a popular public security newspaper:

> Saigonese who are connoisseurs of food and drink like to seek out and enjoy the culinary delights in the small alleys. . . . Famous for the dishes of rice vermicelli and grilled pork, of fried rolls is the Casino alley. . . . Intellectuals, prominent businessmen, and *Việt kiều* [overseas Vietnamese] all know the reputation of the Nguyễn Huệ alley with Mrs. Cả Đọi's shop and her *thịt đông* [cold meat and pickled cabbage], her *mồng tơi* [a country spinach] soup, *cà pháo* [small pickled melons], *mắm tôm* [fermented shrimps], cheap and delightful. . . . If you're nursing some melancholy and want to empty out your sadness, you must stop by the alley of 220 Lê Văn Sỹ in District 3, classy and discreet, known for little sisters beautiful as a dream, who will entertain you by the hour just like the call girls.[75]

In the city, as with the suburbs and outlying towns, these hidden pleasures were accessible only to those with indigenous knowledge or to those initiated into it by the native-as-connoisseur, with his informed discrimination in taste and his art of enjoyment. Native-ness, belonging-ness, could be shown in this repetitive act of sampling those pleasures, culinary and sexual, as the mark of connoisseurship. These rural dishes, not the "peacock hash or phoenix pie" of courtly banquet menus, awaited the connoisseur deep in the labyrinth of the city's bowels. A restless search for what was authentically Vietnamese went on in the inexhaustible depth of an interior soul. One could roam the lush country and its connecting highways in search of this depth or one could find it emboweled in the city. The city dweller could look deep into his city and find its rural soul, to be had in food and women.

Nostalgia for Country Land: The Aesthetics of Vulgarity

Rurality was not the only possible component, just a convenient one, in the construction of native ties to the land. The rural village and its fields with their protective walls of swaying bamboo often were evoked in literary and visual artistic productions in the past as the source and resting place of the Vietnamese soul, beyond the reach of outsiders. Phạm Duy's recovered folk songs of the 1950s and 1960s did much to reinforce this image. Even when the naïveté of this romantic notion was "exposed" in accounts of rural hardships and oppressive ways of life, it served as a prop to offer more complex reworkings of the same motif. Examples include the highly acclaimed literary works coming out of the period of Vietnamese glasnost in the late 1980s and early 1990s, such as Dương Thu Hương's *Những thiên đường mù* (Paradise of the Blind), with its endless descriptions of local rural food, rich and nourishing against the austerity and death inflicted on this rural community by the socialist regime's Land Reform Campaign in the 1950s, or Nguyễn Huy Thiệp's "Những bài học nông thôn" (Rural Lessons) and "Thương nhớ đồng quê" (Nostalgia for Country Land; with a film by the same title), on a rural moral clarity and the sacrifices asked of the countryside by the nation for its projects. For the purpose of social and political critique directed at the regime, these were depictions of the rural as the wronged and forgotten (or even as the neglected cesspool of oppressive backwardness), yet in them, the rural remained the source of strength and renewal for the national consciousness.[76]

The problematization of a Vietnamese identity came now at a time of sweeping changes. Economic liberalization had called into question the socialist revolutionary promise and its utopian time line. But it had put in its place the lure of capitalist modernization and its teleology of progress, its fetish of the new, which, in the case of a Vietnam newly opened to the world, was synonymous with the foreign. But as discussed, this love affair with the new life came with anxieties about native women won over to foreign power and foreign money, that old story about the native whore.

The government slogan Determined Modernization and Industrialization of the Country only underscored the nation's anxious rush toward an unfamiliar future, fraught with the familiar fear of conquest and occupation. Benedict Anderson asks if it was not the novelty of nations that called for their imagined antiquity as a narrative source of nationalist "memory."[77] Territorial boundaries aside, I ask here if it was not also some imagined geographical source that served as one of the Vietnamese nation's anchors as it rushed forward into a future made in the West and the Asian economic "dragons" and "tigers." Yes, the nation narrated itself backward as it moved forward. But it could also take with it such an imagined place as the rural, that clump of earth with the nation's metaphorical roots attached, a source and resting place, a depository of a national soul. This temporally mobile geographical source was not a particular place. Seen from a plane as watery emerald expanses, it was an imagined heartland that ultimately became carry-on luggage as the nation flew toward some modern and foreign future.

In this sense, rurality was imbued with a sense of nationalist nostalgia for when the land was being won and cultivated, a primal connection between man and land, enactable in the sexual connection between man and woman, conflated with the act of ingesting wildly exotic dishes of indigenous edibles. It may be pointed out that not just any woman was to be consumed in this way, but only those who did not have the means to resist such objectification of their bodies in a social hierarchy of domination. The act of eating, and its now twin sex act, vulgar in formulations of bodily functions and gluttony, could now defiantly pronounce its vulgarity as proof of its firm connection to a nostalgic romanticism of nation and geography in literary and artistic evocations of rurality.

Objectification and Ambiguous Subjectivities

Although this search for a Vietnamese essence amid all the profound changes could be rendered comprehensible, the brutality of this act in its transformation of women into ingestible commodities was difficult to overlook. The mixing of metaphors and the mingling of food and sex allowed the performance of nativism in the act of food ingestion to be duplicated in the act of pleasure consumption using women. The women had come to embody this tie to the land, the consumption of which is an attempt at being native. This process demands that these women became objectified as things, the ingestion of which provided the men with the coolness and freshness of native ways. This objectification predicated itself on a gender difference between the women and the men who were to consume them. Doreen Massey has noted that in recent times, "woman" often has been nostalgically constructed as "a place called home."[78]

As the women were objectified and commodified, many felt stripped of a sense of subjectivity. Both Minh and Hằng told me that, among themselves, the women agreed with their "faces" and not with their "insides" to serve the men: "Bằng mặt chứ không bằng lòng."[79] The differentiation between a surface and an interior gave the women a sense of the possibility of preserving a core being beyond the reach of this objectification.

These women were caught between being the Vietnamese object of a foreign fantasy of ravishment and being native offerings that allowed Vietnamese men to reenact their dream of native resistance. Nevertheless, there were makeshift ways in which the women disrupted both the foreign "erotics of ravishment" and the native "erotics of resistance." One way was the above affirmation that sex was a service to be provided for a monetary price, and their feminine surrender to conquest was only a surface exchange. Their hearts and minds remained their own.

The romanticism of erotics of national resistance was refuted when the dozens of working and retired women I interviewed told again and again stories of how foreign men treated them with more respect. These women produced a discourse that insisted foreign men paid more and were more compliant with the women's insistence on condom use. One Ho Chi Minh City Women's Union officer in charge of an AIDS peer education group, consisting of fifteen former sex workers, expressed her amusement at the stories she heard on the street regarding how foreign men would perform "caring gestures" like "feeding" the women and "bathing" and "caressing" them, while the Vietnamese clients would only ask for "all kinds of tricks."[80] More telling was the dismay expressed by the central Women's Union officer in Hanoi who investigated AIDS and prostitution: "The foreign clients are rare compared to the Vietnamese clients. And the women, they all say foreigners are more polite and caring while our men mistreat them. This is a strange finding for me. I'd thought the foreign men's appearance would be perceived as strange, unfamiliar, with alien needs. If it were me, I would be scared to death of them. And it's not just because they pay more, but they actually treat the women better, more fair."[81] The model as used by the Women's Union of woman's sense of familiarity and solidarity with "our men" was thrown into doubt by the sex workers' renditions of the Vietnamese men's behavior. The women's stories show that these representations, and the narratives in which they were situated, were ambiguous enough in their multiplicity and disparity to be contestable. I turn now to the disparate representations of romantic rurality in the pleasure trade and the ambiguous subjectivities of the women who worked this trade.

The romantic vision of a lush-country-for-the-taking stood contested. A reporter for the *Tuổi Trẻ* compares a "love market" in a poverty-stricken area of central Vietnam to those in the south:

> I don't know how lush and alluring the *miệt vườn* love markets in the south might be, but here, it's just rows of low huts thatched with various *tranh, tre, nứa* grasses in Hưng Thủy (kilometers 701st to 708th)

with girls still stained with mud and earth from the field, though covered up with red nail polish, the ruralness and hardship keep showing through. . . . Not all the sisters at this rural love market step into the realm of severed viscera [*đoạn trường*, or pain] because of too much hardship in country life. But when you stand here looking at the bare huts amid the white sand and the wind blowing through all four seasons, and looking at a new generation of youth without jobs while the market spreads to the roots of each new rice seedling, then it is not at all difficult to comprehend why, in some moment, it is possible to sell your body to live.[82]

Despite the common image of lush rurality in the southern "love markets," this ambivalent mix of rural beauty and hardship was present in the southern pleasure scene as well. The same report that detailed the appeal of the hammock and thatched-hut cafés on the outskirts of Ho Chi Minh City also pointed out that the makeshift huts were also called "pens" because they were dirty and mosquito infested.[83] The performance of rurality by those in the pleasure industry often turned out to be a pale imitation of the romantic nativist vision of a soothing, cool, fresh, and lush rurality. The rural native narrative here revealed the contingent character of its construction. Even the practice of eating/drinking snake blood described above was of doubtful origin. The snake-blood custard mimicked the pig- or dog-blood custard seen as a special Vietnamese dish. But drinking snake blood is also found elsewhere, for example, in Thailand. I am not implying that there was a lack of authenticity in these performances. What I am saying is that this authenticity in indigenousness was being produced before our eyes and that this nativist production was contingent on the performances of rurality engaged in by the men and women involved, for the benefit of male consumers' construction of their national identity.

In my conversations with the rural women who worked in the pleasure trade, I kept hearing stories of their desire to return to the countryside with enough money to start a new life. Yet the number of those attempts was matched by the times they ended up back in their trade in the cities, suburbs, and resort towns and along the highways. Hoa, one of these young women, said, "I get so *buồn* [sad, depressed, or bored] in the countryside. Every time I went back there, I could only stay for a few days and I just had to leave." Her lover, who picked her up at the "hen café" where she worked as a prostitute, insisted she go back to the countryside where women stay out of trouble (for safekeeping) to wait out his prison term as a motorcycle thief.[84] The women felt the pressure to embody rurality in their trade.

At the same time, these women kept failing to live up to the standards of rural life. Their trade demanded the embodiment of this rurality, but being a rural woman meant adhering to strict rules of chastity and propriety. Many of the women said they fled their home in the countryside to escape the life that these virtues entailed. Some were fleeing abusive husbands and bad marriages. Some were fleeing marriage altogether, as their fathers tried to arrange it. Whatever the packaging of the goods to be sold, it was imperative in this trade that these women put aside rural values and effectively sell their flesh. Eighteen-year-old Hà, the youngest and most rural looking at a beachside café in Vũng Tàu, told me, "Mai [a coworker] knows how to make love. I'm too country [quê]. I don't know anything. I only know how to go *shop*." She explained that "making love" meant "you got to know how to touch, caress, and serve them in different ways. I am too shy to do it. . . . Going *shop* is like what husbands and wives do." When I asked who among their clients preferred making love and who preferred just plain intercourse (*shop*), she answered, "Westerners [the term may refer to all foreigners] like making love. . . . Vietnamese like *shop* better."[85] But she was ridiculed by her boss for her lack of skills in pleasing the men. The owner of the café where she worked complained to me that, while the men liked Hà's young, innocent appearance in her red *đồ bộ*, she had not been aggressive or business savvy enough: "She should go learn how to sew or something. What kind of 'hen' is she when she has not gone with a customer in three days?"[86] Shortly later, Hà explained to me that her boss was mad at her for not "stuffing [herself with] cotton" as her boss would do to continue working during menstruation. For a country-woman, menstruation had to be kept invisible to men and was a time to avoid sexual contact with them for it might bring illness: "I just will not do it. I refuse to do that."[87] Nevertheless, she did spend the remainder of that night, from one to five o'clock, with a client who paid her VND100,000 (about US$10), 40 percent of which went to the owner of the café.[88]

The pleasure trade and the women who worked it appeared to be failing to completely compress themselves into one single representation, in this case, rural objects. Perhaps this was what might be called a moment of dissonance in which an identity reveals its performative status. Performance does not mean falsehood as opposed to some true essence or reality, such as some true rurality or Vietnamese-ness. What it means is that there are inherent ambiguities, as identities remain contingent on the acts, the deeds. These performances remain incomplete in the face of intersecting or contradictory representational demands, opening up possibilities not otherwise negotiable within the narrow constraints of a single representation. Or perhaps this might have been an instance of Walter Benjamin's dialectical image where the prostitute, being both "saleswoman and wares in one," embodies the bifurcation of commodity as an object of desire that reflexively exposes its presumed worth: "Commodity attempts to look into its own face. It celebrates its human incarnation in the figure of the whore."[89]

In any case, these contradictory demands showed in the women's demeanor and appearance. The ambiguity of this double performance of being fresh and rural and being savvy with the ways of the world hung over their stories about the desire to return to the countryside and the inability to stay confined there for more than a few days at a time. The country prostitute became a "hen with red nails/claws" in this designation's startling combination of rurality and glamour for sale, of the powerlessness in a simple rural girl and the threat of her transformation. While objectifying and commodifying the women into ingestible rural things, the pleasure trade also offered them the possibility of some agency beyond the scope of rural women trapped in rural ways. As Massey has suggested, the very act of the women's leaving their home in the countryside might have opened up possibilities of other ways of being and disrupted the men's efforts to fix firmly the women's identity in the rural home place.[90]

CONCLUSION

With economic liberalization in the 1990s came the problematization of class and national identity. The pleasure scene was one site at which these issues were worked out. If the new rich in Vietnam started out attaining their wealth through contacts with the outside world, as Bạch's study suggests, an emerging class of rich and powerful Vietnamese men began to differentiate themselves, and they distributed themselves on a separate class/status scale than one that might put them below the foreign men. The Vietnamese men of means had to be painfully aware of what Minh said had entered mundane daily exchanges: "Girls of seven and eight. The grown-ups would say, 'Oh, she's pretty. Save her and marry her off to a Taiwanese or a *Việt kiều*.'"[91] Phương, a journalist covering prostitution for a large newspaper, said resentfully that while working undercover as a client at the expensive dancing halls, "I would have to flaunt my money for those girls to even come to me, because I'm obviously not foreign, and I don't have the looks and the style of a *Việt kiều*."[92] Showing one's spending power at these expensive places was a statement of class parity with foreigners. But frequenting pleasure places with a native flavor differentiated Vietnamese men from outsiders.

Travel brochures and publications on Vietnam typically presented the Vietnamese girl in the traditional dress of *áo dài* and the long flowing hair, leaning on one dynastic tomb or another of the national landmarks (if they were not being made to pose as imperial consorts to foreign tourists in regal guise). This image was the state's version of a healthy Vietnamese culture presented to the world. For the large part of the pleasure market geared to Vietnamese men, however, the women had come to typify the nation by embodying the locally exotic, in this case rurality, inaccessible to foreign men, who lacked the discriminate taste/knowledge to enjoy it. This typification of Vietnamese-ness for Vietnamese, as opposed to the courtly motifs in the image of Vietnam presented to the rest of the world, allowed Vietnamese men to perform Vietnamese-ness in two ways. First, it tied them to the land and the history via the ingestion of local offerings in a native aesthetics, transforming the vulgarity of the sexual act. Second, it enabled these men to assert difference through exclusive knowledge. But as with the use of pleasure to mark class, this construction of national identity was reserved for men, as it was built on gender differentiations.

The commodification and consumption of pleasure in women's bodies had to do with liberalizing economic practices in the current distribution of political/economic power, with the new powerful class in a process of social stratification, and with what it meant to be Vietnamese. These practices, visible to ordinary Vietnamese and officials alike, undermined the credibility of the old story of prostitution as vestige of ancient regimes. Instead, commercial sex implicates entrepreneurial men's business practices and their consumption as a source of their class and national identity. The post–Đổi Mới government can no longer eradicate it in the same way it did back at the end of the war. Entrepreneurs must be free to do business, both the male entrepreneurs who fraternize with business partners through the consumption of commercial sex and the entrepreneurs who run establishments that offer sex on the side in various guises. Consumers must be free to buy what they choose, even a night on the town that ends with bought sex. Nevertheless, commercial sex, which was and is integral to the market freedom to do business and to consume, incites government intervention, where modes of control connected to both politics and economics are devised.

PART II

THE REAL AND THE TRUE

Governing by Choice and Coercion

CHAPTER 3

The Rise of the Empirical
and the Case of Medical Expertise

A Genealogy of Governance

IN PART 1, I SHOW how neoliberal choice in entrepreneurial decisions and consumption shaped the sex trade as Vietnam marketized primarily from the late 1980s to the mid-1990s. In part 2, I examine how the government approached prostitution as a social problem through public health, policing, and rehabilitation measures and in doing so show the shift from state socialism toward two simultaneous modes of governance that were based on both choice and coercion and were more amenable to the global market economy.

From the 1950s, the Vietnamese Communist Party and its state apparatuses sought to curb the autonomy of knowledge, folding them into an all-encompassing party-state. This process was most evident in the state's treatment of experts and intellectuals during the Nhân Văn–Giai Phẩm affair of the mid-1950s and the anti-revisionist campaign of the early 1960s. I argue that the feature distinguishing state socialism as led by a Leninist party is not repression per se but the rejection of an imagined social realm separate from the state.

The case of medicine illustrates how the socialist state had started to use expert and empirical knowledge during marketization. The increasing use of expert medical knowledge was symptomatic of a reimagined relationship between the erstwhile all-encompassing socialist state and a society separate from it. The socialist state came to resemble more and more a government in relation to society. Medicine as a body of knowledge became important in the government's dealing with prostitution through public health measures. It is through these health measures that a mode of governance based on knowledge and choice emerged.

EXPERTISE IN SOCIALIST GOVERNANCE

The changing place of expertise in governance can be seen in the shift in the relationship between state and society from socialism to market. The two historical episodes mentioned best exemplify the socialist mode of governing. Besides artistic conflict, the Nhân Văn–Giai Phẩm affair and the anti-revisionist campaign less than a decade later also illustrate the related struggle between the party and experts and their expertise. In modern forms of government, including governance by Leninist parties such as the ruling Communist parties in state socialist countries, expertise occupies an important place. Why then would one find the new socialist government waging a fierce battle against experts?

Analyses of the "totalitarian model" that stress how rulers use expert knowledge as a tool to control and manipulate the population according to the political ends of the regime are not unfamiliar.[1] By comparison, proponents of the industrial convergence model point to the tendency even in Leninist systems toward rule by expert knowledge as a result of the demands of advanced industrial economies.[2] Mark Beissinger points out that both models entail a unidirectional development of Leninist systems toward more total control in the first case and toward more autonomy for experts and their expertise in the second case.[3] Beissinger instead uses organizational theory to suggest that there is a contradiction or tension inherent in bureaucratic organization of hierarchical discipline, on the one hand, and pursuit of rational goals, on the other.[4] The inherent tension here is that between the requirement for cohesion under party rule ensured by hierarchical command and the goal-fulfilling tasks requiring expertise involved in running a command economy. Compared to the more familiar totalitarian and convergence models, Beissinger's suggestion explains better the historical cycles of promotion of expertise and its political suppression in Leninist societies. However, there is also a tension in Beissinger's application of general organizational theory to Leninist systems. On the one hand, he claims that Leninist systems fall prey to the same contradiction besetting bureaucratic organization in general. On the other hand, Marxist-Leninist ideology makes its way into his theory from an external position as the source of the "technocratic utopianism" behind the command economy. As a result, Beissinger mentions the historically recurring official concerns over the class status of experts but does not fully account for such ideological consideration in his organizational explanation.

THE STATIZATION OF EXPERTISE AND LENINIST GOVERNANCE IN VIETNAM

In my analysis of knowledge and governance in Vietnam before the start of economic liberalization, I benefit from Beissinger's insights into this tension in Leninist governance as coming from the need for both expertise and cohesion through hierarchical control by the Leninist party. However, my purpose is not to advance a better theory to account for the use of knowledge and Leninist governance. Rather, from an examination of cycles of tension over expertise in the history of socialist Vietnam, I show how governance was being imagined in relation to society. In this sense, I look at the bourgeois class designation of experts ill accounted for in Beissinger's organizational theory. But rather than chalk it up to the party's ideological assertion of class struggle, I suggest that it points to a certain mentality of governing in which there was no conception of a realm, such as "society," separate from the political state. This mentality was again evident in the assertions by the party of a *raison d'état* in its wartime foreign policy over the dangers posed by experts.

At the beginning of the anticolonial war, the party had identified native possessors of Western knowledge, such as doctors, engineers, lawyers, and those in the natural, technical, and human scientific disciplines, as belonging to the bourgeois class, whose interests essentially conflicted with those of the revolution. Western knowledge was part and parcel of the *mission civilisatrice* of colonial rule, which had to be reformed and put to new uses in a new culture of anticolonialism and socialism.[5] This ambivalence was maintained at various historical moments in the party's position toward the bourgeois intelligentsia. On the one hand, members of the intelligentsia had to be recruited to serve the resistance and the revolution and to build the new society with their Western-learned knowledge and technical skills. On the other hand, their class was iden-

tified as bourgeois, one whose interests conflicted with that of the proletarian revolution and its vanguard party. I turn to examine two major
crises in party-expert relations: in the latter part of the 1950s at the start
of the party's initiation of a command economy right after the anticolonial war and in the 1960s as the anti-imperialist war (the Vietnam
War) intensified. I argue that the class designation of experts and their
expertise in the first instance, the wartime *raison d'état* in the second
instance, and the statist solutions in both instances reflected a configuration of governance that did not see itself as responding to autonomous
realms of life separate from the organization and reasons of state.

In a Party Central Committee resolution setting down the party's 1959
position toward the bourgeois class, the necessity of having the participation of the "bourgeois intelligentsia" in the victorious anticolonial
resistance was affirmed at the same time as the class danger was spelled
out. The resolution stated that in the beginning years of the establishment of a socialist society in the North after the 1954 Geneva Accords
ending the anticolonial war, "the bourgeoisie, while complying with our
policies, always reacts to them." According to the resolution, this reaction came in two forms, both of which were manifestations of essentially reactionary bourgeois class interests: in 1956 and 1957 when this
class's "racketeering" economic practices posed direct obstacles to the
state's "management of prices and market" and from 1956 to 1958 with
cultural opposition in the form of the ill-fated Nhân Văn–Giai Phẩm
movement for intellectual and artistic autonomy from party dictates.[6]
In the view of the party, the economic and cultural are but the two fronts
put up by the same bourgeois class against the proletarian party-led class
struggle. The Nhân Văn–Giai Phẩm episode was a crisis in party-expert
relations at a moment when expertise was crucial to the party's initiation of socialist transformation.

In the late 1950s, demands for autonomous artistic freedom were coupled by demands for the state to "return control over expertise to
experts."[7] Nguyễn Mạnh Tường, a prominent attorney and legal scholar
who participated in the Nhân Văn–Giai Phẩm movement, gave a
speech representing the views of intellectuals at the 30 October 1956
meeting in Hanoi of the party-led mass organization Fatherland Front.

In it, he spelled out the problem facing the new Democratic Republic of Vietnam:

> The intellectual brothers in the resistance often complain that the party does not trust them. They are pained to observe that even though they have gone through difficult trials and made sacrifices, the party still does not trust them. It's not like they ask for much. They do not ask to be made minister or ambassador. No. The majority of intellectuals do not dream of glamorous positions. They are glad to leave those places to politicians, party officials. All they want is to bring their expert ability and experience to their job of serving the people. All they desperately want is to protect the intellectual honor and freedom of thought that they think are necessary for an intellectual's integrity.[8]

At the heart of the problem was the question of whether there was a realm for expertise autonomous from the bureaucratically organized state and its professed ideological preoccupations. Prominent intellectuals in the university such as Paris-trained philosopher Trần Đức Thảo were later denounced for demanding the "expulsion of politics from the area of expertise" and for announcing "expertise is the future and politics is the past."[9] This dichotomous posing of the problem reflected the Western-trained experts' insistence on an autonomous logic in the area of knowledge, beyond reasons of state. The rebel experts argued that their professional activities needed to be autonomous from the control of the party's political cadres simply because these did not concern governors, the "ministers and the ambassadors," with their domestic and foreign policy considerations.

The view from the party, however, was not that simple. The Marxist-Leninist party could not see the demands of the intelligentsia as arising from an ahistorical and classless position. Instead, since these intellectuals-cum-experts belonged to the bourgeois class, their demands were viewed by the party as class positions. There was no such thing as an autonomous logic in the realm of culture, which included the arts and sciences. Subsuming the sciences and arts under the problematics of culture gave the party the advantage of claiming this entire domain as one belonging to a state trying to create a "new culture."[10] Tố Hữu, a writer and high-ranking party official in the Writers Union, put the party's position regarding the problem thus: "They [the Nhân Văn–Giai Phẩm intellectuals] disseminated their fanciful myths about the laws of development of 'art in itself' and 'science in itself.'" Their sins were to "attack the economic organs of the state, especially the state exchange organs [price-fixing agencies]"; "to oppose the regime of the democratic people's state"; "to label us a bureaucratic state under party rule; to oppose the cultural revolution; and to deny the class character and thus the party character of culture." What these intellectuals really wanted to do, continued Tố Hữu, was to "turn our state into a bourgeois state."[11]

A persistent theme in the party-sponsored denunciations was the linkage between the Nhân Văn demands and outside hostile forces.[12] To be bourgeois was not just to be against "our State"; it was to be foreign, alien altogether. There was nothing conceivable outside the state short of the foreign. The mentality of governance was marked by a close identification between the "nation" itself and the state. This was in accordance with Lenin's view of the state as the entity that would take over the class struggle in civil society for the proletariat in a "dictatorship of the proletariat." The state he envisioned was to be simply the proletariat's state, formed by its vanguard party.[13] If the state had little meaningful dynamics autonomous from its base in civil society with a simplified Marxist view, Lenin's "transitional" state assumed agency and took over the dynamics of history, at least until it could usher in the end of history in a Communist society.[14] So even though the "social" was overriding in Marx (hence the socialist solution), it was not a stretch for Lenin to go for the reverse emphasis on the state as taking over the dynamics of civil society, carrying the necessary class struggle for the proletariat, thus conceptually eliminating an autonomous realm of society with its own dynamics. Hence, there was in the Leninist mentality of governing a conceptual unity of ends in a statist rationality that spurred the experts-governors tension that Beissinger identifies. The ideology of class struggle was to provide the unity of ends for a self-referential state since the reference to society as an existing reality was deferred to a yet-to-exist future Communist society.

So in a roundabout way, through the debate about the class character of expert activities, the crux of the disagreement in North Vietnam at the time was what belonged to the political realm and thus the state. From the party's point of view, since all economic, artistic, and scientific activities were class based and thus political, they all belonged to the realm taken over by the proletarian state, which, under the leadership of the party, was waging a class struggle against the exploitative bourgeois class. The party saw experts' demands for autonomy from party supervision as part of the attacks by the bourgeois class directed against the proletarian state. Denouncing renegade intellectuals in the Nhân Văn–Giai Phẩm movement, Nguyễn Đình Thi in the party's theoretical journal *Học Tập* spelled out the ways in which the intellectuals' demands amounted to political attacks on the network of state institutions and on a *raison d'état* of survival against outside attacks by the capitalist and reactionary forces:

> They [the Nhân Văn–Giai Phẩm intellectuals] protest the dictatorship [of the proletariat] while asking for "democracy," "freedom" in the bourgeois sense in the realm of politics, economics, culture. They attack the state's control of market exchange, the state's management through the household registration, the post office, the publicist organs, the hospitals, and even the National Assembly. In short, they attack all the apparatuses of our state, demanding the freedom to form an opposition to the government while the reactionary forces are plotting sabotage and elements of the bourgeoisie are attacking us.[15]

These party-sponsored denunciations point to a conceptual identification between the political regime of the party and the state apparatuses. It must be noted that in addition to the party's selection of personnel for governmental positions, the party's political cadres assigned to a particular governmental unit ensured that unit's adherence to the party line. Political or ideological reasons served as reason of state. It was in this sense that claims to autonomous and apolitical logic in the realm of expertise were seen as direct attacks on the party-led state. The party's ideological assessments and goals provided the coherence and unity for a statist rationality.

The state in this rationality could least of all tolerate autonomous organizations for experts. Trương Tửu, a university professor involved in the Nhân Văn movement, was singled out for fierce attacks because of his activities to set up alternative organizations for intellectuals and artists outside of those provided by the state.[16] These state entities included various unions such as the Writers' Union that belonged to the party's umbrella mass organization called the Fatherland Front. The State Committee for the Sciences included those working in the natural and social sciences. The 1959 plenum resolution cited above spelled out the threefold solution to the bourgeois expert problem: Utilize, Limit, and Reform (*Sử dụng, hạn chế, cải tạo*).[17] Many Nhân Văn participants were sent to labor camps for reform, after which many were condemned to live out their lives in extreme poverty and severe social isolation. Beyond the personal tragedies of those who were made examples, the party moved to reeducate and enclose experts within state organs and set limits as to the focus of their expertise.

In place of autonomous realms of life whose dynamics needed to be uncovered, represented, and known by autonomously generated expertise, the party supplied a ready-made knowledge about human history driven by class struggle. State policy adjustments were to happen within statist praxis by state experts, enclosed in state organs. Rather than "abstract" theories, experts were to use descriptions of the world and of what to do about it in general accordance with the party line. Adjustments were made between the party theoretical line and expertise in praxis gained through what were called "reality trips," or *đi thực tế*. These were designed for state cadres, including experts, to check the correctness, usefulness, or effectiveness of their work by visiting the people and seeing how they lived their daily lives. It was this "practical expertise" that played a role in adjustments of state policy. If experts and expertise other than "practical" were not criticized for their class background, then they were criticized as being too abstract and distant from the material conditions at hand.[18]

The second episode of crisis in party-expert relations came soon after the Nhân Văn–Giai Phẩm movement, and it also was resolved in the name of a *raison d'état*. As Beissinger finds with Soviet cycles of crises, the Vietnamese party soon found itself faced with problems of a lack of expertise to run the state-command economy and carry out its plans for socialist transformation. A 1962 plenum resolution called attention to severe problems because "the bases of scientific and technological research are still too weak and do not possess the necessary conditions to serve sufficiently the purpose of economic and cultural development."[19] Calls for training and promotion of experts, from managers to scientists and engineers, followed. Such state organs as the Cultural Ministry also found its "professional impulse" frustrated by the lack of qualified cadres after the Nhân Văn crackdown.[20]

But before a clear direction in the promotion of expertise could take effect, a foreign policy problem arose. Many experts by this time had been trained in the Soviet Union and influenced by the politically relaxed atmosphere in the sphere of knowledge initiated by Nikita Khrushchev. Khrushchev's foreign policy since the Twentieth Party Congress in 1956 had been promoting the principles of peaceful coexistence, which included two main modifications of Leninist-Stalinist doctrine thus far: (1) a rejection of the thesis of the inevitability of war and (2) an acknowledgment that socialism could be achieved by peaceful means.[21] Peaceful coexistence translated into the Soviet Union's less than enthusiastic support for Hanoi's war efforts against the Republic of Vietnam in the south and into escalating American involvement through the first half of the 1960s.[22] The Moscow Conference of November 1960 marked the confrontation and division of Communist parties into two camps: about seventy parties endorsed the new Soviet principles, and the rest sided with China.[23] Although the Vietnamese party was a signatory to the resolution of the Moscow Conference, the ascending forces headed by Lê Duẩn and Lê Đức Thọ in the Vietnamese party saw the new principles as "revisionist" because they posed a threat to the party's intensified war efforts. By the time of the December 1963 plenum, this faction was dominant, such that it could sponsor Resolution 9. This resolution unleashed a terror campaign against the "revisionist antiparty clique." Lê Đức Thọ, head of the Party Central Organization Committee, announced to party cadres: "The theoretical front to counter contemporary revisionism we will leave to China. The organizational front, we take care of ourselves."[24]

This pronouncement was translated to "administrative measures" to imprison without trials roughly four hundred party members, including scientists. The primary site targeted by the party for censure was the

State Committee for the Sciences, the state organ designed to contain experts. It was here that the party found the greatest concentration of resistance to the party's foreign policy. The legitimating reason for the crackdown on experts in the State Committee for the Sciences this time was nothing less than the survival of the state in an all-out war with the United States and its "puppet regime" in the South.[25]

In the first episode in the late 1950s, the expert problem was over the issue of a realm of activities in the arts and sciences (labeled "culture") and whether it could contain its own logic autonomous from the political state. This was solved by enclosing and setting parameters for experts and expertise within state entities. In the second episode in the 1960s, the need to develop expert knowledge was countered by a foreign policy concern, elevated to the stature of a reason of state, justifying the decimation of the ranks of experts in areas seemingly unrelated to the foreign policy in question. The state and its reasons were posed in ways that precluded the imagination of autonomous realms of life in a society separate from the political state, knowable and manageable through expert knowledge.

THE REORGANIZATION OF GOVERNMENT

With the adoption of marketization in the late 1980s, the all-encompassing socialist state faced challenges to its organizational logic. Since I am dealing with economic liberalization as a set of drastic changes for the society, including its political regime, why not classify groupings as either advocating change or resisting change? The relationships between political changes and economic liberalization are treated in the literature on regime transition from totalitarianism or authoritarianism, which overlaps with the democratization literature. To the extent that this literature talks about political actors, they are for the most part placed on a continuum from conservatives to ideologues, from those resistant to change, on one end, to reformers and radical democrats, on the other. The bargains they strike among themselves and with groups in society in response to demands during the transition are said to determine the political outcome.[26] Following this literature, it is not uncommon for

Vietnam analysts to position the political leadership or elite on this continuum based on its members' advocacy of change.[27] Nevertheless, I would instead propose that loose groupings of government entities be viewed based on the functional demands of their respective entities. This analytical division would allow one to see that, far from any one "faction" resisting change, filling some "conservative" category, all were trying to extend their jurisdiction over the changes gripping the country and to define the functions their respective apparatuses would fulfill in the future. As such, evocation of past Communist Party achievements was not the backward gaze of "conservatives." Reminders of past glories were used, not to bring the country back to a time before economic liberalization, but to fashion future functions for party and government entities.

What I suggest is that the adoption of a market economy changed the alignment of political forces in the state and the mentality of governance in Vietnam. As soon as the economy referred to market mechanisms as opposed to a central five-year plan, it followed that many saw the economy as gaining a status of relative autonomy from statist considerations. Economic planners and state enterprise managers who experimented with the profit incentive thought this market mechanism operated autonomously from statist considerations. Fforde and Vylder document this early experimentation with economic practices outside those prescribed by central planning (i.e., the use of the profit incentive). Economic managers of agricultural cooperatives and certain state enterprises referred to this use of market mechanisms as "breaking the fence" (*phá rào*).[28] Further, write Fforde and Vylder, the "transition itself started to be seen as possessing a momentum of its own. It was seen by some as operating according to 'laws of nature' [*quy luật*]."[29] International bodies such as the Association of Southeast Asian Nations (ASEAN) Free Trade Area and the World Trade Organization further enforced the thinking that the economy operated according to its own laws by requirements attached to loans or programs justified on the basis of knowledge of economics. As a result, state management of the economy became tied to knowledge about the economy and to the ability of state agencies to respond with more flexibility than a party resolution and the party-devised five-year plan could allow. In this mentality, the government agencies dealing directly with economic management would have to make more economic decisions, more knowledgeably and more flexibly, than could the Politburo or the Central Committee. Đặng Phong and Melanie Beresford document such a shift in decision making, from its locus in the party leadership to governmental bodies: "Particularly since 1986, decentralisation of economic decision-making powers and the associated needs for increased market regulation and more transparency in the legal system have shifted both the balance of power and volume of work in the direction of the government and legislature."[30]

The shift of the locus of "power" to governmental activities meant political forces formerly operating mainly on the party stage now had to move to incorporate their respective governmental arms and adopt the latter's governing functions to justify their continued existence. If the Politburo no longer devised the bulk of economic policy, then the "economic bloc" in the Politburo had to pick up the governmental bodies that devised economic measures and champion the latter's cause. Other political blocs in the party likewise picked up the governmental entities performing the appropriate functions.

But the questions of the day were which governing entities should have jurisdiction over what and which (also who) would become obsolete. The result was political contention among these entities for jurisdiction that would secure their roles in a future Vietnam. A 1993–94 nationwide survey found that 70.73 percent to 78 percent of respondents considered prostitution a "dangerous social evil that must be eliminated," while only 2.04 percent to 2.51 percent thought of prostitution as a "normal trade in society."[31] The handling of prostitution had become an area in which the different groupings of Vietnam's governors debated the questions of how and what to govern in their ongoing fight over who among them should yield what in the exercise of state power.

EXPERT KNOWLEDGE: THE CASE OF MEDICINE

To expand on the shift in the organization and imagination of government, I move to a theoretical discussion of the new configuration. To explore contrasts in the modes of governance before and after the start of economic liberalization, I examine medicine under Leninist governance and during marketization since the late 1980s and early 1990s. I make the case that the changing relationship between medical expertise and governance pointed to at least an experimentation in certain areas with a mode of governing that could be called liberal in its conception of a "society" autonomous from the state.

Liberal Governance: Imagining Society

The idea of a "civil society" with dynamics that are autonomous from those of the state is not unfamiliar. Autonomous dynamics may be economic in the form of competing interests and classes;[32] they may be social in the form of social groups, intermediary bodies, and citizens' organizations.[33] Foucault makes the case that the very idea of this independent reality called a "civil society" or a society arose historically with the particular problematization of government that was "liberal": "What was discovered at that time—and this was one of the great discoveries of political thought at the end of the eighteenth century—was the idea of *society*. That is to say that government not only has to deal with a territory, with a domain and with its subjects, but that it has to deal with a complex and independent reality that has its own laws and mechanisms of disturbance. This new reality is society."[34] Foucault contrasts this conceptualization to modes of governance before the eighteenth century based on an autonomous rationality of governing, a *raison d'état*—a rationality intrinsic to the state. This reason was justifiable to no other but its own logic of threats and survival. The state was its own end.[35] Self-reference, says Foucault, was the characteristic of "sovereignty" as a mode of rule, a kind of government. What characterized the ends of sovereignty was "in sum nothing other than submission to sovereignty."[36] The sovereign-as-his-state began to claim autonomy from ecclesiastical power in sixteenth-century Europe through the doctrine of "reason of state" (a pope condemned *raison d'état* as "the devil's reason").[37] The incarnate of *raison d'état* as survival of the state in foreign relations became a premise of realist thought in international relations.[38]

This was soon to change, as "society" became an independent reality in eighteenth-century Europe. The reference for liberal governance became the existing entity of society with its complex multiplicity of aspects knowable and governable with expert bodies of knowledge. The unity of ends in the survival and success of the state was substituted by a multiplicity of ends in liberal governance: health, prosperity, safety, and so forth achieved with a plurality of governing tactics.[39]

Aspects of society, from its economy to the state of health of its population, came to be known through the knowledge disciplines. The development of political economy as a knowledge discipline based on scientific objectivity depended on its autonomy from the preoccupations of state, while the content of this economic science affirmed the limits of what the state could know. Colin Gordon argues that liberalism could thus be characterized as "critique of state reason."[40]

Perpetually unfolding knowledge about the complex dynamics of the economy stood between the formerly all-knowing state and its object of knowledge and of rule. The latter was "society," which was vested with the quasi-natural and autonomous dynamics of civil society to generate its own economic and social order.[41] Society, then, came to be imagined through its being the object of knowledge. How to govern the "social," as in civil society or the private sphere, with its own dynamics became the problem of liberal government.

Liberal government arose historically and changed over time.[42] But as a set of strategies of governing characterized by the way it problematizes society, it has been adopted to solve problems by governors faced with their own historically specific problems. As such, it is analyzable. I make the case that governors in Vietnam, in response to new problems brought on by economic liberalization, adopted an arguably liberal style of governance in the area of public health intervention with its attendant medical and related fields of expertise.

Expertise, Social Problems, and Liberal Governance

In liberal governance, aspects of this complex and independent reality called society—its health and pathology, its prosperity and poverty—

are represented, studied, and known by expertise. This arrangement gives rise to a peculiar relationship between expertise and governance. Expertise is not simply an instrument of rule. Nor is this rule by experts in a technocracy. It is an alliance in a technology of rule. Nikolas Rose argues that the authority in the liberal style of governing arises out of a claim to knowledge, neutrality, and efficacy. Expertise provides the solutions to the contradiction between the need to govern and the need to restrict government in liberal thought.[43] "Liberal strategies," writes Rose, "tie government to the positive knowledges of human conduct" and to the authority of the experts like the psychologists, physicians, epidemiologists, criminologists, sociologists, economists, social workers, and so forth. It is this "'know-how' that promises to render docile the unruly domains over which government is to be exercised, to make government possible and to make government better" (44–45).

This liberal governing arrangement does not mean the withdrawal of government from people's lives or a retreat of the state. Rather, it is governance reconfigured. Governors work out new techniques of rule required for the exercise of governing. Instead of problems of the state or its political regime, certain "disturbances" are recoded as "social problems": epidemics and disease, criminality, indigence, breakdown in marital relations, and so on (46). How to deal with these problems becomes the domain of expert authorities: physicians, criminologists, economists, psychologists, and so forth. Governors and experts can divide a social problem into areas of intervention linked to a number of these areas of expertise. For instance, prostitution could be dealt with in matters of medicine, criminal policing, and social rehabilitation. There was a pluralization of governing tactics dispersed over different areas of expertise. Experts could seek political resources to further their work. Political forces in governing apparatuses could seek expert authority to legitimize their governing functions. Governors and their respective state agencies license, facilitate, promote, carry out, and fashion programs to further the prescriptions of norms and supervision of norms by experts. The authority of expertise facilitates the state's authority to regulate people's conduct down to small details.

Specialized Intervention and Liberal Governance in Vietnam

This style of governing in conjunction with the norm setting and supervision by expertise led to two consequences in the context of Vietnam: (1) the depoliticization of governance and (2) the possibility of the privatization (called "socialization" in Vietnam) of governing functions. By depoliticization, I do not mean that medical practices came to be beyond all contention. Health officials put medical expertise to use in promoting conjugal sex in such a way that it was less offensive to the security and ideological apparatuses in the state. By depoliticization, I mean that governance and state intervention measures acquired their authority from knowledge, purporting to be neutral and efficacious, as Rose suggests. This authority arising from expert knowledge annulled political justifications such as the state's conducting a class struggle against the bourgeoisie in the name of the proletariat to bring about a future classless society. This new kind of governing technology took political problems and recast them in "the neutral language of science."⁴⁴ Whether governance was now actually neutral is another issue. State health measures prescribed behaviors for citizens according to gender and class. Nevertheless, no such claim of partiality was made explicitly. Class and gender reality of state practices became nearly invisible. I am not suggesting the depoliticization was all "deceptive." This depoliticization of governance was "real" in the sense that it freed expertise from the rationality of the state, as the latter's reference for governance was no longer itself but "society." As health was the goal of medicine, health was the goal of the state. It was indeed the normalization of governance in both meanings of the word. It was normalizing governance in terms of the norms promoted by bodies of expertise such as medicine. And it was normalized governing in the sense of doing away with the language of political struggles.

Governing with expertise permitted the option of privatizing some governing functions. Health was promoted by state measures. But if health was the goal of medicine anyway, then health could be promoted by fee-based hospitals, by physicians' private practice, and by health dissemination campaigns of nongovernmental organizations (NGOs). As

Graham Burchell points out, in liberal governance, there are "privately conducted public campaigns aimed at the moralization and normalization of the population through practical systems situated at the interface of society and the state, private and public (medical, psychiatric, educational, philanthropic, social, [etc.])."⁴⁵ These liberal governing strategies in Vietnam allowed for the option of turning certain governing functions over to the dynamics of the market in two ways: (a) supply and demand in the forms of fee-based hospitals and physician private practice and (b) individual choice as health-care consumers were vested with individualized responsibility for health. The privatization of some governing functions meant the state governed in conjunction with outside networks and entities such as private-practice physicians or NGOs. It was somewhat of a paradox that society was conceptually differentiated from the state while the boundary between them was diffuse, with shared governing functions.

In short, I suggest that what was seen in Vietnam in the late 1980s and early 1990s was at least a foray into the liberalization of governance in the sense that there emerged the conception of a society whose autonomous dynamics had to be studied and managed or governed with expertise. This style of governing depoliticized governance, on the one hand, and brought on the possibility of privatization ("socialization") of some governing functions, on the other. This new mode of governance was most visible in the area of medicine and public health.

It might be expected that medical intervention since the early 1990s relating to prostitution should be compared to its counterpart before the start of economic liberalization. Medical intervention in prostitution under socialism was limited to administering medicines for the sexually transmitted diseases of prostitutes upon their entry into a "Camp for the Recovery of Human Dignity," where forced labor would reform them into good socialist subjects. The operating logic then was simply that prostitutes were sick in body and spirit and needed to be cured. There were no equivalent uses of prostitution as a social problem to address the health of the population under socialism. My argument is precisely that the constitution of the social problem of prostitution in a way that allowed for expert intervention to maximize the health of the population was a new phenomenon symptomatic of a different paradigmatic configuration of governance. I explore the differences between the old and new modes of governance through an examination of medicine and public health before and after liberalization.

Medical Expertise under Leninist Governance in Vietnam

Medicine was not an exception to the overall problem of expertise in Leninist governance. The mentality of governing in relation to medical expertise under socialism differed from current uses of medical expertise. In a brief examination of public medicine before liberalization, I highlight certain contrasts with current state uses of medical expertise. A discussion of what these contrasts reveal about the changing mentality of governance follows.

Public medicine in socialist Vietnam developed in the same way as did other expertise in the arts and sciences subsumed under the problematics of "culture," which could not be ahistorical or classless from the point of view of the party. Nguyễn Đình Thi's piece in *Học Tập* had denounced the Nhân Văn movement for criticizing, or "attacking," a host of state institutions including hospitals. Physicians were mobilized in 1958 to denounce the Nhân Văn movement.[46] If practitioners of scientific knowledge insisted on its autonomy from the preoccupations of the state to study aspects of society separate from the state, then this kind of knowledge had to be denounced. What was the correct focus for medicine within the socialist state?

The answer appears in Trường Chinh's 1947 piece on the party-led anticolonial resistance. There, Trường Chinh spelled out his three new criteria for "cultural" contributions by engineers, scientists, physicians, nurses, medical students, architects, educators, writers, and journalists, since these "cultural forces, these literary, scientific and technological talents have not been sufficiently mobilized."[47] The three criteria were nation, science, and the masses (*dân tộc, khoa học,* and *đại chúng*).[48] *Nation* referred to a nativist identification and its resistance to things foreign; *science,* to effectiveness and efficiency; and *the masses,* to the level at which the masses could use, follow, and comprehend these contributions.[49] The party leadership sought science and its effectiveness, but not science unchaperoned. The native and mass identification kept science and scientists from being bourgeois. As I have noted, those conducting the revolution considered Western knowledge bourgeois. Both "Western" and "bourgeois" were attributes of things alien first to the anticolonial resistance and then to the proletarian state. The point here is that scientific expertise, if it were to be autonomous, was not just bourgeois in class character, but it was alien as well.

The party used these same criteria in its 1958 solution to "use" but "limit" expertise after the Nhân Văn episode. Ho Chi Minh's vision of a health-care system was characterized by emphases on nation, science, and the masses.[50] Health officials, doctors, nurses, and state cadres were to maintain a mass-based medicine, which was a mixture of Western and native medicine in basic preventative care, as opposed to advanced medical expertise centering around treatment.[51] "The revolution's health-care system," writes Bùi Mộng Hùng, director of France's National Institute of Medical Research, "felt it had connected itself with the sources of medicine in the national tradition, long looked upon with condescension by the colonial rulers."[52] Health minister Phạm Ngọc Thạch assessed public medical accomplishment during his tenure from the end of the 1950s to the late 1960s in this way: "As I see it, most importantly we were able to establish a whole health-care network, bringing medicine to peasants in even out-of-the-way villages and turning the peasants into their own health and hygiene cadres."[53] This network consisted of small, local, rudimentary clinics and of incessant cadre persuasion and supervision of people's adherence to basic hygiene. Health education centered on encouraging rural dwellers to adhere to basic hygienic practices, such as drinking water from wells as opposed to water from rivers to control diarrhea and typhoid (57).

The revolutionary government also educated people so that they would participate in their health care. However, as opposed to the situation since the early 1990s, the authority of the government's basic hygiene campaigns back then did not depend on independent advances in the medical field. Mobilization for the use of clean water did not change much with advances made in medicine as a field or its subfields of specialties. Nor did this network of preventative and basic health care depend much on experts to develop or keep abreast of medical advances in areas not emphasized by state health practices. The state did not have much use for runaway expertise. Major research accomplishments from this period were exemplified by the work to devise a two-compartment septic tank so human waste could be recycled into fertilizer with minimal spread of parasites and germs (58). The trademark of this system was not the sophistication of medical science and technology but, rather, its successful provision of readily available basic health care for the masses.

Besides satisfying the ideological criteria that marked medical practices as a province of the state to be administered through state hospitals, clinics, and mobilization campaigns, the use of native medicines and the network of local hospitals and clinics also suited the requirements of war in the 1960s. Native medicines made up for the lack of Western medicines. The dispersion of health care away from urban hospitals meant more readily available care for war wounds, childbirth, and routine diseases, while roads were destroyed, transportation disrupted, and northern industrial centers bombed. The management of clinics, the treatment of patients, and even the preparation of medicines were left up to the localities as transportation and communication lines were disrupted (61). A unified field of knowledge and practices in medicine (nationally and internationally) was not feasible, nor would it have been conducive to the state's all-out war efforts. There was tension between the state's mass-based system of basic health care focusing on prevention and the experts' demand for one that would follow medical advances spurred by a focus on treatment led by big urban hospitals. Health minister Thạch said in 1967: "Many physicians urge the government to follow that path [advanced treatment in hospitals]; in these past few years, medicine in the world has made many advances, and our physicians thirst for the opportunities to treat their countrymen with the most modern means. It's a legitimate wish. But I must admit that the government does not direct its main efforts in that direction" (59).

A NEW MODE OF GOVERNANCE: THE ASCENDANCE OF
EXPERTISE AND THE RECODING OF A SOCIAL PROBLEM

In contrast to the system described above, the new Vietnamese health-
care system focused on advances in the field, spurred on by the search
for better treatment concentrated in urban hospitals with access to more
advanced and foreign sources of medicines, equipment, and medical
expertise. I examine current practices in the provision of medical care
to discuss the place of expertise in the new configuration of governance
and show how the recoding of the strategically placed social problem
of prostitution was instrumental in the state's efforts to govern with
expertise in market conditions.

Medicine by Experts

With economic liberalization, the state experimented with a system of
state-owned, yet fee-based, hospitals in Ho Chi Minh City. The fee-based
system was adopted nationwide in 1991.[54] Hospitals and medical import-
export companies could start buying medicines and equipment from foreign sources.[55] Exchanges of knowledge and linkages to the global state
of medical knowledge came with the fee-based hospitals' efforts to update
their treatment of patients, thereby attracting patients, through increasingly specialized training of physicians. Besides trying to train doctors
better during their internships in big hospitals now equipped with some
of the latest technology, hospitals sent their doctors abroad for updated
specialization.[56] France alone accepted in the late 1990s roughly one hundred Vietnamese doctors a year for supplemental training and maintained special medical training programs in Vietnam.[57]

In addition to fee-based hospitals, the state started to allow physician
private practice. In 1994 the 2,682 private doctors in Ho Chi Minh City
treated 8 million cases, while state hospitals and clinics treated 10.32 million cases.[58] Health minister Đỗ Nguyên Phương in 1997 applauded the
state policy to provide health care in the new era:

> The prices of services and investment in activities of diagnosis and
> treatment to safeguard the health of the people are going up, and the

state cannot keep up. Thus the state has had to rely on the private financial resources (of paying patients) and other nonstate sectors in the economy in providing health services in fee collection, health insurance premiums, etc. Besides the state's health-care system, it now must recognize and help develop the network of private providers of health services to the people. This proves the correctness of our state's policies in responding to the pragmatic demands and trends in other countries.[59]

Similarly, Bùi Mộng Hùng lamented the loss of Vietnam's socialist mass-based medicine but suggested directions in which current developments could be utilized to overcome problems posed by the market with its inequitable provision of health care focused on expensive treatment and thus its neglect of basic health promotion for the population at large.[60] Governors, suggested Hùng, could use developments spurred by the market to address the problems of the market. Treatment and prevention, Hùng wrote, could be integrated with advantages not enjoyed under socialism by developing and utilizing the sizable force of highly trained private and state doctors and an extensive network of hospitals and clinics connected to an educated public.[61] Increasing professionalization and specialization would be required if doctors and hospitals were to survive market mechanisms. But that would leave hospitals much better equipped to fill new roles like keeping doctors and other health workers updated in the latest medical knowledge and practices. Hospitals and private-practice physicians would also be in a better position to educate patients and their families in healthful ways as part of preventative care.

These developments were already taking place: medical professionals, with increased expertise and thus authority, were reaching patients for treatment and observation, educating them and assigning them their responsibilities for their health. Much work remained if the state was to effectively pursue this direction in governance, as Hùng pointed out. But the state had already taken the first steps to govern better with the market. This redefined role of the state in ensuring the health of the population was characteristic of a liberal mode of governance. Namely, the state tried to find solutions to the shortcomings of the market without impinging either on the autonomous dynamics of the market or on a knowledge discipline. According to Nguyễn Đăng Thành, the author of a 1997 article in the party theoretical journal, political leadership in a market economy meant finding solutions to the market's failings such as inequality, but with "respect for the natural laws of the dynamics and development of the economy."[62] He further explored this kind of governing and calls it the "art of mobilizing the forces of the market."[63]

Even shortcomings of professionals were to be dealt with differently than before, leaning in the direction of expertise and market mechanisms. Health minister Đỗ Nguyên Phương raised the problem of professional ethics in medical practice in a market economy; he proposed more laws to spell out illegal practices, means to inspect medical practice, and state support for courses on professional ethics in medical school curriculum. But instead of some strictly statist mechanisms of control, he strongly advocated self-policing by professional associations, to be based on expertise, professional ethics, and the realities of providing health services in a market economy, as opposed to a reliance on the state police. The minister even suggested state support for the establishment of an association of health services entrepreneurs as a body to police standards and the quality of health-care services.[64]

Turning the goal of health over to medical expertise and the market was more efficient at least in the sense that it saved the state's coffers. It was certainly less political, drawing attention away from any explicit political agenda of the regime of the ruling party. A section of the Vietnamese state, its Health Ministry with the tacit approval and support of the camps within the party and government that oversaw economic development, had begun to use certain effects of the market such as the increasing professionalism and expertise of hospitals and doctors to help solve problems posed by the market's shortcomings in a treatment-driven medical system at the expense of broad-based preventative care.

The formula of turning the function of providing health over to expertise and the mechanisms of the market included the production of responsible individuals. Medical practices established a patient's (or a potential patient's) dependence on medical expertise, at the same time as they assigned individuals responsibility for their own health. This was individual self-normalizing and self-governance to an extent. This individual responsibility prepared people to be educated about their health and to seek health services when needed. Responsible individuals took care of themselves, and they became health-care consumers in a system that had turned to expertise and market mechanisms.

Social Problems Link Governance to Expertise

Social problems play a crucial role in linking governance to expertise about aspects of society. One must remember that social problems as such did not exist in the Leninist mentality of governance. Trần Độ, a high-ranking party official at the start of economic liberalization, stated in a 1988 publication that party and other policy documents before had mentioned policies for the economy and society, but he admitted that "pertaining to society, I counted a few meager lines. It was not until the Sixth Party Congress [in December 1986, when economic liberalization was officially adopted] that this problem became fully conceptualized, posed as an area for policy next to economic policy."[65] According to Trần Độ, what was becoming clear as economic liberalization picked up speed was the need to "understand" people or "humans" in their various relations, which became the subject of research in the social sciences starting in the late 1980s.[66]

With this mentality that before economic liberalization took society as a non-referent, governors did not see prostitution as a social problem continually arising out of society. It was merely a vestige of past political regimes, soon to disappear in the socialist state. Existing prostitutes were products of the old regimes. Reforming them would be the end of the problem. This definition of prostitution did not require an ever-accumulating and up-to-date knowledge about its medical threats to the rest of the population or about the sex habits of clients and prostitutes, the kinds of crimes arising out of activity-concentrated areas, the class backgrounds and geographical origins of prostitutes and clients, or alternative economic prospects for women of those classes.

Statistics in Leninist countries had always been notorious for their inaccuracy. Production statistics were doctored or conjured to fulfill production quotas and so forth. This practice made sense in a system that did not have an external referent such as society, imagined to be an independent reality. Increasingly now, the issue of more accurate information became urgent as government agencies dealt with newly defined problems.[67] It was a self-reinforcing circle. Changes in society due to the market economy generated areas not hitherto known to governors both at the political leadership level and at the bureaucratic level. But as governors tried to know more, they became more dependent on experts of one kind or another. Expertise subdivided reality and generated ever more information about aspects of society, which in turn rendered society more complex as an object of knowledge and of rule. Governors knew about a social problem such as prostitution as it was subdivided into different aspects by a host of areas of knowledge and intervention agencies: for example, medical expertise on how diseases were transmitted and on sex and the psychology of sex; expertise on crime and policing; and social work expertise that relied on social studies of prostitution and economic studies of employment opportunities for women of certain classes and educational backgrounds. A ruling party with intra-party contention over centrally devised social plans could not adequately respond to the complex world conjured up by the knowledge disciplines. To continue governing this envisioned social realm, party factions had to form governing apparatuses by incorporating government agencies with more specific functions tied to special knowledge.

Phạm Xuân Nam, assistant director of the National Center for the Social and Human Sciences, argued in a 1997 article that governors needed expertise from the social sciences side by side with the natural sciences.[68] He gave the example of the problem of population control, pointing out that governors needed not only medical and technical expertise but also social psychology, as well as sociological studies of public attitudes about family happiness and about the educational levels of the public, and so on (12). Problems requiring governance were thus multifaceted and should be dealt with using a number of specialized areas of intervention linked to special knowledges or expertise. His assertion about the social sciences drew attention to the complexities of social realities knowable and manageable only with special knowledges, which in turn required the development of these sciences. "We must ourselves," wrote Phạm Xuân Nam, "research, seek, and discover systems and conjunctions of laws natural and inherent in existents interacting in a society at a concrete level of development" (10). With a similar argument, a member of the party's Central Training Committee in charge of the subcommittee on the natural, industrial, and environmental sciences recommended that the state help develop expertise by organizing more units aimed at raising standards and the quality of knowledge in state scientific institutes. His recommendation was in accordance with the new party policy of "solving problems of society in the spirit of socialization."[69]

"Socialization" had become a buzzword in Vietnam in recent years. Its meaning came from the old statist context: the turning over of certain state functions to society. The formula for the "socialization of social work," according to the minister of labor, veterans, and social work, consisted of "three legs": the central and local state, the community with international help, and self-reliant individuals.[70] According to the minister, the socialization of social work relied on "mass organizations" and "associations" of many kinds operating in the "community."[71]

In the case of the social problem of prostitution, practices in present processes of commodification made it impossible for governors to keep defining prostitution as a vestige of past political regimes. To govern its ills while leaving the market economy intact, governors had to recode prostitution as a social problem in a real society with its own economic dynamics. Without wanting to take the blame for the party's political decisions to promote market mechanisms with their "side effects," the party's political factions focused on prostitution's social threats to promote intervention measures that would expand their respective governing apparatuses' jurisdiction. Specific state agencies like those of the Health Ministry drove forward the process of governance linked to specialized intervention as they promoted their respective tasks for various specific gains, that is, jurisdiction ensuring jobs, access to foreign sources of money, training that could further career opportunities, and so on.

In these circumstances, the legitimacy to rule increasingly came from the fulfillment of governing functions unrelated to the ideology of a party ruling over a now recognized society with its autonomous economic and social dynamics. The authority necessary to intervene in people's lives in order to fulfill those governing goals increasingly came from knowledge about aspects of society, especially with its "ills," and how to deal with them. A social problem like prostitution was picked up by governing apparatuses because it provided a good vehicle for state involvement in this social realm, thus staking each apparatus's jurisdiction against the encroachment of others. Social problems focused public concern with a sense of urgency for things to be done. The state agencies expanded their activities to influence more behavior in larger segments of the population using special knowledge about the social problem and the expertise required to deal with its effects.

CONCLUSION

The Leninist party enfolded knowledge as a category of intellectual activities into the apparatuses of the state in the 1950s and early 1960s. This official discourse was replaced by calls by party cadres and government officials to acknowledge a lack of expert knowledge about realities in an autonomous social realm that supposedly stood outside the state. From the late 1980s on, particularly in the 1990s, to adapt to the demands of governing with the market, the government did reorganize to incorporate empirical knowledge and a redefined relationship between state and society. Within the state, the government rather than the party became more important in the decisions of running the country. And knowledge became more and more vital to how each government agency governs. A research institute is now attached to the major ministries in Vietnam, including the Ministry of Labor, Invalids, and Social Affairs; the Ministry of Culture and Information; and the Ministry of Foreign Affairs. Hand in hand with this reliance on knowledge is the way in which each government entity may profit from its participation in the intervention into what now is a society operating by autonomous dynamics. Social evils, then, serve as foci of activities. Through these nodes of intervention activities, one can see this reorganization of government.

The new configuration of governance was demonstrable with medical practices and state public health intervention then and now. There was a turning over of some governing functions in the promotion of health to fee-based hospitals, physician private practice, and even health dissemination efforts by some international NGOs. The reliance on the authority of expertise gave the appearance of depoliticized governance in the sense that more and more state measures no longer appeared as part of the political agenda of a Marxist-Leninist party. Did these things add up to the withdrawal of the state?

The evidence does not suggest a withdrawal of the state. The state provided some of the means such as specialized units in state institutes to further the training and generation of more expert knowledge in an array of fields. The fee-based hospitals were state owned. Hospitals sent doctors, technicians, and managers abroad for additional training at the approval and selection of the health bureaus of the Health Ministry.[72] Hospitals imported medicines and medical equipments through the health bureaus' state-owned import-export company, YTECO.[73] Even the sex-health education manuals were published by state-owned publishing houses. Policing and rehabilitation were more obviously state enterprises. The state was still directly involved in many of these new activities. What was different was not just that there were some nonstate activities by physician private practice and NGOs but that the logic of governing had changed. State entities such as the health agencies or the state-owned health import-export company operated with the authority of expertise and with market conditions. Because of this shift in logic, state entities could function in tandem with some nonstate entities and sectors. State agencies translated apparatus-wide claims to combat prostitution into their respective specialized areas of intervention. Intervention measures relied on a special knowledge of some kind; in the case of the health bureaus, it was the expertise of medicine, used to combat the negative effects of prostitution on the health of the population. The health bureaus, whose measures rely on the authority of expertise to intervene in people's lives, could count on state-owned hospitals that charge fees, private-practice physicians, privately paid medical writers, and international NGOs in their efforts to carry out the state policy to combat prostitution and promote health. These measures were the clinical and nonclinical practices that reach, treat, and educate individuals about what to do and what not do to maximize their health, down to minute details.

What did these arrangements do to the state-society divide? State intervention measures could fit into webs of state and nonstate practices, institutions, and organizations that shared governing functions. Yet these arrangements rested on the premise of an autonomous society with autonomous dynamics knowable through autonomous knowledge disciplines. So, on the one hand, many entities in Vietnam were now nonstate entities, from medical private practice to NGOs. On the other hand, it was not easy to distinguish by their functions some of these state entities from nonstate ones. There was not much distinguishing the practice of private doctors from state doctors. Nor was there much difference in the function fulfilled by a private charity rehabilitation center from a state-run one. The redefined role of the state made it seem like the state had been rolled back to just making sure these functions would be filled. Yet the reach of state intervention suggests that it was merely a reconfiguration of governing arrangements in which the state could promote minute intervention in people's daily lives without the explicit social engineering travails of socialist days. I am not suggesting that this configuration of governance was free of tension. This paradox of respect for civil society's autonomy, on the one hand, and the possible reach of the new political technology linked to expertise, on the other, is certainly one source of tension.

Jeremy Paltiel has suggested that Leninist governance is the micromanagement of the system through control over personnel, production, pricing, and consumption by means of meting out rewards and sanctions.[74] Paltiel insists that, in contrast, liberal governance is about macromanagement through laws that guarantee the conditions necessary for a healthy market and society. I suspect that the distinction is not that neat. Liberal government governs "at a distance" or "at arm's length," as characterized by Rose.[75] But it is not just about good laws as macromanagement. The conditions necessary for this macromanagement or remote control are webs of minute intervention carried out by experts and their knowledge, along with state and nonstate institutions and organizations.

CHAPTER 4

Governing Passion

Consumers' Choice and the Production of a Differentiated Citizenry in Public Medicine

IN BOTH GOVERNMENT public health measures and sex education manuals, the Vietnamese government since marketization directly and indirectly promoted health practices that generate and supervise class and gender differentiated norms in sexual conduct linked to birth and disease control. On the one hand, public health measures targeting sex workers were more clinical in their emphasis on diagnostic tests and the treatment of disease. On the other hand, middle-class urban women were invited to acquire knowledge about sex and medicine so that they could make the right consumerist choices to safeguard their health and beauty. Despite the difference in measures targeting different classes of women, public health measures still direct rather than coerce, as they posit some degree of autonomous agency on the part of the women involved. This disciplinary power differs from measures of policing and rehabilitating sex workers.

SEX BY EXPERTS: THE SUPERVISION OF NORMS

Throughout the second half of the 1990s and early 2000s, public health measures addressing the "social problem of prostitution" included (1) mandatory medical exams and testing for HIV and other sexually transmitted diseases (STDs) for women sex workers in rehabilitation camps and also programs to encourage testing among practicing sex workers and other high-risk groups such as their clients; (2) STD treatment and birth control procedures at hospitals and clinics; and (3) sex education efforts aimed at birth and disease control in the form of peer education, counseling, the distribution of health pamphlets and condoms among sex workers and potential clients, sex education in school curriculum, and the promotion of sex education books.

In discussing these measures I build on Foucault's exploration into the supervision of norms in modern modes of power.[1] Through observation and surveillance, professionals like teachers, doctors, psychologists, and social workers teach individuals how to habitually measure themselves against the norm.[2] Professionals are trained to identify the norm in the distribution of traits and individuals, thus upholding what is normal. Professionals promote behavioral norms in accordance with normality as defined by bodies of knowledge like medicine, psychology, sociology, and criminology. It is through this normative power of normality that experts and, by extension, governors can supervise the choices of individuals.

Certain mechanisms of expert norm supervision are identifiable in governmental intervention measures. First, the capture of physical bodies (extending from those of prostitutes, to their clients, and to the wives and children of suspected and potential clients) in clinical settings would allow persons to be tested, monitored, judged against the norm, treated, and educated. Second, the clinical setting would highlight the health threat and make logical the extension of surveillance and education beyond the clinic in outreach programs. Third, medical knowledge, made popular in a variety of sex education manuals, would prescribe a new healthy way of living centering on sex and sexuality. With these supervision mechanisms in the intervention measures, governors and health professionals could prescribe sexual practices and sexuality according to the norms in medicine, but, far from being neutral, these would differentially reproduce class and gender practices. In short, since the 1990s these intervention measures have rendered comprehensible and persuasive, as well as concrete and habitual, certain models of class- and gender-specific sexual behavior through mechanisms of capturing the physical bodies of persons and teaching them how to take care of their health and the health of their family and nation.

SEX OUTSIDE THE HOME

Medical intervention in prostitution before economic liberalization was limited to administering medicines for the sexually transmitted diseases of prostitutes upon their entry into a camp where forced labor would reform them into good proletarian subjects. Prostitutes were simply removed from the population and treated. There, the problem would end because it was defined politically in terms of capitalism, imperialism, and the ancien regime's political servitude, as discussed. Under the revolutionary regime, the private sexual acts of men and women simply could not be problematized within the given ideological framework other than as personal corruption linked to a lingering past or to external contamination. Now, the government uses prostitution as an ongoing social problem to differentially address the health and sexual habits of segments of the entire population.

Life, Death, and Prostitutes in the Nation's Body

A March 1995 article in the very popular *Tuổi Trẻ*, the news publication of the Ho Chi Minh City Youth Union, warns the population of the connection between prostitution and the peril of AIDS for the entire nation.[3] The author cites statistics on projected HIV-positive cases in Vietnam by the year 2000, projected cases linked to prostitution, and interviews of physicians and other health professionals. "Clearly," says the article, "prostitution is becoming a companion to AIDS, and the threat of AIDS exploding from prostitution as in Thailand is no longer a long way off."[4] Although the cited figure of 5.7 percent of HIV cases linked to prostitution does not seem all that high, the quoted interview with the physician from the city's Health Bureau (belonging to the Ministry of Health) drives home the credibility of the prostitution threat.[5] This "Dr. V. P." describes the prostitution scenes, tells stories of practicing prostitutes who are HIV positive and who do not use condoms, and traces the transmission line into the general population. Most striking is the following story: "Through heart-to-heart confessions of an HIV-positive prostitute, he [Dr. V. P.] looked up one of her 'guests at the village of play' to counsel, and the doctor was shocked to see how happy and well-to-do this client's family was. . . . Dr. V. P. advised the client to go in for testing, and the result was positive. Now his wife is pregnant, and he does not have the courage to avoid transmitting the disease to his wife."[6] The news article establishes the links in a population via the lines of transmission of a deadly disease. The main line of transmission goes from infected prostitutes, to their male clients as solid citizens of society, to the unsuspecting wives, and finally to the unborn innocent children in otherwise happy middle-class families.[7] According to this line of reasoning, death threatens the whole population, the whole nation, and the prostitute is its agent. Linh, a Women's Union officer in charge of a peer education group of former sex workers, related to me while on her way to disseminate information on STDs and to distribute condoms among practicing sex workers how her group would try to convert sex workers to condom use: "We would say to these girls you must use condoms, because otherwise you will infect your clients [with HIV], and your clients will infect their wives, and their wives will transmit it to their children. The whole nation will die of this disease."[8]

The point, however, is not that the prostitute is simply vilified as the vessel of disease, to be cast out or eradicated. To the contrary, it is the embeddedness of her body in the nation's body that makes her so connected, so visible as an entity. Public health workers draw attention to prostitutes in order to make visible the links that connect individual bodies to the body of the population, said to be threatened with disease and death. Another newspaper article draws attention to a future generation of "deformed children" in "our world of tomorrow" as a result of the disease-ridden bodies of prostitutes.[9] These disease-ridden female bodies are not just capable of reproduction but are imagined to be always engaged in the very activity of human reproduction. The disease narrative implicates the presence of prostitute bodies in the body of the nation now and in the future. By establishing such understanding, experts and governors could propose and implement health measures to safeguard the well-being of the population as a whole by getting a hold of individual bodies, starting with the bodies of prostitutes.

A Hold on Bodies

Health workers refer sex workers, clients and families to the STD hospital for testing and treatment, including pregnancy termination. But women who are arrested as prostitutes are sent for compulsory testing and treatment. The capture of bodies in the clinical setting thus targets one group more than it does others: women sex workers who often come from the lower classes. The following accounts illustrate the medical hold on bodies in the clinical setting for purposes of testing, treatment, surveillance, and education. I made observations of the normal operation of the abortion program at Ho Chi Minh City's second-largest state-run and fee-based obstetrics and gynecology (ob-gyn) hospital, where many sex workers went to terminate their pregnancies, and the city's STD hospital, where many sex workers and clients were referred for testing and treatment.

At the ob-gyn hospital, I saw young women ushered through a station for quick pelvic examinations performed by nurses. The nurses would scold the women for getting pregnant, ask probing questions, and make decisions on the spot regarding procedures, time, and prices, all in front of the other patients and their families present in the room. The nurses did not hold sex and its consequences in the intimate or private light.

The nurses informed patients that the price for the operation with local anesthesia was VND50,000 (about US$5 at the time); for the use of general anesthesia, it was VND150,000. The latter was available only as an "after-hours" procedure, for which doctors, nurses, and others involved charged service fees on top of hospital facility fees. At the appointed time, groups of women gathered in the hallway of the abortion wing as the doctor went over the charts, yelling out brief questions regarding the heart or kidney condition of each patient. This was followed by a brief preoperation exam, during which male doctors yelled at one woman after another to "pull down your pants, quickly, go." The patients were then sent to the opposite wing to await the procedure, to be performed by two doctors.

At intervals of roughly ten minutes, a woman was wheeled on a stretcher from the operating room to a recovery room, dressed in the same clothes she arrived in, which were now bloody. In the two small recovery rooms, patients doubled up on narrow, rusty beds, as more kept coming from the operation rooms on bloodstained sheets. There was an occasional woman accompanied by her husband. Most were younger women, many of whom were sex workers. The recovery rooms were full of young women groaning, sometimes screaming, as the anesthetics wore off and the contractions began. And these women felt lucky to be able to afford the extra costs of general anesthetics. Patients' relatives and friends busied themselves with applying cold compresses to the young women's lower abdomens. It was a gathering of women's bodies in a spectacle of blood and pain.

This scene was a dramatic instance of the hold on bodies by medicine. Women gathered by medical necessity in the clinical setting to be subjected to extreme physical pain or simply shame in the undignified processing that preceded it. At the city's STD hospital, men and women waited in a large waiting room for preliminary exams by nurses. The nurses there made a determination of the affliction to be written on charts often by asking questions or requesting that the men pull out their genitals in full view of embarrassed onlookers, who responded with laughter. By erasing the consequences through trauma and shame, the clinical procedures forcefully draw attention to the errant sex act as the cause. As doctors and nurses test and treat the bodies of individuals, they also help educate patients and their companions about the connections to be made between one person and another in the population, between certain acts and their consequences in terms of unwanted pregnancy and disease.

This education through the spectacle of consequences is not limited just to patients and their companions in the clinical setting. Health professionals make sure these spectacles are available to the general public. Hospitals take photographs showing how sexually transmitted diseases manifest themselves on the bodies of their patients. These photos of deformed infants, decimated bodies, shriveled genitals, and festering sores are printed in full color on health flyers and blown up into wall-size posters for display at health exhibits such as that put on by the Ho Chi Minh City Health Bureau's Health Information and Education Center (an agency of the Ministry of Health) in May–June 1996. Exhibits of this kind of photographic deterrence continue to this day. Generated from bodies captured in the clinical setting, these photos serve as visual aids to educate health personnel, high-risk groups like prostitutes, and other members of the public outside the clinic. In short, the prostitute body highlights the danger of sexually transmitted diseases; the danger legitimizes the subjection of bodies of prostitutes, clients, wives, and children to testing and treatment; and, finally, treatment makes visible the individual body's errant sex acts through the spectacle of consequences.

Once the body's errant sex acts become visible, medicine has the possibility of reaching the body in these acts, outside the clinical setting. Đỗ Hồng Ngọc, the head of Ho Chi Minh City's Health Information and Education Center, stressed the need to focus on behavior modification through counseling and the distribution of pamphlets and condoms.[10] The focus translated into AIDS counseling cafés for youths, peer education groups, and pamphlet and condom distribution. While Ngọc's center and the city's AIDS Committee trained counselors and peer educators, some of the funding to pay for these outreach programs came from international NGOs. For instance, the Café Condom, a nickname for the counseling center for youths set up by the city's AIDS Committee, received most of its operation costs from Medicin du Monde.[11]

At the Café Condom, counselors advised patrons about dangerous sex acts such as those with prostitutes, gave out free condoms displayed in bamboo baskets placed on tables as centerpieces, and put on entertainment shows featuring Mr. Raincoat (*áo mưa*, slang for condom) to make patrons comfortable with this birth and disease control device. The primary mission of the Café Condom was to make condoms a natural part of sex. Counselor Hùng informed me that the majority of patrons' questions, many of which were from men calling in, concerned the HIV risks of various sex acts with prostitutes. Counselors' answers centered on ways of transmission, the danger posed to those men and their families, and the range of sex acts, which were sorted into safe and unsafe acts with safe and unsafe partners.[12]

The peer education groups, run by the city's Women's Union in conjunction with the health agencies, had a similar mission. At the time of my visit, the city's AIDS Committee and the Health Information and Education Center trained former sex workers, supplied them with health education materials and condoms, and paid them a small salary of between VND200,000 and VND400,000 a month.[13] The local units of the Women's Union ran these peer education groups, whose members would seek out their working peers in the sex trade for health education. At the two groups' weekly meetings I attended in June 1996, peer educators reported urging sex workers to go to the STD hospitals for testing and examination. Peer educators were giving out STDs/AIDS information, free condoms, and health pamphlets. They routinely gave out douches and vaginal inserts to treat infections. The health pamphlets and flyers distributed were also available at the Café Condom and at various clinics and hospitals. Some pamphlets feature forms of safe and unsafe sexual contact. Several feature graphic illustrations of the use of condoms. Some specifically target prostitutes, laying out the facts of HIV transmission and instructions on how to put a condom on a client's penis and how to remove and dispose of it afterward. With these auxiliary programs, governors and medical professionals reach out to minutely intervene at the moment of the sex act that is the cause of disease and unwanted births: with whom should one have sex, how should one have sex, and what should one do right before, during, and after the sex act.

Poor and Female

Men could call in to such places as the Café Condom to ask questions and receive health information about sex acts commercially available to them outside the home. Health agencies put out pamphlets for men educating them about the whats and hows of STDs. But as exemplified by the peer education groups' message to women who work the sex trade, that "you must use condoms, because otherwise you will infect your clients," both the clinical and outreach programs identify sex workers as agents of disease and thus target these women to carry the greater burden in protecting the well-being of the nation. As women, the sex workers' sexualized female bodies are imagined to be always engaged in the errant sex act, resulting in unwanted births and the transmission of disease. The responsibility falls on these women to see to it that pregnancies resulting from their work be terminated in the interest of the nation's well-being now and in the future. Compared to their clients as sex partners, sex workers disproportionately receive the blame and therefore the responsibility regarding these health problems.

The ease with which governors and health professionals could assign sex workers this disproportionate blame might be better understood if one were to consider the class positions of most sex workers. According to one of the increasing numbers of studies done in Vietnam on prostitution as part of the drive for more knowledge, most sex workers come from the poorer classes in indexes of family background and educational level. Of the surveyed 260 arrested and practicing sex workers, 54 percent described their family as poor, another 40 percent described theirs as having just enough to eat, and only 5 percent said they were from "well-off" families.[14] Eighty-seven percent had lower than a ninth-grade education, of which 17.4 percent could not read and 30 percent had between a first-grade and a fifth-grade education.[15]

It was not difficult for health personnel to conjure up for public consumption the connection between the poorer classes and disease. Health professionals often narrated this link between poverty, squalor, and contagion, making it logical and believable. Linh, the Women's Union official in charge of a peer education group, for example, made repeated references to the unhygienic practices of prostitutes that resulted from their poverty. She worded this message in a way that not only showed concern for the women's health but also evoked fear and disgust. Many of these women, said Linh, resorted to simply urinating after intercourse to clean themselves because they had no access to clean water and because they believed this would protect them against disease and unwanted pregnancies.[16] In his story excerpted above, V. P., the health official, juxtaposes the prostitute-as-vessel-of-disease to the much more legitimate class status of the threatened family of the client. The doctor's strong reaction at seeing the "well-to-do" status of the client's family gives off a sense of regret at the mortal wrecking of this picture-perfect and unsuspecting middle-class family. The doctor in his professional capacity makes the link from poor woman, to well-to-do man, to well-to-do woman. The middle-class wife in her innocence would fall victim, followed by her unborn child. The story conveys pathogenic threats to the middle-class family from lower-class women and pits the middle-class woman against the prostitute as the source of her family's pending or potential destruction.

Individualization

The patients were treated as active subjects responsible for their own health. Further, they had to rely on expert knowledge to inform them so they could act responsibly for the purpose of their own well-being and happiness.

In *The Birth of the Clinic*, Foucault talks at length about medicine as a science of the individual, the individual as "both the subject and object of his own knowledge."[17] The species body is embodied by the individual body in its finitude. While medical knowledge is of the species body, medical practice is based on particular knowledge of the individual patient. In Western society, one's medical history is meticulously reconstructed on lengthy questionnaires every time one visits a new doctor or when one enters the hospital. There is the obligatory transfer of an individual patient's medical file to the current place of treatment. The individual patient is thought to hold sovereignty over his or her body and its history of test results, diagnoses, and treatments. The release forms patients must sign to give permission for the transfer of these files serve as testaments of the uniqueness and sovereignty of the individual.

Except for some instances of individualized dignified care such as that recommended by the CARE International compilation (see chapter 2), the more common experience of Vietnamese women at the abortion clinic that I described did not testify to this kind of meticulous attention to the continuity of the individual patient's existence in her medical file. A chart was written up for each patient for the invasive procedure to follow. The doctor's repetitive and casual question posed to each patient, "Do you have a heart, lung, or kidney disease?" was the closest this clinical practice came to documenting a patient's medical history. The body was the body on the medical chart, to be treated at the moment, disjointed from an individual history conducive to the assembling of an individual biographical narrative. As seen with both the clinical practice of abortion and STDs, health professionals were rather condescending, dismissive of the individual dignity of the patient. Little attention was paid to the identity (no verification of identity at any stage in the process), privacy, or dignity of the individual patient. The doctor giving the preoperation pelvic exams to women at the abortion ward kept yelling at the woman to be examined next to "pull off your pants, hurry!" even while the previous patient had not had time to dress herself and leave the curtained examination space.[18]

So the meticulous individualization of Western medical practice did not fully play out in the Vietnamese clinical practice. Nevertheless, I argue that this lack of attention paid to the marking of the individual patient did not prevent the assignment of individual responsibility for one's own health. At the abortion ward described, the doctor who went over the charts before giving the final preoperation pelvic exams kept calling over the confusion of the crowd gathered around him for the patient herself to answer his questions, as opposed to family members, fixing the patient of the moment as the subject and object of her knowledge about herself and as individually responsible for both her condition and her treatment. He had to yell down family members repeatedly so that the patient could answer for her own condition.

A paradoxical relationship between a patient's lack of medical knowledge and her individual accountability was also set up. In one instance, a woman argued that she should be given the abortion procedure even though she informed the doctor that she had a "weak heart." This exchange followed:

Doctor: We can't do it with a weak heart, all right? How many children have you had?

Patient: [inaudible]

Doctor: You go in there, your heart will stop and you'll die. Once we inject general anesthetics, your heart can stop.

Patient: But [inaudible] fetus would be expelled.

Doctor: But after it comes out, we'll have to scrape. You don't know anything. Let others explain it to you. You don't know anything. Let people who are learned tell you.[19]

At the same abortion ward, the nurse at the preliminary examination room inquired about the women's situations and scolded them for "breaking the [population control] plan." The following was a typical exchange that I heard in that room, illustrating the relationship between medical knowledge and individual responsibility:

> Nurse: How can we scrape it at more than five months into your pregnancy? Do you have any health problem?
>
> Patient: I have a heart condition.
>
> Nurse: Who said you have a heart condition?
>
> Patient: Over at Hospital 115.
>
> Nurse: How is it that you knew you were sick and still did not stick to the "plan"? You let it go on 'til you're five months along. How can we scrape it for you now, and with a heart condition?
>
> Patient: I went to see a doctor, and the doctor said to wait until I'm five-months pregnant.
>
> Nurse: Are you crazy? How can we scrape at five months? Now wait and let the doctor decide.[20]

Although the patient could not be trusted to really know what was wrong with her or what was good for her, it was still her responsibility to be informed of medical facts about the human body and her own and to do what was good for her. The patient was scolded for not effectively using birth control and, once pregnant, for letting her pregnancy proceed when she knew she had a heart condition. Medical professionals and their knowledge were made indispensable to the patient, who was treated as ignorant and at the same time made fully responsible for her predicament as the consequence of her lack of knowledge and her uninformed acts.

This paradox of a perpetual lack of knowledge and final accountability for one's own condition in the clinical setting confirmed the individual's need to be instructed. This need for instruction serves as the basis of measures aimed at affecting the care of one's body. Public education of these issues in sex education in school, in the distribution of health pamphlets, and in the issuance of "what you need to know/how-to" manuals reached out both to fix the individuals' responsibility for their health and to show them how to do it. Pamphlets and flyers covered topics from women's and men's anatomy, physiology, and methods of birth control, to STDs (especially AIDS), to types of sexual intercourse, and forms of safe sex.

SEX IN THE HOME

If health officials and professionals effectively use prostitutes to anchor an imagination about public health connected to sex outside of the home, their medical and health discourse urge wives and potential wives of the expanding middle classes to compete for their men's sexual interests against the lure of prostitutes in the marketplace. Once health officials and professionals have shown errant sex with prostitutes to be the cause of unwanted births and disease, the stage is set for them to suggest appropriate and healthy sex. Self-help books in their role as education manuals disseminating knowledge about appropriate and healthy sex also have become popular.

An Invitation to Bourgeois Femininity

Sex education manuals in the form of self-help books have flooded the shelves of urban bookstores in Vietnam in recent years. During my visit in 1996, I made a survey of Ho Chi Minh City bookstores and found that about one-fifth of the total number of books displayed on shelves deal with proper gender roles, dating, family happiness, and sex. Usually, a self-help book would include a combination of the above items.

The sex education self-help books are produced by publishing houses of mass organizations such as those of the city or central youth unions (e.g., Nhà Xuất Bản Thanh Niên and Nhà Xuất Bản Trẻ) or city and provincial government units (e.g., Nhà Xuất Bản Hà Nội, Nhà Xuất Bản Thành Phố Hồ Chí Minh, and Nhà Xuất Bản Đồng Tháp). These publishing houses, along with other enterprises set up by party or governmental work units, operate within a market system, with profits and losses borne by the work units themselves. The houses maintain a degree of relative autonomy from governmental policy dictates, catering to market demands for certain materials. Informal conversations with some newspaper and publishing house editors suggest that they avoid antagonizing party lines and governmental policies and respond to general campaigns like the antiprostitution campaign. Within those parameters, material content can respond to professional dictates or market demands. Although the government has not allowed for privately owned media, the line between the public and private sectors blurs as in the case of the privatization of health care. Health professionals who work for the government in some capacity, such as doctors and other health workers at state-owned clinics and hospitals, could consult for these sex education and self-help venues "after hours," in the same way that doctors and nurses at the abortion hospital charge fees for after-hour services.[21] The "state-owned" media, which operate by gains and losses, would either broadcast or publish government-employed health professionals who consult on health education.

Common to all these books is an enlightened medical discourse on sex and sexuality: the anatomy, physiology, and psychology of sex and reproduction; sexual desire and pleasure; sexual dysfunctions and perversions; and sexually transmitted diseases. If the authors of these books are not themselves physicians, then lengthy lists of medical books are referenced, many of which are Western-language sources. The content focuses on what is normal and what is not. Often, book sections are devoted to normal functioning in sex and then to sexual dysfunction, disorders, perversions, and, finally, methods of correcting them. The usual format presents informed answers to selections from torrents of anxious questions about the normality or abnormality of a condition. Trần Bồng Sơn, physician and author of a number of these sex education books, said in a newspaper interview: "So far, I have received over three thousand letters through the newspaper columns, and five thousand calls through [the radio program] Central Station 108. Over 95 percent of them are inquiries about sex and husband-wife activities."[22]

Clearly, the norm according to medicine as a science becomes the standard against which people are anxiously measuring themselves. This is

the mechanism of expert norm supervision at work. Medical professionals teach people how to monitor themselves and their behavior
against the medically established norm. I point out that these books,
premised on professional medical knowledge and produced by publishing
houses that have begun to blur the line between governmental policy
and expert or market considerations, help to eroticize the conjugal ties
in the bourgeoisified family. This eroticization relies first on a construction of bourgeois femininity. This becomes clear as one considers
who makes up the target readership of these books and how they are
invited to take up practices that will allow them to become bourgeois
and feminine.

First, I take up the question of target readership. Authors pitch their
books to women. Judging from the pricing of these books, I would say
that the readers belong to the middle to high-income brackets. The prices
of these books ranged from less than US$1 to US$3 in 1996. The average monthly salary of a woman garment worker was US$20–$30 at the
time. The rate for domestic workers was roughly US$16. The average
sex worker could earn more than US$100 a month, but she usually had
incredibly high expenditures in terms of clothing, medical costs, remit-
tances to family, and high interest (up to an annual rate of 200–300 percent) debt servicing. Book purchasing would be an exceptional luxury
for these lower-class working women. The main readership then seems
to consist of women who come from the classes of party and government employees, state and private entrepreneurs, professionals, and other
office employees, and who are the wives or potential wives of men also
from these classes. As noted, the main clientele of commercial sex in the
late 1990s consisted of men from these rising classes, primarily the entrepreneurial class. The targeting of the wives and potential wives of these
men would help extend the reach of government-promoted health
measures.[23] I suggest the object is to bring the erotic activities in the marketplace into the middle-class home and keep it there with prescriptions
for healthy sexual behavior.

The identity of the middling classes in Vietnam is far from clear in
an economy and society still in a fervent process of stratification during economic liberalization. Even if a class position could be objectively

determined by the group's access to the means of production and exchange, "a class," writes Bourdieu, "is defined as much by its *being per-ceived* as by its *being*."²⁴ The historical rise of the middle class in nineteenth-century Europe offers some insight into some mechanisms of this class perception. McClintock for instance writes about "the still disorganized middling classes" and their class expression in Victorian domesticity.²⁵ Foucault points out that the discourse of sexual repression in the nineteenth century was about "the body, vigor, longevity, progeniture, and descent of the classes that 'ruled.'"²⁶ It seems that groups rising in economic standing would need to actively engage in practices that would allow their higher status to be perceived as such.

If the expanding middling classes in Vietnam need some active affirmation, and if the narrative of proletarian class superiority no longer serves the new hierarchy of social stratification brought on by economic liberalization, then the conditions of bourgeois-ness and petit-bourgeois-ness make convenient signs to mark a new set of middle-class identities. What have the authors of these self-help books invited women of comfortable means to do in order to be perceived as bourgeois? For one thing, these women should take on the aura of scientific knowledge. Medical knowledge in Vietnam since colonial days has often been synonymous with Western knowledge. Possession of the latter has a long tradition of being perceived as a sign of superior class distinction. In colonial times, Western (French) colonizers occupied the superior class position in relation to the natives; for natives to be learned in Western ways, "to be dusted over with colonial culture," was to set themselves apart in an intermediary class above other natives.²⁷ These native intermediaries were Salman Rushdie's Minutemen, products of colonial education set out in such documents as T. B. Macaulay's "Minute on Education."²⁸ The same semiotics of class and knowledge held in postcolonial Vietnam. Sex education manuals in the wartime South also aimed at the urban bourgeois classes.²⁹ To the revolutionary regime in the North, possession of Western knowledge was the definitive sign of a bourgeois class status to be reformed, redeemed, and held at arm's length.

These self-help manuals encourage the acquisition of knowledge necessary for women to fill new reproductive functions in the bourgeois family. The books invite women to learn and to reproduce an enlightened discourse on sex. One sex education manual for "parents of adolescents," for example, urges a hypothetical mother to offer her child a more medically truthful explanation of sex and reproduction against the advice of the grandmother. An intergenerational contest is waged as the mother champions an enlightened and healthy way of handling children's sexuality in such a matter as masturbation or what to tell them about sex.[30] In the same spirit, mom describes for little daughter sex between mom and dad (thus husband and wife) in loving and gentle details.[31] The bourgeoisified woman is to demonstrate the urbanity of an enlightened discourse on love, sex, pleasure, health, and disease. She needs to make sure this enlightened knowledge informs the sex life of her children and her conjugal relationship with her husband.

The Eroticized Bourgeois Wife

As the woman of comfortable means acquires the knowledge that is to be read as bourgeois class status, she is invited to use some of that knowledge to eroticize herself and the conjugal relationship. In order to protect her family from the dirty sex available to her husband in the marketplace, she would need to keep his interest by taking care of her appearance and by knowing the science of sex and sexual pleasures. The self-help books ask her to perform a bourgeois femininity that reproduces the bourgeois family with gendered spaces and gendered roles.

In the publisher's introduction to a comprehensive encyclopedia for women, the Hanoi Publishing House explains its target audience and purpose as follows:

> Some ask: "Why women?" Because nature created two sexes/genders and endowed each with separate advantages to fulfill separate functions. In the area of love, marriage, and family, we see this most clearly. The men play the active role, but the decision belongs to the women. . . .
> Marriage and family in its true essence is an issue that belongs to women. Here, their interests are most clearly expressed, their skills (or lack thereof) most clearly revealed.
> [Sex] is a completely scientific topic. In many families with prob-

lems like adultery the deep cause is in the partners' lack of sexual sat-
isfaction due to lack of knowledge about the functioning of this
machinery, and because they have not escaped antiquated prejudice,
viewing sex as something dirty and ugly.[32]

The "scientific" knowledge in the above passage justifies anchoring
women of the new middle classes in domestic spaces and using these
women to sexualize such spaces of marriage and family. The same encyclopedia elaborates on the dangers to the conjugal family in these terms:

> First, we need to observe that in capitalist society, where everything
> could be bought and sold, sex becomes a commodity as well. Shameless
> and unethical merchants sell sex retail and wholesale. . . . The sex busi-
> ness [faced with intervention] withdraws to the shadows and claims
> its victims from there.
>
> In our country, the situation is just as threatening. In recent years,
> the divorce rate has gone up very quickly. . .; the divorce rate due to
> lack of sexual satisfaction is rising alarmingly.[33]

To keep middle-class husbands happy, the women must actively "combat" the "boredom" that usually takes over conjugality.

The books tell the middle-class wife that she could do a number of
things. For one, she could take care to create a happy home environment. The psychology of the sexes is a big item that sometimes merits whole volumes on "the psychological differences between men and
women" that lead to "conflict between husbands and wives." The
author of such a volume announces that her readers should condemn
infidelity and "support the young couple's being romantic at the necessary level to understand each other and be gentle, affectionate to one
another;" but if problems, doubts, or infidelity on the husband's part
should arise, the woman should never make a scene and run to the work
unit or denounce her husband to others.[34] The solution cautioned
against had served in the past as one of the primary means of family
resolution when a wife would come asking for intervention by the "collective" in the form of the neighborhood Women's Union, the Neighborhood Citizens' Cell (*tổ dân phố*), or the work unit. The resolution
usually took the form of collective and thus public criticism and surveillance for compliance.[35] Now, however, one should not confuse this

socialist man and woman with the private bourgeois. The middle-class woman in this new context is asked to use her knowledge to ensure bourgeois family happiness and to take care of any problems herself, cut off from the watchful eyes of the collective. The domestic spaces of the bourgeois home have once again been privatized to facilitate conjugal intimacy.

These self-help books tell the middle-class woman that combating boredom to ensure conjugal happiness in her private home means taking care of herself, to feel good and look good for her children and especially her husband. The books present regimes of diet and exercise, makeup, dress, and so forth. They teach the wife to feel and look happy as part of the prop of this pleasant family environment. The *Encyclopedia for Young Women* spells out clearly this necessity: "The wife who busies herself all day in front of the husband, only to prepare herself to look good in front of guests at night, would she have the certainty of having her husband's burning love? So the same goes for makeup. If you wipe clean the makeup to 'let your face breath,' you can be assured that this attention to appear good for others but not for your husband will not earn you your husband's passion."[36] However busy a wife might be, the authors recommend an appearance of leisure in makeup, dress, and demeanor for the sake of keeping the "burning love" of her husband. For her husband's gaze, she is to appear pretty and unburdened by the ugly signs of work. Not only should the bourgeois woman erase the signs of work for outsiders, she should mark herself in the bourgeois home with the status of the leisure class as well.[37]

The campaign to keep in the home the husband's wandering sexual interests in the era of the erotic marketplace settles on conjugal sex as the main line of defense. One staple in these manuals is the incitement to knowledge about sex: how it works and how to maximize pleasure. Unabashed sex physiology and psychology, plus sexology, which speaks of "pleasure spots," "stages," "positions," "variety and techniques," "arousing scents," "appropriate lighting" of the conjugal bed, and so on, occupy large sections in many of these self-help books.

One manual addressed to "the girl who is getting married" explains why

it is extremely important for men to be aroused and get pleasure in the
sexual act in heterosexual terms based on the necessity of biology:

> Why is it [sexual arousal in men] more important? Because the male
> sexual organ cannot be used in normal circumstances; it has to go
> through a process of profound change in the level of firmness to be
> functional. And this happens only when the man is sufficiently
> aroused.
>
> Women, on the other hand, can do it any time, regardless of whether
> there is desire, even when threatened or coerced.
>
> Unlike men, women do not need "recovery time" in between.
> Women can do it anytime, are always ready to return to sensitivity,
> and are the only creatures on earth with the capacity for multiple
> orgasms.[38]

Such description of the "normal" or "natural" state of women in the sexual act reads like what is expected of most practicing sex workers.
Middle-class wifeliness here is about out-whoring prostitutes and doing
it all within the hygienic confines of the conjugal bed. From the above
description of the female sex, the same manual launches into a lesson
in sexology, dissecting sexual pleasure and how to ensure it. Never
before since the revolution has there been such excited discussion about
sex and the conjugal bed.

Through sex education, especially these self-help manuals, those
wielding the medical discourse of knowledge and enlightenment urge
women of the middling classes to take on a certain femininity to be read
as bourgeois. In their grasp of this knowledge, these women are invited
to act, feel, and be seen as distinct from the lower classes of women, even
while employing it to compete with sex workers for the sexual interests
of their men. While governors and medical professionals use prostitutes
in the erotic marketplace to drive home the dangers of uninformed sex
in its relation to disease and undesirable reproduction, health authors
groom women of the middling classes in bourgeois femininity to provide class-appropriate pleasure for their men. Theirs would be a femininity linked to an enlightened and scientific discourse of sexual pleasure
in the context of the progressive, healthy, and satisfying family, one that
would be private and intimate.

CONCLUSION

Governmental measures addressing prostitution in the late 1990s and early 2000s suggest that governors have begun to deploy governing strategies that draw their authority from expert knowledge rather than from the ideological mission of the Marxist-Leninist regime. The new uses of medicine in public health measures allow for governance without the language of political struggles, opening the way for the possibility of the privatization of some governing functions. Expertise-legitimated governance, however, does not entail class or gender neutrality. With medical professionals and their expert knowledge on health and disease, the government attempts to guide sexual behavior in and outside of the home, targeting sex workers and middle-class wives to anchor an imagination of a sexual order based on an eroticized bourgeois conjugality.

One can discern in this governing through health and medicine a reliance on a combination of threat and seduction by medical knowledge. Although differentiated by both class and gender, where the clinical measures targeting sex workers seem more coercive than does the discourse of sex, health, and vitality aimed at men and women of the new middling or higher classes, it still posits to some degree the autonomous agency of the sex workers involved, that they must be persuaded to use condoms and get tested. The mandatory testing takes place only in conjunction with practices of incarceration in rehabilitation camps, where the mode of governance is decidedly coercive and where scientific knowledge takes a backseat to a discourse on authentic Vietnamese culture.

CHAPTER 5

Who You Truly Are

Coercion, Culture, and the Global Imaginary
in the Governmental Rehabilitation of Sex Workers

ONCE A SEX WORKER is arrested by the police, a set of "administrative"
government decrees decides her fate. Government Resolution 53/
CP of 1994 reinforces Article 24 of the Decrees for Administrative
Transgressions by specifying that "those who have been identified as
engaged in selling sex shall be sent to centers for the purpose of education, disease treatment, and labor."[1] The organization of these rehabilitation "centers" resembles the organization of a low-security prison.
Inmates are forcibly committed and incarcerated for the duration of
their "administrative" sentence, which could last anywhere from three
months to twenty-eight months, depending on repeat offenses or further infractions of camp rules such as escape attempts. Rehabilitative
incarceration also entails a strict regimentation of daily tasks and routines, which include STD testing and education, political and ethical
classes, and vocational training for piece-rate global production.

The literature on globalization debates the place of the nation-state
in relation to global capitalist processes. I make the point here that this
is an instance in which a national government reasserts its power of
defining its governable subjects and thereby its relevance in relation to
the global economy. More specifically, the national government in this
instance reinscribes a truth about this group of women. Through policing and incarceration, the government points out the falsity of wayward
prostitutes, who earn more than their worth and who spend above their
class, in order to present the truth of lower-class women as honest workers imagined through the global division of labor in terms of class, gen-

der, and Vietnamese national culture. As the reference to Vietnamese traditional culture helps to justify a coercive mode of control, it also helps one to think about the ruling techniques of a modern government in its particular location within a global economy.

As I discussed earlier, many scholars cast doubt on the demise of the nation-state in relation to forces of globalization. Instead, the role of a national government seems reshaped in a global economy dependent on the use of feminized labor, a model of which projects an imagination about the young Asian female worker who is dexterous, docile, and tolerant of tedious work because of her traditional gender role. In the Southeast Asian context, while Aihwa Ong argues that the Southeast Asian "tiger" states increasingly focus on "producing and managing populations that are attractive to global capital," Jayne Werner points out how the Vietnamese Đổi Mới state is seeking to "make the populace more 'legible' and easier to govern."[2] I find that the Vietnamese national government reasserts its relevance in the global economy by actively projecting truths and "hailing" subjects as imagined through the global division of labor.[3] As Jean and John Comaroff lament the "displacement of class" by "cultural and other forms of identity," I make the case that class identity is being defined by a national government through terms of gender and national culture.[4] Through rehabilitation efforts, the government engages the ideological task of holding up to lower-class Vietnamese women a model of the Asian female worker in a flexible production mode based on subcontracted piecework.

THE FALSITY OF PROSTITUTES

Foucault argues that modern governance, what he calls "governmentality," operates by regimes of truth and disciplinary training that produce the governable subjects and their sense of self.[5] I discuss here how sex workers, using their earnings, try to represent themselves through their consumption of certain objects. I make the case that the government falsifies the sex workers' representations of their "selves" in their consumption by denouncing this work as dishonest and illegal, by arresting sex workers, and by sending them to rehabilitation camps. The government shows it can deploy repressive tools to render certain selves false or unauthentic, to be replaced by those that are "true."

One Hundred Thousand Dong in One Day and Gold Bangles

All the sex workers I interviewed saw sex work as a way for them to eke out a living, if not to move up in the world. Mai, a twenty-nine-year-old woman working at a Vũng Tàu café, said it was vastly better for her there than it was staying in the countryside where she would have to feed herself and her four-year-old daughter by prawning, a whole day's worth of which would fetch her VND3,000, or less than US 30¢ at the time.[6] Each time she went with a client or two, who would sandwich her between them and whisk her away on their motorbike, she was paid from VND50,000 to VND100,00 (about US$5–$10). A night spent with one or two men beginning before ten at night would fetch VND150,000 (a little less than US$15). Forty percent of Mai's receipt went to the owner of the café, since the latter provided the place of business and protection by way of keeping around a band of tough-looking young men and maintaining good relations with the local police to protect them from the government's campaign against social evils.

Minh and Hằng, both *bia ôm* hostesses in Ho Chi Minh City, narrated their trade and high earnings as a means to pull their families out of desperate conditions and to have some control over their lives, as Minh relates:

> My family was so desperate. Back then, we were poor to the extent that with plain rice, you'd count the bowls and never was there enough. I was in the ninth grade. I was a good student. I had to quit after I took the exam. Before I could go to tenth grade, I had to quit to look for work. I hid what I did from my mom. The money I made I brought home to feed the littler ones. Back then, school fees were a few dong for the little ones, and I brought home more than one hundred thousand dong in one day. Can you imagine?[7]

The women often described their work as bitter, but found it necessary to maintain a livable life. The women called themselves working women, whose work provided for themselves and their families in ways that other women among the urban or rural poor could not. Elsewhere in the interview, Minh said she once tried to quit the trade by applying for a position in the garment factory paying VND200,000–VND300,000 (less than US$20–$30) a month. She added that the garment job required an education level and tests that she would not be able to pass. Compared to the pay they would earn doing the kind of "legitimate" work reserved for poor women of modest educational backgrounds, the sex workers' pay was from ten to twenty times higher. To the women, their pay was rightly high because the work was often humiliating. Clients could pick and choose who would wait on them in the most servile ways like wiping their hands and faces and feeding them food or catering to all their sexual demands.

Many sex workers used the high earnings from what they saw as demeaning work to gain some control over their families' living conditions, with "even a bit of security for yourself," as Hằng phrased her future prospects.[8] Both Minh and Hằng made relatively comfortable lives for themselves in small but clean and very well furnished units on the first and fourth floors of an old apartment building in a working-class Ho Chi Minh City neighborhood. Hằng's living room had a ceramic-tiled floor; a solid wood furniture set with a sofa, easy chair, and coffee table; a television and videocassette recorder; and a stereo system.

Many sex workers can afford jewelry and the new products available on the market. Through the acquisition of these products, many women mark themselves with certain signs of status. Minh explained this acquisition of the signs of class and status in this way:

> While you work, you have the motorbikes and the clothes. When you're going down the street, you see all these beautiful girls who ride Dreams and Cubs [the best makes of motorbikes at the time and a sign of money], and who wear gold bangles and such. Their faces would look like nice girls', as though they are from well-off and proper families. No, they are working girls. Taxi dancers. Not nice girls. Outside of work, they look nice. Even I mistake them for nice girls. I think sometimes, I dress like this, I ride this kind of motorbike, who'd know I'm a working girl?[9]

By riding the Dreams and Cubs and by placing certain clothing items and the gold bangles on their bodies, the women represent themselves to be women of the moneyed class. Judith Butler writes that "the process of signification is always material; signs work by appearing (visibly, aurally), and appearing through material means, although what appears only signifies by . . . relations of differentiation."[10] The accessories listed became the material signification of a gendered and classed subjectivity for the women. The femininity projected is not just a body well adorned with pretty clothes and jewelry; these feminine items speak of class as it is perceived. If the servile character of their work denies the women an imagined membership in a class well placed in the relations of production, the objects they consume signify them as "girls from well-off and proper families." These items, according to Minh, could even erase the signs of her work ("Who'd know I'm a working girl?"). The feminine and classy objects present the women either as being well provided for or as being high earners themselves. But the subjectivity enabled by the women's earnings also includes the ability to provide for themselves and their families, as Hằng so proudly affirmed.

Many sex workers exist in constant debt because of the high expenditures on clothes and makeup and on debt servicing on high-interest loans from their bosses and loan sharks. Not all sex workers spend from a leisurely disposable income. And efforts come from many quarters, particularly the government, to erase the classed and gendered subjectivities these women inscribe on their bodies with expensive objects. Nevertheless, these women do actively engage in their own subject making using their relatively high earnings.

Making False: The Police Arrest and Processing of Sex Workers

Certain objects, then, signify class and status, and they are available on the market for purchase by anyone who can pay. However, the construction of subjectivities is not just a matter between spenders and the market. Governments can and do produce truths about the spenders themselves.

The media frequently nullifies the sex workers' efforts in self-making through the acquisition of expensive objects. Sex workers are often portrayed as whores turning their "1,001 tricks."[11] Deception is a pervasive theme in the narrative on prostitutes—from the sex worker deceiving her clients about her HIV-positive status to "whores" being portrayed as dishonest, cheap, gaudy, withered, ugly, even frightening, all hidden under their masks of makeup and clothing.[12] This representation of the prostitute undermines the signs of status and class she puts on with the money she earns. The media enjoys various degrees of autonomy from governmental dictates, although all publicist organs are owned by units of either the government or the party and its mass organizations. In informal conversations, newspaper editors told me they do take their cues from governmental policy lines and high-profile campaigns like the anti-prostitution campaign, and they are ultimately answerable to the party's Ideological Committee (ban tư tưởng và tuyên huấn). But editors do place high priority on the salability as well as the quality of their products.

If the media owned by governmental and party entities other than Public Security could be considered quasi governmental by virtue of their ties to the party and the government, the police see to it that the media renders the self-representation of prostitutes false in the most unmistakable ways. Popular police newspapers often "unmask" the "pretension" of sex workers. For example, a 2005 article in *Công An Nhân Dân*, the newspaper published by the central organ of Public Security, named all the ways in which sex workers deceive those around them.[13] The author told the story as one of revelation about the person behind the lies. Following the process of the police booking and interrogation of a few arrested women, the article revealed their "truth." "I thought she was an honest country girl, but through the police interrogation, I realized she was as she appeared," wrote the author. This "country girl" first produced a false identity card, thinking she could "conceal" herself. Then she tried to pull the wool over the eyes of the police officer by saying that that was her "first time with a customer." The narrative in the article points to police interrogation and documentation as an instrument of truth discovery whereby falsehoods would start to fall away, revealing the woman who should become a recipient of a governmental truth. Such truth went beyond the work of the sex worker to her character in social relations. The truth came out that her parents, and even her lover, had been deceived. Finally, the author cast doubt on even the sex worker's tears as signs of her interior life externalized as a bodily symptom: "After she finished talking, O. even cried. I knew not if those were the tears of shame or the weapon that those like O. use to get pity and empathy from others."

Even more directly or more brutally, police activities to arrest sex workers rely on criminal laws and governmental decrees. Government decrees were and are carried out by governmental entities as administrative orders not subject to judicial procedures established by criminal statutes or even the constitution.

Women selling sexual access to their own bodies do not violate any criminal statutes in Vietnam, but there are criminal laws against the organization of prostitution. Organizers, traffickers, pimps, and other go-betweens could be prosecuted. Article 115 of the 1985 Criminal Codes (still in effect in 2007) reads as follows:

1. Those who buy or sell women are to be punished with prison sentences of five to seven years.
2. Those in the following categories will be given prison sentences of five to twenty years:
   a. organizing
   b. transporting women abroad
   c. buying and selling many women
   d. repeated offense.[14]

Similarly, there were prison sentences for go-betweens (Article 202).

There was no criminal code against prostituting oneself.[15] Instead, these women were "administratively processed" and their activities effectively made illegal according to the Decrees for Administrative Transgression. Article 24 of this document reads, "Narcotic addicts and prostitutes with repeated offenses, who after the local state and people had educated them still had not corrected their ways, shall be committed for the purpose of disease treatment, learning and labor, for the duration of three months to a year."[16] As noted, this was reinforced in 1994 by Government Resolution 53/CP. With anti-social evil resolutions like 87/CP, issued in 1995, the police were given the authority to conduct antiprostitution raids at places where prostitution could be found such as certain streets, parks, hotels, entertainment and food establishments, and whole neighborhoods that had been marked with Social-Ill Area signs posted by the police. Such practices constitute a kind of governmental branding of spaces, activities, and people, negating the ways in which these people might present themselves.

At their meetings, peer education workers reported that sections of streets like Lê Duẩn and Huyền Trân were cordoned off by police at night for "white clearings" (*giải tỏa trắng*) as part of the antiprostitution campaign.[17] Stretches of streets were blocked without warning, and people were taken into custody unless they could prove that they had a legitimate reason to be there. Men, weapons, search lights, and vehicles including transport vehicles with sirens were involved. Mostly women, but some men as well, would be apprehended as prostitutes, along with their clients, and taken to police stations. At certain city parks like Quách Thị Trang, police mobile units were posted from 7:30 a.m. to 9:00 p.m., with frequent patrols after the parks' closing time. The peer educators complained that they were often mistaken for prostitutes and apprehended. The police would let them go only after their cards identifying them as AIDS educators were produced and condoms and health flyers were found in their bags.[18] Rather than be apologetic, the police complained that about 5 percent of the prostitutes apprehended produced false identity cards as "educators, health collaborators."[19] This complaint justified police raids and further demonstrated that sex workers falsify their identity, posing as someone other than who they really are.

At restaurants and other establishments, hospitality hostesses must be identified as such to prevent them from posing as patrons. Unless hostesses could produce papers proving they were registered to work there, they would be arrested:

> Hằng: For example, if I have a business permit for a restaurant with fifty hostesses, the police would come and check the papers of those women found there. Anyone not on that list of fifty registered would

be taken in and fined . . . By the third time, well, they keep you to send to the camps.

Minh: They put you in their vehicles. People on the street would have to wonder what it's about. The sirens go [imitated siren sound].[20]

In other words, the burden of proof of wrongdoing was not on the police. Lack of documentation was sufficient reason for arrests in hospitality establishments.

Beyond these basic information checks, there were "conduct" checks for employment purposes. Minh explained to me that in order to obtain a job at the registered restaurants (not the little corner stalls or cafés), she needed to present her citizen identification, household registration card, a health clearance, and a verification of conduct. Hằng added that this last item was the most important and required by all the state and some nonstate places of employment including, in her experience, garment factories. According to Hằng, the local *phường*, or subdistrict, Public Security used to provide this verification of conduct; "then it changed so that it could verify only residence and address, whereas 'the Justice Committee' [*ban tư pháp*] would verify that I hadn't violated any article in the criminal statutes."[21]

The women had to acquire conduct clearance to be employed as hostesses in the name of controlling the social problem of prostitution. Should they decide to seek a different job, their past arrests (though administrative for prostitutes) might still show up and diminish the women's chances of finding decent employment. But other than being punitive to the women, local police files played a part, linked to the criminal/conviction records of the court system, in the tracking of individuals and their past conduct.

Besides raids of streets and restaurants, the police also conducted raids of hotels. Hà, a young hostess at a café where clients came to arrange for sex in nearby hotels, told me she was arrested while with a client in a hotel room. Being found in a hotel room with a client was incontrovertible proof of sex selling, which landed her in a rehabilitation camp for fourteen months.[22] The following interview excerpt with another

restaurant hostess describes how the police made prostitution arrests in
hotels:

> We don't dare go with clients to hotel rooms now. You're sleeping at
> two, three in the morning. How can you run? Where can you hide?
> They search. My friend, she almost fell to her death. She was sleep-
> ing at two in the morning when they knocked on the door. She threw
> everything under the bed. All the things that were women's: purses,
> shoes, clothes. They came and asked the man whom he was sleeping
> with. He said: "Alone." But the first thing they'd look for are women's
> things. A pair of women's shoes and they'd know. So she was hiding,
> hanging on outside this sixth-floor window. It was windy. There were
> barbed wires down below. She prayed.[23]

The women saw such practice as arbitrary and repressive. The same
restaurant hostess put the matter to me this way: "In Vietnam, there
are only orders. If there is an order issued to go search and sweep all the
bia ôm restaurants, and sweep up all the women without papers, then
it happens."[24]

Such harassment to falsify the women's self-presentation of themselves
depends on documentation, their physical presence at certain places and
times, and also the company they keep. If a native woman was caught
with a foreign man, the police took it as a sure sign that the woman was
a prostitute.[25] But the intimidation in the interrogation process with
allusions to a network of police information and files would usually do
the trick in making the women confess to their trade:

> Hằng: If you say the man is your lover, then they phone your neigh-
> borhood authorities to ask, "What had been this girl's occupations
> in the past?"
>
> Minh: Suppose you say, "He's my lover." They ask for your address,
> and they call the Neighborhood Public Security to see what kind of
> work you do.
>
> Hằng: So, first of all, the young women are shamed.
>
> Minh: They [local authorities where residents' occupations are reg-
> istered] know you work at a restaurant or a dancing hall. [The police
> would say,] "A dancing hall is fine. So you work. And here you are,
> with a client in bed. So you are selling sex. Your work is illegal."
>
> Hằng: Here, they are very good at this. They have all the words to

trap you. But if there's money, then you can escape their mouths. Without money, there's no way.[26]

The police frequently compiled statistics to show the effectiveness of their arrest activities. In 2006, for example, the police reported that they had closed down 255 brothels and arrested 1,476 brokers, pimps, and sex workers.[27] The women countered the police discourse of truth discovery in relation to sex workers with their own stories of using bribe money to escape the grip of the police, while at the same time they unmasked police corruption. But with the whole arsenal of repression at their disposal, the police were clearly in a better position to falsify the women's self-presentations by deploying tactics that identified them as prostitutes in need of governmental rehabilitation.

The police hold clients accountable for their infraction of the laws by fining them. But sex workers are subject to incarceration as a means of rehabilitation. If the sex workers have tried to narrate their work as paid work, the earnings from which they use to represent themselves as capable women or women of the moneyed class, the government, through resolutions, decrees, and policing, clearly *re*-represents them as illegitimate subjects, to be arrested and rehabilitated. One could look at these governmental activities as the crossing out of a certain kind of subjects rather than the total erasure of these women who do sex work and who earn their purchasing power. Instead of denying that prostitutes exist, the government highlights their presence with very vocal anti–social evil / anti-prostitution campaigns. All over the city, there are murals, banners, posters, and exhibits exhorting the eradication of these social evils, often in graphic terms. One huge street poster depicts the busy activities of the police executing the governmental Three Reductions (*ba giảm*) campaign against drugs, prostitution, and crime (figure 5.1). This image, mounted at an actual street corner, casts a prominent police presence in the physical and representational spaces of the city.

A mobilization poster (*tranh cổ động*) in a September 1996 exhibit by the Ho Chi Minh City Cultural Bureau shows a red fist crushing a naked woman with PROSTITUTION written in black across the length of her body (figure 5.2). Besides this image, other social evils like gambling and

5.1 Street billboard of police activities, 2002. Photo by the author.

5.2 Poster in exhibit by the Ho Chi Minh City Cultural Bureau, 1996. Photo by the author.

5.3 Poster in Ministry of Culture and Information exhibit, Ho Chi Minh City, 2002. Photo by the author.

drug use are represented. At the bottom is the caption, "Stopping poisonous culture and social evils is the responsibility of the entire society" (*Ngăn chặn văn hoá độc hại và tệ nạn xã hội là trách nhiệm của toàn xã hội*). It is governmental power that strips the woman of her false adornment and inscribes on her body the visibility of a target subject that must be unmasked in order to be eradicated.

Another poster at a Ministry of Culture and Information exhibit in Ho Chi Minh City in July 2002 shows in stark black and white the words CRIMES, PROSTITUTION, and DRUGS on bars, under an emphatic NO! in bold on top (figure 5.3). Interestingly, the social evils in questions are shown as shadows and extensions of prison bars, the very tool of social repression. It is as if the repressive measures themselves give these social evils their visibility and intelligibility.

In an incitement to talk, to acknowledge a "social problem," to do something about prostitutes, the government first "exposes" them as illegitimate beings, as false subjects who are to be rewritten through rehabilitation in terms that would be legible for the agendas of the government as it interfaces with the global economy at the local and regional levels.

MAKING TRUE: THE REHABILITATION OF PROSTITUTES

Louis Althusser classifies the apparatuses of the state into those that exercise repression and those that enforce the ideological imaginings of subjects.[28] The repressive state apparatus, or RSA, includes the police, army, and prisons, and the ideological state apparatuses, or ISAs, include schools, churches, the media, and so forth (142–43). The differentiation lies in the mode of operation: the RSA functions "massively and predominantly" by physical violence or repression, and the ISAs function massively and predominantly by ideology (144–45). But Althusser, in a manner reminiscent of Foucault, acknowledges that one cannot separate ideology from the physical and material practices, be they violent or not. In his words, the RSA functions "secondarily by ideology," for example, in the "values" the police or army propounds (145). I suggest that in this case the governmental measures of repression from arrest to incarceration perform an ideological task: the making of falsehood and truth in the imaginings of subjects. If the police arrest and "administrative processing" of prostitutes and the terms of incarceration deny the validity of, and thus make false, the sex workers' self-representations, then the actual practices of carceral rehabilitation in the camps attempt to reinscribe a truth about the kind of subjects these women should have been. The descriptions that follow of practices in the rehabilitation camps inform a discussion of the government's deployment of Foucauldian discipline so as to guide Vietnamese women of the lower classes to imagine themselves as natural candidates for the global production line.

Carceral Training

Techniques to rehabilitate sex workers resemble more or less those found in modern prisons with their principles of carceral correction. The camps use confinement and space and time regimentation and proclaim their function to be rehabilitative.[29] The means of correction in government-run rehabilitation camps could be discussed with regard to (1) the spatial confinement of inmates and the organization of surveillance; (2) the regimentation of time for its coordination with tasks—the timetable; and (3) the infantilization of inmates to facilitate this reinscription of discipline. These are the means of discipline to render the inmates docile and useful.

When one speaks of incarceration, the most obvious feature of this correction method is of course the isolation effected by the physical capture of inmates. "Social-evil subjects" were forcibly interned. The New Center for the Education of Women, a camp exclusively for "prostitutes," had enclosed walls and a guarded iron gate. To request entry, I had to present my papers from the proper authorities to the guard through a small window in the wall. Hà, a former inmate at the Center for Social Sponsorship, another governmental rehabilitation camp for female prostitutes and male drug addicts, recited to me the second of fifteen rules from a list that inmates were made to memorize and recite everyday: "All who come to and leave the camp must be subjected to the controls of the wardens [*ban quản giáo*, or committee of supervisors/educators]."[30] Among the gravest punishable offenses was an escape attempt. Mai, another former inmate from the same camp, gave this account: "They laid it out for us: if you were supposed to undergo reform for twelve or fourteen months and you tried to escape, they would increase the duration of reform to twenty-eight months. If you tried to escape, yes, they'd beat you plenty. Women they beat less than men."[31] Would-be escapees were made to kneel by the central flagpole and whipped. As Mai recounted, "Those made to kneel under the flagpole were whipped with an electrical whip. They'd whip you 'til you bled. Wherever they could get you. They hit your butt, your back. If you tried to pull away, they'd hit your face, your head."[32]

Within the enclosure of the compound, inmates were assigned to groups of three, making up teams of thirty. The teams acted to segregate inmates and coordinate their activities. The Center for Social Sponsorship had four teams of women inmates (incarcerated for prostitution), eight teams of men (incarcerated for drug addiction), and one isolated team of AIDS-afflicted or HIV-positive inmates.[33] Team leaders and deputy leaders were selected by the wardens. At the New Center for the Education of Women, these leaders wore armbands printed with the word *bảo vệ* (protector). Inmates reported to their team leaders before the start and end of the day and in between activities and tasks.[34] The inmates watched one another, the team leaders watched the inmates in their teams, and, finally, the wardens watched the teams of inmates. As Foucault observed in modern carceral systems, the organization of authority and surveillance in these camps minimized "horizontal conjunctions," using "procedures of partitioning and verticality" in "compact hierarchical networks," making up an "individualizing pyramid."[35] The wardens had the authority to administer punishment, but they charged the team leaders with this task. Team leaders carried out the whippings and beatings for violations of camp rules such as stealing and for failures to fulfill production quotas.

The foremost object of this form of hierarchical organization is to efficiently minimize the potential for agitation, revolt, alliance, or organization among inmates. At the time of my visit, the New Center

for the Education of Women needed only a staff of thirty-two, including those in administrative functions, to run a camp of six hundred
inmates. But this pyramid, with its power to separate, coordinate, and
supervise, also facilitates the training of habits of docility and utility.[36]
The organization of surveillance ensures adherence to the timetable. At
the Center for Social Sponsorship, the inmates' day went from 7:00 a.m.
to 5:00 p.m.: work and training went from 8:00 a.m. to 11:00 a.m. and
from 1:15 p.m. to 4:45 p.m.; from 7:00 p.m. to 9:00 p.m. was the time
for learning laws or for entertainment. Inmates started and ended their
day by singing three camp songs and reciting camp rules in the central
courtyard marked by the flagpole. Their day was punctuated by bells to
rise, to do the morning exercise, to get their ration of cooked rice for
breakfast, to gather at the flagpole for singing and reciting rules, to start
the work/training day by going to the work areas assigned to their respective teams, to stop and to go to places for rest or for meals, and so on.[37]
Inmates had to internalize the regimentation of time by memorizing
the daily schedule, listed as the eighth rule on the list of fifteen camp
regulations at the Center for Social Sponsorship.[38]

In the camps, wardens made every effort to infantilize inmates. They
treated inmates as though they were now to start over and relearn the
things they should have learned as children, especially as schoolchildren.[39] Mai recited a line in a song taught to inmates: "Tomorrow we shall
learn to be humans."[40]

Wardens carried out the infantilization of inmates by setting up an affec-
tive paternalistic/tutorial relationship between themselves and inmates.
Inmates refer to themselves as *em*, and they are addressed by wardens as
em. This first- and second-person pronoun refers to a younger child, a
younger sibling, or someone in such a role. Songs taught to inmates at the
Center for Social Sponsorship made many references to "the love" inmates
were supposed to feel for their wardens in return for the love their wardens showed them. According to Hà, one refrain went as follows:

Em had followed a life of dust
. . . .
One day *em* turned to this school
A school of love to show the way

Em has awakened and now will change
With friends, learning to progress
Cac anh [older brothers] have taught *em* the boundless love
So *em* can become a good person.[41]

A head warden recited to me the slogan summing up what supposedly made things work at the New Center for the Education of Women: "The awareness of camp members (inmates)[and] the love and responsibility of managers (administrators and wardens)."[42] At the New Center for the Education of Women, the age of inmates ranged from fourteen to fifty years, but the overwhelming majority were in their late teens, twenties, and early thirties. These women, regardless of their age, found themselves locked into these hierarchical and paternalistic relationships with their wardens.

The mechanisms of control in the camps are spatial confinement and organized surveillance, the routinization and coordination of tasks, and the infantilization of inmates. These Foucauldian carceral mechanisms provide the frame of camp life and prepare the women inmates for further training that would inscribe a new sense of who they ought to be in relation to the larger world outside the camp.

Who You Truly Are: Governmental Hailing of Subjects through the Global Imaginary

Work or "vocational training" for inmates was part of the training of bodies through the coordination of space, time, and tasks. The work/ training hours served as the centerpiece of the daily timetable, around which other time slots for exercise, meals, and rests were scheduled. At the time of my field research, women inmates learned primarily how to type, make bamboo curtains, weave baskets, and fill orders for false eyelashes; they also learned business skills including computer usage, hairstyling, mat making, and industrial sewing. Business training was initiated by the international NGO CARE with funding from NOVIB, the Dutch organization for international aid (Nederlandse Organisatie voor Internationale Bijstand), which was later changed to the Dutch organization for international development cooperation (Nederlandse

Organisatie voor Internationale Ontwikkelingssamenwerking).[43] Besides this NGO-initiated training program, the inmates learned job skills that were rather interchangeable. I suggest that these jobs require, not only the specifics of mat making or sewing versus eyelash making, but also patience, dexterity, docility, and a kind of worker accountability connected to a particular narrative about Vietnamese femininity. Not coincidentally, these skills are those required in a global mode of flexible accumulation.

All of the jobs taught to women in the camps make for slow and monotonous work that requires much patience. Most of the jobs require a high degree of dexterity. The men who were in these camps for drug addiction were sent mostly to work the land. Wardens reinforced the thinking that these tasks require too much physical strength and are inappropriate for proper women. Mai said that at the Center for Social Sponsorship, men and women were segregated, with the men doing "labor" like breaking the land, which was used as a form of punishment for the women.[44]

Moreover, the jobs taught to women trained them to be patient, dexterous, and docile in their acceptance of authority. But even among those feminine jobs, not all were viewed with equal importance. At the New Center for the Education of Women, the emphasis was on the industrial sewing workshop, as it absorbed most of the inmates' time. I later found out why. From mid-1996 on, the Ministry of Labor, Invalids, and Social Affairs decided that women being rehabilitated had to contribute to the costs of their incarceration. As a result, they had to work in moneymaking operations. If their earnings fell short of the designated amount, the women would incur a debt to be repaid after they left the camp.[45] The sewing workshop thus increased in size after my 1996 visit, and moneymaking schemes expanded to smaller operations in mat making, embroidery, and matchbox making.[46]

The sewing workshop was presented to me as a class that taught young women job skills. Sewing machines were arranged in straight rows. Each woman sat at a machine, supervised by wardens holding long wooden rulers and walking up and down the aisles. Women learned to do assembling, hems, buttons, and so on. Their productivity was measured by how many pieces, each requiring certain tasks like assembling or button-hole making, they could complete during a work session. The head war-den informed me that the purpose was to train the women so that they could become garment workers doing piecework, not tailors who could measure and cut.[47] Wardens scolded the women for making mistakes that required undoing and restitching. The head warden allowed me less than twenty minutes of observation in the sewing workshop. While I attempted to talk to the women about their work conditions, the head warden hovered and tapped her wooden ruler on the table in front of the women. The wardens were unforthcoming about the whole opera-tion, and therefore I was not able to obtain answers about who supplied the work orders and how the camp or the women were compensated for work performed.

I gained a clearer picture of a similar piecework operation at the Center for Social Sponsorship when I conducted extensive interviews with Mai and Hà, two young women who had just been released after having spent fourteen months there. Even though wardens could assign various other classes to the women, making false eyelashes was mandatory for all female inmates. This was a piecework operation for profit. The camp contracted or subcontracted the work orders. Inmates were not compensated for fulfilling their quotas of twenty sets per daily work session, but if they managed to produce beyond the quotas, they were rewarded based on the number of extra sets they completed. Hà, the younger of the two women, said she almost always exceeded the quotas and received com-pensation in the amount of VND70,000–VND90,000 (less than US$7–$9 at the time) a month. She said the camp director announced that the operation yielded a monthly amount of D30 million (or less than US$3,000), a large sum in Vietnam. At the very least, the camp and the Ministry of Labor, Invalids, and Social Affairs would have recov-ered partial costs of incarcerating the women.

As with other jobs taught in the camp, eyelash making demanded a high degree of patience and dexterity. The women threaded hair through tiny holes and tied, tightened, cut, and evenly spread the strands so that they would not bunch up or leave spaces in between. Hà proudly showed me the nimble fingers of her tiny hands and said, "They imported the hair. They gave us the materials that we threaded, tied, cut. I am very dexterous and quick. See?"[48]

For Hà, dexterity was an existing ability put to work. But for Mai, it was a different story. As each worker was rewarded or punished on the basis of the quality of each piece of work completed, Mai suffered for her lack of the necessary qualities, as she recounted:

> The team leaders, they were allowed to beat you if, say, your work fell short of the required number of products. I got a hundred canes, twenty each night—a thick cane. That was because the products I was assigned got rejected. For each set of eyelashes that got rejected, I got two canes. For the ten rejected each day, I got twenty canes. They said to thread the hair evenly with no spaces in between. Most of mine had spaces in between. Then it was my fault that my products got rejected. At the end of each work session, I turned in twenty pieces with my name clipped to the bundle. Once they got them, they inspected them and would know who was responsible for the rejects. That was how I got a hundred canes. After that, I begged and begged the head warden to let me out of that work or I would kill myself. He felt sorry for me because I had my little daughter with me in the camp and had no family to take care of us.[49]

The forced work in the camp, said Mai, was because "they thought we must work hard to earn money so we would know our true worth. Whereas outside we are 'girls' and make money too easily."[50] If being a "girl" was somehow false, the camp would teach the young woman who she should have been by putting her through the work that would reflect her true value. The assumption seemed to be that the sex market had somehow inflated her value beyond her true self. Who the young prostitute should have been was a true Vietnamese woman of her economic class. The head warden at the New Center for the Education of Women listed the four educational programs that were run in the camp: political education, literacy, HIV education, and job training. When I asked what was taught in political education, the head warden replied that instructors taught "tradition, morality and ethics" (*truyền thống, đạo đức*) in order to make the "girls understand the essence of being a woman" (*bản chất người phụ nữ*).[51] Political education was sometimes referred to as "ethical education." Wardens reinforced the instruction in their speech and in their interaction with the women. When I asked another warden what they did to reinforce the inmates' ethical education, she replied, "We teach them how to be good women because they apparently aren't conscious of it yet. We teach them the role of a woman in the family and in society—a good wife, a good mother—with the Three Obediences and the Four Virtues."[52] The Confucian Three Obediences refer to woman's obedience to father, to husband, and to son. The Four Virtues refer to a woman's appropriate work, appearance, speech, and conduct.

The warden's last reference to Confucian values once denounced as oppressive and feudal by the revolutionary party might have been that particular warden's way of describing what was going on in her camp. But it speaks of the camp's emphasis on "tradition" as being the defining feature of a good Vietnamese woman for these incarcerated women. At the Eighth Congress of the Women's Union in 1997, its president, Trường Mỹ Hoa, stated flatly that "Vietnam is an Oriental country and we preserve the traditional role of women."[53] Within a few years, the emphasis on the family and woman's more traditional role in it has become a matter of stable policy and practice for the Women's Union. An officer of the Central Women's Union in Hanoi explained to me in 2002 that they tried to teach "family at the base" and "traditional cultural values for women."[54]

If terms like "Oriental" and "traditional role of women" sound vague in public pronouncements, the camp gives them concrete meaning with its training of women whose social indexes would place them in the lower classes, according to a study conducted by the Institute of Sociology in conjunction with the Unit for the Fighting and Prevention of Social Evils from the Ministry of Labor, Invalids, and Social Affairs, as mentioned in the previous chapter.[55]

The government, or more specifically, the Ministry of Labor, Invalids, and Social Affairs, seems to use these indexes to devise the type of work for which these classes of women are suited. The suitable type of work is imagined to be that required of poor Asian women doing piecework on the global assembly line. It is a class, nationality, and gender position in the global imaginary of labor division. In the camp, the concrete content of the traditional Vietnamese woman narrative for a lower-class woman is the work they are trained to do. The job skills taught in the camp, as shown, are those that require a high degree of patience for tedious work, dexterity, and docility. The Vietnamese feminine identity attached to such attributes is but a convenient label for a generic model of workers in today's pattern of global production. Angie Tran observes in the Vietnamese garment and textile industries the same tedious work with high expectations for female dexterity and for worker docility, which figure centrally in workers' adaptability to quickly alter types and quantities of products.[56] Tran points to the nature of the pattern of production:

> Producers/contractors (foreign, state, or private) use multi-level subcontracting to deal with fashion clothing seasons and market volatility. They place the burden of adjustment to these fluctuations on workers. During 9 months of clothing seasons (winter clothing season is between May and October; spring between November and January), garment workers operate two to three shifts per day which normally last over 12 hours; during 3 months of off-seasons, they are underemployed or have no garment orders to do. Within the piecework arrangement, they earn nothing. In other words, workers are at the whims of international textile and garment markets (4–5).

There is little time to train workers for specific tasks, as work orders change so quickly. Instead, factories must rely on a baseline dexterity on the part of workers and on an individual worker's accountability for the quality of each piece of product. If one does not get it right, one does not get paid. Quantity fluctuations demand that workers be willing to work long shifts on monotonous tasks during peak seasons, with little or no break even for sanitary purposes such as menstrual care (9–10). The government-run rehabilitation camps train women in the same work requirements as those described to be low-wage work in global production. The garment industries, which employ six hundred thousand workers in Vietnam, 80 percent of whom are women, best exemplify this pattern of global production (2).

Althusser proposes a theory of the workings of ideology in general. Ideology, according to him, "interpellates" individuals into subjects.[57]

Ideological state apparatuses like educational institutions "hail" or call on individuals to imagine their individual relations to the larger whole (i.e., God, society, etc.).[58] Individuals form their subjectivities or senses of selves to be recognized by themselves as well as by their society in moments of mutual recognition. But Althusser did not completely rec-oncile his general theory of ideology with the Marxist paradigm of his-tory as defined by the mode and relations of production. On the one hand, the mode and relations of production for each historical epoch supposedly could be "objectively" identified in the Marxist framework, thus making them "real." On the other hand, the Subject, that larger whole in relation to which individuals are asked to imagine themselves as subjects, seems in his theory to be necessarily imaginary in the same way that God is imaginary in Christian ideology. Yet his Marxist posi-tion still insists that the mode and relations of production must be real and objective as opposed to the individual imaginary sense of self in rela-tion to the former (the structure or base in Marxism). As a result, the opposition between the real and the imaginary becomes less workable. I propose that the very relations (i.e., the global division of labor) in the new flexible mode of production be viewed as imaginary in that they constitute a mental picture of the world available for a governmental agency to reference in its hailing of subjects. In this way, the rehabilita-tion camp draws on the global imaginary of labor division in asking the women inmates to imagine their true selves as low-paid, Asian female, docile, dexterous, and patient pieceworkers.

From the sociological knowledge showing that garment workers for global production and sex workers come from the same classes of women, rehabilitation reinforces the idea in society that the proper work for these classes of women is global production work such as garment work. Journalistic reports on sex work often assume the overlap in pop-ulations of garment and sex workers. One such article begins, "There is nothing wrong with garment work . . . , but the rural girls who liberate themselves from their families often use the excuse of 'I work in sewing.'"[59] The women interviewed in the same news article forcefully point out the disadvantages of such low-wage work. One woman said, "My first month's salary was eighty thousand dong, how could I pay my rent?" Rent apparently was VND300,000 a month.[60] As shown, Minh, the *bia ôm* hostess, also protested the clear disadvantages of garment work over sex work.

Over such protests, what rehabilitation does is to hold up a model of what the proper Vietnamese woman of the lower classes should be for society at large. There is no reason to believe that the camps actually turn most prostitutes into workers for the global production line. According to the study conducted by the Institute of Sociology in Hanoi for the Ministry of Labor, Invalids, and Social Affairs, the average sex worker surveyed had been in the camps 1.5 times; 30 percent had been incarcerated in camps two or more times, some of them five or six times.[61] The study concludes, "Clearly, arresting and sending them to be reeducated have not been effective; too many have returned to their trade after being arrested and after leaving the camps."[62]

One could say the high rate of recidivism is the result of other factors such as the lack of economic opportunities available to the "rehabilitated" young women. However, the main factors seem more intrinsic to the rehabilitation process itself. Most young women are homeless upon their release because their camp sentence has disrupted their ties to family and trade networks.[63] Many incur much larger debts as a result of accumulating interests on previous debts, of new debts taken out by their family in the absence of their income, and of the government's policy of making them pay for their stay.[64] It is not surprising that the women would try again the trade most open to them in their now more desperate situations. As with Foucault's prison, the camp's failure to return women to their true selves is answered with more camp time.[65] Over the period from 1996 to 1998, the New Center for the Education of Women constructed new buildings to house double its former capacity of six hundred inmates.[66]

The point, then, is not that the camp is highly successful in turning prostitutes into workers endowed with Vietnamese feminine patience, dexterity, and docility. Rather, the government fulfills two functions, one toward a domestic population and the other toward the global economy. First, the government ideologically interpellates women of the lower classes about who they truly are. Second, it brands this range of values, thought to be traditional femininity, as *Vietnamese*, a brand name that could be expected to deliver qualities of traditional femininity of motivation (read willingness to accept cheap pay), dexterity, patience, and docility, sought after by managers and contractors of transnational production companies.

As marketization progressed, the government-run camps became more rather than less coercive. Coercion thus could not be a vestige of a more repressive mode of governing from socialist times. From 1995 to 1998, the New Center for the Education of Women allowed CARE International in Vietnam to run a program funded by NOVIB to educate women inmates about wellness, to teach them entrepreneurial and leadership skills, and to empower them with a system of open files that permitted them access to comments instructors made about their progress, although this last feature was met with strong official resistance.[67] The program was discontinued by camp and ministry officials in 1998 as camp officials sought to reorient inmates to their "true nature of womanhood."[68] One CARE officer said camp and ministry officials rejected subsequent efforts by CARE to propose further work there, opting instead for "teaching mainly vocations that go with tradition."[69]

Rather than disappear as a momentary experiment, this governmentally produced ideology seems to have strengthened and acquired a commonsensical quality for society at large over time. To illustrate the spread of this government-induced ideology of gender beyond governmental practices, I cite as an example the Shelter, a nongovernmental center for at-risk girls and mostly underage sex workers. In 1996, funded mostly by international NGOs and private donors in Vietnam and abroad, the Shelter, among other orders, took out subcontracts of mat production for a Japanese producer. The difference was that the enterprise functioned as a cooperative; the young women received their fair shares of the profits, as opposed to being trained to be more docile in the coercive form of discipline and punishment found in the government-run camps. The director of the Shelter in the mid-1990s proudly explained that the aim of the cooperative was to enable the young women to "master their own means of livelihood, master themselves."[70] By 2002, a traditionalist narrative had become apparent at the Shelter, as one of its liaison social workers explained the vocation training (the center was no longer run as a cooperative) in terms of how "East Asian cultures place the responsibility on the woman to help out the family."[71]

CONCLUSION

Rather than just theorize the nation-state or the national government as either adversarial or losing control to global economic forces, I suggest that one look at how governors deploy governmental power in the context of globalization. Governments actively produce truths about their subject populations. In the case of the arrest and rehabilitation of sex workers in Vietnam, the government falsifies the subjectivities inscribed by the women using their market earnings and replaces them with "true" subjectivities. The "truth" of subjects is their legibility and intelligibility within the global imaginary of labor division, where Asian female pieceworkers play a pivotal role in global production. Subjects as inscribed by governments are those differentiated by class in terms of gender and nationality. But this global/local truth making takes governmental deployment of Foucauldian tools of discipline and repression. Therefore, it is not that national governments either serve or resist global capital wholesale, but that governors selectively use governing technologies in ways that ensure their relevance in relation to the global economy.

Police arrests of sex workers and their incarceration in rehabilitation camps deploy cultural authenticity in anchoring identities of citizens and directing their choices according to their gender and their class. This mode of governing is much more coercive. However, it is not a regression to, or a vestige of, an earlier mode of governance where the socialist government would incarcerate large segments of the population for "reeducation." Rather, together with the kind of power based on choices guided by medical expert knowledge covered in the previous chapter, the use of arrests and incarceration as a mode of social control demonstrates the coexistence of vastly different modes of power that target classes and genders differently. The specific ways in which this coercive power operates in tandem with current modes of production in the global economy reveal that the presence of such coercive governing has a material basis and explains its increasing importance as a tool of modern governance. What makes possible the coexistence of such disparate modes of power is the topic of the next chapter.

CHAPTER 6

What Kind of Power?

Specialization of Intervention and Coexisting
Modes of Governance

DURING MARKETIZATION, the rise of medicine as an expert field of knowledge disciplined different segments of the population through its specialized public health intervention. Public health measures taught urban women of the upper and middling classes to become *informed* consumers of health services and beauty products at the same time as other measures pushed testing and other more invasive procedures on sex workers, most of whom came from the lower classes. The use of coercion together with notions of true cultural tradition by the police and the rehabilitation camps allowed the government to cultivate a segment of the population for the demands of the neoliberal global market, namely, to suggest that lower-class Vietnamese women should provide low-wage feminine labor for the global assembly line. It is thus difficult to say that the coercive mode of governance constitutes a vestige from some totalitarian rule. Rather, repression as a governmental technology of rule is produced and reproduced in conjunction with contemporary conditions of the market. The gradation of coercion seemed to increase as governmental measures moved from the upper and middle classes to the lower classes, from men to women, and certainly from the medical mode of intervention to policing and rehabilitation. The kind of knowledge imparted to different segments of the population also changed as the government moved across class lines. While medicine still had to rely on individuals making the right choices using information about empirical reality and expert scientific knowledge, albeit with differences across gender and class lines, policing and rehabilitation measures used outright repressive tactics toward lower-class women justified by notions judged to mark true Vietnamese tradition.

This chapter searches for an explanation as to how these seemingly contradictory modes of governance aimed at producing a differentiated population for the market economy could coexist. I suggest that specialization of intervention keeps the logic of one mode of intervention from canceling out the other. The use of specialized or expert knowledge also allows the justification of governmental measures to be taken up by organizations in society as some governmental functions are turned over to society. But at the same time, there is cause to speculate that specialization may allow critiques or alternative practices to emerge.

This discussion begins with how policing had come to rely on specialized knowledge as marketization proceeded through the 1990s. All three areas of intervention—medicine, policing, and rehabilitation—are then taken up to consider the implications for theories of liberal and neoliberal governance, given the presence of contradictory modes of governance aimed at producing a differentiated citizenry for the neoliberal economy.

POLICING VERSUS PUBLIC HEALTH: WHAT KIND OF POWER?

Policing of the Social: Specialized Knowledge

I make the case that (1) a focus on social problems like prostitution allowed the police to claim a certain expert knowledge on the origins and manifestations of crimes and social disorder and that (2) this represented a shift away from the old socialist conception of crime and policing. I also explore how specialization allows for public health and policing measures, with their different modes of power, to coexist.

Colonel Bùi Quốc Huy, the director of the Ho Chi Minh City bureau of the Ministry of Public Security in 1996, summarizes his vision of police work and the origins of crime in this way: "Let me emphasize that the main mission of Regional Police is to provide security, to prevent and stop the emergence and development of crime. The social ills of gambling, drug addiction, prostitution, decadent culture are the sources of crime."[1]

Reports summarizing police action routinely acknowledged arrests of a host of social-ill targets, among which real criminals were singled out, supporting the view that criminals came from the population of social-ill targets. A typical report reads as follows:

> According to the Kiên Giang People's Inspector General's report, the province as a whole has 301 drug addicts, 33 entrepreneurs dealing in decadent and poisonous videos, 1,887 gamblers, 230 prostitutes, 50 madams and pimps, 34 drug traffickers/dealers. From the total of people mentioned above, after participating in drug use, gambling, poisonous video viewing, prostitution, etc., there have been 33 subjects who committed murder, robbery, burglary, illegal use of weapons, public disorder, rape, and 80 subjects who tested HIV positive (we have discovered and managed them).[2]

Routine news articles in the Public Security presses highlighted how many women started out by prostituting themselves and ended up running sex tours or cross-border trafficking in women.[3]

Once the police established that social ills produced the delinquency behind the crimes, they invited themselves to investigate and discuss these same social problems from a security point of view. Policing a social problem like prostitution became an integral part of criminal policing, linking criminal policing to police views of social order. *Công An Thành Phố Hồ Chí Minh* devoted regular columns to discussing civility in public conduct, in "A Way of Life with Culture"; discussing commendable government and private charity efforts stemming the tide of social problems, in "Eliminating Hunger and Reducing Poverty"; and making examples out of families that fell apart or became involved in crime or other social ills on account of the temptations of the market, in "The Family in the Market Regime." Policing social problems allowed the police to extend their prescription of desirable conduct into social areas not covered by criminal laws such as public, personal, and family life or even into government decrees like the anti-social evil resolutions.

Thus the police installed themselves in a permanent job, not just to rid society of foreign enemies, but to fight against threats ever arising from a now complex socioeconomic reality. Their job was permanent in the sense that they were now implicated in the crime scene through their exposure of crime and their own corrupt dealings. They made themselves needed in keeping the economy going, certifying workers, and ensuring peace and order for people to secure their economic livelihood. In apprehending people, the police sorted them according to their transgressions (clients, prostitutes, pimps, go-betweens, madams, organizers of prostitution rings, etc.). The police created categories of criminals, building a knowledge of types of criminality. The police's own sensational accounts of the perpetual contest between criminal tactics and police response built up the ever more intricate science of policing and criminology, thus perpetuating the police presence as a professional force. In short, the police "tend to assimilate the transgression of the law into a general tactic of subjection" by "laying down the limits of tolerance, giving free reign to some, putting pressure on others," "excluding a particular section, making another useful," "neutralizing certain individuals," and "profiting from others."[4]

In those ways, the police used social problems to police the social. They narrated social problems in ways so as to connect crime and disorder to the complex dimensions of the social. Colonel Thân Thanh Huyền, the deputy director of Ho Chi Minh City Public Security, offered this assessment for an upcoming Party Congress in 1996: "The market regime in our socialist economy also gives rise to many complexities in the social dimensions. Therefore, I propose all levels and units of the Party, government, and branches [which include Public Security] coordinate to develop economic, cultural, and social programs in accordance with calculations of consequences in security and order so as to prevent these [negative consequences]."[5] The police argument seemed to be that they would know about the origins and manifestations of crime and other forms of social disorder and therefore should be consulted on economic, cultural, and social policy. From policing crime, the police extended their claim on the knowledge of policing social order as a way to control the sources of crime.

The police presses demonstrated this special knowledge to their readership on a daily basis. Crime coverage series read like serialized crime novels where the police protagonists were locked in a race with criminal or social evil antagonists. In this narrative, police targets got ever more cunning in their disorderly pursuits. The police therefore had to constantly strive to stay one step ahead of the bad elements in terms of expertise in detection and measures of suppression. This endeavor was portrayed as extremely difficult and thus called for updating and upgrading the quality of police forces.

Public Security had been calling for the professionalization of the police forces in terms of better training. On the occasion of their conference in preparation for the 1996 Party Congress, the party organ within Public Security reiterated the need to "raise the level of professionalism, the level of education and culture, legal knowledge, and knowledge about society" of the members of Public Security forces.[6] The police presses regularly called attention to this necessity and offered statistics on efforts to raise the educational and training levels of their rank and file.[7]

Public Security made efforts to gather a nascent body of expert knowledge in criminal policing and security. *Công An Nhân Dân* proudly reported in 1996 on Public Security efforts to research and write up one thousand items relating to policing and security, four hundred of which were to be selected and placed in the newly compiled *Vietnam Encyclopedia*. The article elaborates on the significance of this knowledge endeavor:

> The encyclopedia reflects the level of cultural and scientific development of a nation and the world in its historical stage. . . . A Chinese scholar had written in 1917: "One could observe the weakness or strength of a society's knowledge by examining the kinds and quantities of dictionaries and encyclopedias [it produces]."
> . . . The ministry has decided to set up the review board headed by a vice minister with heads of departments and bureaus, the [Public Security] colleges, and the Institute of the Science of Public Security to review and approve the items to be entered in the *Vietnam Encyclopedia*.
> The knowledge reflected in the subfields [under the headings] of Security and Order marks a pivotal step in the development of the science of the profession of Public Security in Vietnam.[8]

The article makes the point of including in the body of "security and order knowledge" the accumulated knowledge in the field, even that of socialist Vietnam's enemies, from the Americans to the South Vietnamese. The official ideology of Marxism-Leninism is not used in the article to distinguish legitimate and valid knowledge to protect the socialist motherland from class-based knowledge in the service of the bourgeoisie, capitalism, imperialism, and illegitimate puppet regimes:

> This work entails systematic research into historical documents on Vietnam's People's Public Security: [list of past incarnations of Vietnam's present police and security organizations]; on organizations in other countries like the CIA, FBI, KGB [the U.S. Central Intelligence Agency and Federal Bureau of Investigation and the Soviet State Security Committee], or those belonging to the old [Southern] regime: [list of the South's security, police organizations, and penal networks]. Of special interest is the fact that among the headings, there are those dealing with terminology and concepts. Terms like "national security" and "social safety and order," or "misinformation" and "informant" are extremely important and require a total assessment of the field that is meticulous and scientific to ensure value in their generalizability.[9]

I have quoted this article at length to show that Public Security was compiling a nascent body of positivist knowledge on crime, social order, security, and policing techniques that would sidestep old ideological divides set up by the socialist state in the past. The CIA, FBI, and KGB unceremoniously appear as entries in a unified field of police science. The South's police organizations and prisons, formerly denounced as the instruments of oppression, appear side by side with police organizations that served the revolution. In sifting for scientific knowledge, the elements and social phenomena to be policed and the policing techniques seemed to take precedence over ideological and historical enmity. The police laid claim to this special knowledge that accompanied their area of social intervention and that should give them a say in economic and social policy. The ever-cunning crimes and their origins in complex social ills were explicitly attributed by the police to socioeconomic conditions tied to the market economy. The dangerous reality sensationalized for popular consumption in the police presses came across as being part of a dynamic society, not a shrinking vestige of regimes past. The special police mission of keeping order as a well-portrayed race with crime necessitated their sharpening professionalism and expanding expert knowledge on crime's origins in social problems and on its manifestation and suppression.

Policing as Specialized Intervention and Liberal Political Rationality

As part of the liberal configuration in the form of specialized intervention, policing underwent a process of depoliticization. But if specialized intervention changed policing, it also sustained differences in the kinds of power exercised. Analyzing Marxist criminology, Nancy Travis Wolfe writes, "For Marxist criminologists, [crime] was linked to the concept of class stratification. In the socialist system of the German Democratic Republic, where there was theoretically only one class (the working people) and exploitation has been abolished, crime was perceived as an alien phenomenon."[10]

I have shown that the police now insisted that crime arose from social problems like prostitution and that crimes' manifestations were ever changing as social dynamics necessitated more knowledgeable policing. Crime was no longer narrated as an alien phenomenon. As portrayed by the police, crime brought into view its origins in a society with socioeconomic dynamics autonomous from political ones. Crime as a justification for police activities built up criminal policing to be at least as important as political policing.

Some Public Security pronouncements in official speeches and the organ's presses still drew continuity with a style of policing in which crime as a form of social deviance was political and had alien sources.[11] The task of the police before economic liberalization was defined in terms of protecting the people by protecting the people's political regime against these alien threats. Criminal policing was subsumed under political policing. The achievement of the People's Public Security in its half century of service, said Standing Deputy Interior Minister Phạm Tâm Long, had been to do its part with other branches, especially the People's Army, to "create the unified strength of the entire political system in setting up the strategic front of the People's Security, thus helping to ensure political stability, national security, social safety, and order and protecting the peaceful lives of the people.... [The People's Public Security] had striven to accomplish the two strategic tasks assigned by the Party and State: building socialism and protecting the socialist fatherland."[12]

The main tasks of the police in the past significantly overlapped with the function of the People's Army to protect the people's state from outside threats. The deputy minister emphasized the fact that unnamed external enemies still use "forces inside and outside" to "wipe away the party's leadership and overthrow socialism in our country" in a strategy called "peaceful evolution" (*diễn biến hòa bình*).[13] An important task of Public Security was to prevent this sinister plot from succeeding.

But the deputy minister also hastened to add that Public Security "must forcefully push to realize Decree 406/TTg, Resolution 36/CP, Resolution 87/CP [anti-social evil and other safety and order resolutions] in order to establish rule and order in the management of society, raising security and order to a new level, an important new step."[14]

Managing society for order as a police function seemed to have come out from under the shadow of political policing. It became a justification in its own right, on an equal footing with ensuring national security. This caused a certain awkwardness in determining how to integrate or narrate these two functions. The deputy director of Ho Chi Minh City Public Security found it necessary to raise the need to "tightly integrate the fight against corruption, crime, and social evils with the task of protecting political security."[15] Newspaper writing and official interviews and speeches settled on formulaic phrases in which one police function simply followed the other, in no particular order of importance.

In a speech on the occasion of the National Public Security Conference in 1996, Prime Minister Võ Văn Kiệt commended Public Security forces for ensuring the security of the public through "crime fighting and state management of security and order," down-playing political policing. Unlike high-ranking officials in the Ministry of Public Security and other organs in the party and state that specialized in maintaining security, the prime minister, more concerned with economic development, mentioned no external threats. Vigilance against peaceful evolution (which translated to political policing) had been used by the police as a justification to gain jurisdiction over lucrative economic activities in the new market economy. Those in this field of security also used their political policing function to argue to their rivals that Public Security was protecting on behalf of the latter all the personal privileges that accompanied the Communist Party's monopoly on power.[16] Public Security's dual function was protecting the privileges that accompany the monopoly of political power by the party and crime fighting to ensure the safety of the populace. Political policing against external threats to the regime was used by those in Public Security to secure its foothold in the political contention among different camps within the party and government, while criminal and social policing defined the focus of its governing function. Security justifications that had an air of paranoia about them often translated into simple tasks of criminal and social problem policing to ensure the inhabitants' peaceful lives. In an article featuring interviews with Public Security heads in Ho Chi Minh City on how they would "bring the resolutions of the Eighth Party Congress into [people's] lives," each official detailed efforts to fight crime and social evil and concluded with a statement of the mission of his unit of Public Security as keeping the peace in his unit's geographical jurisdiction so as to keep its inhabitants safe from crime.[17]

As one might recall, the police complained that the health bureau's approach to prostitution (i.e., condom distribution by peer educators) allowed people to engage in this social evil and its accompanying crimes with impunity. And Public Security had not ceased its nagging about a foreign-sponsored (read American) plot of peaceful evolution in conjunction with domestic enemies of the regime. These seams revealed the contradictions in the government that resulted from contention among its camps. But based on the analysis presented so far, I suggest that specialized intervention in social problems as a way to govern the social allowed contending forces and their different governing claims to coexist in all their contradictions. My analysis tentatively suggests that the contending governmental agencies, with their separate claims, not all of which were compatible with a liberal political ideology, could uneasily coexist in the framework of specialized intervention.

I have discussed a liberal configuration of governance in which the social problem was recoded in a way as to reveal its aspects knowable and manageable with separate bodies of expertise. In the case of the state intervention in prostitution as a social problem in Vietnam, each area of specialized intervention claimed access to or possession of bodies of special knowledge. Specialized intervention allowed the police mode of control to coexist with the medical one in two ways. First, this specialized intervention with claims to expert knowledge allowed for the staking of turfs among state agencies that might align themselves with different party leaders. Each set of agencies or measures could focus on different aspects of prostitution, limiting occasions when they did step on each other's toes. Second, this special intervention with expert knowledge translated much of the contentious rhetoric by different sets of agencies (i.e., Public Health, Public Security, and Social Affairs, which runs rehabilitation camps) within the government into knowledgeable and manageable tasks on separate turfs, constituting an area of overlap in their vision of governance. What each set of agencies should do to manage the social is an area of agreement.

This configuration of specialized intervention mediated and thus sustained the existence of differences, as I demonstrate by comparing policing with public health intervention. On the one hand, Public Health might subscribe to a more liberal political rationalization of individual choice suitable for the functioning of a market. The relative autonomy of bodies of expertise like medicine could serve as the basis of critique of state reason. A medical school instructor for courses on public health policy and the "economics of medicine" kept up good relations with the Ho Chi Minh City Health Bureau, but at an informal talk she complained to bureau officials about higher-up state policy. She argued for more "destatization" of social policy: "We must think about economic pressures in order to coordinate programs—which program should accompany which. As of now, we researchers can only make proposals. There is a gap between research and the state."[18] It was the relative autonomy of her knowledge discipline that allowed her to make that critique of state policy.

On the other hand, even as the police professionalized their forces with positivist knowledge, they used repression, not the persuasive technology of medicine, to make their targets comply. The police did not work through the persuasion of optimal choice in terms of health or pleasure; rather, they worked through the deterrence of punishment from job denial to incarceration. It is not unusual to hear advocates of law and order using the vocabulary of "choice" in their argument for more police repression and incarceration. People are arrested and put in prison because of the choices they have made, so the argument goes.[19] But people do not choose to be arrested. Their choices, if they are choices, are often met with the governmental use of repressive power in the form of policing and incarceration.

Consequently, the subjectivity fostered by the medical model of control differed from that of the police model. Even with their controlling or normalizing pressures, public health measures offered and reinforced a sense of subjectivity with limited agency, if to a lesser degree for sex workers. Public Health did this because the success of public health measures depended on a sense of self-interest on the part of their intended targets. Health workers told sex workers to insist on condom use because the latter would ultimately be responsible for their own health. Medical mechanisms of control created and depended on an individual accountability that asked sex workers to do something on their own behalf.

An anecdote illustrates this difference in approach between Public Health and Public Security. During my interviews with peer health educators, I asked whether the sex workers encountered brutality from their clients for asking them to wear condoms. The peer educators, who themselves are former sex workers, told me a story about some policemen who had been circulating among the sex workers they encountered on their rounds. Thanh, one of the peer educators, said she had heard of such brutality not by a client but by the police:

> Public Security men frequently ask the girls they come to arrest for sexual service. This sister she told me two Public Security men demanded sex. She asked that they wear condoms. One agreed. The other one refused. She said to him: "Being Public Security, you should

respect this request more than others." He punched her in the face a few times. That's the one case of beating that I heard; and it was Public Security who did the beating.²⁰

Whether this event actually happened is not the issue here. What is notable is the telling of the story. If indeed it was circulated by sex workers, the story articulates a critique of police repression. The sex workers and the peer educators expressed resistance to police brutality in terms of a transgression, a violation of a healthfully and rightfully self-asserting request, if even from a prostitute.

In contrast to the medical discourse, the police force's repressive tactics did not ask their intended targets to do anything on their own behalf. These tactics forbade and negated agency. A *bia ôm* hostess repeatedly said to me in her telling of police measures against working women like her, "I don't have rights. There are no rights here. Only money can get us out of trouble with the police."²¹ What I want to point out here is not the issue of legal rights or lack thereof but, rather, the sense on the part of targeted women that they themselves were negated, erased by police power to the point where money was the only thing visible and acknowledged.

As with medicine, police intervention also claimed expert knowledge. In this case, it was a nascent body of knowledge about crime, its social origins, and its suppression. Although a full-blown discipline of criminology claiming autonomy from the state had not arrived, the development of this special knowledge was undertaken by Public Security itself, in accumulating field experience and compiling more formal knowledge for transmittal in its colleges and its Institute of the Science of Public Security. Possessing its own institutions of knowledge gathering, the police may or may not in the future rely more on existing and future studies done in the social sciences to improve its policing of the populace.

Nevertheless, if medicine is knowledge that "confronts its own normativity" and "its purpose is to inform government as to the norms proper to this domains," then the technology of policing as presented here does not conform to this model.²² Self-developed police knowledge linked to state intervention in a more direct way than did medicine to public health intervention. Public Security could rely on its claim to special knowledge to criticize its rivals' social policies. But developing its own body of knowledge meant Public Security closed the space between knowledge and governance, thus precluding the possibility of an autonomous critique of state intervention. Health officials, based on arguments of public health, did criticize police intervention, as discussed. But Public Security could easily discredit its outside critics on grounds that they did not possess knowledge of the "science of security." The arrangement of Public Security running its own entities of knowledge collection would leave little room for conflicts and contestation arising from a degree of indeterminacy or mismatch between government and the domain to be governed.

Whatever mismatch there may be in this arrangement came from the contending government agencies and their separate areas of specialized intervention. Health officials could presumably criticize the police or the rehabilitation efforts or vice versa. But specialized intervention put a limit on this kind of contestation by dividing up tasks. The union between the police and its knowledge-generating entities within the security apparatus put further limits on the possibility of a critique of police intervention.

Police measures relied on some of the same microphysics of power—physical presence, surveillance, individual accountability, and the use of specialized knowledge. But on a more macro level, police power worked differently. It did not link to notions of choice and rights or to the possibility of critique of government in political rationalization. Instead, police power drew on justifications of security and order. The result was a coexistence of kinds of governing power.

REHABILITATION VERSUS PUBLIC HEALTH:
WHAT KIND OF POWER?

If what this discussion illustrates is how such contradictory modes or technologies of governance could coexist, what then are the implications for theories of liberal and neoliberal governance? Here, I consider how the justification used by the government in rehabilitation was "socialized" in that such logic spread to nonstate entities in society. Nonstate social work dovetailed with the state model of rehabilitation in important regards, taking over some state functions of social work. Certain differences between the state-run camps and the nonstate ones suggest that innovations in nonstate models of rehabilitation could provide possibilities of critique of state practices. Ultimately, however, policing and rehabilitation constitute a very different mode of power that relied primarily on repression rather than on the self-interested choice of individuals formed through the normativity and normality preached by a body of knowledge like medicine. I revisit the repressive elements in the mode of power operating in the state-run rehabilitation camps and discuss how this power was not productive of a subjectivity of choice. I push further the suggestion that it was the arrangement of specialized intervention that allowed for the coexistence of different modes of power in governance.

Turning Governmental Logic over to Society

To illustrate the spread of this government-induced ideology of gender beyond governmental practices, I discuss two cases, the CARE-run training program at the New Center for the Education of Women and the Shelter, a nonstate home whose job training of women overlapped significantly with the model held up in the state rehabilitation camps.

The program of piecework job training was in two ways social work in response to perceived realities in the social realm: as a realistic assessment of the endowments of these women and the kind of jobs likely to be available to them and as a response to the market that involves the profit to be had from these piecework operations. Social studies by academic units on the subject of prostitutes and prostitution had started to multiply, even those jointly commissioned by the Ministry of Labor, Invalids, and Social Affairs. The already cited study jointly commissioned by this ministry gives many indices regarding the class, occupational background, and educational level of sex workers.[23] Sections of it focus on socioeconomic causes and consequences of prostitution.[24] The study draws attention to economic patterns like surplus labor in rural areas, labor migration, and so on.[25] Job training as described in the camps could be seen as a response to these social realities. Wardens presented job training in the camp as a matter-of-course innovation to direct the low-skilled women toward socially acceptable employment.[26] They drew my attention to the fact that they wrote reports and kept statistics to be collected by their ministry for analysis, thus emphasizing their work as informed innovation in response to complex processes.[27] This reasoning was further helped by the profit incentive. To accept piecework contracts or subcontracts meant money for the camp, at least to compensate for the costs of housing and feeding the inmates. The women were hardly compensated for their work. Only when they exceeded the quotas were the inmates at the Center for Social Sponsorship given a nominal reward. This was the kind of work order available on the market. It was profitable and easy to obtain. Social work officials proved they could use market conditions to accomplish their assigned task.

No longer a utopian ideological mission of the state, the reference for the model of rehabilitation was now a social realm with its cultural and socioeconomic challenges and opportunities. Social scientific studies from the early 1990s referred to an "active/determining and dynamic social [realm]" that solved old problems of stagnation as well as posed new ones like the stratification of society.[28] "Scientific conferences" and study units convened on topics like "Reforming Social Policy and the Regime of Social Management" and "The Systematic Utilization of Social Policy and Social Management in Reality," where academics and government officials stressed a new relationship among socioeconomic dynamics, knowledge, and social policy.[29] Bùi Đình Thành, assistant supervisor of a study unit on this topic of social policy, wrote: "To manage society in a scientific manner is to consciously effect the whole of the social system, or facets and parts of it on the basis of knowledge and the utilization of society's objective laws and trends to ensure its optimal development."[30]

This perception was the basis for the promotion of the "socialization of social policy." Labor, invalids, and social affairs minister Trần Đình Hòan's writings echoed leadership calls for the "socialization of social policy," putting an end to efforts in the past that amounted to "bureaucratic and heavily subsidized social relief."³¹ He proposed the utilization of mass organizations, private associations, and international assistance in tandem with local state organs and citizens.³²

The reconceptualization of social work opened the way for nonstate groups to take over some of the social rehabilitation functions of the state. The Ministry of Labor, Invalids, and Social Work reached an agreement with CARE International allowing for the NGO to set up a training program for inmates at the New Center for the Education of Women in Thủ Đức.³³ The CARE program offered training for various business skills and for living well (3, 16–23). The project as a whole received funding from another international development organization, NOVIB, while some training manuals relied on materials developed with help from the Royal Netherlands Embassy and a local NGO (22, 24). In addition, CARE enlisted a nearby Vietnamese convent in setting up an outreach program to track the progress of the women and to provide them with help like contacts and credit once they left the rehabilitation camp (3, 24–29). Once the state opened the door to social work, the involvement of one nonstate entity led to that of others in a widening network.

Mrs. Ngọc, the head of a Ho Chi Minh City–based NGO serving the needs of children described her place in this period of socialized social work: "NGOs like us have the social capacity and functions to perform, but Mr. State has to push the buttons to allow things to happen."³⁴ Mrs. Ngọc had impeccable revolutionary credentials and formerly served as a government representative abroad. Her credentials allowed her to ease the work of coordinating permissions and cooperation from among the state entities including mass organizations such as the Women's Union and the Youth Union and among national and local governmental bodies. Highlighting nonstate groups' advantages of being close to the targeted people and their immediate social environment, she described their meticulous work in investigating their local projects and making small proposals for funding from a variety of sources including international NGOs and Vietnamese charitable groups abroad. Among the projects to which this NGO, headed by Mrs. Ngọc, contributed funds was the Shelter, a nonstate center for "young prostitutes and at-risk adolescent girls."³⁵

The Shelter served the local population in a poor area with high "social-ill and crime" rates on the outskirts of Ho Chi Minh City. Its tentative beginnings, management, and continued survival depended on a respected local woman, Mrs. Vân, who had done social charitable work since before unification.[36] The idea was to provide a sanctuary for girls who were in the sex trade or girls from impoverished and "contaminated" families and neighborhoods and thus "at risk for prostitution."[37] The place was gradually built up on landfill over swampy areas through much dedication and perseverance by Mrs. Vân and those who supported her. The Shelter provided a "safe, orderly and family-like environment," which included a clean room, daily meals, access to health care, basic literacy education, counseling, and job training for the targeted young women who were there on a voluntary basis.[38]

The discipline was based on "tough family love" and included suspension of privileges, light whipping, and explanations of wrongdoing.[39] Mrs. Ngọc said Mrs. Vân served as the "grandmother of the family while her staff acted as parents."[40] Mrs. Vân insisted her methods of educating the girls came from her own experience as a "mother raising her six surviving children."[41] At the time of my visits, there were twenty-seven adolescent girls (thirteen to seventeen years old) and a staff of three in addition to Mrs. Vân. There were two cells of ten girls each plus an isolation cell of seven pregnant girls. Each cell had a leader. Girls in each cell were responsible for designated tasks in addition to keeping clean their rooms and bathroom. If their cell's rooms and bathroom were found to be untidy or dirty, all girls in the cell would face "minor collective punishments" like having to eat plain rice for lunch without meat and vegetables or going without breakfast. Mrs. Vân said she did not give out big morality lessons but instead relied on time spent working and playing alongside the girls to teach them "concretely and bits at a time" right from wrong. She emphasized the technique of "child-to-child" education, as peers were encouraged to "whisper in one another's ears" what was "the right things to do."[42] Girls who required specialized counseling were taken to see "doctors and specialists for psychological treatment."[43]

Without the explicit teachings regarding the Vietnamese woman marked by tradition, the Shelter's emphasis on the family setting acted as the frame of reference for femininity. Although the organization of cells and cell leaders resembled less the family setting than the basic unit at the school, the military barrack, or the rehabilitation camp, the Shelter fostered an atmosphere and narrative of familial love, individual attention, and reciprocal responsibility and obligation. The staff at the home and supporters did not teach Confucian or "Oriental" values. Nevertheless, there was a clear understanding that the Western lifestyle was not suitable for Vietnam. Mrs. Ngọc noted the "activism" of health intervention in prostitution, but thought it would be "harmful" to "our society." In her opinion, to give out condoms was to "show the way for deer to run wild," with "careless Western sexual practices."[44] Mrs. Vân echoed this sentiment by telling me how she exploded at an antiprostitution meeting with officials from different government agencies:

> They had two slogans up. One said "Fight AIDS"; the other said "Fight Prostitution." I pointed and asked which one were they fighting. I said if you fight AIDS, then pass out the condoms. It means you encourage prostitution. But if you fight prostitution, then you have effectively fought AIDS. We have to teach morality and ethics as the foundation, as the source and end of human existence. Only then would we know what to live for. Condoms are dangerous. They can break apart the moral foundation.[45]

Instead of an explicit reference to a gendered tradition as marking a Vietnamese identity, the Shelter used the "family bond" as a reference to a general morality suitable to "our society" to guide the behavior of the girls.

Accompanying the ideology of family love and suitable values was the job training. Mrs. Vân's daughter had helped set up a "handicraft co-op" workshop. It was a piecework operation open to neighborhood residents as well, although most workers were older girls from the home. There were men in the workshop who were mostly confined to heavy tasks like stacking and carrying bundles of heavy and thick straw mats. The girls engaged in the "last stages of production." At the time of my visits, they were working on tatami subcontracts for a Japanese contractor.[46] They machine embroidered patterns on squares and long strips of blue materials, sewed them as borders onto rectangular pieces of thick straw mats, assembled the pieces into large mats, and trimmed loose threads.[47] All of these tasks required a high degree of patience and dexterity. The co-op was paid by the assembled pieces. Profits were shared according to the "number of pieces each girl completed of the task she was assigned, whether it was the embroidery or the assembling."[48] The girls switched positions with one another, but the more skilled ones embroidered patterns and sewed on the borders. According to Mrs. Vân, some girls threw themselves into the work, even skipping meals, and earned as much as VND600,000 (almost US$60 at the time), almost twice the average monthly income for a garment worker in Vietnam at that time. The girls managed to save about 30 percent of their earnings, which some used to buy gold and gave to Mrs. Vân for safekeeping until they left the home.[49] Workers could exhaust themselves in the demanding work built into the piecework system.[50] At the time of my visits, the workshop was in a frenzy to complete the orders for on-time delivery to the buyer/contractor.

Mrs. Vân said this work enabled the girls to "master their own means of livelihood, master themselves, and avoid relying on others to live."[51] The success stories were about the girls that the home had turned from "stealing" and "swearing" delinquents into self-mastered workers.[52] The model of rehabilitation in this privately run home did not completely mirror the model held up in the state-run camps. The ideological frame was not an explicitly Vietnamese traditional femininity. But the concrete content of a good person of the female gender from the lower classes turned out to be very similar: the patient, dexterous, docile worker on the global assembly line. The innovation of training the women for piecework appeared to state and nonstate social workers as a logical response to the socioeconomic status of the women in the targeted group and to the operation of the global economy. As far as social work was concerned the model of rehabilitation held up by the state-run camps was an innovation in the mentality of governing. With it, the state opened up rehabilitation work to the initiative of nonstate groups, effecting the socialization of social work.

So the difference was that the enterprise functioned as a cooperative, and the young women received their fair share of the profits rather than training to be more docile in the coercive form of discipline and punishment found in the government-run camps. It was not until 2002 that an "East Asian" or "'Oriental" traditionalist narrative became apparent at the Shelter, when one of its liaison social workers explained the vocational training (now no longer run as a cooperative) in terms of how "East Asian cultures place the responsibility on the woman to help out the family."[53] Within half a decade, the discourse about family at the Shelter has been displaced onto East Asian tradition and the role of the woman in the family, matching the governmental discourse.

The Possibility of Critique

As entities in society adopt the justification for government intervention, one begins to see spaces for critique to emerge in contrast to the encompassing ideology of the socialist state before market reforms. In chapter 3, I explored how expert knowledge allows for government intervention in an ideology of nonintervention. Yet liberal government intervenes while exposing itself to critiques of government. This style of governance incorporates in its logic of operation critiques of government in the same way that it incorporates the ideology of free choice. I suggest that the negative space of choice is a political notion based on an assumption of epistemological constraint. The notion of critique of government also builds around the state's or government's lack of immediate knowledge of the workings of the social realm. Both these notions of choice and critique link the microphysics of power to liberal political rationalization. These notions provide the political space in which the individual subject could act even if she or he is created by the disciplinary techniques of power.

As subjective interests cannot be deduced from state reason nor can the totality of reality be induced from these instances, governors cannot directly know the constituted socioeconomic reality that has been variously labeled the "invisible hand of the market" or "civil society." Colin Gordon writes that Adam Ferguson's and other Scottish thinkers' conception of civil society was a political invention: "It signifies the denser, fuller and more complex reality of the collective environment in which men as economic subjects of interests must be located, in order to govern them."[54]

Liberalism thus poses the problem of state reason in light of this dense reality, and liberal government circumvents it with expert knowledge and intervention. In this way, the rationality of liberal governance incorporates the space for critique of government based on knowledge about the complex social reality. In this conceptualization, the legitimate source of critique would be the relatively autonomous knowledge disciplines. One might object that the most likely sort of criticism aimed at the state would be charges of policy inefficiency, negative side effects, and so on. In such cases, the state would have co-opted these critiques to its own advantage since they would justify further more efficient or effective state intervention. This would be the ultimate ideological mystification in the same way that free choice might be a ruse of power. I would suggest that the potential of critique could hold more than just the rationale for more state intervention. I give the following example.

At the start of reforms in the late 1980s, dissidents in Vietnam had relied on "knowledge," and particularly scientific reasoning of the knowledge disciplines, to counter the reasoning of the Leninist state and to push for more political openness. In his writings, Trần Độ, a leading party official turned critic, points to the knowledge vacuum on the part of the party and calls for more studies in the social sciences about "humans in their various aspects and relations" to guide future state policy.[55] Citing the nontransparent nature of social reality, Hà Sĩ Phu, a dissident scientist, objects to the ruling cadres' simple impulse to govern unilaterally. Party cadres, writes Hà Sĩ Phu, have been saying, "Stop all discussions, which will only make society more complicated. Each will have to do good in his or her work . . . and the whole society will be good." This reasoning, insists Hà Sĩ Phu, is irrational and specious because governors cannot assume that "society is the simple sum of its parts." Instead, he proposes that society be viewed in the paradigm of the complex workings of the human body and be the object in a continuing search for knowledge.[56]

This possibility of critique depends on the assertion of a relative autonomy on the part of the knowledge disciplines. In the early push for wider reforms in the late 1980s, Lý Chánh Trung, a university professor and member of the National Assembly, demanded the decoupling of state ideological reason and the empirical knowledge disciplines. "Must Marxism-Leninism," he asked in a 1988 speech, "serve as the foundation, the frame, or even the direction of the disciplines when the social sciences are developing strongly with subfields, such as management, that are ideologically neutral?"[57] Recalling the 1960s anti-revisionist campaign in which expertise was denounced on political grounds, Vietnamese dissidents and reform advocates in their push for reforms in the late 1980s routinely demanded more political openness that would allow a neutral and autonomous space for science and technology to develop.[58] One may question this "neutrality," but its use served the purpose of pitting the empiricism of positivist knowledge disciplines against state justifications in the same way that eighteenth-century Anglo-Scots' empiricist philosophy undermined state reason.[59]

From the early experience of Vietnamese dissident demands for greater participation and political openness in the late 1980s, one can see how critique of governance based on the relative autonomy of the knowledge disciplines worked to disrupt state reason at the start of liberalization, clearing the way for the liberal alliance between knowledge and political power. But the very notion of the inability of governors to claim direct knowledge about the realm they govern (and the consequences of their policies) also continues to provide a space for possible contestation. The presence of alternative practices linked to autonomous bodies of knowledge could proliferate, diverge, and act as the basis of criticizing any one set of practices, as I argue with the rehabilitation camps and the socialization of social work. To put it another way, the continued potential of critique lies in what Thomas Osborne calls "a space of indetermination, and of possible conflict, between the aims and desire of government and the norms of the domain to be governed."[60] Critique of government, like choice, is a feature of classical liberal governance as a component in the operation of political power. One can also go into an involved discussion about the determination of legitimate contestation: experts may monopolize the credentials to speak for the governed. Nevertheless, the potential at least exists in this space for strategies in the practice of critique.[61]

Although the CARE project managers proclaimed with a measure of pride their goal of changing the camp's "training methodologies" and "official attitude," which led to incarceration as the solution to prostitution in the first place, it remains to be seen whether this will be the case.[62] For one, the inmates' participation in the management of the program was rejected from the beginning by the camp administrator (32). Inmates' input into the content, direction, and methodology of the courses was immediately reduced as the program was handed over to camp personnel (32). Another, open enrollment based on "freedom of choice" on the part of the inmates was withdrawn in favor of their compulsory participation in the camp moneymaking piecework operations. The camp was preparing to double its capacity as the CARE project came to a close. In the case of the Shelter, the model of rehabilitation did not stray far from that held up by the rehabilitation camp with its piecework operations. What then can one say about the value of such nonstate or socialized social work? I argue that the socialization of social work opened up the however-limited possibility of critique, at least of state practices.

The presence of differences in practices of rehabilitation indirectly or directly challenges any one set of practices as the only legitimate model of rehabilitation. Most of all, the nonstate entities' practices demonstrated alternatives to state-run rehabilitation. Residence at the Shelter was voluntary. There was no forced incarceration for a certain duration. The Shelter did not rely on repressive state police power to capture and hold the women in the camp. The young women could leave at any time. While it mirrored the state-run camp's money-generating scheme in which women were taught to be workers for the global production line, the Shelter's piecework operation was a cooperative. Profits were shared. It was not exploitation of unpaid prison labor. The young women at the Shelter were not forced to work in order to cover the expenses of their forced incarceration. Indeed, the social workers involved in the Shelter and its supporting NGOs emphasized these features as superior and just practices.[63] Although it was not good politics for the nonstate social workers to spell out explicitly the contrast with state practices,

the listener was left to make the comparison to state practices of rehabilitation. Mrs. Ngọc, at the supporting NGO, informed me that the
Shelter as a model had gained considerable support, prompting even a
state agency on children's welfare to send people to come and study the
privately run home.[64]

Similarly, the CARE training program succeeded in acting as an
alternative and viable model of rehabilitation right in the confines of a
rehabilitation camp. Its emphasis on empowerment and open and participatory training did not fail to make an impression on the camp's wardens, and it elicited their resistance.[65] Such alternative assumptions and
practices could not help but make it harder for wardens to take the infantilization of inmates for granted as part of the natural order of things.
CARE project facilitators and managers had insisted the inmates be
allowed to make assessments of and suggestions for the teaching curriculum and methodologies. These evaluations, suggestions, and trainees/
inmates' work records were all kept in files open to inmates "so the
women would have a sense of control over their files and ownership over
their products from the course" (34–35). Even as the input from inmate
was reduced after the program was turned over to camp staff, this file cab-
inet remained open (34–35). The gender sensitivity sessions that educated
the women and camp staff about gender inequities and power imbalances
could not help but erode the natural intelligibility of the narrative about
the good Vietnamese woman with traditional virtues.

The CARE project produced training manuals that could be used
again in similar projects and offered a model of rehabilitative training
that basically clashed with the incarceration framework.[66] Yet as a
viable model of training with the possibility of being funded by local
and international NGOs it received a good amount of attention. In particular, a drug rehabilitation camp nearby and the General Prison
expressed interest in the CARE project's health component dealing with
sexually transmitted disease and HIV prevention.[67]

Both the Shelter and the CARE project relied on specialized knowledge generated about methods of discipline and social work. As mentioned, in the case of the Shelter, Mrs. Vân boasted of her utilization of
psychology and her use of such methods as the "child-to-child" peer edu-

cation arrangement, now in vogue in Vietnam by way of the work of international NGOs. The CARE project brought into the camp "adult" and "participatory training methodologies" developed elsewhere. It also used a consultant service on the economic viability of setting up businesses in the camp to generate some income for the women and to improve their diet.[68] The nonstate social workers thus brought into the picture a range of knowledge about human behavior, the economic environment, and effective methods of intervention, developed autonomously from the state. Nonstate practices of rehabilitation, linked to autonomous bodies of knowledge, provided alternative models of intervention that could serve as the basis for questioning the validity and legitimacy of state entities' methods, assumptions, and ideological narratives.

Liberal Government and the Genealogy of Freedom

If there was a limited possibility of critique as societal entities took over some functions that dovetailed with governmental intervention, the kind of power deployed in the rehabilitation camps still stands in contrast to that of public health measures as far as the idea of a subject whose choice would be for his or her own good as directed by expert knowledge. In *Discipline and Punish*, Foucault identifies a new mode of power visible by the nineteenth century, which he calls "disciplinary."[69] Disciplinary power individualizes bodies as it normalizes an individual's will through carceral techniques of spatial arrangement, surveillance, and judgment by experts, from the teacher to the doctor, the shop-floor supervisor, the judge, the social worker, and the prison warden (293–308). This "carceral continuum," from the school to the factory, the clinic, and the prison, according to Foucault produces individualized sovereign subjects who will make the "right" choice (297). Many found disturbing the two sides of the same coin in his theory—disciplinary power applied in the carceral continuum, on the one hand, and the idea of a sovereign individual, on the other. Everything can appear part of disciplinary power, even the individual freedom called on to resist incarceration. Hubert Dreyfus and Paul Rabinow, for example, think Foucault's genealogy undermines a stance that opposes the carceral society on the grounds of natural law, human dignity, or subjective preferences of individuals or groups. These writers ask, "What are the resources which enable us to sustain a critical stance?"[70] Similarly, one is left to wonder on what basis would one call for more schools rather than more prisons?

In the *History of Sexuality*, Foucault did pay more attention to the enabling aspects of power in his discussion of bio-power with its production of subjects who seek individual health and vitality in a regime whose goal is the health and vitality of the population. Soon, partly in response to criticism directed at his preoccupation with discipline and partly in response to the rise of neoliberalism in the 1970s and early 1980s with Margaret Thatcher and Ronald Reagan, Foucault started to link the microphysics of disciplinary power to the level of governance. Foucault finally confronted the problematic of freedom, as I discussed my introduction.

Liberal government involves, as Colin Gordon writes, "the idea of a kind of power which takes freedom itself" and the conduct of the free subject as "the correlative object of its own suasive capacity."[71] In more concrete terms, liberal governance persuades and controls by positing the individual subject's freedom to choose according to his or her "particular and personal interests."[72]

I next explore how the microphysics of power relates to governance through the subjectivity of choice. I argue that although there were certain similarities in the microphysics of power employed by health workers, the police, and camp wardens, measures of control used by the police and camp wardens did not connect to a political rationalization based on the disciplining of choice.

The Subjectivity of Choice

Graham Burchell rereads David Hume to explore a liberal formulation of interests. "Every man's interest," writes Hume, "is peculiar to himself."[73] Interests are preferences, the passions and volitions of an individual, irreducible to reasoning; they are "original facts and realities, compleat in themselves."[74] The subject of interest and thus of choice is an empirical subject that exceeds and gives content to the juridical subject in contract theories of sovereignty. If Thomas Hobbes proposes the sovereign as an "epistemic power" rescuing the individuals from the collective dangers arising from utterly subjective realities and thus individual preferences, Hume asserts individual interests and preferences as given, nonexchangeable and nontransferable.[75] If Hobbesian skepticism prompts the need for a unifying public reality provided by sovereignty, Humean skepticism affirms the irreducibility of particular and subjective interests.[76] Burchell writes that for Hume, "the action resulting from individual calculations" makes "an isolated, particular event." Burchell sees this model of the subject of particular interests taken up by theorists of political economy like Adam Smith. "In the game of private interests," writes Burchell, "isolated individuals are situated within an infinite field of immanence in which their action is conditioned by an entire series of accidents and events which escape their knowledge and will."[77] This is Smith's invisible hand. The Humean formulation of the subjects of irreducible interests and preferences marks an important development in the working out of a liberal mode of governance. Instead of just trying to unify individual subjective interests within the juridical realm of sovereignty, governance becomes a problem of governing through and with particular interests, whose workings are not immediately apparent to the state.

In such a formulation, the reality of the empirical individual subjects and their interests are not thought to be deducible from a reason of state. It is this addition of peculiar interests (in theories of political economy) to the juridical subjects of rights (in contract theories) that persuasively imposes limits on state power because it disqualifies justifications that are based on reason of state. As Burchell puts it, "The legal subject of rights says to the sovereign: 'You must not do this, you do not have the right.' The economic subject of interest says: 'You must not do this because you do not and cannot know what you are doing.'"[78]

The absence of this liberal invention of the subject of interest with its epistemological disruption of state reason might to a certain extent explain the inconsequential and nonessential character of legal guarantees of individual rights of juridical subjects in actually existing socialist systems. As I have discussed, the latter operates within a self-referential reason of state. This *raison d'etat* can justify the nullification of individual rights for values deemed more important to the state. In the liberal mentality, individuals should be inviolable not just because of humanist or contractarian principles codified into law but also because individuals and their actions are thought not to be immediately knowable by the state with its reason.

The present line of analysis clearly carries the risk of reproducing the comforting cold war mentality of freedom on one side and tyranny on the other. Critics of liberal governance have long assured that this comfort is unwarranted and that no system has a monopoly on unfreedom. I discuss here some of the analyses of unfreedom in liberal governance in order to understand better the notion of the subject of free choice.

Freedom in liberal political ideology, most importantly, has been conceptualized negatively, in terms of what the state must not do. Isaiah Berlin writes that this negative freedom is about "the area within which the subject—a person or group of persons—is or should be left to do or be what he is able to do or be, without interference from other persons."[79] This space without interference is what laissez-faire governance is purported to be about. The state or government should leave individuals and groups a certain space to do as they choose. This is the cornerstone of liberalism. Liberals "participate in government with an eye to limiting its power," because there is no higher value than negative liberty: no utopia, no "final solution."[80] Thomas Dumm calls this liberal concept the "neutral space" of negative freedom.[81]

Whether the laissez-faire state provides this neutral space is the crux of Marxist critiques of the liberal state. "It must be made clear," writes Antonio Gramsci, "that laissez-faire too is a form of state regulation, introduced and maintained by legislative and coercive means."[82] Marxists have long criticized the non-neutral power of the liberal state based on analyses of it in relation to the mode of production and class relations.[83] To put it quite crudely, negative freedom as a protected neutral space is more or less a ruse for state enforcement of oppressive class relations for Marxists. Smith's invisible hand justifies the workings of the market, which unevenly distributes costs and benefits among groups in society. I have discussed at length how the promotion of individual choice in the medical model worked in favor of the marketization of medicine, with clear winners and losers. Liberal government actively reserves the space of freedom for some groups or classes and not others.

From a Foucauldian angle, Dumm also raises questions about this neutral space of negative freedom. Dumm points out that Berlin admits his conception of negative freedom relies on the limits imposed by what Berlin calls "what it means to be a normal human being," by "what it means to act inhumanly or insanely."[84] Within the neutral space of negative freedom, one chooses to act normally as opposed to "insanely," humanly as opposed to "inhumanly." The Foucauldian can readily supply the answers to questions regarding the normality that undergirds the individual freedom to choose. The "doctor-judge," the "social worker–judge" and so on, draw on their respective bodies of knowledge in the human sciences to devise the norms of what is normal and what is not. These experts oversee the supervision of norms so as to guide individual choice in the minute microphysics of power. As a result, one tends to choose life over death, health over disease, sanity over madness, and so forth. So "free choice" might not be an apt term to describe the exercise of freedom in a liberal system.

But what might be as important as what one chooses is the fact that one chooses. The act of choice within this politically sanctioned space presupposes a subject to do the choosing. Foucault's work has detailed how the individual is subjectified in the web of the microphysics of power. He has emphasized how these minute techniques of disciplinary power create the individual subject of self-mastery, how they form the sovereign soul through the molding of the body in minute daily activities.[85]

Such minute discipline is how the microphysics of disciplinary power connect to liberal governance. The creation of the subject goes beyond the individualization of the microtechniques of control. The individualizing, subjectifying microphysics of power relies on the notion of choice. The individual subject created in the microphysics of power can exercise choice within a seemingly neutral space free from government intervention. The sovereign subject of self-mastery in liberalism is what Berlin refers to as the positive aspect of freedom. "The 'positive' sense of the word 'liberty,'" writes Berlin, "derives from the wish of the individual to be his own master," as in "I wish to be a subject, not an object" and "a doer-deciding, not being decided for."[86]

Liberal governance creates the normal subject who thinks he or she is free. According to Foucauldians, it is a particular kind of power, a logic of governance that goes beyond the ruse of freedom as ideology or false consciousness as the Marxian formulation would have it. As Burchell writes, an "original feature of liberalism as a principle of governmental reason is that it pegs the rationality of government, of the exercise of political power, to the freedom and interested rationality of the governed themselves."[87] The conduct of free subjects becomes the object of government in all its persuasiveness and complications. Its persuasive capacities rely on its purposefully incomplete power. It is incomplete power in the sense that it leaves a space between the creation of the subject and his or her act of choosing however guided by normalizing discipline and conducive to the workings of the market. There is an interstice for agency in this "false" consciousness. It is in this sense of subjectivity and agency from the medical model that young women communicated their criticism of the police and of confinement practices, as mentioned.

Disciplinary power linked to "free" choice is insidious in the sense that it elicits less desire for resistance even while it allows for greater possibility of resistance with its production of deciding subjects. Who wants to resist health, well-being, or happiness? Liberal governance posed in terms of governing the conduct of free subjects of choice is certainly not the sufficient condition for freedom. But it provides one basis of possibility.[88] One tends to choose normality. But there is a possibility that "tend" does not mean "must." To persuade a woman about the necessity of condoms on the basis of health is not the same as arresting and putting her in confinement where she is subjected to a "total education," the repressive mechanisms of which aim to obliterate a subjectivity capable of choice. However crude the methods of persuasion in the medical model with its clinical display of pain and shame, its sex manuals, and promises of conjugal pleasure, health, and happiness, they were qualitatively different from those of the police and the rehabilitation camp. The line of argument that I pursue here is that, in the latter two cases, there was little space if any for the notion of choice.

The Subjectivity of Choice in the Rehabilitation Camp

The professed goal of rehabilitation in Vietnam was to remake the delinquent into a disciplined subject capable of self-mastery. This sounds like the often-declared goal of prison systems of today: incarceration is supposed to be rehabilitative. The rehabilitation camp in Vietnam did not stray too far from the modern prison with its forced term of incarceration and its declared rehabilitative function. Is one then to say that these facilities of rehabilitation produced subjects capable of making choices, thus linking the mode of power used in rehabilitation to a political rationalization of choice? The kind of power operating in the state-run rehabilitation camp in Vietnam was not conducive to the production of a subjectivity of choice. Nor could this power connect to a political ideology of free choice. Instead, it was a repressive power linked to a gendered ideological construct of tradition and national identity.

The practices in the state-run rehabilitation camp infantilized the inmate in a regime of total education, which forcibly captured her body and soul. The camp was to remake the inmate into the disciplined and thus accountable individual subject to be accepted back into society. Dumm suggests that delinquency as a concept implies a failure of discipline in the delinquent.[89] The delinquent fails as a self-mastered and accountable individual subject because she lacks discipline. With this mentality, rehabilitation would treat the delinquent inmate as a child to (re)instill discipline by retraining her from the beginning. A warden at the New School for the Education of Women suggested as much: "These girls are not used to good frames and folds [*nề nếp*, or good foundation and habits], which they see as restricting."[90] The assumption was that if the camp was to rehabilitate the delinquent, it needed to instill discipline anew. The camp thus resembled the schoolyard in its spatial organization, its routines, and its name. The inmates became schoolchildren again to learn anew good habits. All songs, recitations, and forms of address gave the appearance that wardens extended the paternalistic protection of a school or family to their charge.

But I would suggest that the very nature of total education with its infantilization of inmates leads not to the production of the self-mastered subject who would be making choices. Rather, total education treats the inmate as object, not subject. She is to be decided for, not to decide for herself. Total education in the camp did not treat women as subjects capable of making choices for their lives.

First, there was the high rate of recidivism mentioned. Foucault offers the explanation that the ingenious feature of carceral institutions is that they perform the tasks of correction while reinforcing the existence of the very delinquencies supposedly corrected.[91] As with the police, this double economy goes back to the idea of delinquency and how it is used to supervise illegalities, especially those associated with the lower classes. If one takes this interpretation, then the camp claimed to correct delinquents while it produced delinquents. The high rate of recidivism discussed in the previous chapter would support this view. One could attribute recidivism to lack of economic opportunities. However, there still remains the question of how the camp would have produced the self-mastered subject with its regime of total education based on forced incarceration and the infantilization of inmates.

Angela Davis, a prison reform advocate after her own prison experience, recalls "the mind-numbing regime that treated full-grown women like children." Based on her experience, she questions the rehabilitative logic of incarceration: "I've always found it so astonishing that people could assume that prisons can actually be rehabilitative when in prison you have no control over your life. You're told when and how to do absolutely everything."[92]

The question thus remains how the camp could have fostered a self-mastered subject making choices while its techniques of control discouraged any sense of subjectivity and of agency and took away all choices. It would be more conceivable that the camp fostered a sense of frustration, despair, or resistance.

If health education was behavior control through the promotion of an acting subject with choices, the rehabilitation camp was behavior control through repression. It was a mode of power that repressed the women's sense of self in order to replace it with discipline in the logic of total education. Mai and Hà, the young women who just finished their term of fourteen months in the Center for Social Sponsorship, described to me its atmosphere of frustration and despair by recounting stories of suicides. Mai and Hà said they witnessed several cases of women attempting suicide by jumping down the well and one case of successful suicide by hanging, the image of which haunted them for a long time.[93] When I asked what drove the inmates to thoughts of suicide, Mai attempted to explain the suicidal urge in her camp and her threat of suicide as a form of protest and a term of negotiation: "Too many beatings. We were desperate, sad, despairing. Like if you failed at making eyelashes, and they beat you. Me, too. When I couldn't do the eyelashes, I wanted to kill myself. I thought I could not stand all the beatings and that I would rather die. They beat me so hard, and if I moved they beat me harder and longer. But how can you lie still when you are being beaten?"[94]

In contrast, Mai and Hà talked very differently about the health education they received in their camp. Medical doctors from health agencies came to teach health education sessions. In between their stories of difficult eyelash making and painful beatings, Mai and Hà recounted in a positive tone the health exams, the HIV tests, and the health classes:

> Mai: In my fourteen months there, I got to go have five blood tests [for HIV]. And the tests told me I was free of disease. . . . We got physical exams and blood tests. Urine tests and blood tests and everything, very proper. When they found you healthy, they let you go back to your teams.
>
> Hà: One blood test every three months.[95]

Mai and Ha went so far as to use the intelligibility of health education to express their passive protest against the political/ethical education sessions about morality, family, society, and the good Vietnamese woman:

> Mai: The doctors taught us physiology [health]. And these cops or cadres, I don't know what, these boogie men, and the director taught political education. . . . Their classes gave me such headaches.
>
> Hà: We heard it [political/ethical education] and we sat and slept and slept.

Mai: They slapped each of us when we fell asleep. . . . The cadres/wardens, they stood outside the classroom windows to spy on us. If we fell asleep, they ran in and slapped our faces. But their lectures gave me headaches.

Hà: I hated it [political education], so I wouldn't listen.

Mai: I rarely listened.

Hà: Political education I wouldn't listen to. But I understood and listened to AIDS education.[96]

Certainly, one likely interpretation is that medical power provoked less resistance and was the more insidious compared to a crude repressive power. One could say the women were given a sense of integrity even while it was a way of directing their behavior. I would not disagree. Nevertheless, it shows the liberal mode of power as different from the repressive power that outright coerces. The confinement, forced labor, corporal punishment, and justification of Vietnamese tradition in the rehabilitation camp forbade and tried to wipe out by force through her infantilization the inmate's sense of being an active and capable subject. Instead of control through choice, such practices controlled through repression. Instead of incomplete control, which incorporates the space for the subject to choose (even if they were disposed to choose normalizing options), these practices in the camp constituted a mode of power that left no space between the production of the subject and her choices.

This difference in the modes of power became most apparent with the implementation of the CARE skills training program for the inmates at the New Center for the Education of Women in Thủ Đức. The program was a prime example of a liberal mode of power that sought to direct behavior through empowerment or the production of an active subjectivity capable of making choices. The stated objective of the program was to assist the women inmates to "develop relevant life skills and self-esteem."[97] Based on assessments that the women had small business as an economic option, the program taught business skills in planning, credit application, client relations, computer use, and so forth. Besides employment skills, instructors taught classes related to "living well." Among these classes were health and well-being, which included STDs/HIV/AIDS education, art, theater, assertiveness for sexual negotiation (content geared for all women, not just sex workers), and gender sensitivity (15–22). At first, attendance was open to those inmates who met minimum requirements like basic literacy and who wanted to be in those classes. The Ministry of Labor, Invalids, and Social Affairs later withdrew the inmates' "freedom to choose, leaving 'selected' women to attend the sessions," as inmates were compelled to work in the piecework operations for their keep (11).

The CARE project managers realized from the beginning that an approach to training that aimed to empower the women was not compatible with an institution of incarceration and "reeducation" and made changing the camp's "methodologies" and official policy of incarceration their "overall long-term aim" (4, 38). The CARE training procedures, in keeping with its aim of inmate empowerment, followed "adult training methodologies," which utilized existing abilities, and "participatory training methodologies" (3–4). These training methods were in direct opposition to the infantilization of inmates as the central feature of the operation of power in the camp. It was not surprising that the CARE program encountered camp and ministry opposition to input by inmates, refusal of credit offered to inmates, even refusal of the operation of a loan library, all on the assumption that inmates could not be trusted to be responsible (19–22).

Ultimately, the CARE program's promotion of inmates as adult subjects who needed to have their range of choices expanded did not replace the treatment of inmates as objects of reeducation. The narrative of remaking the women into good Vietnamese women with traditional values was compatible with the profitable use of inmates as pieceworkers in the camp. This combination had the support of ministry officials and the wardens of the rehabilitation camp as both a profit-making scheme and an effective response to the economic realities of the women in global economics. The scope of the CARE program was curtailed and finally terminated in favor of putting the women to work on the global assembly line. The political rationalization that went hand in hand with the techniques of control in the camp was not the subjectivity of choice, but a restrictive gendered national identity.

Specialized Intervention

If the techniques and model of state-run rehabilitation represented a different kind of governing power than did the liberal brand arguably present in medical intervention, then how did they coexist? First, there was a certain overlap in the mentality of governance. A socioeconomic realm became the reference point by which ideological pronouncements about a Vietnamese identity in women were translated into concrete, feasible tasks such as the training of women in piecework operations.

Second, similar to the relationship between public health and policing, there was a parceling of tasks, which minimized political or bureaucratic contradiction and confrontation between health and rehabilitation. For example, the CARE program offered health education embedded in wellness and self-assertiveness training, which included assertiveness in sexual negotiations for women and gender sensitivity training. This training component threatened to pose certain contradictions to the model of rehabilitation in the camp. Camp administrators and officials from the Ministry of Labor, Invalids, and Social Affairs reduced the general wellness and assertiveness training and tried to make this whole component "more medical."[98] By making it more medical, state social work officials changed the wellness and assertiveness training to fit the rubric of medical intervention. Public health agencies carried out the large part of medical intervention in the camp by way of compulsory testing, medical examinations, and STDs/AIDS treatment and prevention. By making the CARE wellness and assertiveness component medical, social work officials thereby parceled tasks to minimize the potential for functional overlap between CARE instructors and political/ ethical instructors. At the same time, the content of the wellness and assertiveness component was not incompatible with the medical intervention functions performed by public health agencies. Once the two-year CARE project was over, it would be possible for public health agencies to place health/medical personnel in the position of teaching this medicalized component.[99]

The rehabilitation camp makes a good demonstration of how specialized intervention worked to maintain different modes of power in state intervention in the perceived social realm. Health, police, and rehabilitative intervention all revolved around a perception of a society with its cultural, economic, and social dynamics. These dynamics were autonomous from a reason of state and required specialized knowledge in state intervention. At the same time, governmental agencies had different and separate tasks to perform. In the camp, governing apparatuses had separate functions to fulfill: the police made the arrests to keep the camp going; the public health agencies offered the medical tests, exams, treatment, and education; and the camp wardens gave the lessons in what was good and what was Vietnamese. The camp staff went about enforcing their own function of reeducation, borrowing from the police the narrative of keeping society safe; from the narrative of the Vietnamese woman who would be dexterous, patient, and docile on the global assembly line; and finally from health education the narrative of making healthy the population.[100] By parceling tasks, the camp, led by the ministry, engaged the participation and thus the support of separate agencies with their political and governmental resources. Specialized intervention as a configuration of social intervention thus maintained different kinds of governing power with their separate ideological justifications promoted by separate governing agencies.

CONCLUSION

Public health, policing, and rehabilitation share some features in the alliance between knowledge and governance in Vietnam. The liberal mentality of governance, or governing a social realm with dynamics autonomous from state reason knowable through expert knowledge, gave rise to specialized intervention. Nevertheless, specialized intervention as a configuration of governance made it possible for the coexistence of modes of power differentiated by choice and coercion. I have used two dimensions to discuss modes of governing power that do not rely on the self-interested choice of an individual guided by normalizing knowledges such as medicine. They are the notions of the possibility of a critique of government and a subjectivity of choice. These are notions that link the microphysics of power (or simply the techniques of control) to a liberal political rationalization (or simply ideology). I have found policing and incarceration in the rehabilitation camp to differ from the mode of power used in public health measures on one or both of these two dimensions. Specialized intervention as a configuration of governance allowed for an overlap in the mentality of governing a social realm. At the same time, it parceled tasks, keeping the different government agencies involved in their separate functions.

This picture of governance in Vietnam shows an organizing principle that does not entail one dominant kind of power across institutions. In this case, I identify an organizing principle in the form of the mentality of governing the social. This mentality provided an intelligibility for governance as a whole in the form of the configuration of specialized intervention. But what this configuration promoted was contingent on different government agencies and their negotiations or innovations in response to larger contexts such as global economics. Governing with neoliberal freedoms of the market cannot be based on homogeneous power, neatly categorized as either sovereign or disciplinary, as done by Foucault in his earlier works.[101] Instead, governance was in this case parceled, grafted, and sustained by different governmental entities through the configuration of specialized intervention. Barry Hindess articulates well this dilemma of liberal governance that is not really liberal: "Where does this leave the distinction between liberalism and other positions. . . . Most if not all of the governmental devices that might be seen as falling under the heading of the liberal mode of government could be and were supported by those who had no particular commitment to liberalism as a doctrine."[102]

The shift in the mentality of governance to one oriented to an external reality of the social allowed the state as a whole to function with the market. In that sense, one could say there was a liberalization of governance in Vietnam. But would this liberalization of governance necessarily entail the sources of critique of government or production of free subjects? My analysis falls short of answering in the positive across institutions. Nor is this answer limited to Vietnam. It makes one wonder about "liberal" societies in which there are not just the supervising teachers, doctors, and social workers but also the police and prison wardens.

If, as I mentioned in the introduction, neoliberalism could be distinguished from the more generic liberalism before the 1980s by its emphasis on the freedom to sell and to buy in the cult of the economy, then the governing of neoliberalist freedom must differ in its modes of deployment across different segments of the population to enable the current global market economy to extract profit flexibly from differentiated consumers and workers. It must be emphasized that coercion in the rehabilitation camp happens with marketization in relation to demands of the global economy of today, and thus coercion is being sustained by current conditions, not by a disappearing vestige of totalitarian power left over from socialist days. The fact that one finds gradations of coercion and choice according to gender and class in governmental intervention into the social domain, coupled with very different justifications from what would be good for real men and women to what would be true to the ideal Vietnamese woman, reveals that the Foucauldian thesis that liberal government rules not by ideology as false consciousness must be reexamined. Ideology as a problem reappears. Government practices like rehabilitation ideologically interpellate lower-class women. Further, the government's split emphasis on both empirical knowledge and true tradition provides different ways for Vietnamese to imagine themselves and their social environment. That is an ideological function. Now, however, with the rise of the market, including one for cultural products, government practices are no longer the only sources of ideological production in society. Imaginings about the social world and individuals within them now also come from the domain of popular culture including writings and films.

PART III

TO THE REAL

Ideology and Cultural Production

CHAPTER 7

From Antigone to the Kneeling Woman

A Genealogy of the Real from Socialism to the Preparation for Marketization

IF THE FIRST PART of this book examines market freedom, and the second explores how the government oversees such freedom, this third part focuses on how the realm of cultural production deals with such freedom and its governance. Governing with the market requires the simultaneous deployment of technologies of rule that draw on both an empiricism of social "realities" and an assertion of a cultural truth, on both choice and coercion, to produce a differentiated population of consumers and workers for a neoliberal economy domestically and transnationally. The presence of a market and its incitement to freedom to produce and consume must be processed beyond the domain of government as the Communist Party and its state apparatuses no longer have the monopoly on the production of social imaginaries in society. Yet the problem of ideology reappears with governance that deploys both senses of the real and true, both choice and repression. Clearly citizens are no longer invited to see themselves exclusively in relation to a social scientific truth in the form of a Marxist historiography drawn by its vanguard, the Communist Party. And, apparently, not all citizens are invited to think of themselves in all domains of life as the free subject whose choice need only to conform to what experts say is good for them. The issue of cultural representation of social imaginaries, modes of imagining social reality, and how to reconcile the simultaneous and contradictory modes of differentiated governance now fall under the purview of an emerging commercial popular culture in the form of writings and films. This is the focus of the next two chapters, where this chapter pro-

186 Part III. To the Real

vides a genealogy of realism as the predominant mode of social representation in the popular culture of the day.

In the *Giai Phẩm Mùa Đông* journal of 1956, which would become one of the focal points of intense repression by the new socialist state of the Democratic Republic of Vietnam in the North, the Paris-trained legal and literary scholar Nguyễn Mạnh Tường tells the story of Sophocles' *Antigone*, under the column heading of the relationship between "government and the people." More than thirty years later, a collection published in 1988 to great impact presents another woman appealing to a law truer and more just than that of government officials. The collection bears the title *The Kneeling Woman* and includes mostly selections of reportage on local conditions over the three regions of the country. But rather than simply uphold an alternative vision of the good and true against the actions of the state, the writing of dissent from two points in time—one at the beginning of socialism and the other during the preparation for marketization—in different ways engaged in complex contestations over the sense of the real. Both, however, deployed the feminine as markers of social realities.

This chapter traces both state actions and dissent at the beginning of the socialist state in the 1950s and at the beginning of market reforms in the 1980s to explore the history of the relationship between governance and realism—its senses of the real and the true—in cultural representations of society. As the most continuously and widely available form of cultural production prior to 2000, literature has received the most attention from the government in the five decades since independence. As mentioned in chapter 3, almost immediately after winning the war against the French in 1954, the state in the northern Democratic Republic of Vietnam became embroiled in a battle with intellectuals—writers, artists, and knowledge experts. The socialist state, an entity encompassing government agencies and Communist Party organizations that had begun to penetrate most aspects of the daily lives of citizens, proceeded to curb the autonomy of artists and writers while enfolding their organization into its apparatuses, a process most evident in what was later called the Nhân Văn–Giai Phẩm affair of 1956–58. It had become a commonplace cold war practice simply to point to such an episode as an illustration of the repressive nature of the socialist regime. Such an indictment does not really reveal why the Communist Party would need to crush artistic and intellectual autonomy, nor does it explore the manner in which dissent took place beyond the discourse of political dissent. On the other extreme, there have been explanations of the Vietnamese revolution as being continuous with Vietnamese traditions, overlooking instances of contention.[1] Arguing against these theorists of continuity, Kim Ninh has offered the most convincing and nuanced account by showing the drama of building a modern socialist state, which required the ideological service of writers, artists, and experts in the task of transforming the whole of society. Here, I focus on just one aspect of this contest between some writers and the party: how social reality is to be imagined, and represented. The suppression of dissident writers of the Nhân Văn–Giai Phẩm group has been often explained in terms of opposition to the party. Zachary Abuza, like most analysts of this period, argues that "simply raising literary issues did not threaten the party. What did scare the VCP [Vietnamese Communist Party] was that the movement sought to turn itself into an independent, permanent, and loyal opposition to the party."[2] Against this political focus, Tuấn Ngọc Nguyễn, better known as the critic Nguyễn Hưng Quốc, argues that Nhân Văn–Giai Phẩm "mainly constituted an attack on the theory of socialist realism."[3] These two emphases need not contradict. I would suggest that from the beginning of the socialist state in the 1950s, the party had promoted an idea of socialist realism in its suppression of writers, not so much because the state was interested in realism as a literary genre per se but because of what socialist realism implied for a broader social imagining about the role of the party in relation to the notion of historical truth.

This forcing of the real into the true called forth a particular mode of critique by dissidents in the later period of the 1980s, when the party allowed an opening that would prepare for a shift of policy toward marketization. My discussion follows this shift at the introduction of the market economy by examining dissident critiques denouncing the lack of realism in order to criticize the lack of rational knowledge in governance in the late 1980s. This latter deployment of empiricism reprised from the 1950s the dissident writers' depiction of the real with markers of the feminine in order to detach itself from a masculinist statist truth. Such reprisal of the connection between empiricism and the feminine paved the way for a more commercial brand of realism in contemporary popular cultural production since 2000.

THE SOCIALIST STATE AND THE SUBJECT OF HISTORY

After declaring her obedience to a law higher than that of the political ruler, Nguyễn Mạnh Tường's Antigone pronounces in 1956 the one characteristic of a government that would prohibit her from burying her slain traitorous brother: "That is the power of dictators. Whatever they want people to do and to say, the people must do and say accordingly."[4] As if worried that readers would not make the right association, Tường followed Antigone's speech with his affirmation that the ruler Creon typifies a dictatorial government in that he reacts to reasoned challenges by condemning Antigone to death. Tường especially called readers' attention to Creon's efforts to keep his own son within the folds of the ruler's reason of state, crushing the son's love for Antigone and killing him in the process. Few Vietnamese reading the journal *Giai Phẩm* in 1956 would miss the reference to the socialist state and its insistence on having its own intellectuals in its fold, toeing the party line. Nor would they miss the indictment that the truth upheld by the state is one belonging to a particular rationality of dictatorial rulers. I would argue that contestations over what constituted the truth were vital because they were about who could claim to be a subject of history. Below is an overview of what happened during the Nhân Văn–Giai Phẩm Affair.

In 1954, after Vietnamese nationalist and Communist forces defeated French efforts to reestablish colonial rule in Indochina, the Vietnamese Workers' Party (Đảng Lao Động Việt Nam—the name of the Communist Party at the time) established the Democratic Republic of Vietnam in the North of a now divided country as a result of negotiations among the major powers in the shadow of the cold war. The resulting Geneva Accords temporarily divided Vietnam in two, with the stipulation that elections would take place in 1956 to decide the fate of the entire country. Elections never took place because of American resistance. Vietnam remained divided, preparing the stage for one of the bloodiest wars of the twentieth century.

In 1956, many prominent writers in the North issued a number of periodical publications, most notably *Giai Phẩm* (in three issues: spring, fall, and winter, from February through December 1956) and *Nhân Văn* (in six issues, from September to December 1956), expressing dissent against the party's heavy-handed control over literature, art, and expertise.[5] The movement won urban popular support and soon encompassed new periodicals like *Đất Mới* among college students and energized allied journals like *Trăm Hoa*.[6]

Lê Đạt, one of the principal dissenters who had a hand in the publication of both *Giai Phẩm* and *Nhân Văn*, said in a recent interview that had he known what was in store, he would have been very afraid.[7] After the initial wildfire of urban response, the dissenters had been further encouraged both by Khrushchev's speech criticizing Stalinism at the Twentieth Party Congress in the Soviet Union in February 1956 and by the Hundred Flowers campaign in China in May 1956. The dissenters seemed to have the upper hand as the Vietnamese Communist Party hesitated throughout 1956 and 1957. By February 1958, however, the party had turned to decisive repression.[8] Not too far from the mind of the party's leaders must have been Khrushchev's promotion of peaceful coexistence with the West and the Democratic Republic of Vietnam's looming need for a unification war against the U.S.-supported Republic of Vietnam in the South. Once China started the anti-rightist campaign to bring down those in the Hundred Flowers movement, the Vietnamese party followed suit and staged two "study sessions," one in February 1958 for party members and the other for the masses a month later, unleashing a denunciation campaign, followed by punishments.[9] The state stripped dissenters of their writing or teaching positions and reassigned them to labor in punishing "reality" (*thực tế*) posts in production units like factories or communes in remote rural or mountainous areas, as this was the favorite method to remind those in the intelligentsia that reality lay at the proletarian places of labor in the party's class-based perspective. Among the many punished, Lê Đạt tended buffaloes on a commune for ten years and was socially banished until 1988, when he and some fellow writers were rehabilitated.[10] His fellow editor at *Nhân Văn*, Nguyễn Hữu Đang, was imprisoned until 1973, after which time he was placed under house arrest in a remote spot until the end of the 1980s.[11] Trương Tửu, the movement's Trotskyite theoretician, barely survived by practicing acupuncture.[12] Most endured wrenching poverty and social ostracism. Nguyễn Mạnh Tường, who at the age of twenty-two was hailed as a genius with two doctorate degrees in law and French literature from Montpellier, described their common fate: "Making a living was very hard. But hardest of all was the solitude. No one dared to have anything to do with us."[13] Nguyễn Mạnh Tường remembered seeing the once celebrated philosopher Trần Đức Thảo on the streets in the late 1980s in "wooden clogs and tatters, with one lens missing from his eyeglasses."[14] If the dissenters doubted the reality in the party's truth, they were crushed by the reality of its power. Their fight brought personal tragedies and the consolidation of party and state control over intellectuals, artists, and experts as the socialist state created organizations to incorporate these elements into its apparatuses, as Kim Ninh details in *A World Transformed*.

Socialist Realism against Mimesis

Arguing against Ernest Bloch's defense of expressionism, György Lukács wrote in 1938 that a Marxist literature must grasp "reality as it truly is, and not merely to confine itself to reproducing whatever manifests itself and immediately on the surface."[15] In other words, this was a formula that opposed realism to mimesis in literary representation. An exploration of this split would shed light on the terms of contention between the party and writers.

This identification of the real by what "truly is" in a social totality echoed Ivan Gronsky's concept of socialist realism. Assigned the task of organizing writers into the Union of Soviet writers, Gronsky coined the term *socialist realism* in a 1932 declaration: "The basic demand that we make on the writer is: write the truth, portray truthfully our reality that is in itself dialectic. Therefore, the basic method of Soviet literature is the method of socialist realism."[16] In Vietnam, Trương Tửu was a theoretician and literature scholar who came from the ranks of the Trotskyite Fourth Internationalists who were decimated during the anticolonial war by the now ruling Communist Party that belonged to the Third International. Trương Tửu in the early 1950s tried to serve the new socialist state in his capacity teaching at the university in Hanoi, but he maintained his doctrinal independence from the party. It probably surprised no one that Trương Tửu would provide the elaborate theoretical backbone of the movement against party rule in the arts and knowledge production. In one of the 1956 *Giai Phẩm* issues, Tửu also conceded the correctness of this Marxist emphasis on a total vision of society in literature rather than a partial truth such as that promoted by the bourgeoisie.[17]

Despite what seemed like an agreement over the necessity of a total vision of society reflected in literature, Đặng Thai Mai, a writer on the side of the party, said in 1956 that even the party's writers had not produced very many truly socialist realist works, just revolutionary romanticist ones.[18] If one were to look for grand narratives of realism constituted in Marxist analyses of social relations, then Đặng Thai Mai was basically right for that period and even for the subsequent period of more entrenched socialism in the 1960s and 1970s. One of the few works that would fit such descriptions is Hoàng Ngọc Anh's *The Working Neighborhood of Trường Thi*, written over 1957–58 and 1970–71 and published in 1975, spanning the entire socialist period in Vietnam.[19] The novel depicts the coming into revolutionary consciousness and action of a worker admitted into the Communist Party during French colonialism and the Japanese occupation. Tuấn Ngọc Nguyễn emphasizes *partiinost*, or party-minded spirit (*đảng tính*), as the determining criterion of socialist realism.[20] He cites numerous poets such as Tố Hữu, Xuân Diệu, and Chế Lan Viên and some prose writers such as Nguyễn Khải, Đào Vũ, and Chu Văn who fit the *partiinost* criterion of socialist realism.[21]

But even Tố Hữu, whom Tuấn Ngọc Nguyễn calls "*the* leading poet in Vietnamese realist literature after 1945," produced works that one Hanoi literary scholar characterized as "heroic" and "modern revolutionary sentimental spoken poetry" (*thơ trữ tình điệu nói cách mạng hiện đại*), rather than socialist realism in ways beyond party-mindedness.[22] A good-sized body of major, canonical works of exemplary socialist realism, in the sense of meshing material details with a Marxist social analysis, has not been published. Arguably, the Soviet Union during the Stalinist era produced some major works of this literary mode.[23] But even in the home of socialist realism, party man Andrey Zhdanov declared at the First Writers' Congress that "our literature, which stands with both feet firmly planted on a materialist basis, cannot be hostile to romanticism, but it must be a romanticism of a new type, revolutionary romanticism."[24] So it is hardly surprising that in the Democratic Republic of Vietnam before and during a devastating war against the Republic of Vietnam and the United States, descriptions of material conditions of living were diffused in officially sponsored works that offer a mixture of socialist idealism; praise for the party, its leaders, and its goals of fighting against the southern regime and the Americans; and patriotic sentiments and love toward family and collectivity.

If the production of socialist realist texts per se was not paramount to the party, if the dissenters on the whole agreed that there should be a historical truth in the Marxist sense as Trương Tửu conceded, and if they did not question the party's leadership of the arts as their elder Phan Khôi wrote in *Giai Phẩm*, then what was it that lay at the heart of their demands that the party found so threatening?[25] As if to underscore their nondispute regarding the leadership role of the party, Lê Đạt and Hòang Cầm, both core Nhân Văn–Giai Phẩm writers, were grateful to the party for awarding them honors in March 2007, fifty years after their suppression.[26] Nor was the content of what the party advocated a problem for these writers fifty years ago. It recently came to light that in 1956 Hòang Cầm published a poem that he had written in 1953 lamenting Stalin's death and that rivaled party man Tố Hữu's outpouring of loyal sentiments on the same occasion.[27]

Writing about "thaw literature" in socialist regimes, Hilary Chung notes that such literature "reassessed not the fundamental principle of Party control of literature per se but the way in which it was exercised and the definition of socialist realism (particularly relating to sincerity) rather than its dominion."[28] Chung explains that repression came when writers "overstepped the mark."[29] More precisely, I would argue that the Nhân Văn–Giai Phẩm episode shows that its threat to the party revolved around a series of tightly related questions: What was the truth in relation to observable realities? Who possessed this truth? And who thus could claim to be the subject of true history? As the party contemplated and prepared for war, these questions acquired an immediate importance beyond that of theoretical interest.

The Party as Subject of Historical Truth and the Question of Empiricist Realism

At stake is a Leninist conception of the party as it came out of the First Indochina War against the French and as it entered the Second Indochina War against the United States and the Republic of Vietnam. The socialist-realist writer Mikhail Sholokhov explained, "Socialist Realism is the art of the truth of life, comprehended and interpreted by the artist from the point of view of devotion to Leninist Party principles."[30] But the dissenters plotting at the end of 1955 had barely glimpsed the full significance of their demands to such a Leninist vanguard party. This brief and tragically lopsided contest was about socialist realism insofar as an idea of socialist realism enhanced the position of the Communist Party as the acting subject of history.

The contention was not over whether there should be a total vision of society as the truth through which the real could be apprehended. Rather, it was over who could determine what this total vision might be at any moment. Most Vietnamese Communists at the time, dissident or not, would agree that the Communist Party was *người tiêu biểu cho giai cấp vô sản*, or literally, "the person who typifies the proletarian class."[31] This characterization of the party is Leninist. Writ-

ing in 1902 against what he called the economism of Marxists who
wanted to wait for material conditions to ripen into revolution, Lenin
advocated a party that would comprise professional revolutionaries
who not only would have discipline, tactics, and organizational means
to combat enemies but who also would push the proletariat out of
"trade union consciousness" into consciousness of its historical role
as a class. Lenin's vanguard party serves not merely as a political arm
of the proletarian class but as the very thing that wills for this class
and animates it into the historical class from the inertly termed "mass
of people" indistinguishable from just the inchoate ranks of the
discontented.[32] In Marxist historiography, it is the proletarian class that
delivers history. In Lenin's conceptualization, the party becomes the
sole acting subject of history because it delivers the very class with the
historical mission. In Stalin's pragmatist reworking of this notion,
Lenin's voluntarist party now embodies the proletarian class "by all
the fibers of its being" and becomes the acting subject of history to
the point where it detaches from and stands above the working class.[33]
Should not such a vanguard party as the agent of history determine
what the total historical vision might be and through which one could
interpret empirical evidence? While the leadership position of the
party was not contested, this last question became the point of
contention.

The dissenters contended that realism, as a mode of capturing reality, should be a bottom-up rather than a top-down affair. The inaugu-
ral poem appearing on the first page in the first issue of the 1956 *Giai
Phẩm Mùa Xuân* was penned by Lê Đạt. In it, the poet hopes he could
be "the code receiver / In sleepless night / Recording the words life cables
me." To what purpose would the poet use such connection with "real"
life? "I want the party to call me in / Ask my take on life / Mobilize me
into the Ministry of the soul of the masses / Helping the Center / Build
new men."[34] Lê Đạt and other writers like him wanted to be the ones
to contribute the empiricist real to the historical truth, thereby calling
into question the top-down model of truth the party had in mind. Many
of the most memorable poems from this movement insisted on a

verisimilitude and the verifiability of reality as observed by the writer. One poem by Phùng Quán starts out:

I have gone through
Villages where war has just ended
I have met
Old women in rags
Their skin like charred wood
Their hands bloody from pulling barbed wires
Tilling the old enemy forts to grow rice and corn.[35]

The witnessed images serve as a testimony to realities on the ground, embodied by figures of women, to indict state corruption and waste. The poem claims to have mimicked reality from the ground up, thus evoking an empiricist mode of knowing. From the party's viewpoint, using empirical reality to question the vanguard party's truth meant to question its very being as *the* sovereign subject of history.

Antigone: Empiricism and the Dissenting Humanist Subject

The significance of *Antigone*, says Slavoj Žižek, lies in G. W. F. Hegel's reading of it. Antigone must bury her blood relation Polynices, despite the ruler's prohibition, because she must symbolically repeat nature's truth of death in the burial rites so that she herself can symbolically assume responsibility for the inevitable effects of a force beyond herself. Only in such an act of "symbolization par excellence" could Antigone become a subject of a free act in this symbolic order and not an object of forces of nature.[36] In Nguyễn Mạnh Tường's "Antigone," the dictatorial ruler Creon possesses over Antigone the power of death, which he uses to reassert himself as the sovereign subject constituted in the truth of his power, to which he tries to convert his son. What this Antigone does is not necessarily to wrestle individual sovereignty from that of the monarch in a more typical liberalist interpretation. Rather, she asserts a separate subjecthood, which may or may not be an individual, in competition with the monopolizing subjecthood of the ruling party in the person of Creon.

Such insistence on nonindividualist subjecthood separate from the party could be seen in the dissenters' demands for freedom and democratic forms of social life. Two central figures in the dissent movement from the university, Nguyễn Mạnh Tường and Trần Đức Thảo, called to "extend freedom and democracy" as the actualization of the people's collective ownership of the country.[37] They both demanded that the party allow writers, artists, and experts to pursue their work autonomously from the party line. They asked this of the party in the legacy of Lenin, who inveighed against the reformist calls in the socialist movement of his days for the "bourgeois" "freedom of criticism."[38] Trần Đức Thảo forced the issue of the right to question the party's truth in his identification of freedom as entailing the freedom of critique: "The freedom they [mental and manual laborers] want to develop is definitely not the bourgeois freedom of the old society, the freedom of a minority to exploit the majority. The freedom they want to develop is the freedom for the entire people to criticize leadership. . . . That freedom as the right of a citizen is entirely recognized and guaranteed in our regime."[39] The dissenters proclaimed subjecthood in the citizen-subject of a democracy, which is not defined necessarily in bourgeois or liberal individualist terms. However, such a subject, though it be a collective subject, must be constituted in the freedom to arrive at the truth free of coercion to conform to a preconceived revolutionary telos as interpreted by the party.

Ever keen on observing the workings of "actual socialism," Žižek thinks the vanguard party views "the historical process from the perspective of the "Last Judgment," totalizing historical truth and foreclosing all other possible futures.[40] In their resolution, the Third Writers' Congress in June 1958 attacked the Nhân Văn–Giai Phẩm movement in starkly totalizing terms: "The struggle against the 'Nhân Văn–Giai Phẩm' group is an uncompromising one between the revolution and the counter-revolution, between socialism and capitalism in the realm of art."[41] If the party promoted socialist realism, it was not about verisimilitude to an empirically verifiable reality but about faithfulness to the totality of the social vision that the party possessed, judged from some future point of revolutionary telos.

Lest people thought the dissenters were advocating a liberalist freedom to arrive at some individual sensorial or self-evident truth, Trương Tửu further explained their position vis-à-vis the leadership role of the party and history: "Freedom is the understanding of [historical] necessity.... The truth is the real of the revolution progressing forward. Writers and artists want, together with the proletariat and with the Communist Party, to own the necessary, the inevitable, the historical law, and to own the revolution; they therefore seek to pursue creative work with the party."[42] This formulation of one's relationship to history reads very much like a Hegelian Antigone's understanding that death is something *done* by nature, and what a human being could do is to insert and assert consciousness with the funeral rites, so that such death as "pure being" "shall not belong solely to Nature."[43]

If burying the dead is an act of symbolization par excellence, then art must be a human activity par excellence for the dissenters. The name they chose for their periodical was *Nhân Văn*, or *Humanism*. In Trương Tửu's statement above about artists choosing to produce creative works side by side with the party in order to own the revolution, art becomes the symbolic act through which one becomes an owner/subject of history. The perhaps Hegelian strategy, forced on the dissenters by their predicament, was to show that the real was not discoverable through the lens of the party's truth about history. Rather, one had to become a human subject in order to apprehend reality in a perhaps inevitable truth of an impersonal, even deterministic, history that would constitute one's very being. Such was the dialectics of a human subject. Like a Leninist party, and so in competition with it, humans must come before and after history simultaneously. The dissenters claim their humanist subjecthood in relation to history, in tandem with the party but not in relation to the party as the ultimate subject of history. Czeslaw Milosz sums up well the dilemma of the writer in relation to a vanguard party insistent on possessing the truth of history: "Reality, which is quite disagreeable, has to be passed over in silence in the name of an ideal, in the name of what ought to be.... The battle against socrealism [socialist realism] is therefore, a battle in defense of truth, and consequently in defense of man himself."[44] Trương Tửu, in one of his theoretical articles, used Marx to support his enunciation of the arts: "The essence of art is the truth."[45] Like Antigone's insistence on burying the dead in a free act, these writers insisted on writing the universal humanist truth in a free act, to bring forth the conditions necessary for each and all to undo the alienation of history as an overwhelming force and to recover their place as the owners of such history. This ownership of history and revolution was the becoming of a subject, which Trương Tửu called the desire on the part of writers and artists to "reprise for themselves the legitimate meaning of *being human*, alienated by class society's oppression and violation. This is why they stand under the liberation banner of the Communist Party."[46] Without the means of coming into human subjectivity promised by the Communist revolution, there would be no reason for them to stand with the Communist Party. This freedom to engage in symbolization to become a subject in competition with the party was what the party found intolerable. The party's defenders at the Writers' Congress in June 1958 mocked the dissenters as "Trotskyites" for putting on an air of "absolute freedom" to appear "more Communist than the Communists."[47]

In the mimetic mode of representation, the empiricist real threatened to displace the party's total truth. It was the faithfulness to reality as the writer's truth that Phùng Quán, the youngest of the Nhân Văn–Giai Phẩm writers, at the time proclaimed an autonomous epistemological position that would make possible the humanist subject in "Mother's Words," with lines that would reverberate for Vietnamese to this day:

> I pledge to be an honest writer
> Honest for the whole of my life
> Sugar honey fame will not sweeten my tongue
> Thunder clapping overhead will not fell me
> Paper and pen if someone robs from me
> I will use a knife to write on rock.[48]

Phùng Quán lived out his pledge. For most of his life after the movement was suppressed, he would make a living catching fish on the many lakes of Hanoi.[49]

Antigone: The Feminine Universal as the Real

The party's insistence on its status as the sole subject of history left no room for another competing masculine-acting subject. To champion an alternative subject position that is universalist and humanist in content, the dissenters deployed an imagined sense of the feminine to mark an alterity arising out of the empirically real, disrupting the state's masculinist *raison d'état* masquerading as historical truth.

The masculinity of the party's subject position can be seen in the exemplary socialist realist work mentioned above, Hoàng Ngọc Anh's *The Working Neighborhood of Trường Thi*, first written in 1957–58. In this novel, the protagonist Đồng is the son of a worker at a complex of metallurgical factories called Trường Thi in the city of Vinh. Đồng's journey from lost soul in the 1944 famine to Communist Party cadre is told in categorical terms. He meets a Communist Party agent who initiates him into the ranks of the party. Through the party's view of the total historical conditions, Đồng realizes his own life is the result of capital that conflates itself with foreign domination by the French and the Japanese. At barely halfway through the novel, party cadre Hùng concludes the story of his (their) life (lives) for Đồng in terms of a subject that acts and possesses through becoming a member of the party: "Đồng, the life of workers is like that! We are proletarians who make revolution. We lose nothing but our slavery. And we gain the world."[50]

In this formulation, the feminine is not a source of knowledge, nor is it a way of knowing. Xuân, the protagonist's lover, comes from the petit bourgeoisie. At the end of the novel, Xuân joins the great patriotic anticolonial resistance portrayed as fully under the leadership of the proletarian party. As Đồng, now in a leadership position, sees her off, he asks the question and provides Xuân with the correct answer:

> "Darling, do you know how our country comes to have these moments? Because a whole nation would rather die than be slaves!"
> Xuân walks besides Đồng. She does not know how to respond to such a sudden question. She gently lifts her eyes to look at her

beloved. It's still him with his forehead, his mouth, his smile, still his large frame and his sunburned skin. The dark blue pants and moss color shirt make him seem even more solid. Đồng continues, his voice even more insistent:

"It's only now that I truly understand the meaning of the word 'sacrifice.' People could only sacrifice when they find their true reason to live. The revolution liberated my life. The revolution liberated your life."

"Yes!" Xuân whispers, "The revolution has liberated me from the confines of the family, from my selfish former life."[51]

Earlier in the novel, during the scorched-earth campaign in the anticolonial war, Đồng has to convince Xuân's parents to destroy their family home, built with solid bricks in the French style. The revolution does liberate Xuân from her home with its confining petit-bourgeois mores and within which young women spent their time sewing dainty things. But Xuân will be re-feminized in that she will use her sewing skills to make the new red flag with the yellow star for the revolution and from now on will be a foot soldier in the war led by the real subjects of history who know for her and speak for her—party men like her lover.

In response to such masculinization of both the party's path to historical truth and the subject constituted in that truth, the dissenting writers used figures of women in their writings to introduce a reality on the ground through a mimetic mode of representation as an alternative to the masculinist truth about some social totality derived at by a centralized party. Phùng Quán's poem illustrates this claim to verisimilitude through acts of witnessing:

I have gone through
Villages where war has just ended
I have met
Old women in rags
Their skin like charred wood
Their hands bloody from pulling barbed wires
Tilling the old enemy forts to grow rice and corn.

I have met
Young women who tend flowers
20? 30?
I can't tell

Their sweat boils on their backs
The sun like a blowtorch
Burning their shoulders red.
. . . .

     I have met
Bone-thin children
Five or six years of age
Their rice bowls stuffed with bran and greens
It's only March and they are waiting for New Year's
To eat rice with meat
For one meal, one day.

     I have walked
In Hanoi on nights that drizzle
On winter streets, rain falls like daggers

     I have met
The workers, sisters who empty latrines
Tattered brassiere blouses, bare feet
Pant legs rolled to their knees
Shivering, they enter dark latrines
Carrying vats of shit
That if we were to pay ten thousand each
Most people would not dare
These sisters do this through the night
     By morning, they earn just enough to feed their children.[52]

Phùng Quán, in his celebrated poem, attributes his most cherished value to his mother's words about honesty—the feminine maternal as the facilitator of universal truth. In this poem, Phùng Quán's observable realities consist of old women breaking land and young women growing flowers or cleaning latrines. In the first two stanzas, women work the land to bring forth sustenance and beauty in their proximity to the earth. Transformative labor, the most human of Marxist subjectivity, is embodied by the old and young women down to their charred skin and sunburned shoulders. A passage about children and their hunger explains the nurturing purpose for the labor of the women latrine workers. The mimetic real, in its stark materiality, is fetishized in the bare corporeality of the working women—their skin, their hands, their backs, and their thighs. In a sleight of hand, such fetishization of women in all their corporeality, and thus their material reality, rendered the party's historiographical truth abstract and unreal.

The subject that the dissenting writers called forth into being would be a humanist subject with universalist content against a class society of the present instigated by the party as much as that of some prerevolutionary past. Again, the feminine in its connection to the real is evoked to conjure such position of universality beyond the class-based viewpoint of the party. In another poem, "A Child of Six," Hoàng Cầm writes about a child orphaned by class struggle during the land reform campaign: "The woman fighter takes a step back / looks at the orphaned child / tries to find signs of the enemy / All she sees is a human."[53] Rather than correspondence between the real and Marxist historiography, the empirical reality in the poem reveals a universal human child against the typology of the party's historical truth. The person who sees the child for the child, in his immediate reality, is a woman. The writer uses the nurturing and empathic intincts of a woman—her femininity—to reveal for the reader the universal humanity of the child against the party's damning class typology. It is through such feminine eyes that one sees beyond the party's truth, which the dissenters depicted in masculine figures of heartless brutes.

As historically associated with the feminine, love, love of all kinds, especially romantic love, was praised in so many pieces published in the movement. Lê Đạt denounced the party for driving lovers to suicide in his much remembered poem "On the Occasion of Some People Committing Suicide," in which love appears as a natural and universal human lifeforce against the inhuman dictates of the party. In Nguyễn Mạnh Tường's "Antigone," he insisted on showing the reader the love Creon's son has for Antigone, destroyed by Creon's dictatorial *raison d'état*. When Hoàng Cầm wrote in defense of fellow writer Trần Dần, who had become the target of official attacks and imprisonment early on, he chose to portray Trần Dần in a forbidden love with a young Catholic woman of the urban "usury" class and in full aesthetic exploration against the unfeeling despotism of the new state.[54] In Hoàng Cầm's account, Trần Dần's attributes stood in for all the ordinary strivings and failings of humans to live their lives and to create from such lives. Such human pursuits were contrasted with those of the party's "robotic poet," a figure satirized in a play of the same name, and with the breed of Leninist revolutionary giants depicted as lacking human hearts in a story called "The Giants."[55] The dissenters sought to mark themselves as fallible humans against the breed of Leninist revolutionaries who Lenin said possess the strength of giants.[56] They did so using the feminine dimension of universal humanity to oppose the party and the state, portrayed in masculine terms.

In this episode of dissent, what were often imagined as feminine emotions, feminine qualities, and feminine presence, came to embue the humanist subject of history with universality. In his investigation into the eighteenth-century European bourgeois public sphere, Jürgen Habermas observes the same process of the emergence of sentiments in novels discussed in women's salons as contributing to the claim of universality in the bourgeois individual.[57]

It is not surprising then that the party seized on the historical appropriation of the feminine to construct bourgeois humanist universality to accuse the dissenters of serving the interests of their true classes: the exploiting classes of landowners, bourgeoisie, petit bouregeoisie, and the intelligentsia. The party insisted that these dissenting writers inflated "the exploiting, parasitic, selfish, and corrupt self" in order to "serve the exploiting and oppressing class to sing the praise of a corrupt individualism."[58]

More revealing is the way in which the feminine was attacked by writers and intellectuals serving the party at the time. Those speaking on behalf of the party conjured an imagined excess of two kinds: hysterics and debauchery. Theoretical attacks focused on the Trotskyites' hysterical pursuit of "permanent revolution" when the Leninist party was using nationalism to mobilize for the anticolonial war. From feminine hysterics to treason against the masculinized nation was a short step. Those speaking on behalf of the party charged that these Trotskyites were selling out to French and American colonial powers and their puppet regimes when the party was trying to build a new nation-state.[59]

To underscore the feminization that signaled the degeneration of the dissenters, the party presented these writers as succumbing to places like gambling and opium dens, teahouses, theaters, and dance halls — spaces that were marked by the presence of loose women and prostitutes — and consequently the dissenters were bought off by various agents of the South Vietnamese and Americans.[60] Nguyễn Hữu Đang and Thụy An, two leading figures of the Nhân Văn–Giai Phẩm movement, were thus convicted of treason with connections to the enemy. Party man Tố Hữu vividly tallied the mix: "Their [the dissenters'] material base consisted of 'devil's nests,' salons, tearooms, drama troupes, money, girls, opium lamps, liquor cabinets, pornographic films, and Trotskyite books."[61] To represent the dissenters, the party conjured up a discourse of feminized excess. By attacking hysterical reactions and debauchery that caused dissenters to lose their sovereignty to outside enemies, the party had set the terms of the feminization of its enemies and in turn responded to the dissenters' deployment of the feminine as a marker of the empirically real and the humanly universal.

In short, responding to the party's masculinist discourse of historical truth and subjectivity, the dissenters employed pathos in things feminine to arrive at the knowledge of a self-evident universal humanist truth as the conditions in which one could constitute oneself as a subject, in contrast to the wielding of the truth of Marxist historiography by the Leninist party to become the acting subject of history. The feminine became an epistemological route to an alternative history and its subject. So it was not disagreement over the party's leadership position on the part of the dissenters that the party viewed as a threat. It was both the dissenters' use of empiricism to attack the party's truth and their vision of a humanist subject in competition with the party as the agent standing in for the historically chosen proletariat that made it so difficult for the party to tolerate the dissenters' demands. At the end of the contest, however, the party's masculinist historical truth was successfully inscribed as the real. This state of affairs would last through the decades of socialism and victory over the South. Marked by the sign of the masculine and subsumed under a socialist statist truth, such realism set the stage for another moment of contest in the mid-1980s, when the market made its entrance.

REALISM AND RATIONALISM IN DISSIDENT DISCOURSE
OF THE LATE 1980S AND EARLY 1990S

Once the party began to prepare for economic liberalization in the 1980s, it needed to justify this major departure from the socialist command economy. The party allowed a space from 1985 through the early 1990s for critiques of aspects that did not work in the old socialist system. Dissidents quickly used this "untying" (*cởi trói*) to voice dissent beyond what the party was allowing. The main mode of critique was the reprisal of the empirically real, often represented in feminine figures reminiscent of Nhân Văn–Giai Phẩm, to challenge the party's orthodox truth. K. W. Taylor has argued in relation to literature in the reform period that "who has the authority to decide what is real in history" was the issue.[62] While agreeing with the emphasis on the real, I would not present this new contest in purely oppositional terms. Instead, I would suggest that both the new dissenters in the 1980s and the party took advantage of the link between dissent and a realism that claimed an empiricist mode of knowledge in its mimetic verisimilitude.

From 1986 through 1988, there appeared in major literary periodicals like *Văn Nghệ* (Literature and the Arts) a series of reportage pieces by Phùng Gia Lộc, Trần Khắc, Lâm Thị Thanh Hà, and Hoàng Hữu Các, among others, detailing in a gritty realism the harsh realities in rural communes, villages, and towns, in a tone of outrage against the injustices suffered by ordinary people as a result of illogical and irrational party policies, rogue party-state officials especially at the local level, and an oppressive and corrupt bureaucracy. In the space of three years, from 1986 to 1989, there was a flowering of dissenting works that often claimed a lineage to the Nhân Văn–Giai Phẩm movement appearing in writers' unions' journals such as *Văn Nghệ* in Hanoi and *Sông Hương* in Hue. A wave of novels, stories, poems, plays, and films that quickly acquired the label of dissidence art because of their insistent challenges to official narratives about society and history was produced by writers such as Ngô Ngọc Bội, Nguyễn Khải, Dương Thu Hương, Nguyễn Huy Thiệp, and later Phạm Thị Hoài; by poets such as Nguyễn Duy, Trần Vàng Sao, La Quốc Tiến, Thanh Thảo, Phạm Tiến Duật, and Nguyễn

Trọng Tạo; by playwright Lưu Quang Vũ; and by filmmakers such as Trần Văn Thủy and Đặng Nhật Minh, among others. In the field of literary theory and criticism, Trần Bạch Đằng, Trần Độ, Lữ Phương, Phạm Xuân Nguyên, Hoàng Ngọc Hiến, Lại Nguyên Ân, and others theorized and called for a kind of cultural production autonomous from official truth making. Political treatises by notable intellectuals such as Phan Đình Diệu, Bùi Minh Quốc, Hà Sĩ Phu, Lữ Phương, Vũ Kim Hạnh, and Lê Hồng Hà, among others, and a group calling itself Câu Lạc Bộ Những Người Kháng Chiến Cũ (the Club of Former Resistance Fighters) began a wave of attacks on the "illogic" of socialism in official historical narratives and policies.[63] These writers and journal or publishing house editors, even in the milieu of "untying," still put their own positions and employment on the line to produce or allow the publication of these works that went beyond support for the government's liberalization policies. Solid empiricism served as the main premise of these critiques. By reclaiming empiricism as reality against party-dictated truth, these writers and journalists also reclaimed the position of a subject of sovereign perception apart from the party.

The Feminine as Alternative Epistemology

Lâm Thị Thanh Hà, in the reportage piece "Công lý, đừng quên ai" (Justice, Do Not Forget Anyone), insists she had to write from the local site of official corruption and mishandling of a murder case, "because whatever you want to write, it has to be heard with your ears and seen with your eyes."[64] More precisely, the bite of critique lay in the discrepancy between what was shown to be the empirically real and the revolutionary truth claimed by the party. As an influential documentary film of the period, *Chuyện tử tế*, puts it, "Tragedy and comedy often happen in places where between real life and dogma lies a distance too great."[65]

This discrepant reality became a highly charged site of imagination. The reportage pieces paved the way for works of fiction of a level of controversy unseen since the Nhân Văn–Giai Phẩm affair. Nguyễn Huy Thiệp became the lightning rod for such controversy during this initial adoption of market economy in Vietnam. Nguyễn Huy Thiệp's series of stories including "Tướng về hưu" (The Retired General) appeared in *Văn Nghệ* and were later published in collections in 1988 and 1989. They were met with volleys of attacks and counterattacks by critics defending the party line and those in support of Thiệp. In many of his stories, Thiệp laid claim to a representation of reality with an excessive marking of the real. The very excess of the real packed a shock value that forced open an extraordinary debate about epistemology and historiography. Not surprisingly, the reprisal of the sign of the real this time often picked up where Nhân Văn and Giai Phẩm had left off. The sign of the feminine carried now the reality of the mixture of life under socialism and the new government-sponsored market economy. In "The Retired General," the daughter-in-law practices state medicine, open adultery, and an entrepreneurialism with which she harvests aborted human fetuses to feed to her brood of commercially bred dogs to supplement her state income.[66] The status of the daughter-in-law as an outsider-insider to the patrilineal line allows for her to carry an alternate reality. Thiệp's social criticism often took aim against the feminine embodiment of market greed as social realities, the revelation of which called into question the party's epistemological monopoly since the demise of Nhân Văn–Giai Phẩm.

Even when the feminine appears mythical rather than empirical in Thiệp's stories, it served at the time as an opposing sign to state-sponsored masculinist historiography. In the story "Không có vua" (Without a King), another daughter-in-law, called Sinh (Life), holds on to an affective-ethical (*tình nghĩa*) vision of living amid the utter moral corruption in which the men in her family partake.[67] The materialism that supported the state's telling of history was revealed to be no more than the moral corrosion of a household of men who steal from the government, the market, and women. The teleological progress that the revolutionary party laid claim to was revealed to be nothing but poverty, which turned with a vengeance to materialist values once the market was introduced. In his historical stories "Kiếm sắc" (Sharp Sword) and "Phẩm tiết" (Chastity), Thiệp used the mythical figure of a woman named Ngô Thị Vinh Hoa to undermine the party's nationalist and revolutionary historiography based on official evaluation of past Vietnamese rulers.[68] Thiệp depicted with equal irreverence both Nguyễn Ánh (later Emperor Gia Long), who in 1802 founded the officially reviled Nguyễn dynasty, and the ruler he defeated, Nguyễn Huệ (Emperor Quang Trung) of the Tây Sơn favored by party historians. Both succumb to a lust for fame and fortune raised to a mythical level in the figure of Vinh Hoa, or Glory, as a woman whose body secretes a substance of her sex, heavy with scent. The mark of the feminine, together with Thiệp's use of Borgesian pseudo-documents and unreliable narration, constituted a willful erosion of official historiography that often read in the West like a postmodernist attack because of its rejection of Marxist teleological metanarrative.[69] The shrillest denunciations of Thiệp's writings at the time accused him of exhibiting an "ingratitude" born out of "nihilism," or an "anarchism in historiography."[70] For one author, such charges focused on the figure of Vinh Hoa as a woman so un-Vietnamese in her femininity when compared to that other iconic fictional female figure, Kiều, of nationalized poet Nguyễn Du, a contemporary of Nguyễn Ánh. The critic voiced his distress about Thiệp's attacks on historiography by dwelling on Thiệp's transgression through this Vinh Hoa female figure, who "self-secretes the essence" of her sex upon her first sight of Nguyễn Ánh, the future Nguyễn emperor.[71] The representation of the feminine as the embodiment of an autonomous and alternative position shows itself to be the site of epistemological and historiographical contention.

The Kneeling Woman: Epistemological Relegitimation and the Moral Subject

In both "Sharp Sword" and "Chastity," Vinh Hoa refuses to be sexually possessed first by Nguyễn Huệ of the Tây Sơn and then by Nguyễn Ánh of the Nguyễn dynasty. If Vinh Hoa signifies a pure ideal of glory, whose virtue of chastity lies in her refusal to be sullied by her appropriation in the political projects of two rulers, other feminine figures from the reportage writing of this period also offer formulations of autonomous moral positions, albeit in more conventional ways.

Trần Khắc's "Người đàn bà quì" (The Kneeling Woman) was written in December 1987 and published a few months before Thiệp's series of stories in *Văn Nghệ*, the official publication of the Writers' Union edited at the time by the reform-minded Nguyên Ngọc. This piece became the title piece in a collection of reportage writing published by the journals *Văn Nghệ* and *Nông Nghiệp* (Agriculture) and Nhà Xuất Bản Nông Nghiệp (the Agricultural Publishing House) in July 1988. The coming together of those working in literature and the arts and those working in the rural agricultural sector legitimized a reprised mode of representation of social realities focused on the countryside.

Not unlike the other pieces, "The Kneeling Woman" blends a journalistic tone with a literary mimetic style of local usage of language in dialogues and provides detailed descriptions to bring home realities from the countryside. The piece opens by establishing the village of Tiên Đổng as a quintessential Vietnamese village, with its poverty and its dreams inscribed in its colloquial legends. The changes that the new market economy has brought are also depicted as typical of the new Vietnamese countryside, with small shops springing up along its roads and new local government buildings that signify the new prosperity. Displayed on the walls of such buildings are endless statistics of "achievements with striking numbers on grain, pork, and fowl feathers for export."[72] Local officials claim credit for these market economic achievements.

Such evident empiricism, however, is quickly contested by another reality that goes on under its surface. The author of the piece identifies the person who calls into question the character of local officials who do not behave anything like representatives of an enlightened government: "There is someone who dares . . . call Mr. Châu the local party Secretary, Mr. Thực the chairman of the local People's Committee, and Mr. Bẩn the Public Security (police) chief the three village bullies [*cường hào*]. That person is a woman, and she is sitting right in front of me here."[73] A reality more credible and more immediate than official statistics is carried by a widow, Mrs. Khang, who has been asking for redress from authorities for ordinary villagers who fall victim to local government corruption and oppression. One case has to do with the murder of an outspoken farmer by local officials, and another has to do with the confiscation of Mrs. Khang's residence for public use, which turns out to be a private gain for the same local officials.

The word for the village notable who acts like a bully, *cường hào*, has acquired an emotional charge from an earlier wave of social critique in literature during the colonial period. Vietnamese writers from the 1920s through the 1930s used realism to paint stark pictures of rural life in colonial Indochina as an indictment of French colonialism. Canonized by all the governments of postcolonial Vietnam in a national literature, works such as Ngô Tất Tố's *Tắt đèn* (When the Lights Go Out; 1939), Vũ Trọng Phụng's *Giông tố* (The Storm; 1936) and *Vỡ đê* (The Dam Breaks; 1936–37), Hồ Biểu Chánh's *Con nhà nghèo* (The Poor; 1930), and Nguyễn Công Hoan's *Bước đường cùng* (Dead End; 1938) are all examples in this literary vein of realist social critiques. Prominent in such works is the figure of the village official ruthlessly extracting personal gains as French authorities rely on them to rule and to bring in revenues for the colonial government. The village *cường hào* has since become an icon in Vietnamese social imaginings and a shorthand for oppression and exploitation in a social critique issued as if from the countryside, although many writers came from the urban intelligentsia.

In this literature, the countryside became a prominent site of political and cultural legitimation in tandem with extratextual practices. Because cultural and administrative colonization was maintained from the cities, the countryside became the site for bases of the anticolonial resistance. When faced with the return of French colonial forces to reoccupy Vietnam in 1946, the Việt Minh withdrew to their bases in the countryside and the mountains to mount its armed insurgency until 1954. Subsequent campaigns carried out by the Democratic Republic of Vietnam in the North, from the anti-feudal efforts to the notorious Land Reform of 1954–55, focused on the countryside as an important site of socialist transformation. The Second Indochina War against the South and the Americans was also carried out from both the North and bases in the rural South. After defeating the Republic of Vietnam in the South in 1975 and reunifying the country in 1976, the socialist government sent undesirable classes and elements from the urban South to the new economic zones in the countryside, not only as part of an economic developmental plan, but also to educate these urban groups on the proletarian and rural values espoused by the party. Finally, when it came to marketization, the party and government also started to experiment in the countryside with the *khóan* system and other incentive mechanisms from 1982.[74] The countryside, because of its social and economic significance, has had a history of serving as a major site for contest against local injustices symptomatic of more fundamental social injustice. Fighting for rural local redress has become the very symbolic act of moral legitimation in both the popular imagination and official discourse. It was no surprise that a large number of dissident works in this period, such as those by Tạ Duy Anh, Nguyễn Quang Thân, Nguyễn Huy Thiệp, and Dương Thu Hương, among others, issued from a rural perspective.

Similarly, in the story "The Kneeling Woman," Mrs. Khang tells her own story as a narrative that draws on that iconic history of the countryside as the site of moral claims. Mrs. Khang tells the journalist about her prerevolutionary village's stela inscribed with *Tôn ti hữu tự hương đẳng tiểu triều đình* (Above and below in order, the village hall is a small court). Such "feudal" hierarchy was the target of both anticolonial literature and socialist attacks in the earlier days of the revolution. Pointing out this history, Mrs. Khang presents herself now as continuing that fight for justice and progress in the countryside. She describes herself with this proverb: "A widow concerns herself with the affairs of the court" (*Gái hóa lo việc triều đình*). The widow as an exception, freed of her familial obligations and her subjugation to her husband, brings a certain ideological regeneration of perspective from a peripheral location, which can contest and refresh but ultimately does not overthrow the hegemonic order. In one move, she both inserts herself in a long anticolonial and revolutionary historiography and evokes a tradition regarding Vietnamese women. Her feminine and rural location becomes a location for moral claims. Mrs. Khang shuttles in itinerant journeys from her rural village toward increasingly more urban and central locations of governmental power. Her journeys establish the rural location not only as being on the periphery but from where she has marked a direct path to the center of power, connecting both sites in a mutually constituted and legitimated nexus. The seat of government is at the center only because the other core of an imagined geo-historiography of the countryside allows it to be so, and vice versa. Her iterant trips to the palaces of power only partially vindicate her, but they strengthen her resolve to continue with her incessant quest for justice. As the author of the piece puts it, Mrs. Khang fights for a time when "all progress together" (*bao giờ đồng tiến*). She becomes an activist, organizing her village delegations to the capital to make their cases heard at the highest levels of government. The original historical mission of the party is shown as having been corrupted by bad elements and an imperfect marketization program. The author shows Mrs. Khang to be the woman who tries to restore to the collective itinerary the original revolutionary historiography and the place of the countryside in it. The piece ends with the statuary image of the woman, her incessant journeys to the heart of power frozen in her vigilance and vigil. The author suggests the village, when truly prosperous and just in an unspecified future, should erect a statue of a kneeling woman with arms raised in petition to the power that be. Such a monument, he writes, should be named *The Suing Woman* (*Người đàn bà đi kiện*).

Thus, although Mrs. Khang embodies the immediate empirical reality of a rural location as an alternative truth to current governmental claims of market prosperity and progress in the 1980s, the source of historical and epistemological legitimation remains intact. The state-sponsored empiricism seen in the statistics symptomatic of the new mode of governing the market is rejected in favor of a direct empiricism accessible to everyone, giving rise to a sovereign moral subject. However, in this contest over justice for the countryside, doubled as the local and the real, both the party and its critics drew on this discourse invested in the constitution of a location of critique as being outside the system. For the party, such critique can act in a similar way to the hardworking immigrant narrative in America regenerating its ideological legitimacy or to the narrative of the protagonist in *Mr. Smith Goes to Washington*.[75] The mutual constitution of the location of "dissidence" gives credence to this mimetic mode of representation as "real." Further, such dissident discourse, issued from a rural outside at the moment of marketization, relegitimized and rebound the seat of governmental power to a geo-historical imagining. For critics, the outside status allows for an alternative moral claim to correct the wrongs of the system. Of course what these critics wanted might be more than what the party could use. Many courageous critics paid a price for voicing such demands. Nguyên Ngọc, the editor in chief of *Văn Nghệ*, which published such writings, was dismissed from his position within two years of beginning his tenure.

CONCLUSION

The beginning of the Democratic Republic of Vietnam the North in the mid-1950s and the moment of marketization in the late 1980s in the whole of Vietnam were both highly charged moments during which social and political changes were accompanied by an intense contest over the sense of the real and the true and over who should have the right to determine such truth of history and society. Writers, artists, and other intellectuals have at each of these moments insisted on a reality directly accessible to them as universal human subjects, claiming their right to challenge the historical truth championed by the Communist Party as the sole agent of Leninist historiography. If the party demanded to subsume an empiricist and mimetic realism under the truth of its total view of history in the 1950s, dissident writers of the Nhân Văn–Giai Phẩm movement insisted on recovering mimetic language apart from the language of Marxist historiography. In the 1980s, the party found use for empiricism, not only in managing an emerging market economy it had decided to adopt instead of the command economy, but also in allowing for cultural productions to mobilize mass support for the market that must operate separately from the direct dictates of the party and government. Policies of "untying" art thus made use of such empirical claims to support drastic changes in policies, argued as being necessary in order to respond to new realities. Writers and artists, however, used this opportunity to reprise a more autonomous subject position in relation to this empiricism. To have access to empiricist reality means to be able to claim moral autonomy. To different degrees, writers challenged the official history through this insistence on their access to the socially real.

The mark of the feminine served these efforts in different ways. In the 1950s, reducing women's characters to the embodiment of either a corporeal or material feminine provided an alternative access to the immediately and mimetically real as a form of knowledge other than that of the party, which had been enshrined as the truth. Seeing through the eyes of feminine figures thus served as a way for dissident writers to create a subject position—an Antigone—for themselves in relation to such a sense of the real as an alternative to the masculinist subject position within Marxist historiography monopolized by the party. The feminine, often doubled in this literary imagination as both the empirically immediate and the maternal and eternal, and served as a way to construct that alternative subject within humanist universalism as it "unmasked" the party's truth to be a mere particular version of history and society, namely, a class-based perspective. As the party opened up the space for empiricism as a mode of knowledge and representation in the 1980s, and as critics widened this space, the link between an alternative knowledge and the feminine was reprised. Whereas writers such as Nguyễn Huy Thiệp used feminine figures to undermine official historiography, others in a vein of reportage writing such as Trần Khắc's "Kneeling Woman" reappropriated older figures of rural women dating back to the anticolonial social-realist literature of the 1930s to legitimize a moral subject position apart from governmental authority. The challenge to official historiography posed by the reduction of women figures to an imagined sense of the feminine, however, was uneven. The last, in "Kneeling Woman," for example, succeeded in laying claim to a moral position necessary for social critique. However, it did so by reinvigorating the legitimacy of the party's Leninist and nationalist historiography centered in the rural heartland. In either case, the use of the feminine as the marker of the socially real had been cemented, paving the way for the popular films examined in the next chapter.

CHAPTER 8

Love in the Time of Neoliberalism

Ideology and the New Social Realism in Popular Culture

THE GOVERNMENT HAS BEEN responding to a "social evil" like prostitution as a symptom of market freedom in the social realm, and it has done so in a way that would promote such neoliberalist freedom in a global economy. In doing so, the government projects ideological visions of self and the social world to its citizens, including senses of the empirically real and of the true of Vietnamese tradition. But the government is no longer the sole source of such ideological imagining. An emerging commercial popular culture in Vietnam now takes over some of the production of ideology in its response to market freedom through its representation of society in a self-proclaimed social realism.

There has been a rather long history to the split in the representation of reality and truth as realism's relationship to government has changed. As market freedoms take root, and the governance for those neoliberal freedoms becomes differentiated into two primary modes using empirical normalizing knowledge and traditionalist values, a new way of depicting social reality has emerged with the increasing commercialization of cultural production and consumption. From reality marked by the iconic figures of Antigone in the 1950s and the "kneeling woman" in the 1980s, one arrives at the current era marked by the bar girl. Since the mid-1990s, publishers — owned by the government but operating by market profits — have put out collections of "realist" exposés describing various scenes of fast living, most of it tinged with commercial sex and illicit drugs under titles like *Sàigòn by Night*.[1] These journalistic items sell on the claim to show new "complex" (*phức tạp*) realities that have sprung up with the market. But the tone is almost without exception ambivalent. It seeks to rivet attention to pleasures

215

and desires in consuming clothes, motorcycles in street racing, alcohol, food, dance floors, violence, women, sex, and heroin. Mixed in is an ambiguous alarm about their consequences in terms of wasted lives, social disorder, and corrupted traditions, justifying police activities against these new phenomena. This genre of a newly claimed social realism of vice, crime, and women culminated in the limelight with the 2003 release of the film *Gái nhảy* (Bar Girls), directed by Lê Hoàng and produced by the state-owned Giải Phóng Films.[2] Grossing more than VND10 billion (roughly US$700,000 at the time), it became the sensation that suddenly catapulted Vietnamese cinema into commercial viability in the face of Hollywood's global reach.[3] It cleared the way for a Vietnamese film industry with both state and profitable private production companies. It also unleashed a vibrant public debate about realism and the commercialization of Vietnamese cinema. A sequel by the same director, *Lọ lem hè phố* (Street Cinderella) opened in 2004 to expected high receipts and more debate in the popular press.[4] I suggest here that an examination of this genre of popular culture exemplified by the two most commercially successful and genre-launching films reveals the shifting mode of imagining reality as the market becomes more established in Vietnam after the initial period in the late 1980s and early 1990s. Rather than merely being a reality to be captured through empiricism as in the reportage of the 1980s, the sensational tone of this new social realism depends on the construction of market desires into a danger-laden underside of excess enjoyment. What it borrows from the previous mode of imagining reality in the 1980s is the mark of the feminine. This new market underside is marked with the figure of the bar girl, conveniently combining the dangerous thrills in sex, drugs, and women.

The sensational turn in the new social realism offers some insight into why commercial sex has been such a busy site for both governmental measures and popular culture. Commercial sex and similar vices can easily be used to depict the seductive dangers of freedom in the market and emphasize the need to contain such freedom. For the popular writings and films since the late 1990s, the profitable enterprise has been to capture this underside of market freedom in some symbolic order, to give audiences orienting meanings in social fantasy. This is where popular culture intersects with the terms that government has been using to control market realities as it increasingly relies on different modes and techniques of governing for the exigencies of the neoliberal global economy. And as government can no longer tightly control cultural productions because of their marketization, I follow the evolving modes of imagining reality in the newly commercialized popular culture to explore issues of ideology and neoliberalism.

THE LOGIC OF EXPOSÉ: JOURNALISM AND THE NEW SOCIAL REALISM

As economic liberalization proceeded through the commercialization of governmental units as described, the reprisal of the real for purpose of dissent and critique of governmental power came to serve a different purpose in the mid-1990s and beyond. As with other governmental units, newspapers aimed to turn a profit. Editors began selecting not only items that were not too offensive to the party and government platform but also items that had the power to sell papers. The result has been a flood of extremely popular reportage writing, exemplified by selections collected in the *Sàigòn by Night* series. Readers have seen these in every single newspaper for the past decade, from police tabloids (there are countless of these, as each provincial or city police department sells its own tabloid, offering a steady diet of crime reportage) to party youth organ newspapers such as *Tuổi Trẻ* or *Thanh Niên*.

In the new reporting, the gritty realism of the reportage of the 1980s turns into claims of verisimilitude through impressionistic descriptions of social vice as the "hidden reality" behind some facade of normalcy. It is the act of uncovering that renders the account "real." The presentation takes off at first from an empiricist mode of knowledge. In a recent handbook on how to do investigative reporting in the reformed era, journalist Quang Hùng reminds his reporters that the mission of the press is to uncover (*phát hiện*) phenomena.[5] He insists such a mission requires the careful gathering of material evidence including obtaining documents, taking pictures, and making videos and sound recordings. The motto should be *Đến tận nơi, nghe tận mắt, xem tận tai* (Go to the very place, hear with your ears, and see with your eyes).⁶ This does not mean that readers always receive such good empiricist reporting in newspapers and in collections. Indeed, the same handbook gives an example of bad investigative reporting in an article run by the popular Public Security newspaper *Công An Thành Phố Hồ Chí Minh* in 1999 about activities of commercial sex in Đà Lạt, the accuracy of which was being challenged by the local Đà Lạt–Lâm Đồng authorities.⁷ Without giving credence to either the journalistic account or the factual challenges, what the handbook reveals is that two major newspapers picked up that article and that it rang true to its readers. The article's descriptions—the reporter's discovery that lakeside ghostly manifestations are really women in the flesh and flesh trade, who hide behind trees and under umbrellas in the foggy cold night of Đà Lạt to catch their customers—fits the mold and the mode of uncovering a sensational story. Similarly, the bulk of the new reporting merely gestures toward this empiricist mode of knowledge in its emphasis on the act of uncovering. There is a mutual construction and reinforcement of verity from both the performance of discovery and from the representation of the supposed secrecy of the phenomenon itself.

Practices of commercial sex serve well this formula in its representation of a phenomenon that needs uncovering. The same handbook devotes a long section to discussing the ins and outs of (un)covering and combating "negative phenomena" (*hiện tượng tiêu cực*).⁸ These include corruption and its twin phenomenon of vice. Newspaper reporting on the myriad forms of prostitution has become routine. Almost all collections of reportage include pieces about the various and multiplying aspects of commercial sex.

It seems the revelation of the hidden provides the sensationalism that is then given as "reality." Despite resolute calls to suppress these scenes of debauchery and depravity, the message comes across as morally ambivalent. The aforementioned article on sex in Đà Lạt, a highland tourist resort reemerging from its better colonial days, celebrates local "specialties" that consist of "girls" from the Mekong delta dressing up as young ethnic tribeswomen of the highlands serving local spirits and smokes along with sex. Another article takes the title "Tracing the 'Night

Butterflies'" and chronicles the proliferation of various forms of commercial sex in Ho Chi Minh City, from "landing sites" in Bình Thạnh, to "skirts" in District 3, to "under twenty" next to the cultural center, to "water demons," who may not have looks but can perform water tricks on the Saigon River; from the more pricey call girls and bar girls to the lowliest streetwalkers who perform hand jobs for a pittance across from the Unification Palace.[9]

Underlying this fascinated tone of reporting, which as an act of uncovering resembles the logic of a striptease, is an ambiguous alarm about consequences, about wasted lives, social disorder, and corrupted traditions. The author of "Night Butterflies" takes his readers to "places where the streets are filled with the darkness of night and faces that belong if not to pimps then to thieves, if not to prostitutes then to drug addicts." He goes on to ask, "Could it be that the night belongs to these people?"[10] There is often that tone of discomfort with the contrast between what is presented as the real and some vague notion of the true at times coinciding with notions of Vietnamese culture. The author of the 2002 edition of *Sàigòn by Night* feels compelled to include one piece about children making lanterns for the traditional moon festival among selections that stoke readers' fascination with urban vice.

What has happened to the power of the real in social or political critique? Unlike the earlier reportage of the 1980s, the new reportage seduces with visions of the startling new worlds within one's city or town rather than calling on people's sense of social justice. It deflects rather than holds the authorities, capitalists, or any social group accountable for the things that it does present as problematic. Even on the occasion that justice is demanded in exposés of corruption scandals, or exploitative labor practices, the writing no longer has that rage underlying the critical bite so evident in the earlier reportage of the 1980s exemplified by the "Kneeling Woman." It seems the true, which used to be the revolutionary historical vision held by the party, has been rendered irrelevant by empiricist knowledge needed for governance and by the market as the incarnate of the real. In other words, the empirically real in the new writing no longer has the revolutionary truth held by the party as its formidable foe. In place of revolutionary truth, the government sings the refrain of "maintaining the essence of the nation" (*giữ gìn bản sắc dân tộc*). But the enforcement of such truth pales in comparison to the old revolutionary historical truth enforced by the tentacles of the Leninist vanguard party. The result is a sensibility often caught in that peculiar ambivalence. Take, for instance, a scene covered in a *Sàigòn by Night* volume. The writing tantalizes as it admonishes in an exposé style that claims to uncover social realities most visible by night. A group of young workers from Ryo Export Garment Company wandered the streets between shifts of seasonal overtime. It was two o'clock in the morning, Christmas 2000, near the center of the former capital of South Vietnam, now renamed Ho Chi Minh City. Some were waiting for their shift to start, and others for their boarding house to open in two or three hours. They had nowhere else to go and nothing to do because, as they put it, their "income cannot compare with that of others." Nearby, "Ecstasy T." commented, "With us, there can't be the problem of walking around the whole night without knowing what to do. Buy a ticket to a dance hall to 'exercise,' channel at a bar, scream at a karaoke."[11] The journalist describes dance halls and other places like bars and karaokes as places of the "social evil of prostitution," where pleasure seekers go for the taxi dancers or bar girls, who double as prostitutes (88–89). Yet from the midst of "real" night scenes of seductive consumption, albeit with grossly unequal access, the journalist author laments in the introduction to his collection: "'Searching for myself' in the last years of 19—, I can't see my own form. All I see is the hovering shadow of consumption—the Italian Gucci jeans, the latest models of mobile phones. . . . All I find is the pulsating night of dance floors on fire, of road races, and the narcotic smoke of death." (7). While selling sensationalism in a journalistic realism that convinces readers of its verisimilitude precisely through its dismissal of sanitized views of society, the author feels somehow compelled to make visible a tension between this journalistic real lurking in the shadows of consumers' objects and the true conjured in the lamentation of its absence.

Reflecting a similar ambivalence, another short *Sàigòn by Night* selection describes a table of patrons at a dance hall in the center of Ho Chi Minh City (100–103). A woman had ordered for her table two bottles of Louis XIII, costing VND50 million (a little more than US$3,000). After informing readers of what sums like these could accomplish for poor folks, the author judges, "And all that just for the mad dance steps, the swaying drunken spells," and he asks "When the intoxicant wears off, when the night ends, would you not feel shame like those girls in the 'network of sex-selling models' discovered here recently?" (102). But instead of indignation, the extravagant adjectives, images of intoxication in the shadow of night, and the verbatim phrase from recent news reports of a sex ring of beautiful women at the same dance hall all add up to a power of seduction of the market. The prostitute, as in the governmental designation of her false value necessitating rehabilitation, has become in popular culture a figure that channels a search for truer meanings. The search, however, does not seem to readily yield an answer of any certainty. This feature of market reality as seductive pleasures can be seen playing out in full force with the new commercial films in the early 2000s.

REEL TO REAL: COMMERCIAL SEX AND THE NEW SOCIAL REALISM IN POPULAR FILMS

Similar to recent journalistic reportage, current popular cinema has thrived on the reign of the real, judging by both the content of the films and audience responses to them. The new cinematic verisimilitude is commodified for mass consumption in a full-blown market. *Bar Girls* and its sequel, *Street Cinderella*, the most commercially successful films to date, feature the lives of sex workers. Reflecting the full range of the government's imagination about the social evil of prostitution, these popular cultural productions lay insistent claims to a realism that mimics governmental reliance on empiricist and expert knowledge while it heightens the visibility of contradictions in governmental discourses.

A group from within the Institute of Culture and Information, the research arm of the Ministry of Culture and Information, conducted a survey study of audience response to the *Bar Girls* phenomenon after the release of the sequel. Much of the study revolves around the question of the realism of the two films. The study quotes the comments of

Phạm Thùy Nhân, head of the script department of the same state-owned production company Giải Phóng, complaining that *Bar Girls* brings "shame on us who must look at depraved depictions of what should be the dignity of Vietnamese women."[12] As a defense against such criticism, a psychologist, Nguyễn Hồi Loan, is quoted as saying, "*Street Cinderella* is an extension of a phenomenon that is happening in reality—prostitution—with which we are concerned. . . . Before, few people understood it. People imagined prostitution to be this or that. Coming to see the film, they come to know more about this phenomenon."[13] The study explicitly corroborates such comments by the results of its investigation of audience responses to *Street Cinderella*. The study draws attention to the 66.4 percent of responses that attribute the film's success to its presentation of "a reality that not too many know well." Although the audience was not asked to assess the verisimilitude of the film, the study makes the claim that the 66.4 percent response indicates that the film indeed presents "the real lives [*cuộc sống thật*] of those who live at the bottom of society."[14]

Although the films' director of photography, Phạm Hoàng Nam, gave conflicting comments about the verisimilitude of his projects, realism was enthroned as the goal. At the start of the sequel's filming, Phạm Hoàng Nam said in an interview: "I like to make films that directly penetrate life [*xộc thẳng vào đời sống*]. If *Bar Girls 2* resembles *Bar Girls 1*, it will fail. It [the sequel] must be deeper, 'darker' to reveal the threat in its reality at its deep roots."[15] After the release of the film, however, Phạm Hoàng Nam expressed disappointment in its lack of authenticity: "To depict 'girls' without understanding anything about 'girls' . . . I admit that we made the film in a hasty, arbitrary way for convenience sake, without sufficient understanding of real life."[16] Indeed, there was an empiricist language in the premise of the first *Bar Girls*, a short story titled "Trường hợp của Hạnh" (Hạnh's Case) by Nguy Ngữ, a writer who made a name for himself in the South before its forced unification under socialism in 1976. The script of the first *Bar Girls* was a collaboration between Nguy Ngữ and director Lê Hoàng, whose own credentials as a journalist with the feminine pen name Lê Thị Liên Hoan vouched for the verisimilitude of the film.

The content of both films play on and privilege the empirically real. In *Street Cinderella*, an actress and a bar girl are the two main characters. There is a film inside the film. The actress in this film-in-the-film repeatedly frustrates her director by her inability to project verisimilitude in how a real bar girl might drink, smoke, or seduce her clients. The director threatens to shut down the filming and hire some "real bar girls." At one point, he yells out to his lead actress that she plays a "dead bar girl," to which the actress replies that she will make her character "live" by going out and becoming a bar girl herself, so that she might better embody the real stuff. In her absence, her fiancé falls for a real bar girl, who is transformed like the Cinderella of the film's title. This is the plot around which *Street Cinderella* pivots.

Even more interesting, in *Bar Girls*, the audience encounters a series of deepening levels of reality. *Bar Girls* opens with a crane shot of the Hotel Continental, next to the Opera House, in downtown Ho Chi Minh City, both structures built by the French in their efforts to remake Saigon into a rationally planned colonial city with open vistas that echo Paris. The camera follows two young women in white "traditional" *áo dài* as they set up flower decorations and put up a sign for an international conference on HIV/AIDS, marking out the space of rational knowledge.

The film cuts to a dance hall and introduces the first of the bar girls in the title: Hạnh. Hạnh approaches two men at a table and is asked if she is an "American girl." Hạnh replies, "Arab girl" (*gái Á-rập*). To verify the authenticity of her claim, the men ask if she could belly dance, to which she responds with joyful gyrating moves in a close-up of her midriff. The men agree that she is "the real thing," opening up their negotiation over the price she would charge them for the night. Hạnh is seen here not only as being free to assume an entirely different national/cultural identity in this space where claims are authenticated by commodified sexual performance in an economy of global exoticism, but she is also seen as retaining control over the negotiation of how much her body and labor would be worth. Hoa, the second character, is introduced shaking her head to the music, visibly high on some substance, rebuking a man for not taking her up on her challenge to outdrink him from an outsized bottle of Rémy Martin cognac. The degree of power these women exert over the male pleasure seekers would not be the kind of power they might have over men if they were to perform a traditionalist femininity.

Both Hạnh and Hoa experience a sense of exhilarating freedom in the beginning of the film as they sell sexual labor. Hạnh is drawn in by money, which would both empower her as a consumer and help her support her poor family. Hoa, the daughter of newly rich and absent parents, takes up this work both for thrills and for the money to support her heroin consumption. Both women are seduced by the choices the market offers them as sellers and consumers beyond the confines of their femininity. Their lifestyle is presented with the exhilaration of power fraught with danger.

At the same time as the film presents the dance hall as a space of commodified (primarily masculinist) fantasy where women can take on identities and men can sample these identities, it also tries to convince the audience that this is where real life is happening. Market forces and their juicily sordid choices are the markers of the real. In the film a journalist is planted into this space of the dance hall, trying to report on this scene for her readers. On reading her write-up, her editor berates her for superficiality and sends her back to live and work as a bar girl in order to produce good investigative journalism. So the audience is invited to come along with the journalist through the opening of the dance hall into yet a supposedly deeper level of a social reality as the rest of the film unfolds in the presence/absence of some notion of true cultural values. The audience is invited to walk down dark alleyways where a good girl like the reporter gets beat up by the real bar girls; to see the bar girls' living quarters in neighborhoods not easily accessible even to the police; to see the circumstances in which a bar girl is doused with acid as a punishment, leaving her baby for others to care for; to experience the spaces of pleasure where they lounge with men on beaches, and so on. The audience thus follows the two bar girls to irreducible realities, to Hoa's death by a drug overdose and ending with Hạnh's plea to the HIV/AIDS conference audience to save her life, as she has tested positive for HIV.

From Reality as Feminine to the Feminine Real

From the above discussion, it seems reality is the focus of the new social imagining. But director of photography Phạm Hòang Nam's comments about the "deep, dark" reality hint at something that exceeds the readily accessible. If the reportage of the 1980s relied on such an apprehension of reality through what a journalist could see and hear down on the ground at the local level, the new social realism is marked by this striptease act of the extended revelation of a secret that is more real than a reality accessible via empiricism. If writings in the 1980s challenged official truth with a sense of reality marked by the sign of the feminine, market reality in more recent reportage and in these films is fervently marked by the feminine as well, but with a new twist.

Films like *Bar Girls* that stake a claim on a social realism are often referred to as "phim gái" or "phim trong dòng gái" (films in the genre of "girls").[17] The term *girls* here refers to both young women and prostitutes. There is a conflation of the two in the use of language to describe the new filmic genre of social realism. It is the girls topic that allows the films their claim on realism. From the feminine as empirical and alternative to an official epistemology of the 1980s, the feminine now marks the reality of a market that is believable because of the conflation of the feminine and the market's hidden underside. Reality is recognized as such in its hidden depth and darkness. As in recent reportage, with its numerous references to the night scene marked by the presence of street women as images of "night butterflies," the two films tantalize their audience with promises of the revelation of sex and violence happening under the cover of night. *Bar Girls* and *Street Cinderella* offer many night scenes in which the audience can see bar girls beat up the reporter, sailors on a ship assault the boarding bar girls, pimps and gangs chase a bar girl, a bar girl beat up her madam and clients, or a bar girl shoot the pimps and gangs that pursue her, and so on. *Bar Girls* is the first Vietnamese film that features full frontal female nudity in a night scene of gang sex. It is as if the reality of the market could be apprehended only through the revelation of its secret, its mystery in a surplus existence hidden from mere empiricism aimed at its materiality. Such formulation is similar to the way in which Marx famously commented on "the mystery of commodities" in his discussion of the commodity fetish.[18]

This secret that is the mystery of market reality comes in the form of a feminine presence. This feminine presence has become such a prevalent mode of imagining reality that after stories of sex workers have blazed the way, the mere sign of the feminine can now stand alone, without the explicit sexual content. Director Lê Hoàng confidently announced that even without sex and sex workers, his next film, *Nữ tướng cướp* (Female Bandits), would continue to reap box office successes.[19] He seemed to have had his finger on the pulse of a popular craving for new realities marked by the on-screen presence of women, but often in the form of the exposed female body and its sex. A series of other films followed *Bar Girls* and *Street Cinderella*, such as *Những cô gái chân dài* (Long-Legged Girls) and *2 Trong 1* (Two in One) produced in 2004 and 2005, respectively, by Thiên Ngân Galaxy, the first major private production company in the wake of the success of *Bar Girls*.[20] These films feature the racy lives and tribulations of women caught up in the pleasures and glamour of the market.

If the exposure of the female body marks the reality of the market, the fascination with this mode of representing reality seems to suggest that the feminine real has become the Lacanian feminine Real. In *Bar Girls*, the professor, personifying knowledge, responds to press questions about the causes of the HIV/AIDS crisis: "The HIV/AIDS scourge has exceeded the concern over nuclear weapons. We have the responsibility to issue warnings about this threat. This threat is not coming from environmental issues, or from political hatred, nor is it from ignorance, but from the lack of control over the self, over the pleasures that exceed the bounds of morality." One soon finds out that Hoa, the younger sex worker who injects and dies of an overdose of impure heroine, is the professor's daughter. If reality has previously been imagined at the beginning of marketization as apprehensible via empiricist modes of knowledge, the professor's statement reveals it to exceed such knowledge in the present moment when the market has established itself. The fact that Hoa is his own daughter drives home the point with the force of irony. The threat is posed not by ignorance but by something that breaks the bounds of self-control tied to moral values. If morality marks the true in this symbolic order, reality in this case is marked by an excess in market-generated pleasures. It seems in this new mode of social realism, the market with its reality comes back in full force as the surplus, the remainder, the *jouissance* irreducible to either rational knowledge or cultural values. Žižek identifies this as the Lacanian "'Real' of the global market mechanism," which has detached itself from meaning-generating values within the symbolic order.[21] This tension, this threat, or, one could say, this anxiety has elicited different kinds of efforts to re-enframe the new market reality in meanings. Whether such meanings further promote the market and liberal knowledge or caution against its excesses based on notions of "true" values depends on the agendas of different groups and how they align themselves to profit from the market economy. Instead of some neat dichotomy that could be imagined between market reality apprehensible through empiricism and true Vietnamese cultural values, the new Lacanian twist accounts for the popular fascination with, and the sensationalism of the hidden in, this new genre of social realism of the late 1990s and early 2000s.

One can see these dynamics and the way in which they are gendered in the story of Hoa's overdose. The enjoyment, this Lacanian *jouissance*, in commercial sex cannot be immediately and convincingly cast as that of the sex workers. It is clearly enjoyment on the part of clients, the overwhelming majority of whom are men who have made money using either market mechanism or a combination of market mechanism and political power distributed by the Communist Party in a single-party system. Since the safest way to depict the excess of enjoyment, the market Real, is to shift this enjoyment to the female sex worker, Hoa is presented with a drug habit, the excessiveness of which kills her. Žižek points out that narcotic consumption is a pure *jouissance*, as it does not "take a detour through the symbolic order" but "directly attack[s] our neuronal pleasure centers."[22] As such, drug consumption is an enjoyment purer than the nationalist and class fantasies of masculine erotic consumption taking place in Vietnam, because those fantasies depend on symbolic meanings. In this instance, this pure *jouissance* is staged on the body of the woman. It is she who injects the heroine into her own body. It is she

8.1 First Bar Girls DVD cover

who indulges in enjoyment and dies by its excess. The masculine erotic consumption that fuels the sex market is in this case represented by the excessive enjoyment of the woman whose very body is being consumed in the market. From the male consumption of her body, one arrives at a picture in which the woman is consumed by her own enjoyment. In this way, the Real of the market is conveniently marked in the feminine.

One of the two posters and DVD covers for the film *Bar Girls* visually makes the point about the feminine excess. This poster (figure 8.1) shows a vertical syringe rising out of a pile of one hundred dollar bills, imprinted with the face of Benjamin Franklin. The tip of the syringe needle is poised to penetrate the space between a bar girl's closed legs. One of her two legs is still clothed in a lace stocking. The masculinist erotic fantasy inscribed onto her body in her striptease pose is turned around into something else: She is fucked, not by a penis, but by a phallic syringe rising out of the global market for her own unmediated enjoyment.

The Frustrations of Governance: Symbolic Integration of the Market Real in Bar Girls

The threat this feminine excess poses to a masculinist symbolic order is literalized in the figure of the madam in both films as a man who is perverted by excessive femininity. Rather than represent some liberal statement about the empirical presence in Vietnamese society of trans-gendered persons, both of these madams, or *má mì* (mommies), come to bad ends, paying for their greed and enjoyment in the market as their charges punish them. With the figure of the madam, the two films make visible one mode of the perversion of Vietnamese masculinity. Governmental tourist promotion, Public Security corruption in the sex trade, and acts by men who must live off their women's sex work can easily be read as pimping. The figure of the *má mì* underscores this threat of the perversion of masculinity within a masculinist symbolic order by an excess of the feminine Real.

The second poster (figure 8.2) for *Bar Girls* shows what first appears as a classic virgin-whore split image. Hạnh stands on the left, dressed to kill in a short, side-split hot pink dress and stepping forward with a black high-heeled boot, while Hoa stands on the right, forlorn and innocent in her all-white *áo dài* outfit and straight schoolgirl hair. Rather than the solidity of Hạnh's black boot full of feminine sexual power, Hoa's lower body in the white *áo dài* is blurred in a red smoky glow, as if she were rising out of a phantasm. Wedged in the space between them is the phallic syringe containing a foreign-label cigarette and a dark liquid. If one recalls that it is Hoa who indulges in the drug overdose, then the simple virgin-whore dichotomy demands further analysis. Rather than a temporal and spatial direction of tradition on the left to modernity on the right, or purity to perversion, the reverse is seen. The placement suggests a certain order of reading: the modernity of market reality embodied by Hạnh in the pink dress first, next the socially unmediated excess of enjoyment in the form of the vertical syringe, and then Hoa as the figure of Vietnamese national tradition. The order of placement, suggesting market reality with forms of empowerment and enjoyment, necessitates a nationalist/traditionalist fantasy. The feminine Real, depicted as excessive feminine enjoyment, seems to call for its reintegration into some kind of masculine symbolic order.

But rather than a dichotomous imagination about reality and traditionalist fantasy, the new social realism pits the feminine and irreducible pleasures of the market against two different masculinist symbolic orders, both of which come from governing with a neoliberal global market economy: one based on the true of tradition and the other on the real of empiricist knowledge. *Bar Girls* is more interesting than its sequel because it stages a series of frustrations. It makes gestures toward traditionalist remedies but reveals their failure. The film refutes the effectiveness of the government's use of force in stopping these new dangerous freedoms that have acquired the force of a de facto reality. The police are shown conducting an inspection of the employee registry at the dance hall. At one point, the audience is shown the arrested women in a police jail, with promises of corrective punishment for them. But these police measures neither return the women to respectable life nor remove the danger awaiting them. Their fall toward destruction is only briefly interrupted by promises of love and the return to the innocence of a traditionalist Vietnamese femininity, in other words, by discourse on values true to the Vietnamese nation and its culture. When an overseas Vietnamese man (a *Việt kiều*, as diasporics are called in Vietnam), a sex client, insists on seeing Hạnh as a good girl with true and traditional values after all, she is briefly given a vision of what life could be if she were restored to her "true" self. Hạnh contemplates marrying the man, as she tells her aunt that of course a bar girl could marry only a *Việt kiều*, placing both in the marginal spaces of the nation. It seems her potential redemption into respectable and true Vietnamese femininity could be realistically facilitated only by another marginalized by his distance to the nation as a *Việt kiều* and his lowly profession of dishwasher. It is

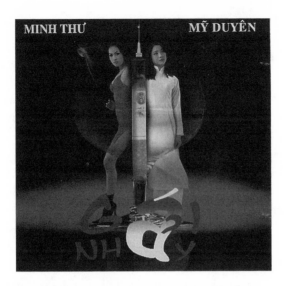

MINH THƯ   MỸ DUYÊN

8.2 Second Bar Girls DVD cover.

for him that she rubs off her butterfly tattoo in the shower while she is with him, and it is because of his sincerity that she looks him up only to find him in what looks like a family scene with a wife and kids. This option, however, remains an ambiguous possibility yet to be realized at the end of the film as he brings a bouquet of flowers to hear her talk at the HIV/AIDS conference.

Similarly, Hoa reenacts a nationalist beginning that remains no more than a fantasy. Awakened by small girls dressed in angelic white after a night during which Hoa has let half a dozen men sleep with her in exchange for heroin, she stumbles into a flock of schoolgirls and their two teachers on the beach. One of the teachers, dressed in the white *áo dài*, chastises Hoa for her whorish outfit and, while tugging down Hoa's top to cover more of her exposed body, offers her another white *áo dài*. Entranced by the apparition of nationalist innocence, Hoa puts on the outfit that has come to signify Vietnamese femininity since colonial times, takes off her wig to reveal jet-black straight schoolgirl hair, and joins the dancing schoolgirls hovering at the water's edge. Seen in the

Benjamin Franklin hundred dollar bills, the Rémy Martin cognac, the American and British cigarettes, the market has also been conveniently marked with the sign of the foreign, partly relieving Vietnamese men of total culpability. Briefly, the audience is invited to substitute dancing girls at the source of the nation for bastardized belly-dancing girls in dance hall spaces of global commodity. These scenes of masculinist nationalist fantasy, however, do no more than give the audience a glimpse of what these wayward lives could be when marked by true Vietnamese values. The beach phantasmic redemption is followed by Hoa's overdose after her revelation to Hạnh that she is HIV positive. The ambulance taking away Hoa's body is shown with a shot from the campsite of the dancing schoolgirls on the beach. The juxtapositioning of the schoolgirls in white and the disappearance of Hoa in the same shot holds the nationalist fantasy in place as a necessary fantasy, a possibility without which there would be only the absolute negativity of death as a result of excessive pleasures.

The severity and finality of these destructive consequences cry out to the audience to contemplate harsh coercive corrective measures like the ones I have discussed with carceral rehabilitation and its traditionalist justifications. But before such measure could become a serious option, carceral rehabilitation is revealed to be futile as the audience finds out after Hoa's death that she had twice gone to drug rehabilitation centers. Neither incarceration nor Vietnamese tradition could save Hoa from the progression of consequences stemming from her lack of control, as her professor father puts it in his statement on the causes of AIDS.

Bar Girls goes on to the other option of the mode of governance that relies on empiricist knowledge and choice. The film does not advocate the suppression of choice as the source of danger and the substitution of model lives and model subjects. Rather, the women undergo a split in their subjectivity: one rooted in the wishful normativity of "Vietnamese traditions," in this case staged in the nationalist fantasy sequence, and one constituted in a proclaimed realism of market choices and the empirical and expert knowledge staged in the form of the HIV/AIDS conference.

In its attempt to integrate the feminine excessive enjoyment underlying the market into a masculinist symbolic order, the film encounters the terms of social imaginings coming from the current paradoxical modes of governance that call both on freedoms in the marketplace and on their suppression in the social realm among certain segments of the population. The result is a series of split subject positions for the women characters. Both films project double images, the mirror inversions of the women. In the films, the women go through rituals of metamorphosis from one kind of woman to another in a series of binaries. In *Bar Girls*, Hạnh swims across the Saigon River to her old aunt's home, where she pours water on herself and is transformed quite completely into a domestic woman nurturing a child. She also rubs off in the shower the butterfly tattoo, called at one point the mark of the devil by her aunt, during the time she spends with the *Việt kiều* who she had hoped would become her husband. Hoa, in the nationalist fantasy at the beach, strips herself of the garments of her trade to metamorphose if momentarily into the innocent Vietnamese girl. *Street Cinderella*, as the title suggests, deliberately plays on transformation and transmutation as the bar girl and the actress trade places.

Beyond this constant splitting and thus shifting back and forth of subject positions by the women characters, however, nothing is resolved. In the last scene of *Bar Girls*, Hạnh makes an appearance before the international audience of the HIV/AIDS conference with which the film opened. This space is marked as masculine in its openness to modern universal knowledge represented by international participants of different races and by the male authoritative professor as its spokesperson. Hạnh shocks the producers of knowledge about HIV/AIDS and public health by insisting that they see her in the makeup and clothes of her work and that they hear her speak out on her own behalf. In the course of her speech, both audiences, at the conference and of the film, learn that she has contracted HIV through her sex work. By challenging them not merely to recognize her but to learn from her as a subject exceeding the object of their liberalist knowledge about those like her in the target population, Hạnh sets up a distance and thus a perpetual and mutually dependent opposition between the producers of empiricist knowledge and their object of knowledge in social realities. The experts can never exhaustively know their object of knowledge because it is also a subject. Hạnh's challenge, however, does not escape the logic of empiricist knowledge itself in the way that Foucault describes in *Discipline and Punish*. As her speech progresses, she becomes increasingly abject with the prospect of her impending death from AIDS and offers herself up as both the object and beneficiary of their knowledge, thus becoming the subject of the discipline that comes with such normalizing bio-knowledge. She promises to quit her sex work and settle down with a man who loves her, alluding both to her willingness to submit to the culturalist normativity of a "traditional" femininity and to her realization of the consequences of the choices she makes as a subject of market freedom. If this seems like a resolution of the paradoxical modes of governance based on empiricism and choice versus tradition and coercion, it does not deliver a happy ending. She ends her speech by imploring the conference participants to find a way to save her life from AIDS, calling out, "I don't want to die." The knowledge she asks for to save her life now shapes her choice to remedy the choices she has made as a subject in the marketplace. But as the audience knows too well, there is no cure for AIDS and existing means of managing the disease most likely would be beyond her financial means. The credits roll and the end music comes on, rendering her plea mute even if her image is held on screen in the silent and repetitive motion of her vocalization. The last frame freezes the despair.

If *Bar Girls* performs the ideological work of reintegrating the feminine Real as the excess of enjoyment in market reality into the two masculinist orders of nationalist fantasy and normalizing knowledge, it also shows the failure of both symbolic orders in different degrees. The nationalist fantasy seems to fail more catastrophically than the empirical knowledge that normalizes through choice. There is no real resolution at the end either in the task of ideological reintegration of the Real into some symbolic order, or in quite reconciling the two symbolic orders at hand, which mirrors the split in governance with public health and rehabilitation measures.

The Way of the Commodity: The New Ideology in Street Cinderella

Coming out in 2004, only a year later, *Street Cinderella* attempts to arrive at an ideological resolution by sidestepping the impasse in *Bar Girls*. First touted with much publicity as *Bar Girls 2*, *Street Cinderella* sharpens a new approach based on the commercialization of both production and the ideological message in the film.

Debates stirred up by *Bar Girls* continued with the publicity and release of *Street Cinderella*. These ranged from complaints of depraved depictions of Vietnamese women to exchanges over the commercialization of Vietnamese cinema. As I have addressed the former in the discussion over the audience's perception of the films' realism, I concentrate here on the exchanges surrounding the commercialization of Vietnamese cinema and the ideological shift to enact the audience members' transformation into middle-class consumers.

From within the state-owned film industry, many criticized Lê Hoàng's use of the sensationalism of sex and women to sell his film, thus lowering the artistic standards of Vietnamese cinema. Others defended the birth of the Vietnamese commercial film that would earn money and thus become less parasitic on state subsidy.[23] Widening the debate, the mentioned report by the Ministry of Culture and Information touts the scientific methods of its investigation and centers the audience in a theoretical argument about "art as process," in which audience members as consumers play a pivotal role, together with investors, intermediaries like critics and marketers, and cultural producers.[24]

This quadripartite model of artistic production curiously assigns a very small role for government censorship, the most pivotal stage in any process of cultural production in Vietnam thus far. Instead, the report steers toward a new standard of censorship by quoting the vice chair of the government management body, the Cinema Section: "The content is not reactionary, so we cannot forbid it."[25] As "reactionary" reads anti-government, anti–Communist Party in Vietnam, it seems there is rising support for an approach to minimal censorship that denies only those works that call for political change. The justification for such an approach is given in the report as the overall governmental policy of the "socialization" of formerly state activities and services, a codeword for turning these domains over to society or marketization. "Socialization of cinema," insists the report, must be "actualized" by stopping the practice of the government's covering production losses, thus the necessity of a commercial success dependent on the reaction of audience members as consumers.[26]

In its effort to insert audience members as consumers into the new model of artistic production, the study counters the criticisms that *Street Cinderella* caters to crass popular desires by citing its findings that 80.1 percent of the film's audience have a university education and above (50). What is even more interesting is the report's emphasis on movie audiences' maturing expectations, which sound like the bourgeoisification of a class of consumers coming out of socialism and the first two decades of market economy. It quotes the director of the National Theater Center extolling the "daily rising needs of the audience for better picture quality, ambience, surroundings, to the service attitude of the staff from the ticket dispensers to the security guards" (44).

The claims of the two films' realism are smoothly grafted onto the new central place of consumers. The report attributes to director Lê Hoàng a "sociological perspective," quoting his insights into the connection between such realism and audience response:

> *Bar Girls* and *Street Cinderella* draw an audience because first of all viewers believe in what is said in the films, like the manner of representation, and finally think about the messages of the films. They believe because although there are mistakes, the issue raised in the film is fundamentally reality. If you understand realism to mean "film whatever there is out there" or "no-avoidance," then you only understand half. The reality of the unfortunate girls always includes their circumstances, way of life, and their desires. If the audience does not empathize with these desires, then the films would not have drawn a large audience.[27]

Again, the Real is not reducible to an empirical reality. And the feminine Real should evoke a sense of identification in audience members and provide a key to their transformation into libidinous market consumers.

While it banks on the continued appeal of, and its claims to, the new social realism, *Street Cinderella* dispenses with the explicit call on empiricist knowledge and nationalist fantasy as solutions to the problem of the market underside. In its place is a consumerist fantasy on several levels of commercialization. The new libidinal economy is reorganized into a story much more formulaic than *Bar Girls*. The production team remained roughly the same, with director Lê Hoàng, director of photography Phạm Hòang Nam, and the state-owned Giải Phóng Films. Given the film's formulaic story, Lê Hoàng went about creating the script himself and dispensed with the writer Ngụy Ngữ. The new story uses the same names of the two main characters from *Bar Girls* but in an entirely different plot. The effect is eerie, as the same ideological impasse from *Bar Girls* is reworked in a parallel universe. The story is set in motion by Hạnh's failure as a professional actress to infuse believability and life into her role as a bar girl. Her acting derided by the fictional director as lacking in authenticity, Hạnh decides to learn by entering the underworld posed as a sex worker. As she endures the humiliations and hardships in the life of a sex worker, Khang Dũng, her pop idol fiancé pays for a night with Hoa, a real bar girl, who slowly conquers his heart not with good tricks but with her heart of gold. In the end, the actress gains the authenticity and anger needed to pull off the make-believe bar girl in her film, and the real bar girl gets the man. The audience is invited to become fascinated with each consumer product that Hoa, the real bar girl, encounters as she becomes initiated into a shopper's paradise through the purchasing power of the successful male pop idol Khang Dũng. The audience watches the bar girl come into her true value, *Pretty Woman*–like, through the visible transformation enabled by classy items that the leading man purchases for her: the expensive boots, the appropriate black dress, the right hairdo, and the right accessories. Without the magic of commodities, Hoa's true value and true self, that is, the Vietnamese girl she has always been, would simply not take form and become visible to her man, to herself, or to the audience.

Marx pointed out that commodities relate to one another in a "social hieroglyphics" that the consumers then decipher.[28] This language of commodities is the new symbolic order into which the Real can be subsumed. Instead of the excessive enjoyment that poses deadly dangers as in the last film, this film shows that the feminine Real can be contained by directing such desires toward some nice things and a heartthrob. As the integration of the Real takes place, it seems the true of the woman's being comes to *be* through a process of subject formation as she works in her delightful bewilderment to decipher the commodity hieroglyphs. The mode of this consumerist subject's interpellation takes the familiar formulaic sentimentalism of a Hollywood romance.

The ideological work in the content of the film is accompanied by product placement for the designer label of Vera Diana, Samsung cellular phones, and the Suzuki Vitara sport-utility vehicle. Market reality indeed includes the familiar global brands that mark out the transnational landscape of daily life. The practice allows the film to draw a bigger profit, which attracts more investors, and in turn liberates it from the socialist system of state-subsidized filmmaking. This is part and parcel of the marketization of Vietnam's film industry. What is noteworthy is the extension of this practice in a manner somewhat similar to the star vehicle from Hollywood. Famous singers, beauty queens, and models in Vietnam often pay filmmakers to star or appear in the new commercial films. The films enhance their price as a pop culture commodity, and their popularity sometimes boosts the receipts of a film. In this case, the male lead, the pop idol Khang Dũng in the film, is played by the real-life pop idol Quang Dũng. The practice of product placement gives viewers the impression that Quang Dũng is the product being placed in the film. The leading man is a mass-market commodity himself, who then initiates the bar girl into the language of commodities. The fantasy of the commodity fills in the place of the fantasy of the true. Hoa is a bar girl with true feminine values, which the right products can help bring out. She is made true in her transformation into a romantic heroine with true love toward her man. He ushers her into an enactment of this fantasy of true love, reified for mass consumption in a stage act replete with lights, smoke, bourgeois and gender-appropriate costumes, and a sappy pop song to the adoration of hundreds in the audience. Hoa, injured by thugs from her life as a prostitute, collapses on stage during their act and is carried, her white dress billowing, by her leading man, down the steps of a glamorous palatial place, away from the crowds and the disappointing gaze of Hạnh, the leading man's actress fiancé. As Hạnh has gained the ability to project authenticity in her film as cultural product, in both Hạnh's and Hoa's transformation verisimilitude effortlessly gives way into reified spectacle. Audience members are invited to share in these sentiments as they consume the filmic product. This identification with the bar girl and her leading man allows for the fantasy to appear as natural desire, rather than governmental discipline as in the first film. The most popular scene by far, according to the above study, is precisely this scene when the pop idol carries the fainted bar girl through adoring crowds after their performance of the sentimental pop song.[29] Lê Hoàng was right in his statement about audience identification with the desires of his "real" characters. In this reified spectacle that draws audience identification, the Vietnamese man at the representational level has undergone a metamorphosis from a sex-consumer culprit for the woman's sexual commodification to the man as a fetishized commodity that could rescue the abject woman and grant her subjecthood through the purchasing power that he earns in the market. This seems to be the more opportune Vietnamese masculinist fantasy, whose workings interpellate the desires and enjoyment of viewers into a sentimentalist consumerism.

CONCLUSION: THE NEW POPULAR CULTURE AND THE QUESTION OF IDEOLOGY

The turn in the new social realism toward sensationalism—the dangerous undertow of excess enjoyment in market freedom—gives some insight into what it is about commercial sex that has captured the imagination of the government and the public. Commercial sex and other vices like drug addiction allow the posing of the dangers of market freedom and spur effort to integrate such freedom into some order at the interrelated policy and symbolic level. In the same way as the containment of market freedom by government must answer to the specific demands of the neoliberal global economy, the new popular culture must answer to the specific demands of a new market for cultural productions at the same time as it must do so within the available discourses of government and the market itself.

Ideology in cultural production used to be the domain of government control in Vietnam. Now there is a separate realm of commercial cultural production that is subjected to less stringent governmental censorship. The split of the representational real and true has a long contentious history with government. Through different periods of socialism, the feminine real acted in various ways as an epistemological challenge and a possible source of critique against the truth issued by the government. In contrast, the current form of the representation of reality takes place within a symbolic field constituted by freedoms in the market and governmental responses using both empirical normalizing knowledge and coercive traditionalist values. This new social realism in the more recent reportage and in popular films offers the kernel of reality as the Lacanian Real in its sensationalist depictions of sex, women, and vice. It proceeds first to gender these pleasures in the feminine and then to integrate them into an order at the symbolic level.

Both the more recent reportage and *Bar Girls* draw on a formulation of the hidden market enjoyment in reality and gender such market Real in the feminine. *Bar Girls* goes on to stage the frustrations resulting from the inadequacy of the dual terms of empiricist and culturalist governance to contain market enjoyment that drive choices. Such frustration sensationalizes market reality at the same time as it reproduces the symbolic terms of the dual modes of governing a neoliberal market in a more conscious, explicit manner. *Street Cinderella*, by comparison, provides a way to capture the enjoyment in the undertow of the market by weaving the empirical real and the traditionalist true into the commodity itself for consumption at a level and in a language more attuned to myth and fantasy. The multilevel fantasy making is signaled by the mechanism of a stage act and a film within the film. Hạnh's stint with empirical reality as a posed bar girl is fetishized into an authenticity reified in the film commodity she is making as an actress. The mark of the real carried by Hoa the real bar girl and the mark of the true in her feminine values are fetishized in expressions of romantic love, brought out by products in visions of consumerist paradise, and staged for mass consumption in the spectacular performance of a sentimental pop song. This approach proves successful in its turn toward the fantasy of commodity at a level more submerged than the comparatively explicit symbolic terms provided by the disciplinary and coercive modes of governance. This film says: the way to deal with the enjoyment in the undertow of market commodity is the commodity fetish itself, into which one can weave the symbolic expressions of the empirical real and the cultural true found in governmental discourses.

The Foucauldian approach to liberal governmentality forecloses the question of ideology prematurely. It claims that liberal governance really takes as its correlate the freedom of subjects to choose; therefore, freedom does not function as a Marxian false consciousness.[30] As a result, there is not enough attention paid to fragmentation at the level of symbolic representation caused by the neoliberal economy's needs for the use of both choice and coercion to produce differentiated labor and segmented access to consumption. Nor is there enough attention paid to ideological constructs in excess of freedom as a governmental notion, such as the justification of traditional Vietnamese femininity. This is where insights into ideology become useful, even if they need to be supplemented. Althusser recognized that investigations into ideology must deal with the structure of representations in which the human subject recognizes itself, hence the importance of the Lacanian process of integration into the symbolic order at the level that seems natural and therefore not entirely conscious.[31] Žižek's insight into ideology is of use because it calls attention to the problem of certain antagonisms around which a society may have to be governed. Žižek does this in a way that addresses the issue of symbolic representation or its failures. He allows for the scenario where "society is always traversed by an antagonistic split," necessitating social-ideological fantasy that would attempt to project society as an organic whole.[32]

The new social realism in current Vietnamese popular culture does not bode well for a basis of social critique or critique against governmental technologies. Whereas Fredric Jameson draws on the Frankfurt School's formulation of mass cultural production as reification into consumable product, he also calls attention to the utopian component of such popular cultural productions. Such utopian dimension can be used to critique by way of making visible the contradictions in the socio-political order through a "realistic faithfulness" to historical facts and attempts to resolve such contradictions.[33] The slightly older form of social realism as seen in the reportage of the 1980s might better fit this description. The limits of this utopianism within realism is of course the reinvigoration of the master narrative to begin with, as seen with the "Kneeling Woman" in the previous chapter. But the current mode of sensational and spectacular social realism has eclipsed the empirical realism of the 1980s. The social realism of today is a far cry from such Jamesonian hopes. The deployment of the language of commodity in the new genre to patch over fragmentations or contradictions at the symbolic level allows the market to be self-referential, short-circuiting the formation of alternative languages. It is not that popular culture in Vietnam can never be a site of contestations and critique, but that perhaps a different language of realism would have to be invented, as the old has become outdated and the new proves capable of translating everything into the monolingualism of commodity.

Looking at the rise of popular culture in Vietnam allows one perhaps to say something more specific about ideology and governance with the neoliberal market: the language of commodity itself can become *the* symbolic order integrating both the enjoyment underlying the freedoms of the market and the terms of their differentiated governance. Ultimately, the most "natural" mode of representation in such a context is that which allows the market to be self-referential in its projections of social fantasy, minimizing the possibilities of critique. The answer to market enjoyment and differentiated governance is given in the hieroglyphs of the commodity fetish as the master language.

Conclusion

AS HANOI WAS PREPARING for a series of Asia Pacific Economic
Cooperation (APEC) summits in the latter half of 2006, the Vietnam
Museum of Ethnology and the Vietnam Revolutionary Museum put on
an exhibit from 16 June to 17 December called "Hanoi Life under the
Subsidy Economy: 1975–1986." APEC is the regional form of a free trade
alliance, putting Asian Pacific countries on the map of global trade.
President George W. Bush was to attend the APEC summit in Hanoi
in November, clearing the way for Vietnam's entrance into the World
Trade Organization (WTO), with its institutionalized neoliberal economics. Vietnam never looked so confidently toward a free and prosperous future. As the Asia Foundation's in-country director Kim Ninh
puts it in the *Wall Street Journal*, "Vietnam's capital city is abuzz with
an unusual spectacle: a museum exhibit that offers a pointed critique
of the country's socialist past."[1] Indeed the temporal and psychical past
was where the exhibit placed the dark ages of the socialist command economy, with all of its deprivation of citizens' desires for material and cultural goods.

As spectators descended into the space of the exhibit, a banner greeted
them with a summation of the "subsidy period" as "a tragi-heroic time
that was also a costly lesson in the law of social development."[2] The
narration highlights an ignorance of empirical and scientific societal
dynamics, paving the way for a backward gaze from a present Vietnamese
location of enlightened knowledge and practices. The subterranean feel
of the dimly lit exhibit space enclosed by earth-tone walls encouraged
an archaeological journey into a layer of memory as sediment. The aestheticization of the displays evoked the tragi-heroic pathos alluded to
by the museum banner. The tragedy of ignorance was matched by the
heroism of the people who withstood the scarcity of goods.

An entire "period" materialized in the viewing of displayed artifacts or recreated spaces of constrained consumption, from rice depots, to bazaar, to living quarters, all allocated according to a distribution system explained in charts as based on rankings of citizens assigned by the state. Snatches of bilingual narration told both domestic and foreign visitors of Hanoians standing in lines from the wee hours of the morning for "moldy, smelly, and wormy rice" and of the heightened desires for goods so rare they acquired a semisacred status. The aesthetically pleasing suspension of these consumers' items suggested such sacred status in the deprived lives of citizens. Spectators saw a precious bicycle suspended in midair and an egg, a bar of Camay soap, and a vial of monosodium glutamate all delicately, elegantly mounted and spotlighted. A set of popular rhymes of the period in large lettering on the wall illustrated an entire libidinal economy revolving around the rarity of goods:

> First, love the man who wears a singlet
> Second, love the man who has dried fish
> Third, love the man who cleans his face with a towel
> Fourth, love the man whose shorts have floral designs.[3]

The lack of choice in consumption was narrated by the exhibit as extending to cultural production. As writers, performers, and other artists "had early on realized the constraints and problems of the reality of life at that time," their "experimentations had met with many difficulties because of a manner of management that bound them in the confines of regimentation."[4] The narration linked the lack of artistic freedom for cultural producers to the lack of freedom for consumers: "Due to a strict and rigid state management of all art forms, a lot of people could not access artwork despite [the artwork's] high artistic and humanistic value."[5] The narration cinched the definition of *freedom* as choice in consumption of material and cultural goods: "The period of *Bao cấp* [subsidy] has been known as a time of hardship, when mechanisms of social-economic management were inappropriate, causing privation in people's material and spiritual life. Productivity was constrained and society stagnated. Humans were limited in their creativity, and they lacked choice in their enjoyment."[6]

The narration of the lack of choice in production and consumption of both material and cultural goods as unfreedom makes evident the current state of freedom enabled by an abundance of goods. Acknowledgement of past unfreedom in nostalgic and tragi-heroic pathos evoked patriotic sentiments, as testified in written comments left by Vietnamese patrons in the exhibit log. One teenager gushed, "I love Vietnam." What the exhibit left unsaid was the very premise upon which such narrative could have been understood: the reorganization of the libidinal economy around a new system of the distribution of goods. At the same time, the exhibit officiated a collective disavowal of the current mix of disciplinary and repressive governmental power sustained by conditions of the neoliberal global economy.

This claim of freedom to produce, to sell, and to consume coincided with the APEC summit and Vietnam's final phases of application into the WTO, symbolic of the complete integration of Vietnam into the regional and global economy based on neoliberal economics. The face of Vietnam that the exhibit put forward to the world asserted a temporal distance between past unfreedom and present freedom, between past scarcity and present prosperity, in short, between past unsuitability for the neoliberal global economy and its fitness for present and future integration.

What was not on display for the eyes of the world was the concurrent rash of arrests in November 2006 and January 2007 of labor organizers who were trying to form an independent trade union called the United Workers-Farmers Organization of Vietnam.[7] These were followed by the high-profile arrests of dissident Catholic priest Nguyễn Văn Lý and two human rights lawyers, Nguyễn Văn Đài and Lê Thị Công Nhân, in February 2007. They were all charged with spreading propaganda against the socialist state. In this media era, images of ongoing unfreedom quickly emerged to compete with the visual message of the Hanoi exhibit putting such things in the past. News clips of Nguyễn Văn Lý's trial in March showed the security police covering his mouth and dragging him out of the courtroom for shouting an antiparty slogan. The image made its way around the world, reproduced in various forms on the multimedia site YouTube.[8] In the wake of the two lawyers' trial in May, news commentators spoke of Hanoi's "zero-tolerance message" to advocates of a multiparty system more conducive for the exercise of political freedom and democracy.[9] It seems Vietnam has two faces when it comes to freedom; I would insist neither is deceptive.

What the case of Vietnam highlights is that governance in current neoliberal globalization may and does take paradoxical forms, sustained not by vestiges of a time passed but by contemporary conditions. Of mutual benefit to both the neoliberal global economy and the ruling party in Vietnam is the use of entrepreneurial and consumer choice differentially among different segments of the population. But also of mutual benefit to both is repression enabled by a ruling party with well-developed apparatuses of coercion from its past. The freedom and unfreedom pair reveals the split personality of the ruling party that enters into the neoliberal global economy.

The rise of commercial sex, its governance and its representation in popular culture, demonstrates well this contemporaneity. The global market brought with it new dynamics hinging on entrepreneurial and consumerist freedoms. Old practices like prostitution now had complex connections to these new dynamics. Sex buying now had to do with entrepreneurs forging personal connections for access to the means of production and exchange in a new economy. Sex consumption also had to do with social stratification, with the emergence of a new class of entrepreneurs and their assertion of class and national identity.

As market dynamics happened outside the central planning of a Leninist state, governors started to perceive them to be part of social and economic laws and regularities autonomous from the state. State officials started to reconceptualize governance as intervention to manage problems in this socioeconomic realm knowable only with expert knowledge. State economic planners and enterprise managers were the first to embrace this new conceptualization of an autonomous socioeconomic realm and its governance through expert intervention by the appropriate government agencies. Others followed. To protect their relevance, factions in the party joined the appropriate government agencies to push for jurisdiction through their participation in the management of such "problems" in the social realm.

Governors from different arms of the government recoded prostitution into an ongoing social problem, with facets to be addressed according to their respective jurisdiction claim. Public health officials claimed they needed to intervene in prostitution to protect the health and well-being of the population. They focused public attention on prostitutes and health threats in order to reach greater numbers of individuals with treatment and health education. Those in Public Security claimed they needed to police prostitution in order to fight crime and ensure social order. They used intervention in prostitution to expand their activities of surveillance. Social work officials claimed they had to incarcerate prostitutes to rehabilitate them. They used their rehabilitation camps to hold up the model of the good woman, "preserving Vietnamese tradition."

Governmental agencies of public health, informed by medicine, controlled the behavior of individuals by making them responsible subjects with choices for their health and well-being. Although they treated lower-class sex workers differently from middle- and upper-class women, state and nonstate health personnel educated individuals and supervised their choices according to the norms of medicine. Health care as such could be taken over by private practice and by the individuals themselves, allowing governors to govern with the market. Medicine as a body of knowledge and practices had its own norms and values from which medical practitioners could criticize government practices like policing.

In contrast, the police made individuals accountable through direct repression. Their claim to expert knowledge depoliticized policing, turning its primary focus to crime fighting. Such claim to expert knowledge was not about teaching this expert knowledge to guide people's choices through persuasion of normative normality as medicine would. Instead, their expert knowledge was to make the police more efficient in their repression to keep law and order. The police did this in ways that would profit them through broader jurisdiction and bribes to protect or actually run hospitality establishments in the market. Far from hampering market activities, the police ensured the functioning of commerce without fostering the liberal subjects of choice among the lower-class sex workers it arrested.

Similarly, the rehabilitation camp was not in the business of producing subjects capable of making choices. Inmates were treated like children in a regime of totalizing education. Imprisonment was a repressive, coercive mode of power; yet it responded to the labor demands of neoliberal globalization. Similar to the other two areas of specialized intervention, rehabilitation as social work referred to knowledge about the socioeconomic environments and their possibilities as they are connected to the global economy. Although its sociological knowledge was not exclusive like the techniques of policing that comprised the domains of police expert knowledge, the state rehabilitation camp held up a model of the good woman, devised as a logical response to socioeconomic demands and making use of what seemed to them local economic opportunities provided by the global economy. This paved the way for the participation in social work by nonstate groups.

The health discipline that relies on an appeal to knowledge and the coercive incarceration as modes of governance existed side by side in Vietnam. Specialized intervention allowed this coexistence by keeping state entities and their tasks separate. Tension exists in this study between an approach that presents, one might say, the necessities of a technology of rule and one that reveals the contingency of conflicts, negotiations, and arrangements among party factions and government agencies. The necessities—specialized intervention that relies on knowledge and market choices—entailed the depoliticization and some privatization of governance. Specialized intervention drew the broad parameters within which groups strategized and innovated in their quest for self-preservation and jurisdiction—the contingent element in this analysis. Specialized intervention did not preclude the use of repressive power in policing or rehabilitative incarceration; nor did it preclude the accompanying justification of fighting crime or promoting national identity. Specialized intervention would allow for those practices as long as these intervention measures came with expert knowledge, which depoliticized (no longer referring to the overt Marxist-Leninist ideology of the state) and paved the way for the government to turn over to entities in society some governing functions, yet ensuring that the overall goals were similar.

Furthermore, government officials in these agencies all profited from their prostitution-related intervention through forms of advancement, jobs, bonuses, or outright corruption. Various sections of the government clearly benefited differently from the equation. For example, Public Health benefited from precisely its emphasis on education of consumerist choices in terms of profit to be made on the health market, but also in terms of grants from international NGOs. The police benefited from a large piece of the pie of commerce related to the very vice and crime they suppress. Rehabilitation benefited from government allocations to run rehab centers, but also from the use of prison labor in subcontracted orders of transnational production.

Above these more narrowly conceived interests, the government as a whole performs ideological functions that help it make use of the transnational market as well as produce differentiated citizens for it. In producing differentiated citizens, the class that would benefit the most and thus would most likely support the ruling party is the class of entrepreneurs and consumers whose rise depended on the Leninist state's possession of the means of production and on its monopolistic power to maximize its profit from such arrangements. If the Hanoi exhibit temporally placed repression in the past, the recent arrests provided contrary evidence that the mode of governing based on freedom of choice would win out over repression in the foreseeable future. They must exist side by side.

This analysis of Vietnam should lead us to reconsider neoliberalism in greater detail. Freedom has been the clarion call of neoliberalism. Among those who examine the question of freedom in neoliberalism, Foucauldians have produced the most in-depth analysis of how power operates in liberal societies. Foucault was critiqued for his earlier notion of the continuum of disciplinary power precluding any meaningful possibility of resistance. As a result, his later work on subjectification as the making of subjects endowed with subjectivity and choice led to a more direct look at liberal government that operates by, and thus produces, the free subject.

Nikolas Rose sees this freedom of the self-interested individual as culminating in the "ethos" of the early period in "the liberal art of government," which in the nineteenth century began to "govern through making people free" in the realm of the market, civil society, and family.[10] Toward the end of the nineteenth century, however, Rose sees the rise of a social imaginary (78–83), discernible in the writings of later liberals like J. A. Hobson and L. T. Hobhouse or the sociology of Émile Durkheim (116). Now, individuals were to realize their pleasures and aspirations "in society" (79). Rose relies on studies into new social strategies of insurance by Jacques Danzelot and François Ewald to argue that the welfare state of the mid-twentieth century culminated at the dusk of this second period of liberal governance, which tried to endow individuals with the conditions to realize their freedom within society (81). Finally, Rose calls "advanced liberalism" the neoliberal/neoconservative governance experienced in the United Kingdom, the United States, and Europe since Margaret Thatcher and Ronald Reagan. This *neoliberal* style of government seeks to revive individual responsibility from its dependence on the welfare state. Rather than a return to laissez-faire or nineteenth-century early liberal government, responsible individualism becomes the code for the active restructuring of social and political relations along the economic model (141). Entrepreneurialism has become the model for both social and governmental entities.[11] For example, schools now are forced to operate within the competitive logic of the market in which teachers and principals must produce the right test scores to receive government funding and to keep their students from going elsewhere. Even an individual is an enterprise. Government downsizing serves both to reduce costs of running society and to make individuals accountable for themselves as entrepreneurs, if not of a firm then at least of themselves as enterprises of human capital. One might say the logic of the market, instead of defending itself against the encroachment of government in the early liberal period of the nineteenth century, has now made the encroachment into government itself. The ends of this enterprising government are to ensure the operation of enterprise in the economic sphere, maximizing the conditions for individuals and firms to make choices and be responsible for their gains and losses.

Although Foucauldian contemplations on styles of liberal governance have been in response to the rise of neoliberalism and neoconservatism in the United Kingdom, the United States, and Europe, and although this line of inquiry has shed much light on the intelligibility of governance in our time, it has not adequately addressed the split personality evident in our difficulty in naming the government under which we live in the United States and the United Kingdom. Is it neoliberalism, or is it neoconservatism? Rose lumps it all under the label "advanced liberalism."

Rose's analysis goes a long way in allowing us to understand new matrices of power in what he thinks is a new diagram of governance, examining everything from the calls to community to Deleuzian nodes of control, and from inclusion and exclusion beyond old disciplinary forms to the management of insecurity.[12] "Community" has been created in such practices of community research, community policing, community development, and so forth and has become the site for government to identify who is to be governed and to work out the relations between governors and the governed.[13] Community bestows civility or withholds it from citizens. Gilles Deleuze has argued that Foucault's work (on individual discipline as a mode of power) was made possible by the dusk of that era.[14] Instead, we have been entering into new matrices of power based on nodes of control through numbers kept and ratings passed and not on individuals per se but aspects thereof, such as assets or the ability to make payments in credit ratings. These new networks determine access to active citizenship.[15]

Most important, in his discussion of the management of insecurity, Rose acknowledges the exclusion of segments of citizens who are barred access to civility via community or via Deleuzian privatized ratings. But strangely enough, the ways in which the homeless, the unemployed, the urban youth, drug traffickers, gang members, migrants, immigrant laborers, and so forth are governed do not present for Rose any fundamental difference to governance organized around notions of freedom, albeit economic freedom. He lumps these illiberal means of coercion under the label of government of insecurity without saying where this insecurity comes from beyond the technologies of community or Deleuzian classification itself. So while acknowledging the rise of prisons in the United Kingdom and particularly in the United States, Rose does not see this as being the innovative counterpart to neoliberal governance, which pushes freedoms in the economic sphere beyond anything we have known. Instead, he writes about the "19th century valorization of self-discipline as the counterpart to political liberty" and "late 20th century valorization of an image of personal freedom marked out in terms such as autonomy, choice, and self-realization as a counterpart to entrepreneurship, innovation and national competitiveness."[16] Even old conservatives in the United States find themselves dismayed by the current neoconservative disregard for individual freedoms inscribed as rights. Mickey Edwards, the former national chairman of the American Conservative Union, for example, laments the "Right's wrong turn," when neoconservatives "fail to place freedom first."[17] This disregard for rights, including the universalist human rights inscribed in the Geneva Convention, seems to have spread from American prisons to American-run prisons in Iraq.

Writing in the vacuum left by the rather bankrupt Left at the end of the cold war, whose history piles with corpses and maimed lives from the Soviet gulag to the Chinese Cultural Revolution, these neo-Foucauldians find themselves unable to leave the safety in the interstices within the liberal system (which does grant limited "freedoms") to go for an explanation outside of the technologies of power themselves. Rose, like other neo-Foucauldian theorists of governance, stakes out a position of inventive politics from within the interstices of the matrices of power in liberalism, using the terrains of freedom therein generated to craft life projects, each with its own telos, a rather understandable if circuitous way back to the basic humanist premise of individual lives as their own ends at a time when such humanist universalism is eroded by neoliberal/neoconservative rule in conjunction with American empire building.[18] While theorists like Rose acknowledge vast numbers of people subjected to vast institutions of confinement, there is no explanation as to why such coercion is at the moment a component of neoliberal rule. It is time we resuscitate a vein of materialist political analysis that would allow for a critique of governance in its particularities.

While indebted to Foucault and Foucauldians for the insights offered by an attention to technologies of rule, I must locate the source of the problem with Foucault in order to push the potentials of this approach. Even the nineteenth-century prisons that Foucault studied in *Discipline and Punish* could not have been counted as part of the carceral continuum that helped to produce and restore the individual to his or her normalized will. Foucault acknowledged the high recidivism rates of prison inmates.[19] But he explained this as a feature of the very carceral system he describes. The failure of prisons to correct inmates and return them to society as individuals restored to their disciplined will, argued Foucault, led often not to the abolition of prisons but to the maintenance or expansion of the penal system.[20] But this disrupts the logic of the continuum. It is much more plausible to recognize that although the prison shares some features with the school or the clinic, it is not a darker version of the latter. In other words, prisons do not often return reformed inmates to the other institutions in society. The prison employs a qualitatively distinct mode of power, one that trains individuals to obey coercion and not to make their own choices, even eventually. Thus, the coercive mode of power in the prison cannot be seen as logically consistent with liberal governance organized around the production of the subject of free choice. It may make more sense to say that it hides behind the "liberal art of government" for particular political agendas.

The case of Vietnam illustrates distinct modes of power that exist side by side, urging us to consider separating the different modes of control rather than subsuming them under an intelligibility. It would then be easier to see how the messy contingencies of politics or economics enter into the equation. Foucault and Foucauldians have often proclaimed their attention to empiricism, the contingencies of the event rather than a structure.[21] Granted, a traditional explanation of political economy has been blind to contingencies and has been too attached to varieties of determinism, breeding dogmatic truths with devastating consequences throughout the twentieth century, including in places like Vietnam. This is what has prompted Foucauldians to drastically curtail structural explanations.

However, the Foucauldian penchant to identify the "episteme," the "discursive formation," the "rationality," and the "mentality" that arise out of social invention and contestation often obscures the plurality of these grids of social imagining, their fragmentary and sometimes utilitarian appropriation directly connected to materialist forces. Perhaps modes of control cannot all be lined up with an entire logic of governance at the level of government. Perhaps it is not just that the model of the economy has been adopted by neoliberal government, but that the requirement of economic arrangements has also been allowed to dictate the different ways in which a particular government conducts the conduct of which segments of its citizenry. The explanation of neoliberalism as an expansion of economic logic into governance could serve as an explanation for such things as privatization of incarceration through subcontracting (the more appalling form of which shows up at Abu Ghraib as interrogation is subcontracted), or the use of prison labor by private companies to offset the costs of running prisons for the government. But the economy-as-model explanation cannot tell us why and which segments of the population must be controlled in this coercive, totalizing mode. Economic globalization and marginalization of certain populations, racialization of the labor force, or even imperialist designs would serve as better exogenous explanations and better bases of social critique. David Harvey, for example, has argued that the current mode of capital accumulation in global capitalism is one by dispossession in which certain people, places, or economic sectors are pushed out of circulation to address crises of overaccumulation.[22] However, it does not seem that all populations are dispossessed in the same way. Although Harvey does not fully develop the connection, his thesis could conceivably be linked to the racialization of different populations for the differentiated labor needs of the transnational economy and for segmented access to consumption. It could also be linked to the militarization and racialization of policing and punishment (i.e., U.S. immigration prisons and overrepresentation of minority races in regular U.S. prisons). Jonathan Simon, for example, has made the connection between globalization and immigration prisons in the United States.[23] Or we could see how the U.S. war on terror globally has necessitated new categories of detention and imprisonment, from more immigration prisons to Guantanamo Bay, where inmates do not fit under any existing subject categories identified by domestic or international laws.

It is no longer news that the neoliberalist transnational economy needs populations with unequal access to wealth so that the mode of flexible accumulation can take advantage of spatial and temporal differences through offshore outsourcing. But what becomes evident in the case of Vietnam is that governing with neoliberalist freedom must differ in its modes of deployment across domestic populations as well as across nation-states. Existing side by side with the government of subjects through the persuasion of their free choice is a much more repressive form of power.

Foucauldian theses dismiss the Marxist argument that ideology is false consciousness by claiming that liberal governance really takes as its correlates the freedom of subjects to choose. But if it is evident from this analysis of Vietnam that we are subjected to different degrees of repression depending on whether we can fill the different ranks of consumers or low-waged labor in the globalized economy, then perhaps we must revisit the question of how we come to imagine our social world and our respective places in it, in other words, the question of ideology. If the prison is not the ignoble truth of liberty, as Rose claims, then the case of Vietnam tells us that it is at least a partial truth.[24] We could look for ideological work in the practices of government. The government in Vietnam used different empirical knowledges to teach women of different classes how to consume health care as well as health and beauty products. Such were the acts of teaching these women their places in their social world and how to behave accordingly. Likewise, the government ideologically interpellated lower-class women in their rehabilitation using a narrative of true Vietnamese tradition, forcing these women to imagine their natural places in the global economy.

Ideological imaginings require symbolic representations. In a market system, symbolization does not reside solely with the government. As Vietnam marketized, the government ceased to be the sole producer of ideology. This becomes evident when the emerging commercial popular culture in Vietnam is examined. As government focused on prostitution to govern market freedom as part and parcel of an empirical social reality, the most commercially successful films to date dealt with social reality in a self-proclaimed realism marked by sexual commerce and the lives of women. Popular cultural representations of reality began to take place within a symbolic field constituted by freedom in the market and the governmental responses using both empirical normalizing knowledge and coercive traditionalist values. A detailed examination of these realist representations marked by the lives of women sex workers yields some insight into market freedom's representation as an empirical reality and its governance beyond the literal confines of government itself.

This examination reveals that neoliberal freedom operates on the reorganization of the libidinal economy. Desires in a world of abundant goods are the premise on which the narrative about past privation as unfreedom is found in the Hanoi exhibit described. The popular films in Vietnam show that such libidinal desires constitute a force that drives market freedom. This force is what remains beyond the actual choices for particular goods. It is a remainder, or, to borrow from Lacan, the Real. It is the excess of this remainder that can readily be signified by such indulgence as the buying and selling of sex.

The popular films also tell us that the language of commodities, the hieroglyphs of the Marxian commodity fetish, can be used both to disarm the dangers of the libidinal market freedom and to sidestep the contradiction in differentiated governance. The impasse in the governance of commercial sex as the symptom of market freedom in the first commercially trail-blazing film *Bar Girls* is resolved in its sequel by turning authenticity in both senses of the real and the true into consumable products, including the filmic product itself.

This examination of market freedom, its governance, and its popular cultural representation tells us why we need a modified Foucauldian approach to governmental imaginings infused with economics and politics, with special attention to the question of ideology. In other words, only by separating the modes of governance can we see the grafting that takes place on exigencies of politics or economics both for the neoliberal global economy and for government. We must be able to see Foucauldian epistemes, rationalities, and mentalities in their plurality and their simultaneity and not just automatically attribute such pluralities to residual contradictions of transitions. We must allow ourselves to see configurations of grafted logics, which in particular contexts at particular points in time respond to exogenous factors of politics and economics. In Vietnam, the response to the introduction of choice in the market has led to the deployment of at least two modes of governance with different justifications, one disciplinary and dependent on expert knowledge about empirical social reality and the other coercive and justified by the authenticity of culture—the real and the true. Both are applied discriminately in relation to gender and class. Thus we cannot say this combination is somehow a necessary response in some structuralist or determinist way. This response is political in that it involves agendas of a ruling government and of the forces in the transnational market.

This approach should enable us to think about governance in a place like the United States. And that we should not be so quick to think freedom is the central organizing principle of governance in the West. It is undeniable that freedom is important in modern governance. But why and how is it important in particular cases? Such questions will have to be empirically studied. Neoliberalist freedom in the marketplace has been politically ensured with greater coercion and suppression against different segments of the population emplaced through racialization or marginalization by the unimpeded market in the United States and the United Kingdom in the past three decades. The expansion of this discussion on governance and freedom in this way would also guard against a cold war or orientalist congratulatory conclusion about how we have freedom and others do not.

Notes

INTRODUCTION

1. David Harvey, *The Condition of Postmodernity* (Cambridge, Mass.: Blackwell, 1990).

2. Pierre Bourdieu, *Firing Back: Against the Tyranny of the Market 2* (New York: New Press, 2001), 9.

3. Jean Comaroff and John L. Comaroff, "Millennial Capitalism: First Thoughts on a Second Coming," in *Millennial Capitalism and the Culture of Neoliberalism*, ed. Jean Comaroff and John L. Comaroff (Durham, N.C.: Duke University Press, 2001), 31, 40.

4. Jürgen Habermas, "The European Nation-State: On the Past and Future of Sovereignty and Citizenship," *Public Culture* 10, no. 2 (1998): 398.

5. Compare Linda Lim, "Capitalism, Imperialism, and Patriarchy: The Dilemma of Third-World Women Workers in Multinational Factories," in *Women, Men, and the International Division of Labor*, ed. June Nash and María Patricia Fernández-Kelly (Albany, N.Y.: SUNY Press, 1983); and Harvey, *Condition of Postmodernity*.

6. Harvey, *Condition of Postmodernity*, 153–56; Harvey, *New Imperialism* (Oxford: Oxford University Press, 2003), 115–24.

7. Chandra Talpade Mohanty, "Women Workers and Capitalist Scripts: Ideologies of Domination, Common Interests, and the Politics of Solidarity," in *Feminist Genealogies, Colonial Legacies, Democratic Futures*, ed. M. Jacqui Alexander and Chandra Talpade Mohanty (New York: Routledge, 1997), 16.

8. Anthony Giddens, *The Consequences of Modernity* (Stanford, Calif.: Stanford University Press, 1990), 55–78.

9. Michael Hardt and Antonio Negri, *Empire* (Cambridge, Mass.: Harvard University Press, 2000); Gopal Balakrishnan, ed., *Debating Empire* (New York: Verso, 2003); Harvey, *New Imperialism*, 26–36.

10. Aihwa Ong, *Flexible Citizenship: The Cultural Logics of Transnationality* (Durham, N.C.: Duke University Press, 1999), 216–17.

11. Michel Foucault, "Governmentality," in *The Foucault Effect: Studies in Governmentality*, ed. Graham Burchell, Colin Gordon, and Peter Miller (Chicago: University of Chicago Press, 1991).

12. Charles Taylor, *Modern Social Imaginaries* (Durham, N.C.: Duke University Press, 2004), 20–21.

13. Ibid., 32.

14. Cited by Harvey, *New Imperialism*, 137.

15. Foucault, "Governmentality."

16. Alan Hunt, "Governing the City: Liberalism and Early Modern Modes of Governance," in *Foucault and Political Reason*, ed. Andrew Barry, Thomas Osborne, and Nikolas Rose (London: University College London Press, 1996), 167.

17. Paul Gordon, "Community Policing: Towards the Local Police State?" in *Law, Order, and the Authoritarian State: Readings in Critical Criminology*, ed. Phil Craton (Philadelphia: Open University Press, 1987), 5.

18. Nikolas Rose, *Powers of Freedom: Reframing Political Thought* (Cambridge: Cambridge University Press, 1999).

19. Ibid., 271. Jonathan Simon, "Refugees in a Carceral Age: The Rebirth of Immigration Prisons in the United States," *Public Culture* 10, no. 3 (1998): 577.

20. See Gareth Porter, *Vietnam: The Politics of Bureaucratic Socialism* (Ithaca, N.Y.: Cornell University Press, 1993); William Turley and Mark Selden, eds., *Reinventing Vietnamese Socialism: Doi Moi in Comparative Perspective* (Boulder, Colo.: Westview Press, 1993).

21. Adam Fforde and Stefan de Vylder, *From Plan to Market: The Economic Transition in Vietnam* (Boulder, Colo.: Westview Press, 1996); Thu-Hương Nguyễn-võ, "Governing the Social: Prostitution and Liberal Governance in Vietnam during Marketization" (Ph.D. diss., University of California, Irvine, 1998); Angie N. Tran, "Global Subcontracting and Its Impacts on the Gender Division of Labor in the Vietnamese Textile and Garment Industries" (paper prepared for the Center for Development Research workshop, Copenhagen, 11–13 June 1998).

22. On the local level, see, e.g., Anne Allison, *Night Work: Sexuality, Pleasure, and Corporate Masculinity in a Tokyo Hostess Club* (Chicago: University of Chicago Press, 1994). On the global level, see, e.g., Kevin Bales, *Disposable People: New Slavery in the Global Economy* (Berkeley: University of California Press, 1999); and Dennis Altman, *Global Sex* (Chicago: University of Chicago Press, 2001).

23. Lauren Berlant, *Intimacy* (Chicago: University of Chicago Press, 2000), 8.

24. Richard Robison, "Neoliberalism and the Future World: Markets and the End of Politics," in *Neoliberalism and Conflict in Asia after 9/11*, ed. Gary Rodan and Kevin Hewison (New York: Routledge, 2006), 28.

25. Ibid., 39.

26. See, e.g., Vedi Hadiz, ed., *Empire and Neoliberalism in Asia* (New York: Routledge, 2006).

27. Aihwa Ong, *Neoliberalism as Exception: Mutations in Citizenship and Sovereignty* (Durham, N.C.: Duke University Press, 2006), 8.

28. For a related discussion with regard to ethnography, see Martyn Ham-

mersley and Paul Atkinson, *Ethnography* (New York: Routledge, 1983), 124–26.

29. Michel Foucault, preface to *The History of Sexuality*, vol. 2, in *The Foucault Reader*, ed. Paul Rabinow (New York: Pantheon, 1984), 335.

30. Following Paul Ricoeur, Hubert Dreyfus and Paul Rabinow call this practice of supplying the hidden motive "the hermeneutics of suspicion," as practiced in Freudian psychoanalysis. Hubert Dreyfus and Paul Rabinow, *Michel Foucault: Beyond Structuralism and Hermeneutics* (Chicago: University of Chicago Press, 1983), 123.

31. Dreyfus and Rabinow suggest that this "interpretive understanding" makes use of the actors' meanings, but the researcher "distances himself from it. This person must undertake the hard historical work of diagnosing and analyzing the history and organization of current cultural practices" (ibid., 124).

32. Michel Foucault, "Questions of Methods," in Burchell, Gordon, and Miller, *Foucault Effect*, 83.

33. Bell pursues the strategy of detaching from "prostitution" bad meanings and attaching good meanings. Shannon Bell, *Reading, Writing, and Rewriting the Prostitute Body* (Bloomington: Indiana University Press, 1994), 2.

1. THE HOOKING ECONOMY

1. For an account of the "mass production of prostitutes" during the Vietnam War by the U.S. war machines and the "liberation" and "emancipation of women" by the socialist revolution, see Arlene E. Bergman, *Women of Vietnam* (San Francisco: People's Press, 1975). Such an account echoes the official line coming from the victorious socialist regime. See, for instance, *Chuyện người đàn bà xin dấu tên* [Story of the Woman Who Must Hide Her Name] (Ho Chi Minh City: Nhà Xuất Bản Phụ Nữ, 1996). Also, Chính Nghĩa, in *Nộc độc văn hóa nô dịch* [Venom Left from a Slave Culture] (Ho Chi Minh City: Nhà Xuất Bản Thành Phố Hồ Chí Minh, 1982), talks about the southern government's "hospitality" to the occupying Americans in providing them with unlimited access to both sex enterprises and to government-organized camps of prostitutes who "meet service standards for foreign guests" (88).

2. *Lịch dử phong trào phụ nữ Việt Nam* [History of the Vietnamese Women's Movement] (N.p., n.d. [late 1970s]).

3. For Marx, the proletarian class is the class that can claim the bare "human title" stripped of civil society's bourgeois relations. See Karl Marx, *Critique of Hegel's "Philosophy of Right,"* ed. J. O'Malley (New York: Cambridge University Press, 1970), 141–42.

4. Vân [pseud.] (head of a private rehabilitation center), interview by the author, Binh Trieu, Vietnam, 14 May 1996; Di [pseud.] (former Women's Union neighborhood leader), interview by the author, Garden Grove, Calif., 28 March 1996.

5. Report on the conference "Mại dâm—Quan điểm và giải pháp" [Prostitution: Perspectives and Solutions], *Khoa Học Về Phụ Nữ* 1 (1999): 36–38.

6. Lê Ngọc Vân, "Mại dâm trẻ em và lạm dụng tình dục trẻ em" [Child Prostitution and Sexual Exploitation of Children], *Khoa Học Về Phụ Nữ* 1 (1997): 37–41.

7. Fforde and Vylder, *From Plan to Market*.

8. David Wank, "Institutional Process of Market Clientelism: Guanxi and Private Business in a South China City," *China Quarterly* 147 (1996): 822–38, 823. See also Dorothy Solinger, "Urban Entrepreneurs and the State: The Merger of State and Society," in *State and Society in China: The Consequences of Reforms*, ed. Arthur L. Rosenbaum (Boulder, Colo.: Westview Press, 1992).

9. See, for instance, "Tệ nạn mua bán dâm và các biện pháp phòng chống tệ nạn mua bán dâm tại Thành Phố Hồ Chí Minh" [The Social Evil of Buying and Selling Sex and Combating Measures in Ho Chi Minh City] (unpublished report, Ho Chi Minh City People's Council and Committee and the Bureau of Science, Industry, and the Environment, 1994).

10. Lê Đức Thúy, "Economic *Doi Moi* in Vietnam: Content, Achievements, and Prospects," in *Reinventing Vietnamese Socialism: Doi Moi in Comparative Perspective*, ed. William Turley and Mark Selden (Boulder, Colo.: Westview Press, 1993), 98.

11. *Asia Yearbook 1987*, ed. Paul Sillitoe (Hong Kong: Far Eastern Economic Review, 1987), 265–66.

12. "Dự thảo báo cáo chính trị của Ban Chấp Hành Trung ương Đảng khóa VII Trình Đại Hội Lần Thứ VIII của Đảng" [Draft Political Report by the Central Committee of the Seventh Congress to the Eighth Party Congress], *Tạp Chí Cộng Sản* 8 (1996): 5–12.

13. Fforde and Vylder, *From Plan to Market*, 243.

14. James Riedel and Bruce Comer, "Transition to a Market Economy in Vietnam," in *Economies in Transition: Comparing Asia and Eastern Europe*, ed. Wing Thye Woo, Stephen Parker, and Jeffrey D. Sachs (Cambridge, Mass.: MIT Press, 1997), 195–200.

15. Porter, *Vietnam*, 128–51.

16. Ibid., 128.

17. Fforde and Vylder, *From Plan to Market*, 7–8.

18. Ibid., 254.

19. Ibid., 12–13. Angie N. Tran, in her study of the textile industry, agrees the process started with bottom-up experimentation and points out that this concept of breaking the fence was first used by Dam Van Nhue and Le Si Hiep back in 1981. Angie N. Tran, "An Analysis of the Developmental State: The Case of the Vietnamese Textile and Garment Industry" (Ph.D. diss., University of Southern California, 1996), 57, 60n. Hy Van Luong also finds piecemeal policies allowing for the gradual emergence of a private sector in the ceramics industry as responses to existent practices. Hy Van Luong, "The Political

Economy of Vietnamese Reforms: A Microscopic Perspective from Two Ceramics Manufacturing Centers," in Turley and Selden, *Reinventing Vietnamese Socialism*, 126–27.

20. Decree 217 in 1987 gave state-owned enterprises' managers "autonomy in management and production decisions, and permitted direct contacts with foreign firms instead of going through many ministers and state officials." A. Tran, "Analysis of the Developmental State," 70. Prime Ministerial Decisions 27/CP, 28/CP, and 29/CP and later the 1991 Law on Private Business recognized different types of private ownership. See ibid., 71–72; and Natalie G. Lichtenstein, *A Survey of Vietnam's Legal Framework in Transition*, Policy Research Working Paper No. 1291 (Washington, D.C.: World Bank Legal Department, 1994).

21. This might be called "state enterprise reform without changing ownership." Danny M. Leipziger, *Awakening the Market: Vietnam's Economic Transition*, World Bank Discussion Paper No. 157 (Washington, D.C.: World Bank, 1992), 23.

22. Fforde and Vylder, *From Plan to Market*, 260.

23. Ibid., 254.

24. "Dự thảo cương lĩnh Đại Hội VII: Xây dựng Chủ Nghĩa xã hội trong thời kỳ quá độ" [Draft Political Platform for the Seventh Party Congress: Building Socialism in the Transition Period], *Tạp Chí Cộng Sản* 1 (1991): 28–35. See also Nguyễn Chơn Trung, "Về việc sử dụng chủ nghĩa tư bản nhà nước tại Thành Phố Hồ Chí Minh," [On the Utilization of State Capitalism in Ho Chi Minh City], *Tạp Chí Khoa Học Xã Hội* 12 (1992): 26–38.

25. "Dự thảo cương lĩnh Đại Hội VII." From 1993 on, the private sector's growth rate had taken off in some areas, but the state sector had steady increases in the share of industrial output, put at roughly 70 percent in 1995 (General Department of Statistics, cited in *Saigon Times*, 21–27 June 1997). The statistics of 1997 showed the state sector to be growing at 8.5 percent, the private at 9.8 percent, and joint ventures (state and foreign) at 22.8 percent (*Diễn Đàn Forum* 66 [September 1997]).

26. Gareth Porter also sees a way to circumvent the inertia of "bureaucratic centralism" in corrupt practices. Porter, *Vietnam*, 137–38. I completely agree with the assessment of deep corruption in the system. However, it was not just bribes to bureaucrats that moved the system. Rather, the bureaucrats themselves had become entrepreneurs with gains at stake in this new game of market economy based on the commercialization of state-owned enterprises. It was a dynamism with costs.

27. Besides vague definitions of legal ownership, especially in the state sector, there were ad hoc interventions by myriad state agencies themselves involved in commercial activities and confusing and contradictory laws and regulations by state planners groping for some economic control (Fforde and Vylder, *From Plan to Market*, 256). See, for instance, Đào Ngọc Lâm, "Problems of Macro-Economic Management at Present," *Nghiên Cứu Kinh*

Tế / Economic Studies 229 (June 1997): 18–23. For example, bank managers, with no clear rules about creditors' rights, could often ignore assessments of financial viability and lend money to even loss-generating enterprises if the right connections and kickbacks were established. Minh Phụng and Epco were cases in point where massive public losses resulted from corrupt practices by lending officials. *Người Việt*, 4 April 1997, 28 April 1997, and 3 June 1997; *Diễn Đàn Forum*, 1 April 1997, 6.

28. Hiếu [pseud.] (private entrepreneur), interview by the author, Ho Chi Minh City, 2 August 1996.

29. A. Tran, "Analysis of the Developmental State," 60.

30. Hiếu, interview, 2 August 1996.

31. Fforde and Vylder, *From Plan to Market*, 268.

32. Many private entrepreneurs had at their disposal small (relative to, say, foreign investment funds) amounts of cash that came from a variety of sources: bank loans taken out on their residences as collateral; pooled savings from relatives and friends, as in the revolving credit clubs (*hụi*); seed capital given by relatives abroad; and even payments on past contracts used as cash accounts before expenses were paid and reinvestment was made.

33. *Statistical Yearbook 1995*, 55.

34. Fforde and Vylder, *From Plan to Market*, 245.

35. While there were only 5,835 new state enterprises registered in 1995 compared to 14,053 new private enterprises, the total "registered capital" of these new state enterprises was VND48.4 billion in 1995 compared to the private enterprises' VND2.2 billion. *Statistical Yearbook 1995*, 45.

36. A 1995 debate in the government centered on the delegated exportation of rice, allowing the state enterprises to charge private sources a "delegation fee" (*phí ủy thác*) of 1–2 percent. The question raised was whether the government would allow private companies to export rice directly, minimizing the difference in the purchasing price from domestic producers and the price on the world market. *Diễn Đàn Forum* 46 (November 1995): 6–7.

37. Đinh Thơm, "Vai trò của nhà nước trong quá trình chuyển thí điểm các doanh nghiệp nhà nước thành công ty cổ phần ở Việt Nam—Những vấn đề cần bàn" [The Role of the State in the Process of Experimental Transformation of Some State-Owned Enterprises into Stock Companies], *Thông Tin Khoa Học Xã Hội* 12 (1995): 23.

38. Hiếu, interview, 2 August 1996.

39. Irregular activities by private companies during the chaotic beginning stages of liberalization up to the mid-1990s included setting up bogus companies to act as clearinghouses for products and services, importing machineries under false pretenses to evade taxation for domestic resale, buying and selling products other than those registered, and exploiting legal loopholes for illegal activities. These activities contributed to the instabilities of the market. See, e.g., Trần Ngọc Dinh, "Thành phần kinh tế tư bản tư nhân ở Thành

Phố Hồ Chí Minh [The Private Economic Sector in Ho Chi Minh City] *Tạp Chí Khoa Học Xã Hội* 13 (1992): 31–39. Given the economic arrangement set up by state policies, these manipulations by private entrepreneurs invariably involved state officials.

40. Lê Minh Triết, "Vài ý kiến về quản lý nhà nước ngành xây dựng" [Comments on State Management of the Construction Industry], *Thời Báo Kinh Tế Sài Gòn* 1 (December 1994).

41. "Đồng chi Tạ Hữu Thanh, Ủy viên Trung Ương Đảng, Tổng Thanh Tra Nhà Nước trả lời phỏng vấn báo *CATPHCM*: Thanh tra phải trở thành tai mắt và công cụ sắc bén chống tham nhũng, tiêu cực," [Comrade Tạ Hữu Thanh, Party Central Committee Member, State Inspector General in an Interview by *CATPHCM* (*Ho Chi Minh City Public Security Magazine*): Inspection Bureau Must Become the Eyes and Ears, as Well as the Sharp Weapons, against Corruption, Negative Acts], *Đặc San Công An Thành Phố Hồ Chí Minh*, 3 August 1996.

42. See also the regular "economic security" columns in the various Public Security publicist organs, for instance, Xuân Xe, "Lấy vốn nhà nước giao tư thương" [Giving State Capital to Private Enterprise], *Đặc San Công An Nhân Dân*, 15 March 1996; Thu Dương, "Lộ chân tướng" [Unmasked], *Đặc San Công An Thành Phố Hồ Chí Minh*, 17 August 1996; Bảo Châu, "Lừa trên 30 tỷ" [The 30 Billion Fraud Scheme], *Đặc San Công An Thành Phố Hồ Chí Minh*, 29 March 1996.

43. Minh [pseud.] (sex worker), interview by the author, Ho Chi Minh City, 19 May 1996.

44. Minh and Hằng [pseud.] (Minh's coworker), interviews by the author, Ho Chi Minh City, 19 May 1996.

45. Compiled from observations and news reports and from interviews with women who worked these scenes: Minh and Hằng (19 and 24 May 1996) and five women at a beachside café in Vũng Tàu (26 and 31 May 1996). See also, e.g., Nhóm Phóng Viên CT-XH, "Cà phê các kiểu" [Café Styles], *Đặc San Công An Thành Phố Hồ Chí Minh*, 29 June 1996; Thanh Hà, "Những quán cà phê gây 'phê'" [Cafés That Can Make You "High"], *Công An Nhân Dân*, 30 March 1996; Sơn Cước, "Vũng Tàu: Bao nhiêu lâu để chấm dứt cuộc chiến này" [Vũng Tàu: How Long Will This Battle Go On?], *Công An Nhân Dân*, 3 June 1996; and Nguyễn Hoan, "Bia ôm ở đâu cũng có" [*Bia ôm* Everywhere], *Công An Nhân Dân*, 4 May 1996.

46. Hiếu, interview, 2 August 1996.

47. Ibid.

48. Hiếu, interview, 4 June 1996. At the time, VND2–3 million was worth about US$200–$300. The contract valued at "a few hundred million dong" was worth a few tens of thousands of U.S. dollars. So the total going into entertainment in this case amounted to more than one-tenth of the contract value.

49. Hiếu, interview, 2 August 1996.
50. Bích Quân, "Bài tổng kết diễn đàn bia ôm, một tệ nạn xã hội cần kiên quyết dẹp bỏ" [Summary of Letters to the Forum: *Bia ôm*, a Social Evil We Need to Abolish Resolutely], *Phụ Nữ Chủ Nhật* (*Phụ Nữ* Sunday edition), 7 July 1996, 5, 8–9.
51. Hiếu, interview, 2 August 1996.
52. See, for instance, Nhóm Phóng Viên CT-XH, "Khi nhà dột từ nóc" [When the Roof Leaks], *Công An Thành Phố Hồ Chí Minh*, 29 May 1996; Nhóm Phóng Viên CT-XH, "Phạm Huy Phước: Quyền lực và sa đọa" [Pham Huy Phuoc: Power and Moral Corruption], *Công An Thành Phố Hồ Chí Minh*, 28 February 1996; and Nhóm Phóng Viên CT-XH, "Bạc tiền giết hết nhân phẩm" [Money Kills Human Value], *Công An Thành Phố Hồ Chí Minh*, 6 March 1996.
53. Lan [pseud.] (married to state-enterprise manager), interview by the author, Ho Chi Minh City, 4 May 1996.
54. Tình, conversation with the author, Ho Chi Minh City, 22 May 1996.
55. Minh and Hằng, interviews, 19 May 1996.
56. Công [pseud.] (entrepreneur), interview by the author, Vũng Tàu, Vietnam, 6 July 2002.
57. Diệu [pseud.] (college instructor), interview by the author, Ho Chi Minh City, 6 May 1996.
58. Hiếu, interview, 2 August 1996.
59. Bích Quân, "Bài tổng kết diễn đàn bia ôm."
60. Nguyễn Trung Thành, "Bia ôm, tôi cứ hỏi vì sao" [*Bia ôm*, I Keep Asking Why], *Phụ Nữ Chủ Nhật*, 12 May 1996, 4, 31.
61. Ngô Vĩnh Long, "Vietnam," in *Prostitution: An International Handbook on Trends, Problems, and Policies*, ed. Nanette J. Davis (Westport, Conn.: Greenwood Press, 1993).
62. Donna Hughes, Laura Sporcic, Nadine Mendelsohn, and Vanessa Chirgwin, *The Factbook on Global Sexual Exploitation* (Coalition Against Trafficking in Women, 1990), http://www.catwinternational.org/factbook/Vietnam.php (accessed 17 April 2007).
63. Rina Jimenez-David, "Anti-Prostitution Ordinance on the Table," *Asia Intelligence Wire* (*Financial Times*) 6 September 2002, http://www.walnet.org/csis/news/world_2002/aiw-020906.html (accessed 17 April 2007).
64. By 2006, the sex tourist industry has grown as well. Establishments range from karaoke bars and massage parlors to five-star hotels that cater to both foreign tourists and rich domestic clients. See, for instance, *Vietnam Economic Times*, "Service Industry," May 2006, 20–21; *Law*, "Ho Chi Minh City Bursts out Ring of Prostitution to Foreigners," 25 May 2005; and Cao Hồng, "Bẽ bàng một kiếp hoa rơi" [Shame on the Life of a Fallen Flower], *Công An Nhân Dân*, 28 July 2005, http://www.cand.com.vn/vi-vn/thoisuxahoi/phongsughichep/2005/7/59418.cand (accessed 1 August 2005).

2. HIERARCHY AND GEOGRAPHY

1. Comaroff and Comaroff, "Millennial Capitalism," 7, 13.

2. On the identity theories of class distinction, see Pierre Bourdieu, *Distinction: A Social Critique of the Judgment of Taste* (New York: Routledge and Kegan Paul, 1984). On performative subjectivity, see Judith Butler, *Gender Trouble: Feminism and the Subversion of Identity* (New York: Routledge, 1990); and Butler, *Bodies That Matter* (New York: Routledge, 1993).

3. Karl Marx and Friedrich Engels, *The Marx-Engels Reader*, ed. Robert Tucker (New York: W. W. Norton, 1978), 220, 473.

4. Poulantzas noted further that "economic relations such as the distinction between productive and unproductive labor are not sufficient to delimit class boundaries." Control of the means of production, together with the political and ideological components, gives a *structural* class determination to those in management and supervision. See Nicos Poulantzas, *Classes in Contemporary Capitalism*, trans. David Fernbach (London: New Left Books, 1975). For a critique of Poulantzas's structuralism, see David Easton, *The Analysis of Political Structure* (New York: Routledge, 1990).

5. Barry Hindess, *Politics and Class Analysis* (Oxford, U.K.: Basil Blackwell, 1987), 37–38.

6. Ibid., 38.

7. Poulantzas, *Classes in Contemporary Capitalism*, 97–98.

8. Hindess, *Politics and Class*, 39–40.

9. Ibid., 40.

10. Bourdieu, *Distinction*, 483 (italics in the original).

11. "Diễn đàn: 'Bia ôm—Vì sao vẫn tồn tại?'" [Forum: "*Bia Ôm*—Why Does It Still Exist?"], readers' column, *Phụ Nữ Chủ Nhật*, 26 May 1996, 4.

12. Hằng, interview, 19 May 1996.

13. Phạm Xuân Phụng, "Bia ôm: Hiện tượng phá rào, hành vi đạp đổ" [*Bia Ôm*: Fence-breaking Phenomenon, Destructive Act], *Phụ Nữ*, 9 June 1996.

14. "Diễn đàn: 'Bia ôm,'" 26 May 1996, 6.

15. Minh and Hằng, interviews, 19 May 1996.

16. Hằng, interview, 19 May 1996.

17. Minh and Hằng, interviews, 19 May 1996.

18. Bourdieu, *Distinction*, 475.

19. Minh and Hằng, interviews, 19 May 1996.

20. *Vietnam Economic Times*, "Service Industry," 20–21.

21. Minh and Hằng, interviews, 19 May 1996.

22. Minh, interview, 19 May 1996.

23. Minh, interview, 24 May 1996.

24. "Diễn đàn: 'Bia ôm,'" 7 July 1996, 4–5; Bích Việt, "Hậu trường bia ôm—Những điều còn chưa nói" [*Bia Ôm* Backstage: Things Not Yet Spoken], *Phụ Nữ*, 7 July 1996.

25. Minh, interview, 19 May 1996.

26. Nguyễn Khắc Hiên, "Kinh tế thị trường và công bằng xã hội" [The Market Economy and Social Justice], *Tạp Chí Cộng Sản* 2 (1994): 36.

27. Bạch Hồng Việt, "Vấn đề giàu nghèo trong cơ chế thị trường" [The Problem of Rich and Poor in the Market Regime], *Tạp Chí Cộng Sản* 8 (1995): 43.

28. Ibid., 45.

29. Ibid.

30. Nguyen Nam Phuong, "Vietnam Struggles to Fight Political Corruption," *Online Asia Times*, 25 May 2005, http://www.atimes.com/se-asia/DE25Ae02.html (accessed 26 May 2005).

31. Barbara Franklin, *Targeting Young Men: Audience-Centered Communication for AIDS Prevention in Vietnam*, Monograph Series no. 4 (Hanoi: CARE International in Vietnam, 1994), 48.

32. Barbara Franklin, *The Risk of AIDS in Vietnam: An Audience Analysis of Urban Men and Sex Workers*, Monograph Series no. 1 (Hanoi: CARE International in Vietnam, 1993), 40.

33. Hiếu, interview, 2 August 1996.

34. Minh and Hằng, interviews, 19 May 1996.

35. Hằng, interview, 19 May 1996.

36. Bourdieu, *Distinction*, 386–87.

37. A series of letters from readers including *bia ôm* clients debated the merits and, of course, demerits of this phenomenon in *Phụ Nữ* through the months of May, June, and July 1996. Of course, denunciations of this activity were overwhelming, in accordance with the official antiprostitution campaign. The obscenity, ugliness, dishonesty, and general vulgarity, however, were somehow disproportionately the responsibility of the *bia ôm* women and not their clients.

38. The vernacular "four pleasures — eat, sleep, fuck, and shit" — are to be understood as vulgar pleasures at the level of bodily functions.

39. David Marr notes that national identity and social discipline and hierarchy came together in the debate over foreign influences. David Marr, "Vietnamese Youth in the 1990s," *Vietnam Review* 2 (1997): 344–45.

40. About this fetish of *áo dài*, Marr writes, "On all occasions when the nation is being presented for foreign scrutiny, for example at international conferences, parades opening sports competitions, films for overseas consumption, ticket counters or hotel desks, women appear in the *áo dài*. In September 1995, a Vietnam Airlines hostess in *áo dài* was voted best dressed participant in an international beauty contest in Tokyo, which stimulated proud domestic comments for months thereafter" (ibid., 344).

41. "Công Ty Du Lịch Hà Nội kiên quyết loại trừ tệ nạn xã hội ra khỏi môi trường du lịch" [Hanoi Tourism Company Is Determined to Eliminate Social Evils from the Tourist Environment], *Người Bảo Vệ Công Lý*, December 1995, 6.

42. See, e.g., Anh Quân, "Chợ người cho khách nước ngoài" [The Human Market for Foreign Guests], *Đặc San Công An Thành Phố Hồ Chí Minh*, 26 May 1996, 11; and Minh Nguyệt, "Điếm deluxe và đêm nhiệt đới" [Whores Deluxe and the Tropical Night], *Công An Nhân Dân*, 23 March 1996. Both are publications of the security police, the former belonging to Ho Chi Minh City Public Security and the latter to the central Public Security organ.

43. Minh and Hằng, interviews, 19 May 1996.

44. Anne McClintock, *Imperial Leather: Race, Gender, and Sexuality in the Colonial Contest* (New York: Routledge, 1995), 354.

45. Xuân Hồng, the five-part weekly series "Từ vũ trường-nhà chứa đến đường dây mại dâm quốc tế" [From Dancing Nightclubs–Whorehouses to International Prostitution Rings], *Công An Thành Phố Hồ Chí Minh*, 27 March 1996–24 April 1996.

46. Among the many cases at the time, that of twenty-year-old ringleader Lâm Thị Bích Thúy received the most publicity. In addition to daily coverage by the public security news organs at the height of the anti-social evil campaign during the first half of 1996, other papers with regular coverage included *Tuổi Trẻ* and *Thanh Niên*. See, e.g., Hoàng Linh, "Lấy chồng đài loan vỡ mộng thiên đường" [Marrying Taiwanese Husbands, Dreams of Paradise Broken], *Tuổi Trẻ*, 3 August 1996; and Thương Hoài Nguyên, "Săn 'gà nước đêm' trên sông Sài Gòn" ["Night Water-Chic": Hunting on the Saigon River], *Thanh Niên*, 21 January 1996. *Tuổi Trẻ* belonged to the Ho Chi Minh City Youth League, and *Thanh Niên* to the Central Youth League. All news organs and journals in Vietnam were either government or party owned.

47. TTV-QT, "Đường dây oan nghiệt" [Vicious Circle], *Đặc San Công An Thành Phố Hồ Chí Minh*, 1992, 33.

48. "Thực hiện cuộc vận động lớn: Thiết lập trật tự kỷ cương trong các hoạt động văn hóa và dịch vụ văn hóa, bài trừ tệ nạn xã hội" [Realizing This Big Movement: Establishing Order, Principles in Cultural Activities and Cultural Services, Eliminating Social Evils], *Tạp Chí Cộng Sản* 2 (1996): 12–14.

49. Ibid. Also compiled from public banners and posters in Ho Chi Minh City and Vũng Tàu and from flyers and poster exhibits at the Ho Chi Minh City Cultural Bureau's "Build and Combat: Exhibition of Government Resolution 87," 1–10 September 1996.

50. See *Những văn bản về phòng chống tệ nạn xã hội* [Official Documents on Preventing and Fighting Social Evils] (Hanoi: Nhà Xuất Bản Chính Trị Quốc Gia, 1995).

51. McClintock writes, "More often than not, nationalism takes shape through the visible, ritual organization of fetish objects—flags, uniforms, airplane logos, maps, anthems, national flowers, national cuisines and architectures as well as through the organization of collective fetish spectacle." McClintock, *Imperial Leather*, 374–75.

52. Since my field research was carried out in the south, I scanned Hanoi

newspapers for the same kind of native or rural appeal in the sex trade. I did find descriptions of such activities. I also checked with a Women's Union officer from the central Hanoi office investigating the issue of prostitution and AIDS and was told that what I found in the south regarding how men sought out exotic pleasures associated with particular geographical places was also common in the northern part of the country (Mỹ [pseud.] [Central Women's Union officer], interviews by the author, Los Angeles and Laguna Beach, Calif., 16–18 March 1997, and Hanoi, 20 July 2002). But I must emphasize that although pleasure-as-native-things had become extremely popular, and has spread across the country, this was certainly not the only form of its commodification.

53. Butler, *Gender Trouble*, 24–25, 134–41.

54. Butler, *Bodies That Matter*, 68. Butler's reworking of her performed subjectivity is the focus of a critique by Timothy V. Kaufman-Osborn, in "Fashionable Subjects: On Judith Butler and the Causal Idioms of Postmodern Feminist Theory," *Political Research Quarterly* 50 (1997): 649–74.

55. McClintock, *Imperial Leather*, 364.

56. Văn Lang, "Cà phê 'de-la-hiên' Sài Gòn: Nơi gặp gỡ của văn hóa đông tây" ["De-la-Hiên" Cafés: Where East Meets West], *Người Việt Online*, 1 October 2006, http://www.nguoi-viet.com/absolutenm/anmviewer.asp?a=49583&p (accessed 2 October 2006).

57. As reported by Marr, "Vietnamese Youth," 343.

58. Ibid.

59. It should be pointed out that this state-sponsored litany of victorious place-names was not the only geography of war. Other place-names, such as Quảng Trị, Kum Tum, Chu-Prong, Asao, Pleime, Dakto, Đồng Xoài, and Bình Giả, had meant the anguish of loss for that part of the population in the South that had memories of the Vietnam War.

60. Hằng, interview, 19 May 1996.

61. Minh, interview, 19 May 1996.

62. "Diễn đàn: 'Bia ôm,'" 26 May 1996, 4–5.

63. Franklin, *Risk of AIDS*, 39.

64. Công, interview, 6 July 2002.

65. Sơn Nam is the author of *Hương Rừng Cà Mau* (The Scent of Camau Jungle), the famed collection of stories about local wisdom that was published in the 1960s, laying Vietnamese claims both on indigenous status in a land long populated by other peoples, including the Khmers, and against foreign knowledge brought in by French colonialism. He invented the term *văn minh miệt vườn* (orchard civilization) and in 1970 authored a book by the same title, which was reissued in Ho Chi Minh City by Nhà Xuất Bản Văn Hóa in 1992. In 1995, he presided over the popular youth newspaper *Tuổi Trẻ*'s forum on the protection and development of national culture.

66. Sơn Nam, "Một khía cạnh của văn hóa xài tiền" [An Aspect of the

Money-Spending Culture], in *An ninh kinh tế và nền kinh tế thị trường Việt Nam—Economic Security and the Vietnamese Market Economy* (Ho Chi Minh City: Nhà Xuất Bản An Ninh Nhân Dân, 1995).

67. Phan Văn Lương, "15 cây số ăn chơi ngày ấy" [Fifteen Kilometers of Eating and Playing in Those Days], *Công An Nhân Dân*, 13 April 1996.

68. Nhóm, "Cà phê các kiểu."

69. Cao Hồng, "Bẽ bàng một kiếp hoa rơi." Similar examples among countless other newspaper reports throughout the 1990s and 2000s include Linh Hoàn, "Đến Bình Dương uống bia . . . thôn nữ" [Come to Bình Dương to Drink Country-Girl Beer], *Công An Thành Phố Hồ Chí Minh* 10 November 2001; Hà Thanh Tú, "Cà phê 'lên bờ xuống ruộng'" [Café "Up the Bank, Down the Rice Field"], *Người Lao Động*, 21 August 2001; and Nhóm PV VHVN, "Karaoke ngoại thành và những nàng 'thôn nữ'" [Suburban Karaoke and "Country Girls"], *Sài Gòn Giải Phóng*, 6 August 2001.

70. Khuất Thu Hồng, Nguyễn Thị Vân, Lê Thị Phương, and Bùi Thanh Hà, *Mại dâm và những hệ lụy kinh tế xã hội* [Prostitution and Its Socioeconomic Corollaries] (Hanoi: Viện Xã Hội Học, 1998), 6.

71. Vũ Quang Việt, "Phát triển kinh tế và phân hóa xã hội" [Economic Development and Social Differentiation], *Diễn Đàn Forum* 49 (1 February 1996): 14–18.

72. *Người Việt*, 24 September 1997.

73. Nhóm, "Cà phê các kiểu."

74. Phan Thế Hữu Toàn, "Tệ nạn mại dâm ở Phú Yên sẽ cáo chung?" [Will the Social Evil of Prostitution in Phú Yên Come to an End?] *Công An Nhân Dân*, 11 May 1996.

75. Khải Quang, "Những con hẻm nổi tiếng nhất Sài Gòn" [The Most Famous Alleys in Saigon], *Công An Nhân Dân*, 26 May 1996.

76. The claim that the rural, the depository of Vietnam's virtuous soul, had been wronged in political and social critique demonstrated its explosive potential in 1997 as peasant demonstrations erupted in the Mekong Delta and in Thái Bình, spreading to other provinces in the north (*Diễn Đàn Forum* 66 [1 September 1997]). Peasants who come to demonstrate in front of government offices in big cities have now become a constant presence. The amount of writing and reportage on rural situations has become increasingly urgent in recent years. Agricultural reforms using the *khoán* system in the late 1980s might have inaugurated economic liberalization and turned Vietnam into a rice exporter, but a rural economic downturn had taken hold as the income gap increased between the city and the countryside.

77. Benedict Anderson, *Imagined Communities: Reflections on the Origins and Spread of Nationalism* (New York: Verso, 1991).

78. Doreen Massey, *Space, Place, and Gender* (Minneapolis: University of Minnesota Press, 1994), 10.

79. Minh and Hằng, interviews, 19 May 1996.

80. Linh [pseud.] (Ho Chi Minh City Women's Union officer), interview by the author, Ho Chi Minh City, 1 June 1996.
81. Mỹ, interview, 17 March 1997.
82. Lê Đức Dục, "Chợ tình mấy nẻo đoạn trường" [The Painful Paths of the Love Market], *Tuổi Trẻ*, 12 October 1996.
83. Nhóm, "Cà phê các kiểu."
84. Hoa [pseud.] (sex worker), interview by the author, Vũng Tàu, Vietnam, 26–27 May 1996.
85. Hà [pseud.] (sex worker), interview by the author, Vũng Tàu, Vietnam, 26 May 1996.
86. Field notes, 31 May 1996.
87. Hà, conversation with the author, Vũng Tàu, Vietnam, 31 May 1996.
88. Field notes, 31 May 1996.
89. Walter Benjamin, *Reflections: Essays, Aphorisms, Autobiographical Writings*, ed. Peter Demetz (New York: Schocken Books, 1978), 156; Alexander Gelley, "City Texts: Representation, Semiology, Urbanism," in *Politics, Theory, and Contemporary Culture*, ed. Mark Poster (New York: Columbia University Press, 1993), 256n, 257n.
90. Massey, *Space, Place, and Gender*, 11.
91. Minh, interview, 19 May 1996.
92. Phương [pseud.] (journalist), interview by the author, Ho Chi Minh City, 4 June 1996.

3. THE RISE OF THE EMPIRICAL AND THE CASE OF MEDICAL EXPERTISE

1. See, for instance, Carl J. Friedrich and Zbigniew Brzezinski, *Totalitarian Dictatorship and Autocracy* (New York: Praeger, 1956), 263–73. To be fair, Friedrich and Brzezinski acknowledge Barrington Moore's point about an "apparent contradiction" in the Soviet Union between scientific decisions as domestic or foreign policy decisions and the recognition of the importance of the autonomy of the sciences. But the authors in the end stress that the "Bolsheviks do not, and perhaps cannot, fully realize the nature of scientific truth, since they make truth a function of the political order" (267).
2. See, for instance, John Kenneth Galbraith, *The New Industrial State*, 2nd ed. (New York: Mentor, 1971); and James Burnham, *The Managerial Revolution: What Is Happening in the World* (New York: John Day Co., 1941).
3. Mark Beissinger, *Scientific Management, Socialist Discipline, and Soviet Power* (Cambridge, Mass.: Harvard University Press, 1988), 286–87.
4. Jeremy Paltiel forwards a similar argument about this inherent tension. Jeremy Paltiel, "China: Mexicanization or Market Reforms?" in *The Elusive State: International and Comparative Perspectives*, ed. James A. Caporaso (Newbury Park, Calif.: Sage, 1989), 261–62.
5. Trường Chinh, the party's theoretician at the time, elaborated this notion

of a cultural revolution to counter the *mission civilisatrice* in a section titled "Kháng chiến về mặt văn hóa" [Resistance in the Realm of Culture] in his 1947 seminal piece "Kháng chiến nhất định thắng lợi" [The Resistance Shall Triumph], in *Lịch sử Đảng Cộng Sản Việt Nam: Trích văn kiện Đảng* [The History of the Vietnamese Communist Party in Party Documents] (Hanoi: Nhà Xuất Bản Sách Giáo Khoa Mác–Lê-nin, 1979), 2:49–143.

6. "Nghị Quyết của Hội Nghị Trung Ương Lần thứ XVI (4–1959) về vấn đề cải tạo Xã Hội Chủ Nghĩa đối với công thương nghiệp tư bản tư doanh" [Resolution of the Sixteenth Plenum (April 1959) on the Socialist Transformation of Capitalist and Private Commercial and Industrial Enterprises], in *Lịch sử Đảng*, 3:29–55.

7. From College of Pedagogy professor Nguyễn Lân's 1958 denunciation of Trần Đức Thảo in the newspaper *Cứu Quốc* (13 April 1958), reprinted in *Bọn Nhân Văn Giai Phẩm trước tòa án dư luận* [The Nhân Văn–Giai Phẩm Clique in the Court of Public Opinion] (1959; Hanoi: Nhà Xuất Bản Sự Thật, 1985), 266.

8. Quoted in Hoàng Văn Chí, *Từ thực dân đến cộng sản* [From Colonialism to Communism], translated into Vietnamese by Mặc Định (Tokyo: Người Việt Tự Do, 1980), 308 (English translation is mine).

9. Phạm Huy Thông's denunciation of Nhân Văn–Giai Phẩm in *Nhân Dân* (5 April 1958), reprinted in *Bọn Nhân Văn Giai Phẩm*, 73.

10. See, for instance, Trường Chinh's writings on building a new culture, including "Kháng chiến nhất định thắng lợi," 2:79–83.

11. Tố Hữu, "Những luận điệu chính trị phản động" [Reactionary Political Arguments], in *Bọn Nhân Văn Giai Phẩm*, 143–55, 151.

12. See, for instance, Như Phong and Phương Dung's denunciations of the Nhân Văn members as "servants to imperial forces" (*Bọn Nhân Văn Giai Phẩm*, 39–44). They denounced a key member in particular, the writer Thụy An, who was said to whore herself to French colonial officials, among her other, if less concrete, connections to hostile outside forces.

13. See in particular V. I. Lenin, "The Economic Basis of the Withering Away of the State," in *State and Revolution*, vol. 2 of *V. I. Lenin: Selected Works* (Moscow: Progress Publishers, 1977), 298–313.

14. Marx, *Critique*, 8, 72–79. In this work, Marx establishes civil society as the "subject," the "real active thing," as opposed to Hegel's universal idea embodied by the state. Marx takes the separation of civil society from the state (thus the dualism of our social and political existence resulting in unequal power) as empirical. He proposes the unity of the two, not in the abstract state, but in a fully realized civil society through universal suffrage and the recovery of bare humanity through the propertyless class, to be later amended by his proposal for the socialization of the means of production. See also Lenin, "Economic Basis."

15. Nguyễn Đình Thi, "Rõ ràng là những âm mưu luận điệu phản cách mạng có hệ thống" [Clearly Those Plots and Arguments Are Systematically

Anti-revolutionary], *Học Tập* (3 March 1958), excerpt reprinted in *Bọn Nhân Văn Giai Phẩm*, 112–15, 113.

16. Bùi Huy Phong's denunciation of Trương Tửu in *Văn Nghệ* (12 May 1958), "Trương Tửu, một tên phản cách mạng đội lốt Mác-Xít" [Trương Tửu: An anti-revolutionary in the guise of a Marxist], reprinted in *Bọn Nhân Văn Giai Phẩm*, 58–63.

17. In *Lịch sử Đảng*, 3:37.

18. Kim Ninh discusses the debate with regard to school curriculum in the latter half of the 1950s. Most prominent was longtime party member and vice minister Nguyễn Khánh Toàn's complaint that existing school curriculum was too "abstract" for the material conditions of Vietnam. According to Toàn, this was a sure sign that schools had not been sufficiently "politicized," resulting in the politicization of the academic disciplines. Kim Ninh, "Revolution, Politics, and Culture in Vietnam, 1945–1965" (Ph.D. diss., Yale University, 1996), 374–78.

19. "Nghị Quyết của Hội Nghị Trung Ương Lần thứ bảy về nhiệm vụ và phương hướng xây dựng và phát triển công nghiệp (tháng 6 năm 1962)" [The Seventh Plenum Resolution on the Tasks and Directions of Industrial Construction and Development (June 1962)], in *Lịch sử Đảng*, 3:239.

20. Ninh, "Revolution, Politics, and Culture," 311–18.

21. Joseph Nogee and Robert H. Donaldson, *Soviet Foreign Policy since World War II*, 3rd ed. (New York: Pergamon, 1988), 28.

22. Ibid., 192.

23. Hòang Minh Chính, "Thư ngỏ của công dân Hòang Minh Chính" [Open Letter from Citizen Hòang Minh Chính], *Đối Thoại* 3 (August 1994): 11–23.

24. Ibid., 15. Hòang Minh Chính was a central figure against whom the party's anti-revisionist campaign was waged. At the time, he held the post of president of the Institute of Philosophy and had just come back from training in the Soviet Union (1957–60).

25. Lê Xuân Tá, "Hồi ức về cuộc khủng bố chủ nghĩa xét lại ở Việt Nam" [Reminiscences on the Terror Campaign against Revisionism in Vietnam], *Đối Thoại* 3 (August 1994): 27–36. Lê Xuân Tá was a chemist assigned to the State Committee for the Sciences at the time.

26. See, for instance, the rational choice approach of Adam Przeworski in *Democracy and the Market* (New York: Cambridge University Press, 1991); and Przeworski, "Problems in the Study of Transition to Democracy," in *Transition from Authoritarian Rule: Tentative Conclusions about Uncertain Democracies*, ed. G. O'Donnell, P. Schmitter, and L. Whitehead (Baltimore: Johns Hopkins University Press, 1986). Although focusing on the compromises among elite groups, O'Donnell, Schmitter, Whitehead also organize elites around rulers who are resistant to change and challengers who advocate change.

27. For instance, Brantley Womack adopts Przeworski's framework in his

analysis of Vietnam's hardliners and reformers, moderates and radicals. Also, David Wurfel talks about the various state organs such as the National Assembly, the press, and the Peasant Union but still uses the analytical barometer of openness to change with regard to the political leadership. David Elliott, however, cautions against "judgements from the outside about the internal politics of reforms" and warns against classifying certain leaders and groups as either conservatives or reformers. In Turley and Selden, *Reinventing Vietnamese Socialism*, see Brantley Womack, "Political Reforms and Political Change in Communist Countries: Implications for Vietnam"; David Wurfel, *"Doi Moi* in Comparative Perspectives"; and David Elliott, "Dilemmas of Reforms in Vietnam."

28. Fforde and Vylder, *From Plan to Market*, 12–13.

29. Ibid., 14.

30. Đặng Phong and Melanie Beresford, *Authority Relations and Economic Decision-Making in Vietnam: An Historical Perspective* (Copenhagen: Nordic Institute of Asian Studies, 1998), 104.

31. "Tệ nạn mua bán dâm và các biện pháp phòng chống tệ nạn mua bán dâm 1993–1994 tại Thành Phố Hồ Chí Minh" [The Social Evil of Buying and Selling Sex and Combating Measures in Ho Chi Minh City, 1993–1994] (unpublished report, in the private official collection of the Ho Chi Minh City Council and Committee and the Bureau of Science, Industry, and the Environment, 1994), 16.

32. In *Philosophy of Right*, Hegel works out the idea that classes and competing particular interests in civil society are to be objectified and universalized by the state. Marx turns Hegel "right side up" by stating that the state is an abstraction of and is determined by civil society. But he agrees civil society moves by the laws of political economy. See G. W. F. Hegel, *Hegel: The Essential Writings*, ed. F. G. Weiss (New York: Harper, 1974); and Marx, *Critique*.

33. See, for instance, Alexis de Tocqueville, *Democracy in America*, trans. G. Lawrence, ed. J. P. Mayer (New York: Doubleday, 1969); Émile Durkheim, *Selected Writings*, ed. Anthony Giddens (New York: Cambridge University Press, 1972); and Talcott Parsons, "Political Aspect of Social Structure and Process," in *Varieties of Political Theory*, ed. David Easton (Englewood Cliffs, N.J.: Prentice Hall, 1966).

34. Michel Foucault, "An Ethics of Pleasure," in *Foucault Live*, ed. S. Lotringer (New York: Semiotext(e), 1989), 261, quoted in Andrew Barry, Thomas Osborne, and Nikolas Rose, eds., introduction to *Foucault and Political Reason*, 9.

35. Foucault, "Governmentality," 95.

36. Ibid.

37. Colin Gordon, "Governmental Rationality: An Introduction," in Burchell, Gordon, and Miller, *Foucault Effect*, 8–9.

38. See, e.g., James E. Dougherty and Robert L. Pfitzgraff Jr., *Contending*

Theories of International Relations, 3rd ed. (New York: Harper and Row, 1990), 90–93.

39. Foucault, "Governmentality," 95.

40. C. Gordon, "Governmental Rationality," 15.

41. Ibid.

42. A genealogy of the welfare state reveals an invention of "the social," as in social welfare programs, in response to problems arising out of early liberal government. Neoliberalism does away with the naturalism of society that characterized early liberalism and substitutes an entrepreneurial model to society and governance. But the premise of society with autonomous (usually economic) dynamics characterizes in the West nineteenth-century early liberal government, the twentieth-century liberal welfare state, and more recently neoliberalism. See, e.g., Jacques Danzelot, *L'invention du social* (Paris: Fayard, 1984); and Graham Burchell, "Liberal Government and Techniques of the Self," in Barry, Osborne, and Rose, *Foucault and Political Reason*.

43. Nikolas Rose, "Governing Advanced Liberal Democracies," in Barry, Osborne, and Rose, *Foucault and Political Reason*, 39.

44. Dreyfus and Rabinow, *Michel Foucault* (Chicago: University of Chicago Press, 1983), 196.

45. Burchell, "Liberal Government," 25.

46. See, for instance, the letter of Hồ Đắc Di, a physician, to the editor regarding the Nhân Văn movement in the official paper *Nhân Dân* (18 May 1958), excerpted in *Bọn Nhân Văn Giai Phẩm*, 267–69. A professor of medicine announced that the "whole medical profession" and the Medical Association of Vietnam "are enraged and join all the classes of the people who agreed and participated in the administrative measures . . . to stop the publication of the journal *Nhân Văn*." Trần Hữu Tước, letter to the editor, *Nhân Dân* (18 May 1958), excerpted in *Bọn Nhân Văn Giai Phẩm*, 269.

47. Trường Chinh, "Kháng chiến nhất định thắng lợi," 2:80.

48. Ibid., 2:81–83. These criteria were first set out in his 1943 piece "Đề cương văn hóa Việt Nam" [Thesis on Vietnamese Culture]. For a careful discussion of Trường Chinh's thesis and his subsequent theoretical elaborations of the party's policy on culture, see Ninh, "Revolution, Politics, and Culture," 54–89.

49. Trường Chinh, "Kháng chiến nhất định thắng lợi," 2:82.

50. "Hội thảo khoa học: Chủ Tịch Hồ Chí Minh với công tác bảo vệ sức khỏe" [Summary of the Scientific Conference on Chairman Ho Chi Minh and the Task of Protecting Health], *Tập Chí Cộng Sản* 515 (March 1997): 60.

51. Ibid.

52. Bùi Mộng Hùng, "Hệ y tế Việt Nam trước thử thách của thực tại: Liên tục và gián đoạn" [Vietnamese Health Care in the Face of Challenges: Continuities and Discontinuities], *Thời Đại* 1 (1997): 54–55.

53. Phạm Ngọc Thạch quoted in ibid., 57.

54. Ibid., 65.

55. Ibid.; and Kim [pseud.] (Ho Chi Minh City physician), interview by

the author, Anaheim, Calif., 27 April 1996. Kim was in the United States for an updated training as a cardiologist.

56. Kim, interview, 26 April 1996.

57. Bùi Mộng Hùng, "Hệ y tế," 65.

58. Ibid., 70, 66.

59. Đỗ Nguyên Phương, "Nâng cao đạo đức của người thầy thuốc" [Raising the Professional Ethics of Physicians], *Tạp Chí Cộng Sản* 7 (April 1997): 21.

60. Hùng, "Hệ y tế," 73–81.

61. Ibid., 75–76.

62. Nguyễn Đăng Thành, "Những yêu cầu của lãnh đạo chính trị đối với nền kinh tế thị trường theo định hướng xã hội chủ nghĩa ở nước ta" [Demands on Political Leadership Facing the Market Economy following the Socialist Orientation in Our Country], *Tạp Chí Cộng Sản* 3 (February 1997): 34.

63. Ibid., 35.

64. Đỗ Nguyên Phương, "Nâng cao đạo đức của người thầy thuốc," 19–21.

65. Trần Độ, *Đổi mới và chính sách xã hội văn hóa* [Reforms and Social, Cultural Policy] (Ho Chi Minh City: Nhà Xuất Bản Thành Phố Hồ Chí Minh, 1988), 27.

66. Ibid., 31.

67. There was a "need to study, research, solve problems posed by the reality of life," writes Phạm Xuân Nam in "Phát huy sức mạnh tổng hợp của các khoa học liên ngành phục vụ sự nghiệp đổi mới đất nước" [Building the Unified Strength of Multidisciplines in the Sciences to Serve the Enterprise of Reform in Our Country], *Tạp Chí Cộng Sản* 2 (January 1997): 9. This was a recurring theme in conversations I had with people working in state agencies. It is notable that a great deal more effort had gone into improving statistics. Courses on how to collect and process data were given to bureaucrats as part of their "supplemental training." In recent years, the General Statistical Office has published statistical yearbooks that have become increasingly hefty from year to year.

68. Ibid., 9–13.

69. Nguyễn Văn Thụy, "Xã hội hóa hoạt động khoa học và công nghệ ở miền núi, vùng sâu, vùng xa" [Socializing Scientific and Industrial Activities in Mountainous and Remote Regions], *Tạp Chí Cộng Sản* 24 (December 1996): 21.

70. Trần Đình Hoàn, "Chính sách xã hội và trách nhiệm của ngành lao động-thương binh, xã hội" [Social Policy and the Responsibilities of the Branch of Labor, Invalids, and Social Work], *Tạp Chí Khoa Học Xã Hội* 19 (1994): 103.

71. Ibid.

72. Kim, interview, 26 April 1996; and N. T., "Sở y tế TPHCM: Nhập nhằng ở đâu?" [The Ho Chi Minh City Health Bureau: Where Are the Tangles?], *Diễn Đàn Forum* 55 (1 September 1996): 12.

73. N. T., "Sở Y Tế TPHCM," 12.
74. Paltiel, "China," 260–61.
75. Rose, "Governing Advanced Liberal Democracies," 40, 46.

4. GOVERNING PASSION

1. Foucault discusses such techniques of discipline in his *Discipline and Punish: The Birth of the Prison* (New York: Vintage, 1995).

2. Ibid., 304.

3. P. V. [Phóng Viên (Reporter)], "Hiểm họa bùng nổ AIDS từ tệ nạn mại dâm" [The Explosive Threat of AIDS from the Evil of Prostitution], *Tuổi Trẻ Chủ Nhật* (*Tuổi Trẻ* Sunday edition), 12 March 1995.

4. Ibid., 32.

5. Xuân, a physician and head of the Ho Chi Minh City AIDS Committee, put it this way: "We anticipate the transmission rate through passive sex—from husbands who shoot up and those who have sexual relations with prostitutes—will increase dramatically." Xuân [pseud.], interview by the author, Ho Chi Minh City, 9 May 1996.

6. The last sentence reads in the original: "Nay thì vợ ông đang mang thai, còn ông ta không đủ can đảm để tránh lây lan cho vợ." P. V., "Hiểm họa AIDS," 33.

7. This use of prostitutes to show the connectedness of the social body across individuals, classes, and generations via disease and birth has been a familiar theme since the latter half of the nineteenth century. Alain Corbin writes of the nineteenth-century fear of syphilis in *Women for Hire: Prostitution and Sexuality in France after 1850*, trans. Alan Sheridan (Cambridge, Mass.: Harvard University Press, 1990). For discussions of the Contagious Disease Acts enforced in parts of England and Ireland between 1864 and 1884, see Linda Mahood, *The Magdalenes: Prostitution in the Nineteenth Century* (New York: Routledge, 1990); and Judith Walkowitz, *Prostitution and Victorian Society* (Cambridge: Cambridge University Press, 1980).

8. Linh, interview, 1 June 1996.

9. Tiến Đạt, "Chợ tình lộ thiên ở Đông Hà-Quảng Trị" [The Open Love Market in Dong Ha, Quang Tri], *Cong An Nhân Dân*, 15 September 1995.

10. Đỗ Hồng Ngọc, interview by the author, Ho Chi Minh City, 16 May 1996.

11. Xuân, interview, 9 May 1996.

12. Hùng [pseud.] (counselor at the Café Condom), interview by the author, Ho Chi Minh City, 8 May 1996.

13. Xuân, interview, 9 May 1996; Ngọc, interview, 16 May 1996; and Huyen [pseud.] (local Women's Union officer in charge of peer education groups in two Ho Chi Minh City districts), interview by the author, Ho Chi Minh City, 4 June 1996.

14. Khuất et al., *Mại dâm và những hệ lụy kinh tế xã hội*, 4, 10.
15. Ibid., 6.
16. Linh, interview, 1 June 1996.
17. Michel Foucault, *The Birth of the Clinic: An Archaeology of Medical Perception* (New York: Vintage, 1994), 197.
18. Field notes, 7 May 1997.
19. Tape recording, abortion ward of ob-gyn hospital, Ho Chi Minh City, 7 May 1996.
20. Field notes, 7 May 1996.
21. For example, Đỗ Hồng Ngọc, head of the Health Information and Education Center, has authored at least one such book. Đỗ Hồng Ngọc, *Viết cho tuổi mới lớn* [For Adolescents] (Ho Chi Minh City: Nhà Xuất Bản Trẻ, 1995).
22. Thúy Ngân, "Vấn đề giáo dục giới tính và bệnh phụ sản ở giới trẻ" [Sex Education and Gynecological Disorders in Youths], *Thanh Niên*, 16 June 1996.
23. I observed that physicians who worked for the Health Bureau, particularly the AIDS prevention units, made extensive use of studies that provided demographic data on sex clients, on their habits and preferences. These sources included, for instance, two CARE International Australia studies prepared by Barbara Franklin, *Targeting Young Men* and *Risk of AIDS in Vietnam*, and an extensive report for health agencies in Vietnam by John B. Chittick, *The Coming Wave—HIV/AIDS in Vietnam: Observations and Recommendations on Ho Chi Minh City's HIV/AIDS Program* (Ho Chi Minh City: John B. Chittick, 1995).
24. Bourdieu, *Distinction*, 483 (italics in the original).
25. McClintock, *Imperial Leather*, 162.
26. Michel Foucault, *The History of Sexuality: An Introduction* (New York: Vintage), 1:123.
27. Frantz Fanon, *The Wretched of the Earth* (London: Penguin, 1963), 47, quoted in McClintock, *Imperial Leather*, 62.
28. Rushdie quoted Macaulay as advocating the formation of "a class of persons, Indians in blood, but English in opinions, in morals, and in intellect," to become "interpreters between us and the millions whom we govern." Salman Rushdie, *The Moor's Last Sigh* (New York: Pantheon, 1995), 376.
29. These kinds of sex education manuals were common in the South before unification with the North in 1976. Many authors of manuals from the mid-1990s on are well known because they had been in the same business in the South before the end of the war. These materials include new manuals by Trần Bồng Sơn and Đỗ Hồng Ngọc and reprints of manuals by Nguyễn Ngọc Bảy.
30. Nguyễn Thành Thông, *Giáo dục giới tính cho thanh niên: Dành cho các bậc phụ huynh* [Sex Education for Adolescents: A Guide for Parents and Guardians] (Ho Chi Minh City: Nhà Xuất Bản Trẻ, 1994), 147.
31. Ibid., 102–9.

32. *Bách khoa phụ nữ trẻ* [An Encyclopedia for Young Women] 5th ed. (Hanoi: Nhà Xuất Bản Hà Nội, 1995), 5–6.

33. Ibid., 177–78.

34. Ánh Nga, *Tâm lý khác biệt giữa nam và nữ* [Psychological Differences between Men and Women] (Đồng Thap, Vietnam: Nhà Xuất Bản Đồng Tháp, 1995), 268–69.

35. A woman official from the Ho Chi Minh City Health Bureau lamented the loss of the old way: "Now we don't pay as much attention to social control. Before, if any husband wandered off the path, all the wife had to do was to go tell the neighborhood Women's Union, and the Union would drag the man up for a lecture that would put him in his place." Hiền, interview, 6 May 1996.

36. *Bách khoa phụ nữ trẻ*, 262.

37. This manner of conduct is reminiscent of the Victorian disappearance act of housewifery that McClintock persuasively presents. She writes, "[The housewife's] parlor game—the ritualized moment of appearing fresh, calm, and idle before the scrutiny of husbands, fathers, and visitors—was a theatrical performance of leisure, the ceremonial negation of her work." McClintock, *Imperial Leather*, 162.

38. Trần Bồng Sơn, *Giáo dục giới tính cho thanh thiếu niên: Người con gái lấy chồng* [Sex Education for Youths: The Girl Who Is Getting Married] (Ho Chi Minh City: Nhà Xuất Bản Trẻ, 1995), 55–56.

5. WHO YOU TRULY ARE

1. *Những văn bản về phòng chống tệ nạn xã hội*, 47.

2. Ong, *Flexible Citizenship*, 216; Jayne Werner, "Gender, Renovation, and State: *Đổi Mới* as Embedded Social Process in Vietnam," in *Gender, Household, State: Đổi Mới in Vietnam*, ed. Jayne Werner and Daniele Belanger (Ithaca, N.Y.: Cornell Southeast Asia Program, 2002), 45.

3. Foucault, "Governmentality"; and Louis Althusser, *Lenin and Philosophy and Other Essays*, trans. Ben Brewster (New York: Monthly Review Press, 1971).

4. Comaroff and Comaroff, "Millennial Capitalism," 7.

5. Foucault, "Governmentality"; C. Gordon "Governmental Rationality."

6. Mai [pseud.] (sex worker), interview by the author, Vũng Tàu, Vietnam, 1 June 1996.

7. Minh, interview, 19 May 1996.

8. Hằng, interview, 19 May 1996.

9. Minh, interview, 19 May 1996.

10. Butler, *Bodies That Matter*, 68.

11. Bích Việt, "Hậu trường bia ôm."

12. See P. V., "Hiểm họa AIDS," 32–33; and the prostitution series in *Phụ Nữ*, May–July 1996.

13. Cao Hồng, "Bẽ bàng một kiếp hoa rơi."

14. *Những văn bản về phòng chống tệ nạn xã hội*, 12–13.

15. Ibid., 12, 14.
16. Ibid., 25.
17. Field notes, 1–2 June 1996.
18. Peer educators, in two groups, interviews by the author, Ho Chi Minh City, 1–2 June 1996.
19. Quang An-Mộc Khoa, "Một nhiệm vụ, hai cách nhìn" [One Duty, Two Perspectives], newspaper title unknown, date unknown [June 1996].
20. Minh and Hằng, interviews, 19 May 1996.
21. Ibid.
22. Hà, interview, 26 May 1996.
23. Minh, interview, 24 May 1996.
24. Minh, interview, 19 May 1996.
25. Ibid.
26. Minh and Hằng, interviews, 19 May 1996.
27. *Vietnam Economic Times*, "Service Industry," 20–21.
28. Althusser, *Lenin and Philosophy*.
29. Foucault, *Discipline and Punish*.
30. Hà, interview, 1 June 1996.
31. Mai, interview, 1 June 1996.
32. Ibid.
33. Hà, interview, 1 June 1996.
34. Mai and Hà, interviews, 1 June 1996.
35. Foucault, *Discipline and Punish*, 219–20.
36. Ibid.
37. Mai and Hà, interviews, 1 June 1996.
38. Hà, interview, 1 June 1996.
39. School instruction of ethics for children was de-emphasized in favor of political education and auxiliary party activities for youths during the socialist years. Since the mid-1990s, the government has been trying to bring it back. This is evident at schools around the country from banners proclaiming the classical priority of correct behavior over academics ("Tiên học lễ, hậu học văn" [Learn first the rites and rituals, then the literature]) and from the enforcement of new school codes and regulations.
40. Mai, interview, 1 June 1996.
41. Hà, interview, 1 June 1996.
42. Warden One, interview by the author, Thủ Đức, Vietnam, 4 June 1996.
43. Ibid.; CARE International in Vietnam, "On the Skills Training for Incarcerated Women Programme, Thủ Đức, Women's Center, October 15, 1995–April 18, 1998" (final report to NOVIB, CARE International in Vietnam, Hanoi, 1998).
44. Mai, interview, 1 June 1996.
45. CARE International in Vietnam, "Skills Training," 11, 31.
46. Ibid., 38.
47. Warden One, interview.

48. Mai, interviews, 27 May and 1 June 1996.
49. Mai, interview, 1 June 1996.
50. Ibid.
51. Warden One, interview.
52. Warden Two, interview by the author, Thủ Đức, Vietnam, 4 June 1996.
53. Chalmers, "Fairer Sex Seeks Fairer Deal."
54. Hồng [pseud.] (an officer of the Central Women's Union in Hanoi), interview by the author, Hanoi, 20 July 2002.
55. Khuất et al., *Mại dâm và những hệ lụy kinh tế xã hội*, 10.
56. Tran, "Global Subcontracting."
57. Louis Althusser, "Ideology and Ideological State Apparatuses," in Althusser, *Lenin and Philosophy*, 162–83.
58. Ibid., 173, 177–79.
59. Võ Khối, "Gái quê trong làng chơi Sài Gòn" [Rural Girls in the Village of Play in Saigon], *Thanh Niên* 157 (1 October 1997): 15.
60. Ibid.
61. Khuất et al., *Mại dâm và những hệ lụy kinh tế xã hội*, 22.
62. Ibid.
63. CARE International in Vietnam, "Skills Training," 25.
64. Thành and Trang [pseuds.] (camp inmates), interviews by the author, Thủ Đức, Vietnam, 5 June 1996; CARE International in Vietnam, "Skills Training," 11.
65. Foucault, *Discipline and Punish*, 264–82.
66. CARE International in Vietnam, "Skills Training," 31.
67. Ibid.
68. Ibid., 30.
69. Trân (CARE International in Vietnam officer), interview by the author, Ho Chi Minh City, 30 July 2002.
70. Vân [pseud.] (head of a private rehabilitation center), interview by the author, Tân Thuận Tây, Vietnam, 21 May 1996.
71. Thi [pseud.] (director at the Shelter), interview by the author, Tân Thuận Tây, Vietnam, 12 July 2002.

6. WHAT KIND OF POWER?

1. Bùi Quốc Huy, interview by Bảo Chân, *Công An Thành Phố Hồ Chí Minh*, 5 June 1996.
2. Hà Thế Cương, "Công tác phòng chống tệ nạn xã hội ở Kiên Giang" [The Task of Preventing and Fighting Social Ills in Kien Giang], *Công An Nhân Dân*, 20 April 1996.
3. See, for instance, Xuân Hồng, "Chặt đứt đường giây mãi dâm quốc Tế" [Severing the Line of International Prostitution], *Công An Thành Phố Hồ Chí Minh*, 23–24 July 1996.
4. Foucault, *Discipline and Punish*, 272.

5. Thân Thanh Huyền, "Góp ý vào văn kiện trình Đại Hội Đảng Toàn Quốc lần thứ VIII: Ba vấn đề mấu chốt để thực hiện thắng lợi nhiệm vụ bảo vệ an ninh chính trị, trật tự an toàn xã hội" [Contributions to Documents to be Presented at the Eighth Party Congress: Three Issues Pivotal to the Successful Realization of the Mission to Protect Political Security and Social Safety and Order], *Công An Nhân Dân*, 2 June 1996.

6. P. V. [Phóng Viên (Reporter)], "Đại hội đảng bộ công an Thành Phố Hồ Chí Minh" [Conference of the Ho Chi Minh City Public Security's Party Organ], *Công An Nhân Dân*, 20 April 1996.

7. Ibid.; and Bùi Quốc Huy, interview.

8. Tiến Triển-Mạnh Thắng, "Công an nhân dân với từ điển bách khoa Việt Nam" [The People's Public Security and the *Vietnam Encyclopedia*], special New Year's issue, *Công An Nhân Dân*, 1996.

9. Ibid.

10. Nancy Travis Wolfe, *Policing a Socialist Society: The German Democratic Republic* (New York: Greenwood Press, 1992), 7.

11. The authorities routinely attributed character failings and criminal activities to links with enemy forces, thus making transgressions crimes against the state. There was a fluidity among the categories of transgressions. It was not at all unusual for the authorities to accuse transgressors of all three at once. See, for instance, the official compilation of denouncements against those involved in the Nhân Văn movement and documents relating to the anti-revisionist campaign, in *Bọn Nhân Văn Giai Phẩm* and "Nghị Quyết của Hội Nghị Trung Ương Lần thứ bảy."

12. Phạm Tâm Long, interview by Phạm Miên, special New Year's issue, *Công An Nhân Dân*, 1996.

13. Ibid.

14. Ibid.

15. Thân Thanh Huyền, interview by Phạm Miên, special New Year's issue, *Công An Nhân Dân*, 1996.

16. "The People's Public Security," said Interior Deputy Minister Phạm Tâm Long, "has been the trusted instrument of, and the place to lean on for, the Party." Phạm Tâm Long, interview.

17. "Công An Thành Phố Hồ Chí Minh góp phần đưa Nghị Quyết Đại Hội 8 của Đảng vào cuộc sống" [Ho Chi Minh City Public Security Contribute to Bringing Resolutions from the Eighth Party Congress into Life], Trần Xuân Trí, Lê Thanh Ngọc and Trương Thanh Sơn, interviews by P. V., *Công An Thành Phố*, 21 August 1996.

18. Thu (public health policy instructor), interview by the author, Ho Chi Minh City, 9 May 1996.

19. For example, the director of a California conservative group, the Criminal Legal Justice Foundation, is quoted as saying of prisoners, "they're there [in prison] because of the choices that they made." Michelle Locke, "'60s Icon Spotlights Prison Reform," *Orange County Register*, 27 September 1998.

20. Thanh (AIDS peer educator), interview by the author, Ho Chi Minh City, 2 June 1996.

21. Hằng, interview, 19 May 1996.

22. Thomas Osborne, "Security and Vitality: Drains, Liberalism, and Power in the Nineteenth Century," in Barry, Osborne, and Rose, *Foucault and Political Reason*, 101.

23. Khuất et al., *Mại dâm và những hệ lụy kinh tế xã hội*, 5–8.

24. Ibid., 43–50.

25. Ibid., 15–16, 53.

26. Warden One and Warden Two, interviews.

27. Field notes, 5 June 1996.

28. Phạm Xuân Nam, "Đổi mới kinh tế-xã hội ở nước ta va mấy vấn đề cấp bách" [Socioeconomic Reforms in Our Country and Urgent Social Issues], *Tạp Chí Khoa Học Xã Hội* 19 (1994): 93. Also see, for instance, Tương Lai, "Tính năng động xã hội, sự phân tầng xã hội trong sự nghiệp đổi mới của nước ta" [The Dynamism of Society and Social Stratification in Our Country's Reforms], *Tạp Chí Khoa Học Xã Hội* 19 (1994): 115–27.

29. The "Reforming Social Policy and the Regime of Social Management" conference was jointly convened by the Program Unit on Sciences at the State Level KX04 and the Ho Chi Minh City Social Science Committee. The papers presented were published in *Tạp Chí Khoa Học Xã Hội* 19 (1994). The "Systematic Utilization of Social Policy and Social Management in Reality" study unit was headed by Trần Đình Hòan, minister of the Ministry of Labor, Invalids, and Social Affairs. See Trần Đình Hòan, "Chính sách xã hội."

30. Bùi Đình Thành, "Những vấn đề cần trao đổi ý kiến trong cuộc hội thảo khoa học thực tiễn về chính sách xã hội tại Thành Phố Hồ Chí Minh" [Discussion Points for the Scientific Conference on Social Policy in Ho Chi Minh City], *Tạp Chí Khoa Học Xã Hội* 19 (1994): 72.

31. Trần Đình Hòan, "Chính sách xã hội," 103.

32. Ibid.

33. CARE International in Vietnam, "Skills Training," 7.

34. Ngọc (head of a Ho Chi Minh City NGO), interview by the author, Ho Chi Minh City, 14 May 1996.

35. Ibid.

36. I obtained background information on the Shelter in interviews with the head of the supporting NGO in Ho Chi Minh City (14 May 1996), the head of another supporting Vietnamese-American charitable group based in the Los Angeles area (27 April 1996), and Mrs. Vân herself (14 and 21 May 1996). Detailed descriptions of the Shelter come from my notes on two days of field observation, 14 and 21 May 1996.

37. Ngọc, interview.

38. Vân (head of a private rehabilitation center), interview by the author, Binh Trieu, Vietnam, 14 June 1996. The Shelter also ran *lớp học tình thương*, or "love classes," which taught basic reading, writing, and arithmetic to chil-

dren in the area who were poor and/or on the street. In addition, a small, separate wing of the compound was reserved for pregnant girls, who would stay until after the births of their babies. Most girls were persuaded to turn over their babies to a group of nuns who would place them in orphanages or homes.

39. Mrs. Vân stressed familial love and empathy in discipline. Even physical "beatings," she said, "have to be done in the right way." She told the story of a girl who caused a big fight and bit her roommate while there was a board meeting at the home. Mrs. Vân said she later that evening lit a bonfire and gathered everyone: "The girl explained that she just lost it and went mad. I asked if then she would agree to three whips. She consented. So I gave her three whips on the buttocks. She agreed to it. Afterward, she even hugged me and cried. I didn't expect it. It was a strange and wonderful moment. She needed our attention, even if it was in the form of a beating. We beat them and punished them, but the attention made them happy. It was that deep and twisted, the psychology involved" (Vân, interview by the author, Binh Trieu, Vietnam, 21 May 2006).

40. Ngọc, interview.

41. Vân, interview, 14 May 1996.

42. Ibid.

43. Ngọc, interview.

44. Ibid.

45. Vân, interview, 14 May 1996.

46. Ibid.

47. Field notes, 14 May 1996.

48. Vân, interview, 14 May 1996.

49. Ibid.

50. Angie Tran notes the tendency in workers to exhaust themselves to earn more by the quantity of pieces they finish in order to make up for loss of income when there are no work orders. Tran, "Global Subcontracting," 8–12.

51. Vân, interview, 14 May 1996.

52. Ibid.

53. Thi, the Shelter's director, interview.

54. Colin Gordon, "Foucault in Britain," in Barry, Osborne, and Rose, *Foucault and Political Reason*, 257.

55. Trần Độ, *Đổi mới và chính sách xã hội văn hóa*, 27.

56. Hà Sĩ Phu, "Biện chứng và ngụy biện trong công cuộc đổi mới" [Dialectics and Specious Reasoning in the Reform Process], in *Trăm hoa văn nở trên quê hương: Cao trào văn nghệ phản kháng tại Việt Nam, 1986–1989* [A Hundred Flowers Still Bloom: The Dissidence Movement in Literature and the Arts, 1986–1989], ed. Trăm Hoa Group (Reseda, Calif.: Nhà Xuất Bản Lê Trần, 1990), 545–46.

57. Lý Chánh Trung, "Thử tìm giải pháp cho một môn học thầy không muốn dạy trò không muốn học" [Let's Find a Solution for a School Subject

That Teachers Do Not Want to Teach and Students Do Not Want to Learn], speech reprinted in *Những vấn đề Việt Nam* [Vietnam: Problems and Issues], ed. Trăm Hoa Group (Garden Grove, Calif.: Nhà Xuất Bản Trăm Hoa, 1992), 366–70.

58. See, for instance, Hoàng Minh Chính, "Góp ý kiến về dự thảo cương lĩnh," [Contributions toward the Proposed Party Platform], in *Những vấn đề Việt Nam*; and Phan Đình Diệu, "Kiến nghị về một chương trình cấp bách nhằm khắc phục khủng hoảng và tạo điều kiện lành mạnh cho sự phát triển đất nước" [Proposal for an Urgent Program to Overcome Crisis and Create Healthy Conditions for the Development of the Country], in *Những vấn đề Việt Nam*, 409–23. Phan Đình Diệu is the founder of the Science and Technology Club, a gathering of scientists who pushed for greater political openness in the late 1980s and early 1990s.

59. C. Gordon, "Foucault in Britain," 257.

60. Osborne, "Security and Vitality," 101.

61. Please see Jon Simmons for a discussion of agonal politics and freedom, where the contestation in the former serves as the condition of possibility for the exercise of the latter. Jon Simmons, *Foucault and the Political* (New York: Routledge, 1995), 116–25.

62. CARE International in Vietnam, "Skills Training," 38–39.

63. Ngọc, interview; Vân, interview, 14 May 1996.

64. Ngọc, interview.

65. CARE project managers reported discussions and demonstration to convince the wardens of the ability of inmates to participate to a greater extent in their education. For camp staff there were also training sessions of CARE methodologies through role modeling by CARE trainers. Care International in Vietnam, "Skills Training," 10, 39.

66. The project report states, "Self-esteem building in any place of incarceration is very difficult." Ibid., 35.

67. Ibid., 39.

68. This scheme was not given permission to operate by the Ministry of Labor, Invalids, and Social Work, even while the camp ran the moneymaking piecework operations. Ibid., 23.

69. Foucault, *Discipline and Punish*.

70. Dreyfus and Rabinow, *Foucault*, 206.

71. C. Gordon, "Governmental Rationality," 5.

72. Graham Burchell, "Peculiar Interests: Civil Society and Governing 'the System of Natural Liberty,'" in Burchell, Gordon, and Miller, *Foucault Effect*, 127.

73. David Hume, *Enquiries Concerning Human Understanding and Concerning Principles of Morals* (Oxford: Oxford University Press, 1975), 228, quoted in Burchell, "Peculiar Interests," 127.

74. David Hume, *A Treatise of Human Nature* (Oxford: Oxford University Press, 1978), 647, quoted in Burchell, "Peculiar Interests," 130.

75. Richard Tuck, ed., introduction to *Hobbes: Leviathan* (New York: Cambridge University Press, 1991), xvii.

76. Ibid., xiv-xviii.

77. Burchell, "Peculiar Interests," 133.

78. Ibid., 137.

79. Isaiah Berlin, *Four Essays on Liberty* (Oxford: Oxford University Press, 1969), 121–22.

80. Thomas L. Dumm, *Michel Foucault and the Politics of Freedom* (Thousand Oaks, Calif.: Sage, 1996), 54.

81. Ibid., 48.

82. Antonio Gramsci, *A Gramsci Reader*, ed. D. Forgacs (London: Lawrence and Wishart, 1988), 210.

83. Marx writes that the "legal relations and forms of state are rooted in the material conditions." Cited by Norberto Bobbio, "Gramsci and the Concept of Civil Society," in *Civil Society and the State*, ed. John Keane (New York: Verso, 1988), 78. Gramsci writes that dominant groups exercise their hegemony and domination through civil society and the juridical government, respectively, the former being the ideological trenches of the latter, yet providing the site of resistance. See Gramsci, *Gramsci Reader*, 306, 234. From Gramsci's dual function of (the laissez-faire) state regulation, Louis Althusser develops his theory of the repressive and ideological functions of the state apparatuses, where the latter maintains the individual's imagined relation to the relations of production. See Louis Althusser, "Ideology and Ideological State Apparatuses," in *Lenin and Philosophy and Other Essays*, 85–126.

84. Dumm, *Foucault and the Politics of Freedom*, 54.

85. The soul, writes Foucault, "is produced permanently around, on, within the body by the functioning of a power that is exercised on those punished—and, in a more general way, on those one supervises, trains and corrects, over madmen, children at home and at school, the colonized, over those who are stuck at a machine and supervised for the rest of their lives." Foucault, *Discipline and Punish*, 29–30.

86. Berlin, *Four Essays on Liberty*, 131.

87. Burchell, "Peculiar Interests," 139.

88. Simmons argues that Foucault's later work on the care of the self, or "aesthetics of existence," as an exercise of self-creation above and beyond subjectifying power requires the conditions of a radicalized liberal democracy. See Simmons, *Foucault and the Political*, 116–25.

89. Dumm, *Foucault and the Politics of Freedom*, 109–12.

90. Warden One, interview.

91. Foucault, *Discipline and Punish*, 264–82.

92. Michelle Locke, "'60s Icon Spotlights Prison Reform," *Orange County Register*, 27 September 1998.

93. Mai and Hà (sex workers), interviews, 1 June 1996.

94. Mai, interview, 1 June 1996.

95. Mai and Hà, interviews, 1 June 1996.

96. Ibid.

97. Care International in Vietnam, "Skills Training," 4, 38.

98. Ibid., 15, 18.

99. This remains speculative based on the ongoing process of the medicalization of wellness training in this camp. At the time of writing, the CARE project had just ended.

100. The camp, said the head warden at the New Center for the Education of Women, "contributes to the establishment of order in society." She also explained to the women that prostitution was wrong because it made "themselves and others sick," whereas the camp provided them with medical help and the prospect of health (Warden One, interview).

101. Foucault, *Discipline and Punish*, 3–31. Foucault later modifies this interpretation of discontinuity in his work by writing that one need not see things in terms of replacement of one mode of power by another, but that "in reality, one has a triangle, sovereignty-discipline-government." Foucault, "Governmentality," 102.

102. Hindess, "Liberalism, Socialism, and Democracy," 76.

7. FROM ANTIGONE TO THE KNEELING WOMAN

1. Kim Ninh very effectively counters the continuity thesis in the scholarship of Nguyễn Khắc Viện, Frances Fitzgerald, and later John Whitmore, to draw attention to the drama and contingency of the revolution. Kim Ninh, *A World Transformed: The Politics of Culture in Revolutionary Vietnam, 1945–1965* (Ann Arbor: University of Michigan Press, 2002), 2–8.

2. Zachary Abuza, *Renovating Politics in Contemporary Vietnam* (Boulder, Colo.: Lynne Rienner, 2001), 52.

3. Tuấn Ngọc Nguyễn, "Socialist Realism in Vietnamese Literature: An Analysis of the Relationship between Politics and Literature" (Ph.D. diss, Victoria University, Melbourne, 2004), 235.

4. Nguyễn Mạnh Tường, "Hai câu chuyện" [Two Tales], *Giai Phẩm Mùa Đông* 1 (December 1956): 49.

5. For more comprehensive accounts of this movement, the individuals involved, and the events of this period, see Ninh, *World Transformed*; and Georges Boudarel, *Cent fleurs écloses dans la nuit du Vietnam: Communisme et dissidence, 1954–1956* (Paris: Éditions Jacques Bertoin, 1991).

6. Ninh, *World Transformed*.

7. Lê Đạt, interview by Thụy Khuê, *Hợp Lưu* 81 (February–March 2005): 29–75.

8. Ibid.; Ninh, *World Transformed*, 121–63.

9. On the study sessions, see Lê Đạt, interview by Thụy Khuê. Articles attacking dissenters appeared in various newspapers and journals more firmly in the party's control. These were later collected in *Bọn Nhân Văn Giai Phẩm*.

10. Lê Đạt, interview, 56; Hòang Cầm, telephone interviews, *Hợp Lưu* 81 (February–March 2005): 81–97.

11. Nguyễn Hữu Đang, telephone interview by Thụy Khuê, *Hợp Lưu* 81 (February–March 2005): 76–80.

12. Trương Tửu's obituary, *Diễn Đàn* 93 (February 2000): 47.

13. Nguyễn Mạnh Tường, interview by Phẩm Trần, "Hạnh ngộ cụ Nguyễn Mạnh Tường" [Encountering Nguyễn Mạnh Tường], in *Trăm hoa văn nở trên quê hương*, 435.

14. Ibid.

15. György Lukács, "Realism in the Balance," in *The Norton Anthology of Theory and Criticism*, ed. Vincent B. Leitch (New York: W. W. Norton, 2001), 1037.

16. Quoted in Nicholas Luker, ed., *An Anthology of the Classics of Socialist Realism: From Furmanov to Sholokhov* (Ann Arbor, Mich.: Ardis, 1988), 18.

17. Trương Tửu, "Tự do tư tưởng của văn nghệ sĩ và sự lãnh đạo của Đảng Cộng Sản Bôn-Sê-Vích" [Writers' and Artists' Freedom of Thought and the Leadership of the Bolshevik Party], *Giai Phẩm Mùa Đông* 1 (December 1956): 64.

18. Quoted by Trương Tửu, "Bệnh sùng bái cá nhân trong giới lãnh đạo văn nghệ" [The Disease of Personality Worship among the Leadership of the Arts], *Giai Phẩm Mùa Thu* 2 (September 1956): 6.

19. Hòang Ngọc Anh, *Xóm thờ Trường Thi* [The Working Neighborhood of Trường Thi] (Hanoi: Nhà Xuất Bản Lao Động, 1975).

20. Tuấn Ngọc Nguyễn, "Socialist Realism," 209.

21. On the poets, see ibid., 209–14. I thank Tuấn Ngọc Nguyễn for these conversations (e-mail communications, 26 April 2007).

22. Trần Đình Sử, "Ngôn từ trong thơ Tố Hữu" [Word Deployment in Tố Hữu's Poetry], *Nhà văn Việt Nam thế kỷ XX* [Twentieth-Century Writers of Vietnam] (1985; repr., Hanoi: Nhà xuất bản hội nhà văn, 1999), 4:634.

23. See Luker, *Anthology*.

24. Quoted in ibid., 20.

25. Phan Khôi, "Phê bình lãnh đạo văn nghệ" [A Critique of the Leadership of the Arts], *Giai Phẩm Mùa Thu* 1 (September 1956): 3–16.

26. The state awards were given in March 2007 to Lê Đạt, Hòang Cầm, Phùng Quán, and Trần Dần, the last two posthumously. Hòang Cầm on this occasion said, "The government has done a beautiful thing, made a beautiful gesture." Hòang Cầm, "Yêu thương và tha thứ là cốt lõi của cuộc sống" [Love and Forgiveness Is the Core of Life], interview in *An Ninh Thủ Đô*, reprinted in *Talawas*, 2 March 2007, http://www.talawas.org/talaDB/showFile.php?res=9358&rb=0102 (accessed 13 April 2007). Likewise, Lê Đạt called this award a "beautiful gesture on the part of the authorities." See T. Văn, "Nghĩ về những 'cử chỉ đẹp' của nhà nước" [Thinking about the Beautiful Gestures of the Government], *Talawas*, 27 March 2007, http://www.talawas.org/talaDB/showFile.php?res=9577&rb=0102 (accessed 13 April 2007).

27. Hòang Cầm, *Bên kia sông đuống* (Hanoi: Nhà Xuất Bản Văn Nghệ, 1956), 49–52, cited by Nguyễn Tấn Hưng, letter to *Talawas*, 13 April 2007, http://www.talawas.org/talaDB/showThu.php?res=9735&rb=12&von=20 (accessed 13 April 2007).

28. Hilary Chung, ed., "Introduction: Socialist Realism," in *In the Party Spirit: Socialist Realism and Literary Practice in the Soviet Union, East Germany and China*, Critical Studies 6 (Amsterdam: Editions Rodopi, 1994), xii.

29. Ibid.

30. Quoted in Luker, *Anthology*, 18.

31. Nguyễn Kiến Giang, "Bàn về sự lãnh đạo của đảng" [On the Party's Leadership], in *Tuyển tập Nguyễn Kiến Giang* [Nguyễn Kiến Giang: Selected Writings] (Garden Grove, Calif.: Nhà Xuất Bản Trăm Hoa, 1993), 71.

32. V. I. Lenin, *What Is to Be Done?* (1902; repr., Moscow: Progress Publishers, 1973), 125.

33. Joseph Stalin, *Foundations of Leninism* (New York: International Publishers, 1939), 110.

34. Lê Đạt, "Làm thơ" [To Write Poetry], *Giai Phẩm Mùa Xuân*, February 1956, 3–4.

35. Phùng Quán, "Chống tham ô lãng phí" [Against Corruption and Waste], *Giai Phẩm Mùa Thu* 2 (September 1956): 39–42.

36. Slavoj Žižek, *The Sublime Object of Ideology* (London: Verso, 1989), 218–19.

37. Nguyễn Mạnh Tường, interview in "Mở rộng tự do và dân chủ" [Expanding Freedom and Democracy], *Nhân Văn* 1 (20 September 1965): 1; Trần Đốc Thảo, "Nội dung xã hội và hình thức tự do" [Social Content and the Form of Freedom], *Giai Phẩm Mùa Đông* 1 (December 1956): 15–21.

38. Lenin, *What Is To Be Done?* 8–11.

39. Trần Đức Thảo, "Nỗ lực phát triển tự do dân chủ" [Efforts to Develop Freedom and Democracy], *Nhân Văn* 4 (15 October 1956): 1.

40. Žižek, *Sublime Object*, 142.

41. Writers' Congress, "Nghị quyết của ban chấp hành hội liên hiệp văn học nghệ thuật Việt Nam" [Resolution by the Executive Committee of the Association of Arts and Letters], in *Bọn Nhân Văn Giai Phẩm*.

42. Trương Tửu, "Tự do tư tưởng," 66.

43. Hegel, quoted in Žižek, *Sublime Object*, 218.

44. Czeslaw Milosz, "Introduction to Abram Tertz's 'On Socialist Realism,'" in *The Trial Begins, and On Socialist Realism*, ed. Abram Tertz [Andrei Sinyavsky] (1960; repr., Berkeley: University of California Press, 1982), 135.

45. Trương Tửu, "Tự do tư tưởng," 64.

46. Ibid., 66–67 (emphasis added).

47. "Resolution at Writers' Congress III, 4 June 1958," in *Bọn Nhân Văn Giai Phẩm*, 338.

48. Phùng Quán, "Lời mẹ dặn" [Mother's Words], in *Nhớ Phùng Quán*

[Remembering Phung Quan: Selected Writings], ed. Ngô Minh (Ho Chi Minh City: Nhà Xuất Bản Trẻ, 2003), 334.

49. Phùng Quán, "Người bạn lính cùng một tiểu đội" [The Soldier Friend from My Unit], *Diễn Đàn* 93 (February 2000): 41–47.

50. Hoàng Ngọc Anh, *Xóm thợ Trường Thi* [The Working Neighborhood of Trường Thi] (Hanoi: Nhà Xuất Bản Lao Động, 1975), 123.

51. Ibid., 410.

52. Phùng Quán, "Chống tham ô Lãng phí," 39–40.

53. Hoàng Cầm, "Em bé lên sáu tuổi" [A Child of Six], *Giai Phẩm Mùa Thu* 1 (September 1956): 15.

54. Hoàng Cầm, "Con người Trần Dần" [The Person of Trần Dần], *Nhân Văn* 1 (20 September 1956): 2, 4.

55. Như Mai (Châm Văn Biếm), "Thi sĩ máy" [Robotic Poet], *Nhân Văn* 5 (20 November 1956): 3–4; Trần Duy, "Những người khổng lồ" [The Giants], *Giai Phẩm Mùa Thu* 2 (September 1956): 32–38.

56. Lenin, *What Is To Be Done?* 105.

57. Jürgen Habermas, *Structural Transformation of the Public Sphere: An Investigation into a Category of Bourgeois Society* (Cambridge, Mass.: MIT Press, 1991).

58. "Resolution of the Writers' Congress III, 4 June 1959," in *Bọn Nhân Văn Giai Phẩm*, 339.

59. Hoài Thanh, *Văn Nghệ*, no. 11, in *Bọn Nhân Văn Giai Phẩm*, 64–67.

60. See, e.g., Tố Hữu, "Nhìn lại 3 năm phá hoại của nhóm 'Nhân Văn Giai Phẩm'" [Looking Back at Three Years of Sabotage by the "Nhân Văn–Giai Phẩm Group"], in *Bọn Nhân Văn Giai Phẩm*, 22–36.

61. Ibid., 32.

62. K. W. Taylor, "Locating and Translating Boundaries in Nguyễn Huy Thiệp's Short Stories," *Vietnam Review*, no. 1 (Autumn–Winter 1996): 441.

63. For an overview and a most complete compilation of writings in this period, see *Trăm hoa vẫn nở trên quê hương*.

64. Lâm Thị Thanh Hà, "Công lý, đừng quên ai" [Justice, Do Not Forget Anyone], in *Người đàn bà quỳ* [The Kneeling Woman] (n.p. [Vietnam]: Báo Văn Nghệ, Báo Nông Nghiệp, and Nhà Xuất Bản Nông Nghiệp, 1988), 91.

65. *Chuyện tử tế* [The Story of Goodness], VHS, directed by Trần Văn Thủy (Hanoi: Xí Nghiệp Phim Tài Liệu Và Khoa Học Trung Ương, 1986).

66. Nguyễn Huy Thiệp, "Tướng về hưu" [The Retired General], in *Những ngọn gió Hua Tát* [The Winds of Hua Tát] (Hanoi: Nhà Xuất Bản Văn Hóa, 1989).

67. Nguyễn Huy Thiệp, "Không có vua" [Without a King], in *Những ngọn gió Hua Tát*.

68. Nguyễn Huy Thiệp, "Kiếm sắc" [Sharp Sword] and "Phẩm Tiết" [Chastity], in *Nguyễn Huy Thiệp tác phẩm và dư luận*.

69. Greg Lockhart raises the issue of Thiep's postmodernism in "Nguyễn

Huy Thiệp's Writing: Post-Confucian, Post-modern" *Journal of Vietnamese Studies* (Australian Association of Vietnamese Studies) 6 (January 1993): 32–49. On the Vietnamese context, Peter Zinoman has argued that Thiệp draws on premodern Vietnamese and socialist literary genres, giving rise to the appearance of postmodernism in his writing. See Peter Zinoman, "Declassifying Nguyễn Huy Thiệp," *Positions: East Asia Cultures Critique* 2, no. 2 (1994): 294–317. K. W. Taylor also convincingly argues that Thiệp has more in common with other writers like Milan Kundera of post-socialism or late socialist realism. See K. W. Taylor, "Locating and Translating Boundaries."

70. See, for instance, Đỗ Văn Khang, "Sự 'mơ mộng' và sự 'nghiêm khắc' trong truyện ngắn 'Phẩm Tiết'" ["Dreaming" and "Seriousness" in the Short Story "Chastity"] in *Nguyễn Huy Thiệp tác hẩm và dư luận*, 126–36. This collection pulls together writings about Thiệp's works in 1988, after the first batch of his stories ran in the journal *Văn Nghệ*.

71. Ibid., 135–36.

72. Trần Khắc, "Người đàn bà quỳ" [The Kneeling Woman], in *Người đàn bà quỳ*, 16–51.

73. Ibid., 17.

74. Đặng Phong and Beresford, *Authority Relations*.

75. *Mr. Smith Goes to Washington*, DVD, directed by Frank Capra (1939; Culver City, Calif.: Sony Pictures, 2000).

8. LOVE IN THE TIME OF NEOLIBERALISM

1. Cù Mai Công, *Sài gòn by Night: Nửa mùa trước gió* [Saigon by Night: Mid-season in the Wind] (Ho Chi Minh City: Nhà Xuất Bản Trẻ, 2002). Another recent title in the series is Cù Mai Công, *Sài gòn by Night: Thời xuyên thế kỷ* [Saigon by Night: The Trans-century Era] (Ho Chi Minh City: Nhà Xuất Bản Trẻ, 2001).

2. *Gái nhảy* [Bar Girls], DVD, directed by Lê Hoàng (Ho Chi Minh City: Giải Phóng Films, 2003).

3. Bùi Quang Thăng, "Báo cáo điều tra khán giả phim *Lọ lem hè phố*" [Audience Analysis on *Street Cinderella*] (Hanoi: Viện Văn Hóa Thông Tin [Vietnamese Institute of Cultural and Information Studies], Ministry of Culture and Information, March 2004).

4. *Lọ lem hè phố* [Street Cinderella], DVD, directed by Lê Hoàng and produced by Hãng Phim Giải Phóng (Westminster, Calif.: Thanh Hằng Productions, 2004).

5. Quang Hùng, *Phóng sự điều tra* [Investigative Reporting] (Ho Chi Minh City: Nhà Xuất Bản Tổng Hợp Thành Phố Hồ Chí Minh, 2004), 177.

6. Ibid., 181.

7. Quang Hùng included a reprint version of Nguyễn Khương, "Đà Lạt—

Một vòng ôm" [Đà Lạt: A Round of Hugs], which first appeared in *Công An Thành Phố Hồ Chí Minh* (30 September 1999), and of documents surrounding the controversy over the article. See Quang Hùng, *Phóng sự điều tra*, 221–37.

8. Quang Hùng, *Phóng sự điều tra*, 162–96.

9. Hùynh Dũng Nhân, "Theo dấu 'bướm đêm'" [Tracing the "Night Butterflies"], in *Tôi đi bán tôi: Tập phóng sự* [I Sell Myself: A Reportage Collection] (Ho Chi Minh City: Nhà Xuất Bản Văn Nghệ Thành Phố Hồ Chí Minh, 1999), 197–208.

10. Ibid., 205.

11. Cù Mai Công, *Sàigòn by Night: Nửa mùa trước gió*, 32.

12. Phạm Thùy Nhân, comments in *Người Lao Động*, 2 July 2004, quoted in Bùi Quang Thăng, "Báo cáo điều tra," 12–13.

13. Nguyễn Hồi Loan, comments in *Người Hà Nội Cuối Tuần*, 22 February 2004, quoted in Bùi Quang Thăng, "Báo cáo điều tra," 17.

14. Ibid., 18.

15. Phanxine, "Phỏng vấn: Gái nhảy 2, sự bất ngờ không lường" [Interview: *Bar Girls 2*, a Surprise], *Yxine*, 22 July 2003, http://yxine.com.

16. Phạm Hoàng Nam, comments in *Lao Động*, no. 365 (2003), quoted in Bùi Quang Thăng, "Báo cáo điều tra," 22.

17. See, for instance, the reference to this genre in Phanxine, "Ba phim tết 2006: An tòan hay bức phá" [Three New Year's Films: Safe or Innovative?], *Yxine*, 28 January 2006, http://yxine.com.

18. Karl Marx, *Capital*, vol. 1 of *Marx-Engels Reader*, 324.

19. *Nữ tướng cướp* [Female Bandits], DVD, directed by Lê Hòang (Hanoi: Thiên Ngân, 2005); Bùi Quang Thăng, "Báo cáo điều tra," 19.

20. *Những cô gái chân dài* [Long-Legged Girls], DVD, directed by Vũ Ngọc Đăng (Hanoi: Thiên Ngân, 2004); and *2 trong 1* [Two in One], DVD, directed by Đào Duy Phúc (Hanoi: Thiên Ngân, 2005).

21. Slavoj Žižek, *The Parallax View* (Cambridge, Mass.: MIT Press, 2006), 181.

22. Ibid., 190.

23. Bùi Quang Thăng, "Báo cáo điều tra," 20–22. This report cites comments from Nguyễn Thị Hồng Ngát, vice director of the state Cinema Section, and from directors Lưu Trọng Ninh, Phi Tiến Sơn, and Vĩnh Sơn supporting the commercial direction opened up by the two films. Among the few negative comments about the crassness and depravity of the films, the report mentions director Đỗ Minh Tuấn, who recently made the commercial flop *Ký ức Điện Biên* [Điện Biên Memory], an expensive state film valorizing the Việt Minh victory over French colonial forces in 1954. See also Đỗ Minh Tuấn, "Thư ngỏ gửi đạo diễn Lê Hòang—Đồng tiền, đạo lý và nỗi cô đơn" [Letter to Lê Hòang: Money, Principle, and Solitude], *Talawas*, 3 December 2004, http://talawas.org.

24. Bùi Quang Thăng, "Báo cáo điều tra," 4–11.

25. Nguyễn Thị Hồng Ngát, interview in *Nhà Báo và Công Luận* 7 (19 February 2004), quoted in Bùi Quang Thăng, "Báo cáo điều tra," 20.

26. Bùi Quang Thăng, "Báo cáo điều tra," 46.

27. Lê Hòang, comments in *Tuổi Trẻ Thứ Bảy,* 7 February 2004, quoted in Bùi Quang Thăng, "Báo cáo điều tra," 16.

28. Marx, *Capital,* 322.

29. Bùi Quang Thăng, "Báo cáo điều tra," 63.

30. See, e.g., Rose, *Powers of Freedom,* 68–69.

31. Louis Althusser, "Freud and Lacan," in *Lenin and Philosophy and Other Essays,* 133–50.

32. Žižek, *Sublime Object,* 126.

33. Fredric Jameson. "Reification and Utopia in Mass Culture," *Social Text* 1 (Winter 1979): 145.

CONCLUSION

1. Kim Ninh, "Home Truths in Hanoi," *Wall Street Journal Online,* 7 July 2006, http://online.wsj.com/article/SB115222298564299979.html.

2. Narration on banner; translation provided in exhibit.

3. Một yêu anh có may ô / Hai yêu anh có cá khô để dành / Ba yêu anh rửa mặt bằng khăn / Bốn yêu anh có cái quần đùi hoa. Wall display at exhibit; English translation provided in exhibit.

4. Displayed narration; my translation.

5. Displayed narration, translation provided in exhibit.

6. Displayed narration; my translation.

7. Human Rights Watch, "Vietnam: Crackdown on Dissent in Wake of WTO and APEC," 9 March 2007, http://hrw.org/english/docs/2007/03/09/vietna15466.htm (accessed 26 May 2007).

8. See, e.g., the BBC news clip of Nguyễn Văn Lý's trial, YouTube, http://www.youtube.com/watch?v=k2CfXeoMlsE (accessed 25 May 2007).

9. Grant McCool, "Vietnam Trials Send Zero-Tolerance Message," *Reuters,* 5 May 2007, http://www.reuters.com/article/worldNews/idUSHAN9920820070506 (accessed 25 May 2007).

10. Rose, *Powers of Freedom,* 69.

11. Burchell, "Liberal Government," 27–30.

12. Gilles Deleuze, "Postscript on the Society of Control," *October* 59 (Winter 1992): 3–7.

13. Rose, *Powers of Freedom,* 187–88.

14. Deleuze, "Postscript."

15. Rose, *Powers of Freedom,* 246.

16. Ibid., 282.

17. Mickey Edwards, "Right's Wrong Turn," *Los Angeles Times,* 9 May 2004.

18. Rose, *Powers of Freedom,* 282–84.

19. Foucault, *Discipline and Punish,* 265–72.

20. Ibid., 272.

21. See Foucault's claim that he was a pluralist, in "Politics and the Study of Discourse," in Burchell, Gordon, and Miller, *Foucault Effect*; on his notion of "eventalization," see his "Questions of Methods." Rose, *Powers of Freedom*, 275–79.

22. Harvey, *New Imperialism*.

23. Simon, "Refugees in a Carceral Age."

24. Rose, *Powers of Freedom*, 68.

Bibliography

INTERVIEWS

Interviews listed here are those that appear in the text. Unless indicated, all names have been altered to protect identities. Designations in parentheses are there to indicate only the interviews' relevance to this study.

Công (entrepreneur), Vũng Tàu, Vietnam, 6 July 2002.
Di (former Women's Union neighborhood leader), Garden Grove, Calif., 28 March 1996.
Diệu (college instructor), Ho Chi Minh City, 6 May 1996.
Đỗ Hồng Ngọc (physician and Ho Chi Minh City Health Bureau official; permitted use of true name), Ho Chi Minh City, 16 May 1997, 26 July 2002.
Hà (sex worker), Vũng Tàu, Vietnam, 26–27 May and 1 June 1996.
Hằng (sex worker), Ho Chi Minh City, 19 and 24 May 1996; Ho Chi Minh City, 28 July 2000.
Hiền (Ho Chi Minh Health Bureau official), Ho Chi Minh City, 6 May 1996.
Hiếu (private entrepreneur), Ho Chi Minh City, 4 June 1996 and 2 August 1996.
Hoa (sex worker), Vũng Tàu, Vietnam, 26–27 May 1996.
Hồng (an officer of the Central Women's Union in Hanoi), Hanoi, 20 July 2002.
Hùng (counselor at Café Condom), Ho Chi Minh City, 8 May 1996.
Huyền (local Women's Union officer in charge of peer education groups in two Ho Chi Minh City districts), Ho Chi Minh City, 4 June 1996.
Kim (Ho Chi Minh City physician), Anaheim, Calif., 27 April 1996.
Lan (married to state-enterprise manager), Ho Chi Minh City, 4 May 1996.
Lịch (senior scholar at Research Institute for Ministry of Labor, Invalids, and Social Affairs), Hanoi, 18 July 2002.
Linh (Ho Chi Minh City Women's Union officer in charge of peer education group), Ho Chi Minh City, 1 June 1996.
Mai (sex worker), Vũng Tàu, Vietnam, 26–27 May and 1 June 1996.
Minh (sex worker), Ho Chi Minh City, 19 and 24 May 1996.
Mỹ (Central Women's Union officer working on prostitution-related programs), Los Angeles and Laguna Beach, Calif., 16–18 March 1997; Hanoi, 20 July 2002.

Ngọc (head of a Ho Chi Minh City NGO), Ho Chi Minh City, 14 May 1996.
Peer educators in two groups, Ho Chi Minh City, 1–2 June 1996.
Phương (journalist), Ho Chi Minh City, 4 June 1996.
Sáu (sex worker / camp inmate), Thủ Đức, Vietnam, 5 June 1996.
Thanh (AIDS peer educator), Ho Chi Minh City, 2 June 1996.
Thành (camp inmate), Thủ Đức, Vietnam, 5 June 1996.
Thi (director at the Shelter), Tân Thuận Tây, Vietnam, 12 July 2002.
Thu (public health policy instructor), Ho Chi Minh City, 9 May 1996.
Tinh (entrepreneur), Ho Chi Minh City, 22 May 1996.
Trân (CARE International in Vietnam officer), Ho Chi Minh City, 30 July 2002.
Trang (camp inmate), interview by the author, Thủ Đức, Vietnam, 5 June 1996.
Vân (head of a private rehabilitation center), Tân Thuận Tây, Vietnam, 14 and 21 May 1996.
Warden One (New Center for the Education of Women), Thủ Đức, Vietnam, 4 June 1996.
Warden Two (New Center for the Education of Women), Thủ Đức, Vietnam, 4 June 1996.
Xuân (physician and Ho Chi Minh City Health Bureau official), Ho Chi Minh City, 9 May 1996.

BOOKS, FILMS, JOURNALS, AND DOCUMENTS

2 trong 1 [Two in One]. DVD. Directed by Đào Duy Phúc. Hanoi: Thiên Ngân, 2005.
Abuza, Zachary. *Renovating Politics in Contemporary Vietnam*. Boulder, Colo.: Lynne Rienner, 2001.
Allison, Anne. *Night Work: Sexuality, Pleasure, and Corporate Masculinity in a Tokyo Hostess Club*. Chicago: University of Chicago Press, 1994.
Althusser, Louis. "Freud and Lacan." In Althusser, *Lenin and Philosophy and Other Essays*, 33–50.
———. "Ideology and Ideological State Apparatuses." In Althusser, *Lenin and Philosophy and Other Essays*, 85–126.
———. *Lenin and Philosophy and Other Essays*. Translated by Ben Brewster. New York: Monthly Review Press, 1971.
Altman, Dennis. *Global Sex*. Chicago: University of Chicago Press, 2001.
Anderson, Benedict. *Imagined Communities: Reflections on the Origins and Spread of Nationalism*. New York: Verso, 1991.
Ánh Nga. *Tâm lý khác biệt giữa nam và nữ* [Psychological Differences between Men and Women]. Đồng Tháp, Vietnam: Nhà Xuất Bản Đồng Tháp, 1995.

Anh Quân. "Chợ người cho khách nước ngoài" [The Human Market for Foreign Guests]. *Đặc San Công An Thành Phố Hồ Chí Minh*, 26 May 1996.

Asia Yearbook 1987. Edited by Paul Sillitoe. Hong Kong: Far Eastern Economic Review, 1987.

Bạch Hồng Việt. "Vấn đề giàu nghèo trong cơ chế thị trường" [The Problem of Rich and Poor in the Market Regime]. *Tạp Chí Cộng Sản* 8 (1995): 42–45.

Bách khoa phụ nữ trẻ [An Encyclopedia for Young Women]. 5th ed. Hanoi: Nhà Xuất Bản Hà Nội, 1995.

Balakrishnan, Gopal, ed. *Debating Empire.* New York: Verso, 2003.

Bales, Kevin. *Disposable People: New Slavery in the Global Economy.* Berkeley: University of California Press, 1999.

Bảo Châu. "Lừa trên 30 tỷ" [The 30 Billion Fraud Scheme]. *Đặc San Công An Thành Phố Hồ Chí Minh*, 29 March 1996.

Barry, Andrew, Thomas Osborne, and Nikolas Rose, eds. *Foucault and Political Reason.* London: University College London Press, 1996.

———. Introduction to *Foucault and Political Reason.* London: University College London Press, 1996.

Basserman, Lujo. *The Oldest Profession: A History of Prostitution.* New York: Dorset, 1993.

BBC. News clip of Nguyễn Văn Lý's trial. YouTube. http://www.youtube .com/watch?v=k2CfXeoMlsE (accessed 25 May 2007).

Beissinger, Mark. *Scientific Management, Socialist Discipline, and Soviet Power.* Cambridge, Mass.: Harvard University Press, 1988.

Bell, Shannon. *Reading, Writing, and Rewriting the Prostitute Body.* Bloomington: Indiana University Press, 1994.

Benjamin, Walter. *Reflections: Essays, Aphorisms, Autobiographical Writings.* Edited by Peter Demetz. New York: Schocken Books, 1978.

Bergman, Arlene E. *Women of Vietnam.* San Francisco: People's Press, 1975.

Berlant, Lauren. *Intimacy.* Chicago: University of Chicago Press, 2000.

Berlin, Isaiah. *Four Essays on Liberty.* Oxford: Oxford University Press, 1969.

Bích Quân. "Bài tổng kết diễn đàn bia ôm, Một tệ nạn xã hội cần kiên quyết dẹp bỏ" [Summary of Letters to the Forum: *Bia Ôm*, a Social Evil We Need to Abolish Resolutely]. *Phụ Nữ Chủ Nhật*, 7 July 1996.

Bobbio, Norberto. "Gramsci and the Concept of Civil Society." In *Civil Society and the State*, edited by John Keane. New York: Verso, 1988.

Bọn Nhân Văn Giai Phẩm trước tòa án dư luận [The Nhân Văn–Giai Phẩm Clique in the Court of Public Opinion]. 1959. Reprint, Hanoi: Nhà Xuất Bản Sự Thật, 1985.

Boudarel, Georges. *Cent fleurs écloses dans la nuit du Vietnam: Communisme et dissidence, 1954–1956* [One Hundred Flowers Close in the

Vietnam Night: Communism and Dissidence, 1954–1956]. Paris: Éditions Jacques Bertoin, 1991.

Bourdieu, Pierre. *Distinction: A Social Critique of the Judgment of Taste.* New York: Routledge and Kegan Paul, 1984.

———. *Firing Back: Against the Tyranny of the Market 2.* New York: New Press, 2001.

Bùi Đình Thành. "Những vấn đề cần trao đổi ý kiến trong cuộc hội thảo khoa học thực tiễn về chính sách xã hội tại Thành Phố Hồ Chí Minh" [Discussion Points for the Scientific Conference on Social Policy in Ho Chi Minh City]. *Tạp Chí Khoa Học Xã Hội* 19 (1994): 70–82.

Bùi Huy Phong. "Trương Tửu, một tên phản cách mạng đội lốt Mác-Xít. [Trương Tửu: An Anti-Revolutionary in the Guise of a Marxist]," *Văn Nghệ,* 12 May 1958. Reprinted in *Bọn Nhân Văn Giai Phẩm.*

Bùi Mộng Hùng. "Hệ y tế Việt Nam trước thử thách của thực tại: Liên tục và gián đoạn" [Vietnamese Health Care in the Face of Challenges: Continuities and Discontinuities]. *Thời Đại* 1 (1977): 50–84.

Bùi Quang Thăng. "Báo cáo điều tra khán giả phim *Lọ lem hè phố*" [Audience Analysis on *Street Cinderella*]. Hanoi: Viện Văn Hóa Thông Tin [Vietnamese Institute of Cultural and Information Studies], Ministry of Culture and Information, March 2004.

Bùi Quốc Huy. Interview by Bảo Chân. *Công An Thành Phố Hồ Chí Minh,* 5 June 1996.

Burchell, Graham. "Liberal Government and Techniques of the Self." In Barry, Osborne, and Rose, *Foucault and Political Reason.*

———. "Peculiar Interests: Civil Society and Governing 'the System of Natural Liberty.'" In Burchell, Gordon, and Miller, *Foucault Effect.*

Burchell, Graham, Colin Gordon, and Peter Miller, eds. *The Foucault Effect: Studies in Governmentality.* Chicago: University of Chicago Press, 1991.

Burnham, James. *The Managerial Revolution: What Is Happening in the World.* New York: John Day Co., 1941.

Butler, Judith. *Bodies That Matter.* New York: Routledge, 1993.

———. *Gender Trouble: Feminism and the Subversion of Identity.* New York: Routledge, 1990.

Cao Hồng. "Bẽ bàng một kiếp hoa rơi" [Shame on the Life of a Fallen Flower]. *Công An Nhân Dân,* 28 July 2005. http://www.cand.com.vn/vivn/thoisuxahoi/phongsughichep/2005/7/59418.cand (accessed 1 August 2005).

CARE International in Vietnam. "On the Skills Training for Incarcerated Women Programme, Thủ Đức Women's Center, October 15, 1995–April 18, 1998." Final report to NOVIB (the Dutch organization for international development cooperation). CARE International in Vietnam, Hanoi, 1998.

Chalmers, John. "Fairer Sex Seeks Fairer Deal in Confucian Vietnam." *Reuters*, 18 May 1997. http://global.factiva.com/ha/default.aspx (accessed 8 May 2007).

Chính Nghĩa. *Nọc độc văn hóa nô dịch* [Venom Left from a Slave Culture]. Ho Chi Minh City: Nhà Xuất Bản Thành Phố Hồ Chí Minh, 1982.

Chittick, John B. *The Coming Wave—HIV/AIDS in Vietnam: Observations and Recommendations on Ho Chi Minh City's HIV/AIDS Program.* Report for Ho Chi Minh City AIDS Committee and other agencies. Ho Chi Minh City: John B. Chittick, 1995.

Chung, Hilary, ed. "Introduction: Socialist Realism." In *In the Party Spirit: Socialist Realism and Literary Practice in the Soviet Union, East Germany and China*. Critical Studies 6. Amsterdam: Editions Rodopi, 1994.

Chuyện người đàn bà xin dấu tên [Story of the Woman Who Must Hide Her Name]. Ho Chi Minh City: Nhà Xuất Bản Phụ Nữ, 1996.

Chuyện tử tế [The Story of Goodness]. VHS. Directed by Trần Văn Thủy. Hanoi: Xí Nghiệp Phim Tài Liệu và Khoa Học Trung Ương, 1986.

Cohen, Stanley. *Visions of Social Control*. New York: Basil Blackwell, 1985.

Comaroff, Jean, and John Comaroff. "Millennial Capitalism: First Thoughts on a Second Coming." In *Millennial Capitalism and the Culture of Neoliberalism*, edited by Jean Comaroff and John Comaroff. Durham, N.C.: Duke University Press, 2001.

"Công ty Du Lịch Hà Nội kiên quyết loại trừ tệ nạn xã hội ra khỏi môi trường du lịch" [Hanoi Tourism Company Is Determined to Eliminate Social Evils from the Tourist Environment]. *Người Bảo Vệ Công Lý*, 6 December 1995.

Corbin, Alain. *Women for Hire: Prostitution and Sexuality in France after 1850*. Translated by Alan Sheridan. Cambridge, Mass.: Harvard University Press, 1990.

Cù Mai Công. *Sàigòn by Night: Nửa mùa trước gió* [Saigon by Night: Midseason in the Wind]. Ho Chi Minh City: Nhà Xuất Bạn Trẻ, 2002.

Đặng Phong and Melanie Beresford. *Authority Relations and Economic Decision-Making in Vietnam: An Historical Perspective*. Copenhagen: Nordic Institute of Asian Studies, 1998.

"Đảng ta: Di sản vô giá của một học thuyết đầy sức sống" [Our Party: The Invaluable Legacy of a Thriving Ideology]. *Tạp Chí Cộng Sản* 3 (February 1996): 3–6.

Đặng Xuân Kỳ. "Vững bước đi con đường xã hội chủ nghĩa" [Sure Steps on the Socialist Path]. *Tạp Chí Cộng Sản* 4 (February 1996): 3–6.

Danzelot, Jacques. *L'invention du social*. Paris: Fayard, 1984.

Đào Ngọc Lâm. "Problems of Macro-Economic Management at Present." *Nghiên Cứu Kinh Tế / Economic Studies* 229 (June 1997): 18–23.

Deleuze, Gilles. "Postscript on the Society of Control." *October* 59 (Winter 1992): 3–7.

"Diễn đàn: 'Bia ôm—Vì sao vẫn tồn tại?'" [Forum: *"Bia Ôm*—Why Does It Still Exist?"]. Readers' column. *Phụ Nữ,* May–July 1996.

Đinh Thơm. "Vai trò của nhà nước trong quá trình chuyển thí điểm các doanh nghiệp nhà nước thành công ty cổ phần ở Việt Nam—Những vấn đề cần bản" [The Role of the State in the Process of Experimental Transformation of Some State-Owned Enterprises into Stock Companies]. *Thông Tin Khoa Học Xã Hội* 12 (1995): 23–28.

Đỗ Hồng Ngọc. "Chung quanh khẩu hiệu phòng chống sida" [Around the Anti-AIDS Slogan]. *Sức Khỏe Thành Phố Hồ Chí Minh* 3 (September–October 1995): 3.

———. *Viết cho tuổi mới lớn* [For Adolescents]. Ho Chi Minh City: Nhà Xuất Bản Trẻ, 1995.

Đỗ Kim Thịnh. "Yếu tố mới đang sống động trong đời sống văn hóa cơ sở" [New Lively Factors in Local Cultural Life]. *Tạp Chí Cộng Sản* 4 (February 1996): 33–36.

Đỗ Minh Tuấn. "Thư ngỏ gửi đạo diễn Lê Hoàng—Đồng tiền, đạo lý và nỗi cô đơn" [Letter to Lê Hoàng: Money, Principle, and Solitude]. *Talawas,* 3 December 2004. http://www.talawas.org/talaDB/showFile .php?res=3351&rb=0204.

Đỗ Mười. "Trong hành trình đưa đất nước tiến lên, cần luôn luôn trân trọng, giữ gìn và phát huy bản sắc văn hóa dân tộc" [In the Country's Forward Journey, We Need to Always Value, Maintain, and Develop the Colors, Identity of Our National Culture]. Speech read by the Party Secretary General at the Conference of the Union of Literature and the Arts, Hanoi, 9 September 1995. *Tạp Chí Cộng Sản* 13 (October 1995): 3–5.

Đỗ Nguyên Phương. "Nâng cao đạo đức của người thầy thuốc" [Raising the Professional Ethics of Physicians]. *Tạp Chí Cộng Sản* 7 (April 1997): 19–21.

Đỗ Văn Khang. "Sự 'mơ mộng' và sự 'nghiêm khắc' trong truyện ngắn 'Phẩm Tiết'" ["Dreaming" and "Seriousness" in the Short Story "Chastity"]. In *Nguyễn Huy Thiệp tác phẩm và dư luận*

"Đồng Chí Tạ Hữu Thanh, Ủy viên Trung ương Đảng, Tổng Thanh Tra Nhà nước trả lời phỏng vấn báo *CATPHCM*: Thanh tra phải trở thành tai mắt và công cụ sắc bén chống tham nhũng, tiêu cực" [Comrade Tạ Hữu Thanh, Party Central Committee Member, State Inspector General in an Interview by *CATPHCM* (*Ho Chi Minh City Public Security Magazine*): Inspection Bureau Must Become the Eyes and Ears, as Well as the Sharp Weapons, against Corruption, Negative Acts]. *Đặc San Công An Thành Phố Hồ Chí Minh,* 3 August 1996.

Dougherty, James E., and Robert L. Pfitzgraff Jr. *Contending Theories of International Relations.* 3rd ed. New York: Harper and Row, 1990.

Dreyfus, Hubert, and Paul Rabinow. *Michel Foucault: Beyond Structuralism and Hermeneutics.* Chicago: University of Chicago Press, 1983.

"Dự thảo Báo cáo Chính trị của Ban chấp hành Trung ương Đảng Khóa VII trình Đại Hội lần thứ VIII của Đảng" [Draft Political Report by the Central Committee of the Seventh Congress to the Eighth Party Congress]. *Tạp Chí Cộng Sản* 8 (1996): 5–12.

"Dự thảo cương lĩnh Đại Hội VII: Xây dựng Chủ Nghĩa Xã Hội trong thời kỳ quá độ" [Draft Political Platform for the Seventh Party Congress: Building Socialism in the Transition Period]. *Tạp Chí Cộng Sản* 1 (1991): 28–35.

Dumm, Thomas. *Michel Foucault and the Politics of Freedom*. Thousand Oaks, Calif.: Sage, 1996.

Dương Thu Hương. *Paradise of the Blind* [*Những thiên đường mù*]. Translated from Vietnamese by Phan Huy Duong and Nina McPherson. New York: Morrow, 1993.

Durkheim, Émile. *Selected Writings*. Edited by Anthony Giddens. New York: Cambridge University Press, 1972.

Easton, David. *The Analysis of Political Structure*. New York: Routledge, 1990.

Edwards, Mickey. "Right's Wrong Turn." *Los Angeles Times*, 9 May 2004.

Elliott, David. "Dilemmas of Reforms in Vietnam." In Turley and Selden, *Reinventing Vietnamese Socialism*.

Evans, Peter B., Dietrich Rueschemeyer, and Theda Skocpol, eds. *Bringing the State Back In*. New York: Cambridge University Press, 1985.

Fanon, Frantz. *The Wretched of the Earth*. London: Penguin, 1963. Quoted in McClintock, *Imperial Leather*, 62

Fforde, Adam, and Stefan de Vylder. *From Plan to Market: The Economic Transition in Vietnam*. Boulder, Colo.: Westview Press, 1996.

Foucault, Michel. *The Birth of the Clinic: An Archaeology of Medical Perception*. New York: Vintage, 1994.

———. *Discipline and Punish: The Birth of the Prison*. New York: Vintage, 1995.

———. "An Ethics of Pleasure." In *Foucault Live*, edited by S. Lotringer. New York: Semiotext(e), 1989. Quoted in Barry, Osborne, and Rose, Introduction to *Foucault and Political Reason*, 9.

———. "Governmentality." In Burchell, Gordon, and Miller, *Foucault Effect*.

———. *The History of Sexuality: An Introduction*. Vol. 1. New York: Vintage, 1990.

———. "Politics and the Study of Discourse." In Burchell, Gordon, and Miller, *Foucault Effect*.

———. Preface to *The History of Sexuality*, vol. 2. In *The Foucault Reader*, edited by Paul Rabinow. New York: Pantheon, 1984.

———. "Questions of Methods." In Burchell, Gordon, and Miller, *Foucault Effect*.

Franklin, Barbara. *The Risk of AIDS in Vietnam: An Audience Analysis*

of Urban Men and Sex Workers. Monograph Series no. 1. Hanoi: CARE
International in Vietnam, 1993.

————. *Targeting Young Men: Audience-Centered Communication for
AIDS Prevention in Vietnam.* Monograph Series no. 4. Hanoi: CARE
International in Vietnam, 1994.

Friedrich, Carl J., and Zbigniew Brzezinski. *Totalitarian Dictatorship
and Autocracy.* New York: Praeger, 1956.

Gái nhảy [Bar Girls]. DVD. Directed by Lê Hoàng. Ho Chi Minh City:
Giải Phóng Films, 2003.

Galbraith, John Kenneth. *The New Industrial State.* 2nd ed. New York:
Mentor, 1971.

Gelley, Alexander. "City Texts: Representation, Semiology, Urbanism."
In *Politics, Theory, and Contemporary Culture,* edited by Mark Poster.
New York: Columbia University Press, 1993.

Giddens, Anthony. *The Consequences of Modernity.* Stanford, Calif.:
Stanford University Press, 1990.

Gilfoyle, Timothy. "City of Eros: New York City, Prostitution, and the
Commercialization of Sex, 1790–1920." Ph.D. diss., Columbia University, 1987.

Gordon, Colin. "Foucault in Britain." In Barry, Osborne, and Rose,
Foucault and Political Reason.

————. "Governmental Rationality: An Introduction." In Burchell,
Gordon, and Miller, *Foucault Effect.*

Gordon, Paul. "Community Policing: Towards the Local Police State?"
In *Law, Order, and the Authoritarian State: Readings in Critical
Criminology,* edited by Phil Craton. Philadelphia: Open University
Press, 1987.

Gramsci, Antonio. *A Gramsci Reader.* Edited by D. Forgacs. London:
Lawrence and Wishart, 1988.

Hà Sĩ Phu. "Biện chứng và ngụy biện trong công cuộc đổi mới"
[Dialectics and Specious Reasoning in the Reform Process]. In *Trăm
hoa văn nở trên quê hương.*

Hà Thanh Tú. "Cà phê 'lên bờ xuống ruộng'" [Café "Up the Bank,
Down the Rice Field"]. *Người Lao Động,* 21 August 2001.

Hà Thế Cương. "Công tác phòng chống tệ nạn xã hội ở Kiên Giang"
[The Task of Preventing and Fighting Social Ills in Kien Giang].
Công An Nhân Dân, 20 April 1996.

Hà Xuân Trường. "Định hướng xã hội chủ nghĩa: Một khái niệm
khoa học" [Socialist Orientation: A Scientific Concept]. *Tạp Chí
Cộng Sản* 7 (April 1996): 18–21.

Habermas, Jürgen. "The European Nation-State: On the Past and Future
of Sovereignty and Citizenship." *Public Culture* 10, no. 2 (1998): 397–416.

————. *Structural Transformation of the Public Sphere: An Investigation
into a Category of Bourgeois Society.* Cambridge, Mass.: MIT Press, 1991.

Hadiz, Vedi, ed. *Empire and Neoliberalism in Asia*. New York: Routledge, 2006.

Haggard, Steven, and Robert Kaufman. *The Political Economy of Democratic Transitions*. Princeton, N.J.: Princeton University Press, 1995.

Hammersley, Martyn, and Paul Atkinson. *Ethnography*. New York: Routledge, 1983.

Hardt, Michael, and Antonio Negri. *Empire*. Cambridge, Mass.: Harvard University Press, 2000.

Harsin, Jill. *Policing Prostitution in Nineteenth-Century Paris*. Princeton, N.J.: Princeton University Press, 1985.

Harvey, David. *The Condition of Postmodernity*. Cambridge, Mass.: Blackwell, 1990.

———. *The New Imperialism*. Oxford: Oxford University Press, 2003.

Hegel, G. W. F. *The Essential Writings*. Edited by F. G. Weiss. New York: Harper, 1974.

Hershatter, Gail. *Dangerous Pleasures: Prostitution and Modernity in Twentieth-Century Shanghai*. Berkeley: University of California Press, 1997.

Hindess, Barry. "Liberalism, Socialism, and Democracy: Variations on a Governmental Theme." In Barry, Osborne, and Rose, *Foucault and Political Reason*.

———. *Politics and Class Analysis*. Oxford, UK: Basil Blackwell, 1987.

Hồ Biểu Chánh. *Con nhà nghèo* [The Poor]. 1930. Reprint, Ho Chi Minh City: NXB Văn Nghệ, 1999.

"Ho Chi Minh City Bursts out Ring of Prostitution to Foreigners." *Law*, 25 May 2005.

Ho Chi Minh City Cultural Bureau. "Build and Combat: Exhibition of Government Resolution 87." Exhibition, Ho Chi Minh City, 1–10 September 1996.

Hoài Thanh. *Văn Nghệ*, no. 11. In *Bọn Nhân Văn Giai Phẩm*, 64–67.

Hoàng Cầm. "Con người Trần Dần" [The Person of Trần Dần]. *Nhân Văn* 1 (20 September 1956): 2, 4.

———. "Em bé lên sáu tuổi" [A Child of Six]. *Giai Phẩm Mùa Thu* 1 (September 1956): 15.

———. Telephone interviews by Thụy Khuê. *Hợp Lưu* 81 (February–March 2005): 81–97.

———. "Yêu thương và tha thứ là cốt lõi của cuộc sống" [Love and Forgiveness Is the Core of Life]. Interview in *An Ninh Thủ Đô*. Reprinted in *Talawas*, 2 March 2007. http://www.talawas.org/talaDB/showFile.php?res=9358&rb=0102 (accessed 13 April 2007).

Hoàng Linh. "Lấy chồng Đài Loan vỡ mộng thiên đường" [Marrying Taiwanese Husbands, Dreams of Paradise Broken]. *Tuổi Trẻ*, 3 August 1996.

Hoàng Minh Chính. "Góp ý kiến về dự thảo cương lĩnh" [Contributions toward the Proposed Party Platform]. In *Những vấn đề Việt Nam*.

————. "Thư ngỏ của công dân Hòang Minh Chính" [Open Letter from Citizen Hòang Minh Chính]. *Đối Thọai* 3 (August 1994): 11–23.

Hoàng Ngọc Anh. *Xóm thợ Trường Thi* [The Working Neighborhood of Trường Thi]. Hanoi: Nhà Xuất Bản Lao Động, 1975.

Hoàng Văn Chí. *Từ thực dân đến cộng sản* [From Colonialism to Communism]. Translated into Vietnamese by Mặc Định. Tokyo: Người Việt Tự Do, 1980.

"Hội thảo khoa học: Chủ Tịch Hồ Chí Minh với công tác bảo vệ sức khỏe" [Summary of the Scientific Conference on Chairman Ho Chi Minh and the Task of Protecting Health]. *Tạp Chí Cộng Sản* 515 (March 1997).

Horwitz, Allan V. *The Logic of Social Control.* New York: Plenum Press, 1990.

Hughes, Donna, Laura Sporcic, Nadine Mendelsohn, and Vanessa Chirgwin. *The Factbook on Global Sexual Exploitation* (Coalition Against Trafficking in Women, 1990). http://www.catwinternational.org/factbook/Vietnam.php (accessed 17 April 2007).

Human Rights Watch. "Vietnam: Crackdown on Dissent in Wake of WTO and APEC." 9 March 2007. http://hrw.org/english/docs/2007/03/09/vietna15466.htm (accessed 26 May 2007).

Hume, David. *Enquiries concerning Human Understanding and Concerning Principles of Morals* Oxford: Oxford University Press, 1975. Quoted in Burchell, "Peculiar Interests," 127.

————. *A Treatise of Human Nature.* Oxford: Oxford University Press, 1978. Quoted in Burchell, "Peculiar Interests," 130.

Hunt, Alan. "Governing the City: Liberalism and Early Modern Modes of Governance." In Barry, Osborne, and Rose, *Foucault and Political Reason.*

Hùynh Dũng Nhân. "Theo dấu 'bướm đêm'" [Tracing the "Night Butterflies"]. In *Tôi đi bán tôi: Tập phóng sự* [I Sell Myself: A Reportage Collection], 197–208. Ho Chi Minh City: Nhà Xuất Bản Văn Nghệ Thành Phố Hồ Chí Minh, 1999.

Jameson. Fredric. "Reification and Utopia in Mass Culture." *Social Text* 1 (Winter 1979).

Jimenez-David, Rina. "Anti-Prostitution Ordinance on the Table." *Asia Intelligence Wire (Financial Times)*, 6 September 2002. http://www.walnet.org/csis/news/world_2002/aiw-020906.html (accessed 17 April 2007).

Kaufman-Osborn, Timothy V. "Fashionable Subjects: On Judith Butler and the Causal Idioms of Postmodern Feminist Theory." *Political Research Quarterly* 50 (1997): 649–74.

Khải Quang. "Những con hẽm nổi tiếng nhất Sài Gòn" [The Most Famous Alleys in Saigon]. *Công An Nhân Dân*, 26 May 1996.

Khuất Thu Hồng, Nguyễn Thị Vân, Lê Thị Phương, and Bùi Thanh Hà. *Mại dâm và những hệ lụy kinh tế xã hội* [Prostitution and Its Socioeconomic Corollaries]. Hanoi: Viện Xã Hội Học, 1998.

Kitschelt, Herbert. "Political Regime Change: Structure and Process-Driven Explanations?" *American Political Science Review* 86, no. 4 (1992): 1028–34.

Kooiman, Jan, ed. *Modern Governance: New Government-Society Interactions*. London: Sage Publications, 1993.

Lâm Thị Thanh Hà. "Công lý, đừng quên ai" [Justice, Do Not Forget Anyone]. In *Người đàn bà quỳ* [The Kneeling Woman]. N.p. [Vietnam]: Báo Văn Nghệ, Báo Nông Nghiệp, and Nhà Xuất Bản Nông Nghiệp, 1988.

Lê Đạt. Interview by Thụy Khuê. *Hợp Lưu* 81 (February–March 2005): 29–75.

———. "Làm thơ" [To Write Poetry]. *Giai Phẩm Mùa Xuân*, February 1956.

Lê Đức Dục. "Chợ tình mấy nẻo đoạn trường" [The Painful Paths of the Love Market]. *Tuổi Trẻ*, 12 October 1996.

Lê Đức Thúy. "Economic *Đổi Mới* in Vietnam: Content, Achievements, and Prospects." In Turley and Selden, *Reinventing Vietnamese Socialism*.

Lê Minh Triết. "Vài ý kiến về quản lý nhà nước ngành xây dựng" [Comments on State Management of the Construction Industry]. *Thời Báo Kinh Tế Sài Gòn* 1 (December 1994).

Lê Ngọc Vân. "Mại dâm trẻ em và lạm dụng tình dục trẻ em" [Child Prostitution and Sexual Exploitation of Children]. *Khoa Học Về Phụ Nữ* 1 (1997): 37–41.

Lê Xuân Tá. "Hồi ức về cuộc khủng bố chủ nghĩa xét lại ở Việt Nam" [Reminiscences on the Terror Campaign against Revisionism in Vietnam]. *Đối Thoại* 3 (August 1994): 27–36.

Leipziger, Danny M. *Awakening the Market: Vietnam's Economic Transition*. World Bank Discussion Paper no. 157. Washington, D.C.: World Bank, 1992.

Lenin, V. I. "The Economic Basis of the Withering Away of the State." In *State and Revolution*, 298–313. Vol. 2 of *V. I. Lenin: Selected Works*. Moscow: Progress Publishers, 1977.

———. *What Is to Be Done?* 1902. Reprint, Moscow: Progress Publishers, 1973.

Lịch dử phong trào phụ nữ Việt Nam [History of the Vietnamese Women's Movement]. N.p., n.d.

Lichtenstein, Natalie G. *A Survey of Vietnam's Legal Framework in Transition*. Policy Working Paper no. 1291. Washington, D.C.: World Bank Legal Department, 1994.

Lim, Linda. "Capitalism, Imperialism, and Patriarchy: The Dilemma of Third-World Women Workers in Multinational Factories." In

Women, Men, and the International Division of Labor, edited by June Nash and María Patricia Fernández-Kelly. Albany, N.Y.: SUNY Press, 1983.

Linh Hoàn. "Đến Bình Dương uống bia . . . thôn nữ" [Come to Bình Dương to Drink Country-Girl Beer]. *Công An Thành Phố Hồ Chí Minh*, 10 November 2001.

Linh Sơn. *Chủ động sinh con theo ý muốn* [Actively Conceiving the Children You Want]. Ho Chi Minh City: Nhà Xuất Bản Thành Phố Hồ Chí Minh, 1990.

Lọ lem hè phố [Street Cinderella]. DVD. Directed by Lê Hoàng and produced by Hãng Phim Giải Phóng. Westminster, Calif.: Thanh Hằng Productions, 2004.

Lockhart, Greg. "Nguyễn Huy Thiệp's Writing: Post-Confucian, Post-modern." *Journal of Vietnamese Studies* (Australian Association of Vietnamese Studies) 6 (January 1993): 32–49.

Luebbert, Gregory. *Liberalism, Fascism, or Social Democracy*. New York: Oxford University Press, 1991.

Lukács, György. "Realism in the Balance." In *The Norton Anthology of Theory and Criticism*, edited by Vincent B. Leitch. New York: W. W. Norton, 2001.

Luker, Nicholas, ed. *An Anthology of the Classics of Socialist Realism: From Furmanov to Sholokhov*. Ann Arbor, Mich.: Ardis, 1988.

Luong, Hy Van. "The Political Economy of Vietnamese Reforms: A Microscopic Perspective from Two Ceramics Manufacturing Centers." In Turley and Selden, *Reinventing Vietnamese Socialism*.

Lý Chánh Trung. "Thử tìm giải pháp cho một môn học thầy không muốn dạy trò không muốn học" [Let's Find a Solution for a School Subject That Teachers Do Not Want to Teach and Students Do Not Want to Learn]. Speech reprinted in *Những vấn đề Việt Nam*.

Mahood, Linda. *The Magdalenes: Prostitution in the Nineteenth Century*. New York: Routledge, 1990.

Marr, David. *Vietnamese Tradition on Trial, 1920–1945*. Berkeley: University of California Press, 1981.

———. "Vietnamese Youth in the 1990s." *Vietnam Review* 2 (1997): 288–354.

Marx, Karl. *Capital*. Vol. 1 of *The Marx-Engels Reader*, edited by Robert Tuck. New York: W. W. Norton, 1978.

———. *Critique of Hegel's "Philosophy of Right."* Edited by J. O'Malley. New York: Cambridge University Press, 1970.

Marx, Karl, and Friedrich Engels. *The Marx-Engels Reader*. Edited by Robert Tuck. New York: W. W. Norton, 1978.

Massey, Doreen. *Space, Place, and Gender*. Minneapolis: University of Minnesota Press, 1994.

McClintock, Anne. *Imperial Leather: Race, Gender, and Sexuality in the Colonial Contest.* New York: Routledge, 1995.

McCool, Grant. "Vietnam Trials Send Zero-Tolerance Message." *Reuters,* 5 May 2007. http://www.reuters.com/article/worldNews/idUSHAN9920820070506.

Migdal, Joel, Atul Kohli, and Vivienne Shue. *State Power and Social Forces: Domination and Transformation in the Third World.* New York: Cambridge University Press, 1994 (decessed 25 May2007).

Milosz, Czeslaw. "Introduction to Abram Tertz's 'On Socialist Realism.'" In *The Trial Begins, and On Socialist Realism,* edited by Abram Tertz [Andrei Sinyavsky]. 1960. Reprint, Berkeley: University of California Press, 1982.

Minh Nguyệt. "Điếm deluxe và đêm nhiệt đới" [Whores Deluxe and the Tropical Night]. *Công An Nhân Dân,* 23 March 1996.

Mohanty, Chandra Talpade. "Women Workers and Capitalist Scripts: Ideologies of Domination, Common Interests, and the Politics of Solidarity." In *Feminist Genealogies, Colonial Legacies, Democratic Futures,* edited by M. Jacqui Alexander and Chandra Talpade Mohanty. New York: Routledge, 1997.

Mr. Smith Goes to Washington. DVD. Directed by Frank Capra. Culver City, Calif.: Columbia Pictures Corporation, 1939; Sony Pictures, 2000.

"Nghị Quyết của Hội Nghị Trung Ương Lần thứ XVI (4–1959) về vấn đề cải tạo xã hội chủ nghĩa đối với công thương nghiệp tư bản tư doanh" [Resolution of the Sixteenth Plenum (April 1959) on Socialist Transformation of Capitalist and Private Commercial and Industrial Enterprises]. In *Lịch sử Đảng Cộng Sản Việt Nam: Trích văn kiện Đảng, tập III* [The History of the Vietnamese Communist Party in Party Documents, vol. 3]. Hanoi: Nhà Xuất Bản Sách Giáo Khoa Mác–Lê-nin, 1979.

"Nghị Quyết của Hội Nghị Trung Ương Lần thứ bảy về nhiệm vụ và phương hướng xây dựng và phát triển công nghiệp (tháng 6 năm 1962)" [The Seventh Plenum Resolution on the Tasks and Directions of Industrial Construction and Development (June 1962)]. In *Lịch sử Đảng Cộng Sản Việt Nam: Trích văn kiện Đảng, tập III* [The History of the Vietnamese Communist Party in Party Documents, vol. 3]. Hanoi: Nhà Xuất Bản Giáo Khoa Mác–Lê-nin, 1979.

Ngô Ngọc Bội. *Ác mộng* [Nightmare]. Westminster, Calif.: Hồng Lĩnh, 1992.

Ngô Tất Tố. *Tắt đèn* [When the Lights Go Out]. Ho Chi Minh City: Nhà Xuất Bản Văn Nghệ, 1939. Reprinted 1999.

Ngô Vĩnh Long. "Vietnam." In *Prostitution: An International Handbook on Trends, Problems, and Policies,* edited by Nanette J. Davis. Westport, Conn.: Greenwood Press, 1993.

Nguyễn Chơn Trung. "Về việc sử dụng chủ nghĩa tư bản nhà nước tại Thành Phố Hồ Chí Minh" [On the Utilization of State Capitalism in Ho Chi Minh City]. *Tạp Chí Khoa Học Xã Hội* 12 (1992): 26–38.

Nguyễn Công Hoan. *Bước đường cùng* [Dead End]. Ho Chi Minh City: Nhà Xuất Bản Văn Nghệ, 1938. Reprinted 1999.

Nguyễn Đăng Thành. "Những yêu cầu của lãnh đạo chính trị đối với nền kinh tế thị trường theo định hướng xã hội chủ nghĩa ở nước ta" [Demands on Political Leadership Facing the Market Economy following the Socialist Orientation in Our Country]. *Tạp Chí Cộng Sản* 3 (February 1997): 33–36.

Nguyễn Đình Thi. "Rõ ràng là những âm mưu luận điệu phản cách mạnh có hệ thống" [Clearly Those Plots and Arguments Are Systematically Anti-revolutionary], *Học Tập* (3 March 1958). Excerpt reprinted in *Bọn Nhân Văn Giai Phẩm*, 112–15.

Nguyễn Đức Bình. "Vì một nền văn hóa đậm đà bản sắc dân tộc " [For a Culture Deeply Colored by Our National Identity]. *Khoa Học Xã Hội* 19 (January 1994): 12–19.

Nguyễn Hữu Đang. Telephone interview by Thụy Khuê. *Hợp Lưu* 81 (February–March 2005): 76–80.

Nguyễn Huy Thiệp. "Không có vua" [Without a King]. In *Những ngọn gió Hua Tát.*

———. "Kiếm sắc" [Sharp Sword]. In *Nguyễn Huy Thiệp tác phẩm và dư luận.*

———. *Nguyễn Huy Thiệp tác phẩm và dư luận.* [Nguyễn Huy Thiệp: Works and Criticism]. Phú Nhuận, Vietnam: Nhà Xuất Bản Trẻ and Tạp Chí Sông Hương, 1989.

———. "Những bài học nông thôn" [Rural Lessons]. In *Truyện ngắn chọn lọc Nguyễn Huy Thiệp.*

———. *Những ngọn gió Hua Tát* [The Winds of Hua Tát]. Hanoi: Nhà Xuất Bản Văn Hóa, 1989

———. "Phẩm tiết" [Chastity]. In *Nguyễn Huy Thiệp tác phẩm và dư luận.*

———. "Thương nhớ đồng quê" [Nostalgia for Country Land]. In *Truyện ngắn chọn lọc Nguyễn Huy Thiệp.*

———. *Truyện ngắn chọn lọc Nguyễn Huy Thiệp* [Selected Stories by Nguyễn Huy Thiệp]. Hanoi: Nhà Xuất Bản Hội Nhà Văn, 1995.

———. "Tướng về hưu" [The Retired General]. In *Những ngọn gió Hua Tát.*

Nguyễn Khắc Hiến. "Kinh tế thị trường và công bằng xã hội" [The Market Economy and Social Justice]. *Tạp Chí Cộng Sản* 2 (1994): 34–38.

Nguyễn Khắc Khanh. "Giữ gìn bản sắc văn hóa dân tộc: Một vấn đề cho toàn xã hội" [Keeping the Color of Our National Culture: A Problem for the Whole Society]. *Tạp Chí Cộng Sản* 8 (April 1996): 45–47.

Nguyễn Kiến Giang. "Bàn về sự lãnh đạo của đảng" [On the Party's Leadership]. In *Tuyển tập Nguyễn Kiến Giang* [Nguyễn Kiến Giang: Selected Writings]. Garden Grove, Calif.: Nhà Xuất Bản Trăm Hoa, 1993.

Nguyễn Lân. Letter to the editor. *Cứu Quốc*, 13 April 1958. Reprinted in *Bọn Nhân Văn Giai Phẩm.*

Nguyễn Mạnh Tường. "Hai câu chuyện" [Two Tales]. *Giai Phẩm Mùa Đông* 1 (December 1956): 49–52.

———. Interview by Phạm Trần. "Hạnh ngộ cụ Nguyễn Mạnh Tường" [Encountering Nguyễn Mạnh Tường]. In *Trăm hoa vẫn nở trên quê hương.*

———. Interview in "Mở rộng tự do và dân chủ" [Expanding Freedom and Democracy]. *Nhân Văn* 1 (20 September 1965): 1, 5.

Nguyen Nam Phuong. "Vietnam Struggles to Fight Political Corruption." *Online Asia Times*, 25 May 2005. http://www.atimes.com/se-asia/ DE25Ae02.html (accessed 26 May 2005).

Nguyễn, Tuấn Ngọc. "Socialist Realism in Vietnamese Literature: An Analysis of the Relationship between Politics and Literature." Ph.D. diss., Victoria University, Melbourne, 2004.

Nguyễn Tấn Hưng. Letter to *Talawas*, 13 April 2007. http://www .talawas.org/talaDB/showThu.php?res=9735&rb=12&von=20 (accessed 13 April 2007).

Nguyễn Thành Thống. *Giáo dục giới tính cho thanh niên: Dành cho các bậc phụ huynh* [Sex Education for Adolescents: A Guide for Parents and Guardians]. Ho Chi Minh City: Nhà Xuất Bản Trẻ, 1994.

Nguyễn Trung Thành. "Bia ôm, tôi cứ hỏi vì sao" [*Bia Ôm*, I Keep Asking Why]. *Phụ Nữ Chủ Nhật* 6 (12 May 1996): 4, 31.

Nguyễn Văn Thụy. "Xã hội hóa hoạt động khoa học và công nghệ ở miền núi, vùng sâu, vùng xa" [Socializing Scientific and Industrial Activities in Mountainous and Remote Regions]. *Tạp Chí Cộng Sản* 24 (December 1996): 20–22.

Nguyễn-võ Thu-Hương. "Governing the Social: Prostitution and Liberal Governance in Vietnam during Marketization." Ph.D. diss., University of California, Irvine, 1998.

Nhóm Phóng Viên CT-XH. "Bạc tiền giết hết nhân phẩm" [Money Kills Human Value]. *Công An Thành Phố Hồ Chí Minh*, 6 March 1996.

———. "Cà phê các kiểu" [Café Styles]. *Đặc San Công An Thành Phố Hồ Chí Minh*, 29 June 1996.

———. "Khi nhà dột từ nóc" [When the Roof Leaks]. *Công An Thành Phố Hồ Chí Minh*, 29 May 1996.

———. "Phạm Huy Phước, Quyền lực và sa đọa" [Phạm Huy Phước: Power and Moral Corruption]. *Công An Thành Phố Hồ Chí Minh*, 28 February 1996.

Nhóm PV VHVN. "Karaoke ngoại thành và những nàng 'thôn nữ'"

[Suburban Karaoke and "Country Girls"]. *Sài Gòn Giải Phóng*, 6 August 2001.

Như Mai (Châm Văn Biếm). "Thi sĩ máy" [Robotic Poet]. *Nhân Văn* 5 (20 November 1956): 3–4.

Những cô gái chân dài [Long-Legged Girls]. DVD. Directed by Vũ Ngọc Đặng. Hanoi: Thiên Ngân, 2004.

Những văn bản về phòng chống tệ nạn xã hội [Official Documents on Preventing and Fighting Social Evils]. Hanoi: Nhà Xuất Bản Chính Trị Quốc Gia, 1995.

Những vấn đề Việt Nam [Vietnam: Issues and Problems]. Garden Grove, Calif.: Nhà Xuất Bản Trăm Hoa, 1992.

Ninh, Kim. "Revolution, Politics, and Culture in Vietnam, 1945–1965." Ph.D. diss., Yale University, 1996.

————. *A World Transformed: The Politics of Culture in Revolutionary Vietnam, 1945–1965.* Ann Arbor: University of Michigan Press, 2002.

Nogee, Joseph, and Robert H. Donaldson. *Soviet Foreign Policy since World War II.* 3rd. ed. New York: Pergamon, 1988.

Nữ tướng cướp [Female Bandits]. DVD. Directed by Lê Hoàng. Hanoi: Thiên Ngân, 2005.

N. T. "Sở y tế TPHCM: Nhập nhằng ở đâu?" [The Ho Chi Minh City Health Bureau: Where Are the Tangles?]. *Diễn Đàn Forum* 55 (1 September 1996).

O'Donnell, Guillermo, Philippe Schmitter, and Lawrence Whitehead, eds. *Transition from Authoritarian Rule: Tentative Conclusions about Uncertain Democracies.* Baltimore: Johns Hopkins University Press, 1986.

Ong, Aihwa. *Flexible Citizenship: The Cultural Logics of Transnationality.* Durham, N.C.: Duke University Press, 1999.

————. "Gender, Periphery, and Hierarchy: Gender in Southeast Asia." In *Gender and Anthropology: Critical Reviews for Research and Teaching,* edited by Sandra Morgen. Washington, D.C.: American Anthropological Association, 1989.

————. "Japanese Factories, Malay Workers: Class and Sexual Metaphors in West Malaysia." In *Power and Difference: Gender in Island Southeast Asia,* edited by J. Atkinson and S. Errington. Stanford, Calif.: Stanford University Press, 1990.

————. *Neoliberalism as Exception: Mutations in Citizenship and Sovereignty.* Durham, N.C.: Duke University Press, 2006.

O'Neill, John. *The Market: Ethics, Knowledge, and Politics.* New York: Routledge, 1998.

Osborne, Thomas. "Security and Vitality: Drains, Liberalism, and Power in the Nineteenth Century." In Barry, Osborne, and Rose, *Foucault and Political Reason.*

Paltiel, Jeremy. "China: Mexicanization or Market Reforms?" In *The Elusive State: International and Comparative Perspectives*, edited by James A. Caporaso. Newbury Park, Calif.: Sage, 1989.

Parsons, Talcott. "Political Aspects of Social Structure and Process." In *Varieties of Political Theory*, edited by David Easton. Englewood Cliffs, N.J.: Prentice Hall, 1966.

Pasquino, Pascal. "Theatrum Politicum: The Genealogy of Capital." In Burchell, Gordon, and Miller, *Foucault Effect*.

Perry, Mary Elizabeth. *Gender and Disorder in Early Modern Seville*. Princeton, N.J.: Princeton University Press, 1990.

Phạm Huy Thông. Letter to *Nhân Dân*, 5 April 1958. Excerpted in *Bọn Nhân Văn Giai Phẩm*.

Phạm Tâm Long. Interview by Phạm Miên. Special New Year's issue, *Công An Nhân Dân*, 1996.

Phạm Xuân Nam. "Đổi mới kinh tế-xã hội ở nước ta và mấy vấn đề cấp bách" [Socioeconomic Reforms in Our Country and Urgent Issues]. *Tạp Chí Khoa Học Xã Hội* 19 (1994): 88–97.

———. "Phát huy sức mạnh tổng hợp của các khoa học liên nghành phục vụ sự nghiệp đổi mới đất nước" [Building the Unified Strength of the Multidisciplines in the Sciences to Serve the Enterprise of Reform in Our Country]. *Tạp Chí Cộng Sản* 2 (January 1997): 9–13.

Phan Đình Diệu. "Kiến nghị về một chương trình cấp bách nhằm khắc phục khủng hỏang và tạo điều kiện lành mạnh cho sự phát triển đất nước" [Proposal for an Urgent Program to Overcome the Crisis and Create Healthy Conditions for the Development of the Country]. In *Những vấn đề Việt Nam*.

Phan Khôi. "Phê bình lãnh đạo văn nghệ" [A Critique of the Leadership of the Arts]. *Giai Phẩm Mùa Thu* 1 (September 1956): 3–16.

Phan Thế Hữu Toàn. "Tệ nạn mại dâm ở Phú Yên sẽ cáo chung?" [Will the Social Evil of Prostitution in Phú Yên Come to an End?]. *Công An Nhân Dân*, 11 May 1996.

Phan Văn Lương. "Cà phê các kiểu" [Café Styles]. *Công An Nhân Dân*, 13 April 1996.

———. "15 cây số ăn chơi ngày ấy" [Fifteen Kilometers of Eating and Playing in Those Days]. *Công An Nhân Dân*, 13 April 1996.

Phanxine. "Ba phim tết 2006: An toàn hay bức phá" [Three New Year's Films: Safe or Innovative?]. *Yxine*, 28 January 2006. http://yxine.com.

———. "Phỏng vấn: Gái nhảy 2, sự bất ngờ không lường" [Interview: *Bar Girls 2*, a Surprise]. *Yxine*, 22 July 2003. http://yxine.com.

Phùng Quán. "Chống tham ô lãng phí" [Against Corruption and Waste]. *Giai Phẩm Mùa Thu* 2 (September 1956): 39–42.

———. "Lời mẹ dặn" [Mother's Words]. In *Nhớ Phùng Quán* [Remember-

ing Phung Quan: Selected Writings], edited by Ngô Minh. Ho Chi
Minh City: Nhà Xuất Bản Trẻ, 2003.

———. "Người bạn lính cùng một tiểu đội" [The Soldier Friend from
My Unit]. *Diễn Đàn* 93 (February 2000): 41–47.

Pike, Douglas. *History of Vietnamese Communism, 1925–1976.* Stanford,
Calif.: Hoover Institution, 1978.

Porter, Gareth. *Vietnam: The Politics of Bureaucratic Socialism.* Ithaca,
N.Y.: Cornell University Press, 1993.

Potter, David. "Democratization in Asia." In *Prospects for Democracy,*
edited by David Held. Cambridge, U.K.: Polity, 1993.

Poulantzas, Nicos. *Classes in Contemporary Capitalism.* Translated by
David Fernbach. London: New Left Books, 1975.

Poznanski, Kazimierz, ed. *Constructing Capitalism: The Reemergence
of Civil Society and Liberal Economy in the Post-Communist World.*
Boulder, Colo.: Westview Press, 1992.

Przeworski, Adam. *Democracy and the Market.* New York: Cambridge
University Press, 1991.

———. "Problems in the Study of Transition to Democracy." In *Tran-
sition to Authoritarian Rule: Tentative Conclusions about Uncertain
Democracies,* edited by G. O'Donnell, P. Schmitter, and L. Whitehead.
Baltimore: Johns Hopkins University Press, 1986.

P. V. [Phóng Viên (Reporter)]. "Hiểm họa bùng nổ AIDS từ tệ nạn mại
dâm" [The Explosive Threat of AIDS from the Evil of Prostitution].
Tuổi Trẻ Chủ Nhật, 12 March 1995, 32–33.

P. V. [Phóng Viên (Reporter)]. "Đại hội đảng bộ công an Thành Phố
Hồ Chí Minh" [Conference of the Ho Chi Minh City Public Security's
Party Organ]. *Công An Nhân Dân,* 20 April 1996.

Report on the conference "Mại dâm—Quan điểm và giải pháp" [Prosti-
tution: Perspectives and Solutions]. *Khoa Học Về Phụ Nữ* 1 (1999):
36–38.

Riedel, James, and Bruce Comer. "Transition to a Market Economy in
Vietnam." In *Economies in Transition: Comparing Asia and Eastern
Europe,* edited by Wing Thye Woo, Stephen Parker, and Jeffrey D.
Sachs. Cambridge, Mass.: MIT Press, 1997.

Robison, Richard. "Neoliberalism and the Future World: Markets and the
End of Politics." In *Neoliberalism and Conflict in Asia after 9/11,* edited
by Gary Rodan and Kevin Hewison. New York: Routledge, 2006.

Rockman, Bert A. "Minding the State or a State of Mind?" In *The Elusive
State: International and Comparative Perspectives,* edited by James A.
Caporaso. Newbury Park, Calif.: Sage, 1989.

Rose, Nikolas. "Governing Advanced Liberal Democracies." In Barry,
Osborne, and Rose, *Foucault and Political Reason.*

———. *Powers of Freedom: Reframing Political Thought.* Cambridge:
Cambridge University Press, 1999.

Rueschmeyer, Dietrich, Evelyne Stevens, and John Stevens, eds. *Capitalist Development and Democracy*. Chicago: University of Chicago Press, 1992.

Rushdie, Salman. *The Moor's Last Sigh*. New York: Pantheon, 1995.

Sơn Cước. "Vũng Tàu: Bao nhiêu lâu để chấm dứt cuộc chiến này" [Vũng Tàu: How Long Will This Battle Go On?]. *Công An Nhân Dân*, 3 June 1996.

Simmons, Jon. *Foucault and the Political*. New York: Routledge, 1995.

Simon, Jonathan. "Refugees in a Carceral Age: The Rebirth of Immigration Prisons in the United States." *Public Culture* 10, no. 3 (1998): 577–607.

Solinger, Dorothy. "Urban Entrepreneurs and the State: The Merger of State and Society." In *State and Society in China: The Consequences of Reforms*, edited by Arthur L. Rosenbaum. Boulder, Colo.: Westview Press, 1992.

Sơn Nam. *Hương rừng Cà Mau* [The Scent of Camau Jungle]. Ho Chi Minh City: Tuổi trẻ, 1998.

———. "Một khía cạnh của văn hóa xài tiền" [An Aspect of the Money-Spending Culture]. In *An ninh kinh tế và nền kinh tế thị trường Việt Nam—Economic Security and the Vietnamese Market Economy*. Ho Chi Minh City: Nhà Xuất Bản An Ninh Nhân Dân, 1995.

———. *Văn minh miệt vườn* [Orchard Civilization]. Ho Chi Minh City: Nhà Xuất Bản Văn Hóa, 1992.

Stalin, Joseph. *Foundations of Leninism*. New York: International Publishers, 1939.

Statistical Yearbook 1995. Hanoi: Statistical Publishing House, 1996.

T. Văn. "Nghĩ về những 'cử chỉ đẹp' của nhà nước" [Thinking about the Beautiful Gestures of the Government]. *Talawas*, 27 March 2007. http://www.talawas.org/talaDB/showFile.php?res=9577&rb=0102 (accessed 13 April 2007).

Taylor, Charles. *Modern Social Imaginaries*. Durham, N.C.: Duke University Press, 2004.

Taylor, K. W. "Locating and Translating Boundaries in Nguyễn Huy Thiệp's Short Stories." *Vietnam Review*, no. 1 (Autumn–Winter 1996).

"Tệ nạn mua bán dâm và các biện pháp phòng chống tệ nạn mua bán dâm 1993–1994 tại Thành Phố Hồ Chí Minh" [The Social Evil of Buying and Selling Sex and Combating Measures in Ho Chi Minh City]. Unpublished report. Ho Chi Minh City People's Council and Committee and the Bureau of Science, Industry and the Environment, 1994.

Thân Thanh Huyền. "Góp ý vào văn kiện trình Đại Hội Đảng Toàn Quốc lần thứ VIII: Ba vấn đề mấu chốt để thực hiện thắng lợi nhiệm vụ bảo vệ an ninh chính trị, trật tự an toàn xã hội" [Contributions to Documents to be Presented at the Eighth Party Congress: Three Issues Pivotal to the Successful Realization of the Mission to Protect

Political Security and Social Safety and Order]. *Công An Nhân Dân*, 2 June 1996.

———. Interview by Phạm Miên. Special New Year's issue, *Công An Nhân Dân*, 1996.

Thanh Hà. "Những quán cà phê gây 'phê'" [Cafés That Can Make You "High"]. *Công An Nhân Dân*, 30 March 1996.

Thu Dương. "Lộ chân tướng" [Unmasked]. *Đặc San Công An Thành Phố Hồ Chí Minh*, 17 August 1996.

"Thực hiện cuộc vận động lớn: Thiết lập trật tự kỷ cương trong các hoạt động văn hóa và dịch vụ văn hóa, bài trừ tệ nạn xã hội" [Realizing This Big Movement: Establishing Order, Principles in Cultural Activities and Cultural Services, Eliminating Social Evils]. *Tạp Chí Cộng Sản* 2 (1996): 12–14.

Thương Hoài Nguyên. "Săn 'gà nước đêm' trên sông Sài Gòn" ["Night Water-Chic" Hunting on the Saigon River]. *Thanh Niên*, 21 January 1996.

Thúy Ngân. "Vấn đề giáo dục giới tính và bệnh phụ sản ở giới trẻ" [Sex Education and Gynecological Disorders in Youths]. *Thanh Niên*, 16 June 1996.

Tiến Đạt. "Chợ tình lộ thiên ở Đông Hà–Quảng Trị" [The Open Love Market in Đông Hà, Quảng Trị]. *Công An Nhân Dân*, 15 September 1995.

Tiến Triển-Mạnh Thắng. "Công an nhân dân với từ điển bách khoa Việt Nam" [The People's Public Security and the *Vietnam Encyclopedia*]. Special New Year's issue. *Công An Nhân Dân*, 1996.

Tố Hữu. "Nhìn lại 3 năm phá hoại của nhóm 'Nhân Văn Giai Phẩm'" [Looking Back at Three Years of Sabotage by the "Nhân Văn–Giai Phẩm Group"]. In *Bọn Nhân Văn Giai Phẩm*, 22–36.

———. "Những luận điệu chính trị phản động" [Reactionary Political Arguments], in *Bọn Nhân Văn Giai Phẩm*, 143–55.

Tocqueville, Alexis de. *Democracy in America*. Translated by G. Lawrence. Edited by J. P. Mayer. New York: Doubleday, 1969.

Trăm hoa vẫn nở trên quê hương: Cao trào văn nghệ phản kháng tại Việt Nam 1986–1989 [A Hundred Flowers Still Bloom: Dissident Art in Vietnam, 1986–1989]. Edited by the Trăm Hoa Group. Reseda, Calif.: Nhà Xuất Ban Lê Trần, 1990.

Tran, Angie N. "An Analysis of the Developmental State: The Case of the Vietnamese Textile and Garment Industry." Ph.D. diss., University of Southern California, 1996.

———. "Global Subcontracting and Its Impacts on the Gender Division of Labor in the Vietnamese Textile and Garment Industries." Paper prepared for the Center for Development Research Workshop, Copenhagen, 11–13 June 1998.

Trần Bồng Sơn. *Giáo dục giới tính cho thanh thiếu niên: Người con gái lấy*

chồng [Sex Education for Youths: The Girl Who Is Getting Married].
Ho Chi Minh City: Nhà Xuất Bản Trẻ, 1995.

Trần Đình Hoàn. "Chính sách xã hội và trách nhiệm của nghành lao
động-thương binh, xã hội" [Social Policy and the Responsibilities of
the Branch of Labor, War Invalids, and Social Work]. *Tạp Chí Khoa
Học Xã Hội* 19 (1994): 98–106.

Trần Đình Sử. "Ngôn từ trong thơ Tố Hữu" [Word Deployment in
Tố Hữu's Poetry]. In *Nhà văn Việt Nam thế kỷ XX* [Twentieth-
Century Writers of Vietnam]. 1985. Reprint, Hanoi: Nhà Xuất Bản
Hội Nhà Văn, 1999), 4:634.

Trần Độ. *Đổi mới và chính sách xã hội văn hóa* [Reforms and Social,
Cultural Policy]. Ho Chi Minh City: Nhà Xuất Bản Thành Phố Hồ
Chí Minh, 1988.

Trần Đức Thảo. "Nội dung xã hội và hình thức tự do" [Social Content
and the Form of Freedom]. *Giai Phẩm Mùa Đông* 1 (December 1956):
15–21.

———. "Nổ lực phát triển tự do dân chủ" [Efforts to Develop Freedom
and Democracy]. *Nhân Văn* 4 (15 October 1956): 1.

Trần Duy. "Những người khổng lồ" [The Giants]. *Giai Phẩm Mùa Thu*
2 (September 1956): 32–38.

Trần Khắc. "Người đàn bà quỳ" [The Kneeling Woman]. In *Người đàn
bà quỳ*. N.p., [Vietnam]: Báo Văn Nghệ, Báo Nông Nghiệp, and Nhà
Xuất Bản Nông Nghiệp, 1988.

Trần Ngọc Dinh. "Thành phần kinh tế tư bản tư nhân ở Thành Phố
Hồ Chí Minh" [The Private Economic Sector in Ho Chi Minh City].
Tạp Chí Khoa Học Xã Hội 13 (1992): 31–39.

Trường Chinh. "Kháng chiến nhất định thắng lợi" [The Resistance Shall
Triumph]. In *Lịch sử Đảng Cộng Sản Việt Nam: Trích văn kiện Đảng,
tập II* [The History of the Vietnamese Communist Party in Party
Documents, vol. 2]. Hanoi: Nhà Xuất Bản Sách Giáo Khoa Mác–Lê-
nin, 1979.

Trương Tửu. "Bệnh sùng bái cá nhân trong giới lãnh đạo văn nghệ"
[The Disease of Personality Worship among the Leadership of the
Arts]. *Giai Phẩm Mùa Thu* 2 (September 1956): 6.

———. "Tự do tư tưởng của văn nghệ sĩ và sự lãnh đạo của Đảng Cộng
Sản Bôn-Sê-Vích" [Writers' and Artists' Freedom of Thought and
the Leadership of the Bolshevik Party]. *Giai Phẩm Mùa Đông* 1
(December 1956): 64–67.

TTV–QT. "Đường dây oan nghiệt" [Vicious Circle]. *Đặc San Công
An Thành Phố Hồ Chí Minh*, 1992.

Tuck, Richard, ed. Introduction to *Hobbes: Leviathan*. New York: Cambridge University Press, 1991.

Tương Lai. "Tính năng động xã hội, sự phân tầng xã hội trong sự nghiệp
đổi mới của nước ta" [The Dynamism of Society and Social Stratifica-

tion in Our Country's Reforms]. *Tạp Chí Khoa Học Xã Hội* 19 (1994): 115–27.

Turley, William, and Mark Selden, eds. *Reinventing Vietnamese Social-ism:* Doi Moi *in Comparative Perspective.* Boulder, Colo.: Westview Press, 1993.

Văn Lang. "Cà phê 'de-la-hiên' Sài Gòn: Nơi gặp gỡ của văn hóa đông tây" ["De-la hien" Cafés: Where East Meets West]. *Người Việt Online,* 1 October 2006. http://www.nguoi-viet.com/absolutenm/anmviewer .asp?a=49583&p (accessed 2 October 2006).

Vietnam Economic Times. "Service Industry." May 2006.

Võ Khối. "Gái quê trong làng chơi Sài Gòn" [Rural Girls in the Village of Play in Saigon]. *Thanh Niên* 157 (1 October 1997): 15.

Vũ Quang Việt. "Phát triển kinh tế và phân hóa xã hội" [Economic Development and Social Differentiation]. *Diễn Đàn Forum* 49 (1 February 1996): 14–18.

Vũ Thư Hiên. *Đêm giữa ban ngày* [Night at Day]. Westminster, Calif.: Văn Nghệ, 1997.

Vũ Trọng Phụng. *Giông Tố* [The Storm]. In *Tuyển tập Vũ Trọng Phụng, tập 1* [Vũ Trọng Phụng: Selected Works, vol. 1]. 1936–37. Reprint, Hanoi: Nhà Xuất Bản Văn Học, 1998.

———. *Vỡ đê* [The Dam Breaks]. In *Tuyển tập Vũ Trọng Phụng, tập 1* [Vũ Trọng Phụng: Selected Works, vol. 1]. 1936–37. Reprint, Hanoi: Nhà Xuất Bản Văn Học, 1998.

Walkowitz, Judith. *Prostitution and Victorian Society.* Cambridge: Cambridge University Press, 1980.

Wank, David. "The Institutional Process of Market Clientelism: Guanxi and Private Business in a South China City." *China Quarterly* 147 (1996): 820–38.

Werner, Jayne. "Gender, Renovation, and State: *Doi Moi* as Embedded Social Process in Vietnam." In *Gender, Household, State:* Doi Moi *in Vietnam,* edited by Jayne Werner and Daniele Belanger. Ithaca, N.Y.: Cornell Southeast Asia Program, 2002.

Wolfe, Nancy Travis. *Policing a Socialist Society: The German Democratic Republic.* New York: Greenwood Press, 1992.

Womack, Brantley. "Political Reforms and Political Change in Communist Countries: Implications for Vietnam." In Turley and Selden, *Reinventing Vietnamese Socialism.*

Writers' Congress. "Nghị quyết của ban chấp hành hội liên hiệp văn học nghệ thuật Việt Nam" [Resolution by the Executive Committee of the Association of Arts and Letters]. In *Bọn Nhân Văn Giai Phẩm.*

Wurfel, David. "*Doi Moi* in Comparative Perspective." In Turley and Selden, *Reinventing Vietnamese Socialism.*

Xuân Đào. "Giáo dục đồng đẳng là gì?" [What Is Peer Education?]. *úc Khỏe* 3 (September–October 1995): 2.

Xuân Hồng, "Chặt đứt đường giây mãi dâm quốc Tế" [Severing the Line

of International Prostitution], *Công An Thành Phố Hồ Chí Minh*, 23–
24 July 1996.

———. "Từ vũ trường–nhà chứa đến đường dây mại dâm quốc tế" [From
Dancing Nightclubs–Whorehouses to International Prostitution Rings].
Công An Thành Phố Hồ Chí Minh, 27 March 1996–24 April 1996.

Xuân Nguyên. "'Quả đấm thép' của cảnh sát nhân dân Vietnam."
[The Steel Fist of the Vietnamese People's Police Force]. *Đặc San
Công An Nhân Dân*, 13 May 1996.

Xuân Xe. "Lấy vốn nhà nước giao tư thương" [Giving State Capital
to Private Enterprise]. *Đặc San Công An Nhân Dân*, 15 March 1996.

Zinoman, Peter. "Declassifying Nguyễn Huy Thiệp." *Positions: East
Asia Cultures Critique* 2, no. 2 (1994): 294–317.

Žižek, Slavoj. *The Parallax View*. Cambridge, Mass.: MIT Press, 2006.

———. *The Sublime Object of Ideology*. London: Verso, 1989.

NEWSPAPERS AND OTHER PERIODICALS

Công An Nhân Dân (Hanoi and Ho Chi Minh City)

Công An Thành Phố Hồ Chí Minh (Ho Chi Minh City)

Đặc San Công An Nhân Dân (Hanoi and Ho Chi Minh City)

Đặc San Công An Thành Phố Hồ Chí Minh (Ho Chi Minh City)

Diễn Đàn Forum (Bourg-La-Reine, France)

Giai Phẩm Mùa Đông (Hanoi)

Giai Phẩm Mùa Thu (Hanoi)

Giai Phẩm 1956 (Hanoi)

Người Bảo Vệ Công Lý (Ho Chi Minh City)

Người Việt (Westminster, Calif.)

Orange County Register (Santa Ana, Calif.)

Phụ Nữ (Ho Chi Minh City)

Phụ Nữ Chủ Nhật (Ho Chi Minh City)

Saigon Times (Ho Chi Minh City)

Thanh Niên (Ho Chi Minh City)

Thời Báo Kinh Tế Sài Gòn (Ho Chi Minh City)

Tuổi Trẻ (Ho Chi Minh City)

Tuổi Trẻ Chủ Nhật (Ho Chi Minh City)

Việt Báo Kinh Tế (Westminster, Calif.)

Index

business: contacts, 13; contracts, 14, 15; and illegal practices, 13–14, 16–18; sub-contracts, 16, 20
Butler, Judith, 46, 119

"Camp for the Recovery of Human Dignity," 81
capital accumulation, flexible mode of, xiii, 134
carceral training. *See* rehabilitation
CARE International, 37, 49, 103, 133, 141, 279n23; and rehabilitation, 157, 159, 166–68, 177–79, 288n99
Center for Social Sponsorship, 131–32, 135, 158, 176
Central Committee. *See* Party Central Committee
Central Training Committee, 90
"Chastity" (Phẩm tiết), 207, 208
China, xxi, 73, 189
Chung, Hilary, 193
Chuyện tử tế (documentary), 206
CIA (Central Intelligence Agency), 149
cinema. *See* film, Vietnamese
citizenship, flexible, xvi
city, 53–54. *See also* femininity; women
civil society: autonomy and tension, 93; and Foucault, 77; idea of, 77, 163–64. *See also* knowledge
class: and aesthetics, 41; and Bourdieu, 28, 31–32, 109; and consumption, 26, 144, 240–41; differentiation, 36–37, 94–95, 142, 144–45; distinction, 25–42, 109; and division of sexual labor, 39; entrepreneurial, 37–41; in Europe, 109; expression in commercial sex, 28–41; and gender, 116, 142; and global division of labor, 115, 137–38, 142; and governance, iv, xxvii, 94–95, 97, 141–42, 144, 182, 257; and knowledge, 109, 114, 144–45, 149; in Lenin's view, 70, 194; and market economy, 145; Marxist approaches to, 25–26, 194; middle, 26–27, 109, 111, 255; and national identity, 116, 142, 246; Neo-Marxist approach to, 26; norms, 94–95; notions of 25–28; and power, 41, 61–62, 142, 182; and rehabilita-

tion, 136, 144–45; and sexual domination, 33–35, 40; and sex workers' consumption, 30, 34, 35, 118; and sex workers' services, 29–35, 94, 97, 101–3; status of experts, 67; status of male clients, 36–41, 47, 102, 108; stratification, 108–9, 246; superiority, 109; and truth, 115–16, 191; and Vietnamese film, 227, 235–36; Weberian approach to, 25–26, 27, 28. *See also* bourgeois class; commercial sex; consumption; family: middle-class; history; proletarian class; women
class struggle, 67–68, 70–71; and human history, 72, 196. *See also* ideology
coercion. *See* governance: coercion and/or coercive; power: and coercion; rehabilitation: and coercion
Comaroff, Jean, xiv–xv, 25, 116
Comaroff, John, xiv–xv, 25, 116
command economy, 66–67, 213; lack of expertise, 72. *See also* economic liberalization; socialist state
commercial sex: clientele, 23, 24, 43–44, 47, 108; current volume of, 4–5; in entrepreneurial transactions, xxvi, 18–24, 36–38; in expression of class, 29–41, 246; in expression of national identity, xxvi, 41–62, 246; food in, 49, 51–54; forms of, 18–19; growth of, 5, 246; as leisure, 28–30; post-colonial, 109; and tourism, 43–45; in Vietnamese journalism, 219–21. *See also* AIDS; class; consumption; economic liberalization; film, Vietnamese; freedom; HIV; prostitution; sex worker
commodification, of sex, 48, 49, 51–54, 111
Communist Party. *See* Vietnamese Communist Party
Communist society, 70
Confucian values, 137
consumption: nativist, 46–56; neoliberal, 25; of sex, 23, 28–30, 37–39, 49, 51–54; by sex workers, 116; by urban women, 144; of Vietnamese film, 227–29, 239. *See also* class; women
contract theories, 170

economy *(continued)*
217, 241–42, 243; and power, xxii;
socialist, 7–8, 150; two-price system,
8. *See also* global economy; market;
neoliberalism
Edwards, Mickey, 252
Elliott, David, 275n27
empirical realism. *See* empiricism
empiricism: and choice, 169–70; and
the feminine, 199–213, 214, 216,
225–27; Foucauldian approach to,
253; and freedom, 195–98; and governance, xx, 65, 91; and knowledge,
xiv, xxi–xxiii, xxviii, 91, 144, 165, 182,
217–19, 255–56; and prostitution,
xiii; of rurality, 206–12, 213; of social
reality, xxvii, 185, 188, 193–213; in
Vietnamese journalism, 217–19. *See
also* dissent; feminine; femininity;
film, Vietnamese; governance; government; knowledge; medicine; social
realism
entrepreneurs, 14, 19, 29, 38, 40, 41; as
commercial sex clientele, 23; state, 11,
21, 23
erotics, 48, 56, 227–29
Europe, 77, 78, 109, 203, 250–51. *See
also* commercial sex; film, Vietnamese; prostitution; sex
Ewald, François, 250
expertise, 76; as alien, 83; as bourgeois,
83; and governance, 78–80, 246; and
medicine, 76–77, 82–84, 144–45;
and prostitution, 103–5, 114, 247;
and rehabilitation, 168; in socialist
governance, 66–67; the statization of,
67–74. *See also* experts; governance;
knowledge
experts: and foreign policy, 74; and medicine, 85–87; and problems in the arts
and sciences, 74; and relations with
governors, 79, 89; in socialist governance, 66–67; training of, 85. *See also*
expertise; knowledge

family: and marriage or conjugal relationship, 110–13; middle-class, 97,
102–3, 108, 110, 112–14; and the

nation, 95; and privatization of
domestic space, 112; in rehabilitation
models, 160–63
Fanon, Frantz, 48
Fatherland Front, 68, 72
FBI (Federal Bureau of Investigation),
149
feminine: in dissident writings, 186,
199–205, 214; embodiment of market, 207; and humanist universalism,
199–204, 214. *See also* culture and
tradition, Vietnamese; empiricism;
femininity; film, Vietnamese; gender;
humanism; ideology; literature,
Vietnamese; masculinity; rurality;
social realism; Vietnamese Communist Party; women
femininity: and bourgeois class, 106–14;
governance, xiv, xxi, xxvii, 116, 140–
41, 144, 160–63; and labor, 116, 140–
42, 144. *See also* class; culture and
tradition, Vietnamese; feminine; film,
Vietnamese; gender; ideology; literature, Vietnamese; masculinity; social
realism; truth; women
Ferguson, Adam, 163
Fforde, Adam, 6, 8–11, 75
film, Vietnamese: and audience, 236,
239; and the body of woman, 227–
39; and censorship, 235; and class,
227, 235–36; commercialization of,
235, 237; and commercial sex, 215–
42; commodification of, 225–26,
237–38, 239; consumption of, 227–
29, 239, 240–41; and empiricism,
223, 225–27, 230, 233, 240; and the
feminine, 225–30, 240–41; and freedom, 216, 230, 232, 239, 241–42; and
government, 215–217, 221, 235; and
ideology, 235–41; and knowledge,
221; and market, 224–27, 230, 232,
234, 238–39, 242; and masculinity,
227–29, 239; and morality, 226–27;
and national identity, 227, 230, 233–
34; and Public Security, 229; and
social realism, 215–42, 255–56; and
symbolic order, 227, 229, 242; and
Vietnamese culture and tradition,

Health Information and Education
Center, Ho Chi Minh City, 99–101
Health Ministry, 87, 90, 92
Hegel, G.W. F., 195, 275n32
Hindess, Barry, 27, 181
history: and class, 194, 204, 214; in
Marx's view, 185, 192, 204, 214; and
revolution, 197–98, 212; in social
realism, 196–98; and subjecthood,
196–98, 200–204; and Vietnamese
Communist Party, 199, 207–8. *See
also* empiricism; feminine; literature,
Vietnamese; Marx, Karl; Marxist
approach to; masculinity; socialist
state; Vietnam, Democratic Republic
of; Vietnam, Republic of; Vietnamese
Communist Party; women
HIV (human immunodeficiency virus):
and public health, 94, 96, 97, 100,
101; and rehabilitation, 120, 131,
136, 146, 167, 176, 177; in Vietnamese film, 223–24, 226, 231, 232, 233.
See also AIDS; commercial sex; medi-
cine; prostitution; public health;
rehabilitation; sex; sex worker
Hoàng Cầm, 192, 202, 289n26
Hoàng Minh Chính, 286n58
Hoàng Ngọc Anh, 191, 199
Hobbes, Thomas, 170
Hobhouse, L. T., 150
Hobson, J. A., 250
Hồ Chí Minh, 83
Ho Chi Minh City, xxiii, 52; bookstores,
106; cafes, 48, 53; dance halls, 220–
21; hospitals, 85, 98
Ho Chi Minh Trail, 48
Học Tập, 71, 82
Hue, 48
humanism, 171, 197–99, 202–4, 214,
252. *See also* empiricism; feminine;
femininity; social realism
Hume, David, 169–70
Hundred Flowers Campaign, 189
Hunt, Alan, xvii

ideology: and Althusser, 129, 138–39,
241; of class struggle, 170; and depoliticization, 248; as false conscious-

ness, xxviii; of family, 161; Foucauldian approach to, xxvii, 172, 182,
241, 255–56; and freedom, 163, 171,
173–74, 241; of gender, 141, 157,
174; and governance, xiv, 185, 241–
42; and government, xiv, 141, 157,
163, 181–82, 215, 240, 248–49,
255; and literary works on, 129–30,
138–39; and market, xx, xxvii, 215;
Marxist approach to, 139, 255; and
Marxism-Leninism, 149, 248; and
neoliberal freedom, 182; and popular
culture, xiv, 215, 217, 239–42; of
socialist state, 163; and state, 129–
30; and state agencies, 152–53; and
Vietnamese culture and tradition,
215; Žižek's insight into, 241. *See also*
empiricism; expertise; film, Vietnamese; Foucault, Michel; freedom; governance; journalism, Vietnamese;
knowledge; literature, Vietnamese;
market; medicine; neoliberalism;
social realism; truth
incarceration, xi, xxii, xxvii, 114, 125,
142; and choices, 154; cost of, 134–
35; and the falsity of prostitutes,
130–31; and historical documents,
174; and labor, 115–16, 121, 133–34,
139, 142, 144, 166, 177, 249; practices of, 115, 130. *See also* governance;
police; policing; power; prostitution;
rehabilitation; sex worker; social work
Indonesia, xxi
industrial convergence model, 66
Institute of Culture and Information,
221
Institute of Sociology, 137, 140
Institute of the Science of Public
Security, 155
intelligentsia. *See also* bourgeois class;
dissent; expertise; knowledge; literature, Vietnamese
ISA (ideological state apparatuses), 129

journalism, Vietnamese, 217–21

KGB, 149
khoán (contracting out land use), 7

marketization, xxvii; adoption of, 74–75, 77; and autonomy of intellectuals, 186–88; and cultural production, 217; and public health intervention, 144–56; and rehabilitation camps, 141, 182; and socialist state, 65. *See also* economic liberalization
Marr, David, 268n40
Marx, Karl, xvi, 70, 261n3, 273n14, 275n32; and the arts, 197–98; on commodity fetish, 225–26, 237–38; and historiography, 185, 192, 204, 208, 214; on labor, xvi; on state, 139. *See also* class; Foucauldian approach to; Marxist approach to; Marxist-Leninist ideology
Marxist approach to: class, 25–27, 194; commodity, 256; criminology, 150; false consciousness, xxviii, 173, 241, 255; history and historiography, 139, 185, 192, 194, 202, 204, 208, 213; labor, xvi, 201; production, 139; social realism, 190–92; society, 191; state, 70, 171. *See also* Marx, Karl
Marxist-Leninist ideology, 66, 149, 165
masculinity: and commercial sex, xx; and Marxist historiography, 214; and the state, 199, 203–4, 207. *See also* commercial sex; culture and tradition, Vietnamese; empiricism; film, Vietnamese; feminine; femininity; gender; ideology; literature, Vietnamese; prostitution; sex worker; socialist state; truth; Vietnamese Communist Party; women
Massey, Doreen, 56, 60
McClintock, Anne, 44, 48, 269n51; and class, 109, 280n37
Medicin du Monde, 100
medicine: and choice, 173; under Leninist governance, 77, 82–84; during marketization, 144; and norms of sex and sexuality, 107, 247; and rehabilitation, 179–80; in socialist Vietnam, 82–83; and subjectivity, 154; Western, 104. *See also* expertise: medicine; governance; knowledge; prostitution; public health; sex worker

Mekong Delta, 50, 53
methodology, xxii–xxvi
micro-adaptation, 6, 8–9
militarization, 254
Milosz, Czeslaw, 197
Ministry of Culture and Information, 91, 129, 221, 235
Ministry of Foreign Affairs, 91
Ministry of Health, 100
Ministry of Labor, Invalids, and Social Affairs, xxiii, 91, 134, 135, 137, 157, 159, 286n68. *See also* commercial sex; prostitution; rehabilitation; sex worker; social work
Ministry of Public Security, 151
mission civilisatrice, 67
modes of governance. *See* governance
Mohanty, Chandra Talpade, xv
Moore, Barrington, 272n1
morality, 218
Moscow Conference of November 1960, 73
Mr. Smith Goes to Washington, 212

National Assembly, 71, 165
National Center for the Social and Human Services, 89
national identity: and aesthetics, 41; and anti-colonialism, 48; and class, 116, 142; and consumption of sex and pleasure, 44–45, 46–54; and global economy, 115, 142; nostalgia in, 54–56; and prostitution, 95–97; and rurality, 52–54, 57–59; Vietnameseness in, 43, 45. *See also* class; commercial sex; feminine; femininity; gender; Marx, Karl; nationalism; women
National Institute of Medical Research, 83
nationalism: anti-colonialism, 48, 67–68, 83, 186, 188, 193, 191, 199, 203, 210–11, 214; anti-imperialism, 68; First Indochina War, 193; Second Indochina War, 210
National Public Security Conference in 1996, 151
nation-state: and globalization, xv, xvi–xvii, 115–16, 142; and sovereignty, xv.

Osborne, Thomas, 165
overseas Vietnamese, 53, 61, 230, 233

Paltiel, Jeremy, 93
party. *See* Vietnamese Communist Party
Party Central Committee, 68, 76
Party Central Organization Committee, 73
peasants, 52–53
peer educators. *See* prostitution: peer educators
People's Army, 150–51
Phạm Hoàng Nam, 222, 225, 237. See also *Gái nhảy; Lọ lem hè phố*
Phạm Tâm Long, 150–51, 283n16
Phạm Thùy Nhân, 222
"Phẩm tiết" (Chastity), 207, 208
Phạm Xuân Nam, 89
Phan Đình Diệu, 286n58
Phùng Quán, 195, 200–201, 289n26
plenum resolutions, 72, 73
police: arrests of sex workers, 119–25, 142; corruption, 125, 147, 247, 249; depoliticization, 150–56, 247; and economic liberalization, 150; and policing of crimes, 89, 125, 145–56; and public health, 145–56; and repression, 154–57, 166, 247; socialist conception of, 145–56; and truth, 120, 125; in Vietnamese journalism, 217–18. *See also* governance; policing; Public Security
policing: and coercion, xxvi; criminal, 145–47, 152; and expertise, 89; and governance, 94, 115, 123, 144–56; militarization of, 254; political, 150–56; of prostitution, 65, 79, 94, 125; racialization of, 254; and repression, 154–57; and social order, 146–47, 149, 247; as state enterprise, 92; and Vietnamese traditional femininity, xxi. *See also* crime; governance; police; power; Public Security
policy: anti-prostitution campaigns, 107, 120, 122, 125; economic, 76; five-year plan, 75; foreign, 73, 74; management of the economy, 75; and "practical expertise," 72; public health, 153;

and publishing houses, 107–8; on the rehabilitation of sex workers, 140; against social evils, 117, 125; socialization of, 158–59; and social realism, 213; Three Reductions (*ba giảm*) campaign, 125. *See also* Đổi Mới; governance; government
Politburo, 76
political changes, xix, xxii
political economy, theories of, 170
popular culture: and freedom, xiii, 216, 239; and governance, xiv, 185, 242; and government, xiii–xiv, 216; and ideology, xiv, 215, 217, 239–42; and market, xiii–xiv, 216, 239. *See also* empiricism; film, Vietnamese; literature, Vietnamese; social realism
Porter, Gareth, 263n26
Poulantzas, Nicos, 25–27, 267n4
power: bio-, 169; and choice, 163–65, 172, 174, 177, 180, 249, 253, 255; and class, 41, 61–62, 142, 182; and coercion, 94, 177, 180, 182, 248, 253; differentiated population, xvii, 26; disciplinary, xvi–xvii, 94, 163, 168–69, 172–73, 181; and economic liberalization, 8, 26; and economy, xxi, xxii, 142–43, 182, 245, 248; of empires, xxi; foreign, 55; Foucauldian approach to, xvi–xvii, 95, 168–69, 173, 181, 249; and freedom, xvi–xvii, 169, 171, 173–74, 249, 252; and gender, 142, 167, 174, 182; and globalization, 142, 248; and governance, xiii, xvi–xvii, 142, 156, 172–73, 251; government, xxii, 76, 115, 172; and hybrids, xxi; and ideology, 182; and incarceration, xxii, 154, 181, 248; kinds of, 144–82, 253–54; and market, xxviii, 5, 221; and Marxists, 171; medical, 177, 179, 180; and methods, xxv; microphysics of, xvii, 156, 163, 169, 172, 180; modern, 95; modes of, 142–43, 145, 152–53, 156–57, 177, 179–80, 248; monopolized, xiii; and national identity, 174; neo-Foulcauldian approach to, 152; neoliberal, 181, 245, 252; normative, 95; police, 166; policing, 14, 154–56,